Beyond Slavery and Abolition

The first full-length historical study of pre-abolition black British writing, this book challenges established narratives of eighteenth-century black history that focus almost exclusively on slavery and abolition. Ryan Hanley expands our perspectives to encompass the often neglected but important black writers of the time and highlights their contribution to politics, culture and the arts. He considers the lives and works of contemporary black literary celebrities alongside largely forgotten evangelical authors and political radicals to uncover how they came to produce such diverse and powerful work. By navigating the social, religious, political and professional networks that surrounded these authors and their writing, he also reveals that black intellectuals were never confined to the peripheries of British culture. From the decks of Royal Navy ships to the drawing rooms of country houses, from the pub to the pulpit, black writers, and the work they produced, helped to build modern Britain.

RYAN HANLEY is a British Academy Postdoctoral Fellow in the Department of History at University College London.

Beyond Slavery and Abolition

Black British Writing, c. 1770–1830

Ryan Hanley

University College London

CAMBRIDGE
UNIVERSITY PRESS

CAMBRIDGE
UNIVERSITY PRESS

University Printing House, Cambridge CB2 8BS, United Kingdom

One Liberty Plaza, 20th Floor, New York, NY 10006, USA

477 Williamstown Road, Port Melbourne, VIC 3207, Australia

314-321, 3rd Floor, Plot 3, Splendor Forum, Jasola District Centre, New Delhi - 110025, India

79 Anson Road, #06-04/06, Singapore 079906

Cambridge University Press is part of the University of Cambridge.

It furthers the University's mission by disseminating knowledge in the pursuit of education, learning and research at the highest international levels of excellence.

www.cambridge.org
Information on this title: www.cambridge.org/9781108468756
DOI: 10.1017/9781108616997

First published 2019
First paperback edition 2020

A catalogue record for this publication is available from the British Library

Library of Congress Cataloging in Publication data
Names: Hanley, Ryan, author.
Title: Beyond slavery and abolition : Black British writing,
    c.1770-1830 / Ryan Hanley.
Description: Cambridge ; New York, NY : Cambridge University Press, 2019. |
    Includes bibliographical references and index.
Identifiers: LCCN 2018026109| ISBN 9781108475655 (hardback : alk. paper) |
    ISBN 9781108468756 (pbk. : alk. paper)
Subjects: LCSH: English literature–Black authors–History and criticism. |
    Blacks–Great Britain–Intellectual life.
Classification: LCC PR120.B55 H36 2019 | DDC 820.9/896041–dc23
    LC record available at https://lccn.loc.gov/2018026109

ISBN 978-1-108-47565-5 Hardback
ISBN 978-1-108-46875-6 Paperback

For J.P.

Contents

Figures

Acknowledgements

This book began life as a doctoral thesis at the Wilberforce Institute for the study of Slavery and Emancipation (WISE) at the University of Hull. I am indebted especially to my supervisors, Douglas Hamilton and Nicholas Evans, and to the two directors of the Institute during my tenure there, David Richardson and John Oldfield, for their mentorship and encouragement. Brycchan Carey, the external examiner of my thesis, also deserves a special share of thanks for his continuing mentorship and support for this project. The thesis became a book during my years as Salvesen Junior Fellow at New College Oxford, and I am very grateful to all the Fellows there, but most especially to David Parrott, Ruth Harris, Jan Machielsen, Anne Hanley and Aaron Graham for their friendship and support for the project.

Beyond these institutions, I would like to thank (in no particular order) Richard Huzzey, Katie Donington, Sheryllnne Haggerty, David Killingray, John Saillant, Paul Lovejoy, Helen Thomas, Suzanne Schwarz, Markman Ellis, Vincent Carretta, Kate Hodgson, James Walvin, John Barrell, John Mee, Richard Blackett, Sue Thomas, Madge Dresser, Olivette Otele, Margot Finn, Catherine Hall and Cassandra Pybus, all of whom have helped me to make sense of this research, sometimes concretely through advice and feedback, sometimes ineffably through their friendship and moral support. At Cambridge University Press, I would like to thank Liz Friend-Smith and the anonymous peer reviewers and editors whose advice was invaluable.

I wish to thank the University of Hull; New College Oxford; the Institute for Historical Research; The Royal Historical Society; the Omohundro Institute at William and Mary College, Virginia; the British Society for Eighteenth Century Studies; Queen Mary, University of London; and the Huntingdon Library, California, for their financial assistance at various points, without which I would not have been able to write this book.

Most importantly, I could not have written this book without the support of my partner and teammate Jessica Moody.

x

Abbreviations

AVB	*Authorised Version Bible* (1611 translation)
BL	The British Library, London
Ch.F.	Cheshunt Foundation, Westminster College, University of Cambridge
DMBI	John Vickers (ed.), *A Dictionary of Methodism in Britain and Ireland* (London: Wesley Historical Society, 2011), available at www.wesleyhistoricalsociety.org.uk/dmbi/
ECCO	Eighteenth Century Collections Online, Gale Cengage, available at http://find.galegroup.com/ecco/
GRO	Gloucestershire Records Office, Gloucester
HRO	Hampshire Record Office, Sussex
JRL	John Rylands Library, University of Manchester
MNC	Methodist New Connexion
ODNB	*The Oxford Dictionary of National Biography* (Oxford: Oxford University Press, 2004), available at www.oxforddnb.com
OED	*Oxford English Dictionary*, available at www.oed.com/
SEAST	London Committee of the Society for Effecting the Abolition of the Slave Trade
TNA	The National Archives, London

Introduction

It must have been quite a sight at the Court of King's Bench on 9 May 1820, when the infamous 'mulatto' revolutionary Robert Wedderburn, half-blind, dressed in rags and covered in the accumulated filth of six months in gaol, stood up and began to lecture the judge on legal ethics. Wedderburn had been arrested the previous December for preaching blasphemy and sedition at his hayloft chapel on Hopkins Street in London. He was held without charge until February 1820 before he was allowed to stand trial. The jury found him guilty at the February hearing, but recommended him to leniency due to the extenuating circumstance of his being raised on a Jamaican slave plantation, without 'the benefit of parental care'. As Wedderburn himself had argued, how could the son of an enslaved black woman, with no access to education, who had been abandoned by his rapacious white father before he was even born, be expected to know any better? The presiding judge – no less a figure than the Lord Chief Justice, Sir Charles Abbot – declared that Wedderburn was to be sentenced at a separate hearing in May.[1]

At the sentencing, he was supposed to appear contrite and respectful, to acknowledge his guilt, to reiterate his unfortunate origins and to throw himself on the mercy of the judge, Justice Bailey. In 1820, it was possible to 'diminish the quantum of punishment' for blasphemy, by proclaiming one's repentance and prostrating oneself before the court. If he chose, Bailey could then issue a fine, or perhaps a short custodial sentence, and thus demonstrate how merciful and fair-handed the British justice system could be, especially toward those who had been degraded by slavery. But contrition was never Wedderburn's style. Instead, he stood defiant and read out a statement which laid the blame for his notoriety on the authorities now charged with sentencing him. 'Those doctrines which would have been confined to my obscure chapel – to my small

---

[1] Erasmus Perkins [pseud. George Cannon] (ed.), *The Trial of the Rev. Robt. Wedderburn, a Dissenting Minister of the Unitarian Persuasion, for Blasphemy* (London: W. Mason, 1820), 20.

congregation, – are now by the fostering aid of my prosecutors, published to the whole world', he harangued. 'They have effectually advertised the very thing which they dislike. By preventing me from preaching, they have compelled me to become an author. They have dragged me from obscurity into public notice.' This line of reasoning could hardly have recommended him to Bailey's mercy – and he was not yet finished. '[S]ince they have made me a member of the Republic of Letters, I beg leave to recommend to their attention a critical, historical and admonitory letter, which I have just published, *"Addressed to the Right Reverend Father in God, his Grace the Lord Archbishop of Canterbury, on the Alarming Progress of Infidelity; and the means which ought immediately to be resorted to, to check its frightful career."*[2] Given the opportunity to mitigate his legal punishment for blasphemy, Wedderburn had instead advertised a blasphemous publication to the court. Justice Bailey was clearly unimpressed by his entrepreneurial spirit; the revolutionary preacher got two years' hard labour in Dorchester Gaol.

Wedderburn's complaint, and his brazen advertisement of new writing, pose the two key questions this book sets out to answer. The first he mentioned directly: how did black celebrities, preachers and radicals in late eighteenth- and early nineteenth-century Britain become authors? Wedderburn seemed to be suggesting that the decision to publish his work was never his at all, but that circumstances, helped by a designing network of influential figures, gave him no choice. Even as he staked his claim to authority over his 'doctrines', he acknowledged that they would never have been put into print without 'the fostering aid' of a group of interacting individuals, who had come together to further their own interests. Black authors during this period, perhaps more than any others, were likely to depend on networks – of friends, co-religionists, conspirators, and even those we might think of as their enemies – for publication, financial support or social prestige. Uncovering the composition of these networks, therefore, is essential to understanding how and why black writing came to be published in eighteenth- and nineteenth-century Britain.

The second key question for this book is also raised by Wedderburn's mitigation plea, though it requires some hidden knowledge to access. Specifically, we must be aware that he did not write it. Or, at the very least, he alone was not responsible for its contents. George Cannon,

---

[2] Erasmus Perkins [pseud. George Cannon] (ed.), *The Address of the Rev. R. Wedderburn, to the Court of King's Bench at Westminster, on Appearing to Receive Judgement for Blasphemy* (London: T. Davison, 1820), 15; 10–11.

a white, déclassé-radical, classically educated amateur lawyer and some-time pornographer, was the man chiefly responsible for Wedderburn's foolhardy courtroom speech. The two had met a couple of years earlier through their mutual involvement in London's ultra-radical scene, and perhaps Wedderburn entrusted Cannon with the task of composing the speech because of his superior education. In any case, it was misplaced trust. This is not to say that Wedderburn necessarily objected to its contents, much less its defiant overtones. But Cannon stood to gain, financially and professionally, from a sensational trial and an overly harsh sentence: he edited the published transcripts of Wedderburn's prosecution and sentencing hearing. He was also the true author and publisher of the 'critical, historical and admonitory letter' to which he'd had Wedderburn allude in court. (He was, of course, a ghost writer; Wedderburn's name appeared on the cover of this scurrilous publication as author, again shielding Cannon from prosecution.)[3] It was Cannon who reaped the financial and reputational profits from the harsh sentence passed down to Wedderburn, and it was his speechwriting that ensured any such sentence could not be anything other than exemplary.

Our second question thus emerges. How did networks – whether social, professional, political, or religious – influence the *content* of early black writing, and to what extent did they affect how it was published, distributed and read? When we return to the published mitigation speech, aware that it was (in large part if not completely) written by Cannon, its true, mercenary purpose becomes clear. Moreover, we come to agree with scholars of early African American writing: that evaluating the level of authority or control an author had over the work attributed to them is centrally important to understanding slavery-era black literature.[4] This does not mean that black intellectuals were the unwitting dupes of designing or self-interested networks of white intrigue; far from it. Black authors were respected comrades, beloved friends and intellectual authorities in eighteenth- and nineteenth-century Britain. In many cases, they were powerful and influential people. But, like all authors,

---

[3] Robert Wedderburn [pseud. George Cannon], *A Critical, Historical, and Admonitory Letter to the Right Reverend Father in God, His Grace the Lord Archbishop of Canterbury* (London: W. Mason, 1820). Iain McCalman convincingly attributes this pamphlet to Cannon in *Radical Underworld: Prophets, Revolutionaries and Pornographers in London, 1795–1840* (Oxford: Oxford University Press, 1988), 153–154.

[4] William Andrews, *To Tell a Free Story: The First Century of Afro-American Autobiography, 1760–1865* (Urbana: University of Illinois Press, 1986), 34–37; John Blassingame, 'Using the Testimony of Ex-Slaves: Approaches and Problems', in Charles T. Davis and Henry Louis Gates Jr. (eds.), *The Slave's Narrative* (Oxford: Oxford University Press, 1985), 78–98; Francis Smith Foster, *Witnessing Slavery: The Development of Ante-Bellum Slave Narratives* (Westport, CT: Greenwood Press, 1979).

they adjusted their writing according to the needs of patrons, publishers, editors and their likely readership. Like all of us, their world-view was affected by those around them. And like all published books, their work went through careful processes of revision and edition, passing through several pairs of hands before readers ever encountered it. When we read a text by an eighteenth-century black author such as Wedderburn, just as when we read one by Charles Dickens or Toni Morrison, we are never reading the work of just one person.

This book examines the lives and works of eight early black authors in Britain: Ignatius Sancho, Olaudah Equiano, Mary Prince, Ukawsaw Gronniosaw, Boston King, John Jea, Ottobah Cugoano and Robert Wedderburn. It uncovers the influential networks that surrounded them and their published works during the period falling roughly between 1770 and 1830. It demonstrates that black intellectuals, as literary celebrities, evangelical preachers and leaders of domestic political radicalism, participated in the full gamut of British social, religious and political culture.

Of course, the black presence in Britain long pre-dated the late eighteenth century. But while Peter Fryer's famous pronouncement that there 'were Africans in Britain before the English came here' is perfectly accurate in itself, he was referring to a largely transient population of a few hundred Roman soldiers temporarily stationed here.[5] The earliest evidence of a substantial resident black population dates back to the sixteenth century, culminating in Elizabeth I's well-known declaration that 'there are of late divers blackamoores brought into this realm, of which kinde of people there are allready to manie'.[6] As Jeremy Brotton has illustrated, the presence of black or 'Moor' populations in early modern Britain was related to crucial trade links with the Islamic world.[7] Accounts of black individuals and families recurred throughout the sixteenth and seventeenth centuries – the Resonable family of Southwark, for instance, may have influenced Shakespeare's depiction of his most

---

[5] Peter Fryer, *Staying Power: The History of Black People in Britain* (London: Pluto, 1984), 1–32 (quotation at 1). For the early history of black people in Britain, see also Paul Edwards, 'The Early African Presence in the British Isles', in Jagdish S. Gundara and Ian Duffield (eds.), *Essays on the History of Blacks in Britain* (Aldershot: Ashgate, 1992); David Olusoga, *Black and British: A Forgotten History* (London: Macmillan, 2016), 29–76.

[6] Cited in Fryer, *Staying Power*, 10. For black people in early modern England, see Miranda Kaufmann, *Black Tudors: The Untold Story* (London: OneWorld, 2017); Onyeka, *Blackamoores: Africans in Tudor England, Their Presence, Status and Origins* (London: Narrative Eye, 2013).

[7] Jeremy Brotton, *This Orient Isle: Elizabethan England and the Islamic World* (London: Allen Lane, 2016).

famous black character, Othello.[8] However, it was not until the expansion
of the slave trade with its deregulation in 1712 and the Treaty of Utrecht
in 1713 that the black presence in Britain began, slowly, to expand.[9] To
an unprecedented degree, black people became enmeshed in British culture during the eighteenth century. As immortalised in William Hogarth's
chaotic paintings, young, black, serving boys became prized fashion acces-
sories among Britain's fashionable elite.[10] Slave-trading African dignitar-
ies Ayuba Suleiman Diallo and William Ansah Sessarakoo caused quite a
stir in such circles when they visited the country after having themselves
been mistakenly enslaved and subsequently 'rescued' by British traders.[11]
At the other end of the social hierarchy, black sailors and soldiers, along
with formerly enslaved young men and women, firmly established themselves in working-class British society, much to the alarm and bemuse-
ment of some social commentators.[12]

The exact size of the black population during the eighteenth century is
hard to gauge, partly because of the lack of reliable census information
(the first national census was taken in 1801, but ethnicity was not
recorded in any standardised way until as late as 1991). When they were
noted, as an aside in ships' muster rolls, criminal proceedings or local
church and government documents, racial or ethnic groupings were
recorded inconsistently.[13] In fact, the term 'black' as used in this book –
that is, in reference exclusively to people of African descent – is something of a linguistic and conceptual anachronism. As Roxann Wheeler
has pointed out, a number of different characteristics besides skin colour
were used to define 'race' in the eighteenth century.[14] While comparative

[8] Imtiaz Habib and Duncan Salkeld, 'The Resonables of Boroughside, Southwark: An Elizabethan Black Family Near the Rose Theatre', *Shakespeare*, 11:2 (2015), 135–156.
[9] See William Pettigrew, *Freedom's Debt: The Royal African Company and the Politics of the Atlantic Slave Trade, 1678–1752* (Chapel Hill: University of North Carolina Press, 2013), 153–178.
[10] For black people in Hogarth, see David Dabydeen, *Hogarth's Blacks: Images of Blacks in Eighteenth-Century English Art* (Manchester: Manchester University Press, 1987); Catherine Molyneux, *Faces of Perfect Ebony: Encountering Atlantic Slavery in Imperial Britain* (Cambridge, MA: Harvard University Press, 2012), 178–218.
[11] See Ryan Hanley, 'The Royal Slave: Nobility, Diplomacy and the "African Prince" in Britain, 1748–1752, *Itinerario* 39:2 (2015), 329–347.
[12] See, for example, James Tobin's complaints about 'the great numbers of negroes at present in England' and 'the strange propensity shewn for them by the lower orders of women'. James Tobin, *Cursory Remarks upon the Reverend Mr. Ramsay's Essay* (London: James Phillips, 1785), 118.
[13] See Kathleen Chater, *Untold Histories: Black People in England and Wales during the Period of the British Slave Trade, c. 1660–1807* (Manchester: Manchester University Press, 2009), 22–23.
[14] Roxann Wheeler, *The Complexion of Race: Categories of Difference in Eighteenth-Century British Culture* (Philadelphia: University of Pennsylvania Press, 2000), 288–302.

anatomy and pseudo-scientific attempts to fix particular intellectual characteristics to certain races began to take hold in Britain toward the end of our period, thinking around human difference for most commentators remained characteristically muddled and contradictory.[15] Enlightenment climatic theory, stressing the influence of region and climate on civilizational development, retained currency, as did the ancient concept of the 'Great Chain of Being', whereby all living beings (including the supposedly separable races of man) could be placed in a linear hierarchy.[16] Stadial theories of civilizational progress, as propounded by Adam Smith and others, were also deeply imbricated in debates over race and heredity, and in turn impacted on moral discussions of slavery and Empire.[17] This unsettled theoretical and ideological landscape had ramifications as to how people saw, and chose to record, their encounters with African people and their descendants in Britain. One eighteenth-century recorder might see someone from South Asia and someone from Africa as equally 'black', by virtue of the fact that they were both equally not 'white'.[18] Another might take great care distinguishing a 'Negroe' from a 'Quadroon' or a 'Mustee'.[19] Another recorder might not see race as relevant and omit it from their record altogether, leaving us to speculate as to whether, for example, the 'Francis Othello' who was indicted at the Old Bailey for theft in May 1786 was a member of London's black community or not.[20]

---

[15] Dror Wahrman, *The Making of the Modern Self: Identity and Culture in Eighteenth-Century England* (New Haven, CT: Yale University Press, 2013), 83–156; Francisco Bethencourt, *Racisms: From the Crusades to the Twentieth Century* (Princeton, NJ: Princeton University Press, 2013), 247–270; Ivan Hannaford, *Race: The History of an Idea in the West* (Washington, DC: Woodrow Wilson Center Press and Baltimore, MD: Johns Hopkins University Press, 1996), 205–215; Felicity Nussbaum, *The Limits of the Human: Fictions of Anomaly, Race, and Gender in the Long Eighteenth Century* (Cambridge: Cambridge University Press, 2003); Ryan Hanley, 'Slavery and the Birth of Working-Class Racism in England, 1814–1833', *Transactions of the Royal Historical Society*, 26 (2016), 103–123.

[16] Silvia Sebastiani, *The Scottish Enlightenment: Race, Gender, and the Limits of Progress* (Basingstoke: Palgrave Macmillan, 2013), 23–44; Nancy Stepan, *The Idea of Race in Science: Britain, 1800–1960* (London: Macmillan, 1982), 1–19.

[17] See Sebastiani, *Scottish Enlightenment*, 45–72.   [18] See Chater, *Untold Histories*, 22–23.

[19] Edward Long, one of the most outspoken and committed racist ideologues of the eighteenth century, outlined some of these perceived distinctions in his chapter on 'Creoles' in *The History of Jamaica, or a General Survey of the Antient and Modern State of That Island*, 3 vols. (London: T. Lowndes, 1774), vol. 2, 260–263; see Catherine Hall, 'Whose Memories? Edward Long and the Work of Re-Remembering', in Katie Donington, Ryan Hanley and Jessica Moody (eds.), *Britain's History and Memory of Transatlantic Slavery: Local Nuances of a 'National Sin'* (Liverpool: Liverpool University Press, 2016), 129–149.

[20] *Old Bailey Proceedings Online*, s17860531-1, 'Punishment summary, 31 May 1786', available at www.oldbaileyonline.org.

Despite these challenges, through careful and extensive archival work, scholars have been able to sketch some outlines of the approximate size and shape of the African diaspora in Britain. Historians very tentatively (and, some claim, rather conservatively) suggest that around 10,000 black people were resident in Britain between 1780 and 1830.[21] However, as demonstrated by the recent discovery of records pertaining to more than 2,500 black prisoners of war held at Portchester Castle near Portsmouth during the late 1790s, this figure was prone to significant fluctuations over time.[22] As might be expected, the largest resident urban black population in Britain was in London (0.55 per cent of the total population in the late 1780s), with other significant concentrations in port towns around the coast, notably in the capital of the European slave trade, Liverpool.[23] In common with most migrant communities, and no doubt accentuated by regular replenishment of Royal Navy personnel in the Caribbean, the black British population was skewed significantly in favour of young men throughout the period.[24] For similar reasons, occupations often centred on maritime industries and military service, though domestic service, agricultural labour and even street arts have all been noted as ways black people made a living in eighteenth-century Britain.[25] Indeed, as Kathleen Chater has pointed out, within these broad brush-strokes, a key characteristic of the black population in Britain during this period was diversity: diversity of experience, diversity of interest and diversity of perspectives.[26] Accordingly, writings produced by black people during this period reflected not a homogenous 'black perspective' but a staggering *diversity* of views and experiences.

This study therefore contests the notion of black writing as concerned wholly, or even mostly, with slavery and abolition and reintroduces some of the other concerns affecting the authors and their networks. These texts were never published in a social vacuum. Like all writers, black authors had to interact with the world around them, and not only with one or two issues. While the life stories of a few early black authors (especially Equiano and Prince) are now well known, and their writings

---

[21] Norma Myers, *Reconstructing the Black Past: Blacks in Britain, 1780–1830* (London: Frank Cass, 1996), 35. Chater suggests this figure could be higher when rural populations are taken into account. Chater, *Untold Histories*, 29.

[22] At the time of writing, these archives were undergoing preservation and cataloguing and were not available for consultation. See Abigail Crippins, 'Black Prisoners of War at Portchester Castle', available at www.english-heritage.org.uk/visit/places/portchester-castle/history-and-stories/black-prisoners/.

[23] Myers, *Reconstructing the Black Past*, 29, 24.   [24] Chater, *Untold Histories*, 30–31.

[25] Well-known black street musicians during this period included the fiddlers Billy Waters and Shadrack Furman. See Fryer, *Staying Power*, 231.

[26] Chater, *Untold Histories*, 35–73.

widely available, the specific circumstances surrounding the composition, production and dissemination of much of this corpus remain obscure or undiscussed. Early black British writing is often incorporated into the later, American tradition of the abolitionist 'slave narrative', denoting an assumption about these texts as confining themselves to the issues of slavery and race.[27] We should be clear: black intellectuals and enslaved people were fundamental to the abolition movements, and as Manisha Sinha has demonstrated so convincingly, the global antislavery cause could not have succeeded without them.[28] But while there is no doubt that black contributions were and are of central importance to these discussions, it must be acknowledged first that eighteenth-century black authors' work was produced with a much more diverse range of interests in mind, and second that early black British writing was not always uncomplicatedly abolitionist.

These two factors were often interrelated – for example, in Chapter 4 of this book, I explore how Ukawsaw Gronniosaw's relationships with prominent slave-owning Calvinists helps to explain his autobiography's apparently ambivalent attitude toward slavery. More to the point, black authors were more likely to be poor or illiterate than their white contemporaries. Their texts therefore often underwent more direct forms of outside influence before publication – i.e. edition, transcription and censorship. In Gronniosaw's case, he himself, his amanuensis and his editor were all followers of his slave-owning patron, the Countess of Huntington. Author, editor, amanuensis and sponsor – each of them held dear, as a fundamental precept of their world, the Calvinist belief that corporeal freedom was not necessary to achieve spiritual salvation. We should not be surprised, then, to find that Gronniosaw's autobiography was not a radically abolitionist political tract.[29] We must use precisely this type of contextual detail if we are to gain a more complete understanding of early black writing, one rooted firmly in the historical realities in which it was produced. Joseph Miller has called for slavery to be understood 'through the lens of a rigorously historical epistemology', as something influenced by – indeed, *emerging from* – contexts specific to

---

[27] Writers as diverse as Jupiter Hammon, John Marrant, Ukawsaw Gronniosaw, Phillis Wheatley and Robert Wedderburn are all incorporated into the 'slave narrative' paradigm in Helen Thomas, *Romanticism and Slave Narratives: Transatlantic Testimonies* (Cambridge: Cambridge University Press, 2000), 167–271.

[28] Manisha Sinha, *The Slave's Cause: A History of Abolition* (New Haven, CT: Yale University Press, 2016).

[29] See Chapter 4, below, and Ryan Hanley, 'Calvinism, Proslavery and James Albert Ukawsaw Gronniosaw', *Slavery & Abolition*, 36:2 (2015), 360–381. For an opposing reading, see Jennifer Harris, 'Seeing the Light: Re-Reading James Albert Ukawsaw Gronniosaw', *English Language Notes*, 42:4 (2004), 43–57.

a particular time and place.[30] This should apply to black writing, too. Texts were produced in, and in a very significant sense created by, the specific social and cultural contexts of the author's life, experiences and associative networks.

Instrumental networks of association like these – 'actor networks', as sociologist Bruno Latour calls them – are commonly visualised as consisting of 'nodes' and 'vertices'. In network analysis, nodes represent actors (for instance, people, organisations or private companies), and vertices, which link nodes together, represent various types of relationship (such as kinship, business ties, or epistolary exchanges).[31] Historians have traditionally focussed on the individual attributes of the actors or nodes, such as personal wealth or area of residence, as explanations for the extent of their personal influence.[32] But if social change, as Latour suggests, is driven not by individual actors themselves but by the relationships between them, then any node's social influence is not necessarily derived from its individual attributes, but rather by the number and nature of its relationships with other actors within the network. A node at the centre of a network, with many vertices linking it to other nodes, is therefore more likely to exercise influence over it than one at the periphery. However, we should always bear in mind that the number of relationships alone is not sufficient to explain social influence. The nature and strength of the bonds themselves is also a significant factor in determining influence. Blood is thicker than water: a strong bond carries greater influence than a weak one.

In an eighteenth-century context, 'networks' have most often been taken to mean mercantile systems of exchange, distribution and information sharing, but scholars continue to emphasise inter-actor relationships as galvanising social change.[33] For example, in her study of the

[30] Miller, 'The Biographical Turn', in Lisa Lindsay and John Wood Sweet (eds.), *Biography and the Black Atlantic* (Philadelphia: University of Pennsylvania Press, 2014), 26.
[31] Bruno Latour, *Reassembling the Social: An Introduction to Actor-Network Theory* (Oxford: Oxford University Press, 2005), 1–18; Stanley Wasserman and Katherine Faust, *Social Network Analysis: Methods and Applications* (Cambridge: Cambridge University Press, 1994), 148–150.
[32] One of the best-known examples of this type of network research is J. F. Padgett and C. K. Ansell, 'Robust Action and the Rise of the Medici, 1400–1434', *American Journal of Sociology*, 98 (1993), 1259–1319. For an overview of this trend, see Bonnie H. Erickson, 'Social Networks and History: A Review Essay', *Historical Methods*, 30:3 (1997), 149–157.
[33] See, for example, Tijl Vanneste, *Global Trade and Commercial Networks: Eighteenth-Century Diamond Merchants* (London: Pickering and Chatto, 2011); Tilottama Mukherjee, *Political Culture and Economy in Eighteenth Century Bengal: Networks of Exchange, Consumption and Communication* (Hyderabad: Orient Blackswan, 2013).

development of Liverpool business relationships, Sheryllnne Haggerty stresses the importance of influence as 'the critical and defining feature of a network'. Haggerty emphasises that 'we cannot . . . simply say because a group of people know each other that they belong to a network. There has to be something that binds them together, that makes them instrumental.'[34] Similarly, the networks of influence that concern this book are only defined as such when they were instrumental in the production and distribution of early black writing. Much of this book is dedicated to unpicking the exact nature of these relationships and considering precisely how instrumental they were.

Importantly, we must be aware that sometimes the relationships that most influenced the contents of early black writing did not even involve the author directly. As I discuss in Chapter 5 of this book, for example, the affiliation between leading Methodists Thomas Coke and George Whitfield profoundly affected how Boston King's *Memoirs* were edited and distributed, despite the fact that King never even met Whitfield. Moreover, we should remember that the connections between actors were not always social. The people affecting (and sometimes effecting) the composition and distribution of early black autobiography were bound together by a variety of different types of tie. Of course, human relationships are complicated and resist static definition, and so a black author might have a patron who was also a friend, or know a fellow Unitarian who also attended the same radical political meetings. Finally, we should always bear in mind that relationships do not need to be positive or cordial to facilitate influence.

Understanding these networks is especially important for the study of early black writing. Unlike most authors, the majority of the writers that appear in this book – Gronniosaw, Cugoano, King, Jea, Wedderburn and Prince – had quite limited literacy. This meant they needed to use an amanuensis, an editor, or both. The role of these figures, and their implications for authorial independence and 'authenticity', has been discussed at length by scholars. Editorial interventions are often seen as unwelcome obfuscations of the 'true meaning' lying encoded within a compromised text. John Blassingame claimed that because 'slave narratives were frequently dictated to and written by whites, any study of such sources must begin with an assessment of the editors'.[35] William

---

[34] Sheryllynne Haggerty, *'Merely for Money'? Business Culture in the British Atlantic, 1750–1815* (Liverpool: Liverpool University Press, 2012), 163; see also John Haggerty and Sheryllynne Haggerty, 'Visual Analytics of an Eighteenth-Century Business Network', *Enterprise and Society*, 11:1 (2010), 1–25.

[35] John Blassingame, 'Using the Testimony of Ex-Slaves: Approaches and Problems', in Davis and Gates (eds.), *The Slave's Narrative*, 79.

Andrews went further still, insisting that if one is to 'open such a narrative to discussion, one must recognise, in order to discount, the white influence informing and enforcing the putative meaning and purpose of that narrative'.[36] Clearly, an understanding of the relationships between nominal author and their amanuensis/editor is essential to the process of historicising and understanding them. However, the notion of a representative, 'authentic' black voice waiting to be excavated from these sources is less convincing. It seems to take for granted that a static, monolithic 'black perspective' is to be found in these texts, and again that it would be framed primarily by debates around slavery. Perversely, these readings tend to limit both the usefulness of the texts and the agency of the authors. For example, they discount the very notion of proslavery black writing from the outset. Apparently proslavery texts nominally written by black authors are read as having been hopelessly compromised by self-interested white editors, who overwrote the underlying antislavery 'black perspective'. Andrews makes this point quite explicitly about Gronniosaw's *Narrative* when he advises readers to 'pay special regard to the seams or cuts in these enclosed narratives when facts are revealed – made tellable – in a way subversive to the text'.[37] But, as we will explore in detail later in this book, a close examination of the networks surrounding both Gronniosaw and the production of his text indicate that he had every reason to produce an autobiography which appeared to support the idea that enslavement could be a kindness, so long as African slaves were converted to Christianity. Indeed, he would have actively endangered himself and his family by doing otherwise, since their survival depended on financial assistance from a slave-owning patron.[38]

Clearly, the networks of influence mapped out in this book were not always benign, and the power dynamics between author, editor, amanuensis and patron were not often stacked in favour of the author. This book does not purport to recover an 'uncontaminated' black perspective from archival sources or through close interpretive reading. It is concerned rather with how the texts came to be as they are. As Lyn Innes perceptively notes, 'the age did not demand or expect an essential self to be revealed, nor did it use the criteria of authenticity and sincerity, and it

---

[36] Andrews, *To Tell a Free Story*, 35.   [37] Andrews, *To Tell a Free Story*, 36.
[38] Laura Browder has acknowledged that, for nineteenth-century antebellum black autobiography, 'authenticity depended on a strict adherence to a set of generic conventions.' Laura Browder, *Slippery Characters: Ethnic Impersonators and American Identities* (Chapel Hill: University of North Carolina Press, 2000), 20–21.

is as post-Romantic critics that we judge by such criteria.'[39] This study therefore accepts and celebrates that early black writing never sought to reveal an 'essential self' nor a definitive expression of individual political, religious or intellectual genius. It understands the production of these texts as a consisting of pragmatic, often collaborative processes with identifiable goals. Black authors, whether operating in networks of celebrity, evangelicalism or radicalism, were seen as key allies in these movements.

In approaching the study of the historic black presence in Britain through the lives of a few individuals, this book contributes to the ongoing project of recasting British and Atlantic world history. Historians, influenced by postcolonial theory, are increasingly interested in the 'connectedness' of Britain, reframing it not as the centre of the world's affairs but as just one of many global sites of exchange, dominance and resistance.[40] While this has galvanised a welcome move away from the traditional focus on the wealthy and powerful in British history, the huge scale at which these histories sometimes operate can lead us to risk losing sight of the individuals who ultimately comprised these global systems. In other words, by focusing exclusively on structures and systems, we lose sight of the human element. As Linda Colley puts it, global histories 'sometimes seem as aggressively impersonal as globalization can itself'.[41] This is an especially important consideration when we think about the lives of the people caught up in the transatlantic slave system: the intended victims of a specifically dehumanising, deindividuating regime. Historians of slavery and the Atlantic world more generally (notably Colley, Cassandra Pybus and Randy Sparks) have responded with a wave of studies seeking to reconstruct individual stories in detail.[42] Their findings have cast new light on global-scale systems from the perspective

[39] Lyn Innes, 'Eighteenth-Century Men of Letters: Ignatius Sancho and Sake Dean Mahomed', in Susheila Nasta (ed.), *Reading the 'New' Literatures in a Postcolonial Era* (Cambridge: D. S. Brewer, 2000), 24.

[40] Dipesh Chakrabarty, *Provincializing Europe: Postcolonial Thought and Historical Difference* (Princeton, NJ: Princeton University Press, 2000), 3–26; Catherine Hall, *Civilizing Subjects: Metropole and Colony in the English Imagination, 1830–1867* (Chicago, IL: University of Chicago Press, 2002); Kathleen Wilson, *A New Imperial History: Culture, Identity, and Modernity in Britain and the Empire, 1660–1840* (Cambridge: Cambridge University Press, 2004).

[41] Linda Colley, *The Ordeal of Elizabeth Marsh: A Woman in World History* (London: HarperCollins, 2007), xxxi.

[42] Colley, *Ordeal of Elizabeth Marsh*; Cassandra Pybus, *Epic Journeys of Freedom: Runaway Slaves of the American Revolution and Their Global Quest for Liberty* (Boston: Beacon Press, 2006); Randy Sparks, *The Two Princes of Calabar: An Eighteenth-Century Atlantic Odyssey* (Cambridge, MA: Harvard University Press, 2004); see also the contributions in Lindsay and Sweet (eds.), *Biography and the Black Atlantic*.

of those who were caught up in them. The effect of this 'biographical turn', as Miller has termed it, has been to reinstate the individual and his or her network as a key scale of historiographical analysis, especially in relation to the black Atlantic world.[43]

However, examining the lives of black individuals in eighteenth- and nineteenth-century Britain *exclusively* in reference to histories of slavery and abolition, as has most commonly been done, profoundly limits our understanding of them. It tends to 'flatten' the black intellectual contribution to British and Atlantic culture. This book therefore moves to embrace the inherent 'messiness' of these writings, their refusal to adhere perfectly to established explanations for the proliferation of antislavery thought or indeed to offer a straightforwardly authentic 'black perspective'. An investigation into *how* these complicated perspectives were forged enables a fundamental reconsideration of these texts as historical, literary, commercial and politically discursive artefacts and puts black authors back into the 'mainstream' narratives of British cultural and social history.

Before we embark on such a revaluation, it is important to take stock of the historical contexts in which black writing has traditionally been read. It bears reiteration that this book does not seek to divorce black intellectuals from the antislavery movements they so profoundly affected.[44] Rather, it prompts a broader view of their personal interactions as a means of better understanding both their work and their roles in facilitating links between abolitionism and other contemporaneous movements. We will return to the specific interactions between slavery, abolition and the authors' networks in more detail throughout the chapters of this book. However, situating them in broad terms within the now familiar history of British abolitionism – that is, outlining how historians and literary critics have traditionally tended to see them – is an important first step in our exploration of their links to other movements and interests.

Black Writing, Slavery and Abolition in Britain

Black writing was first published in Britain amid a controversy over slavery. *A Narrative of the Most Remarkable Particulars in the Life of James Albert Ukawsaw Gronniosaw, an African Prince* appeared in Bath in December 1772, a few months after the first key legal victory in the

---

[43] Miller, 'The Biographical Turn', 26.
[44] For black leadership of the antislavery movements in Britain and America during this period, see Sinha, *The Slave's Cause*, 9–191.

long campaign against slavery was won, in the Somerset ruling.[45] The case of James Somerset, an enslaved man who had run away in Britain and whose former owner had attempted to forcibly deport back into bonded servitude in the Caribbean, captured the imagination of the public. Crowds of black people (among them a fifteen-year-old Ottobah Cugoano, who would go on to publish two books of his own) gathered around the Court of King's Bench each day to follow the proceedings. After months of deliberation, Lord Chief Justice Mansfield delivered his verdict: 'No master ever was allowed here to take a slave by force to be sold abroad ... therefore [Somerset] must be discharged.'[46] This was an equivocal ruling: Mansfield had never suggested that Somerset was no longer a slave – only that his former owner could not compel him to leave Britain. Regardless of its limited legal impact, the case brought debates over slavery into the mainstream of political consciousness and generated a new market for texts by black authors.

On first reading, the earliest black British writing seemed to have conscientiously divorced itself from the political questions that emerged as a result of the Somerset case. Gronniosaw's *Narrative* was first and foremost a piece of devotional literature. This it bore in common with what little Anglophone black writing had already been published – a short autobiographical pamphlet by Briton Hammon released in Boston in 1760 and a single poem by Jupiter Hammon published in New York the same year.[47] Similarly, when the black epistolarian Ignatius Sancho died in December 1780, his letters were collected and then published in 1782 with the view (then still more or less politically unobjectionable) of 'shewing that an untutored African may possess abilities equal to an European'.[48] Though this would prove a key issue in the abolition debates that were to follow, in 1782 it had more to do with notions of sensibility,

---

[45] For British abolitionism before 1772, see Christopher Brown, *Moral Capital: Foundations of British Abolitionism* (Chapel Hill: University of North Carolina Press, 2006), 33–101, 90–95. For the Somerset case, see Brown, *Moral Capital*, 90–101; Hugh Thomas, *The Slave Trade* (New York: Simon and Schuster, 1997), 474–479; James Walvin, *Black Ivory: A History of British Slavery* (London: Harper Collins, 1992), 13–17; Seymour Drescher, *Abolition: A History of Slavery and Antislavery* (Cambridge: Cambridge University Press, 2009), 99–104; Adam Hochschild, *Bury the Chains: The British Struggle to Abolish Slavery* (London: Macmillan, 2005), 48–53.

[46] *London Evening Post*, 23 June 1772; 'Substance of Lord Mansfield's Speech on the Cause between Mr. Stuart and Somerset the Black', *The London Magazine, or Gentleman's Monthly Intelligencer*, 41 (1772), 268.

[47] Briton Hammon, *Narrative of the Uncommon Sufferings and Surprizing Deliverance of Briton Hammon* (Boston: J. Green and J. Russell, 1760); Jupiter Hammon, *An Evening Thought: Salvation by Christ, with Penetential Cries* (New York, 1760).

[48] Ignatius Sancho, *Letters of the Late Ignatius Sancho, an African*, 2 vols. (London: J. Nichols et al., 1782), 1:ii.

charity and class than slavery. The work of Gronniosaw and Sancho laid the foundations for a popular strand of antislavery humanitarianism, which insisted that black and white people were capable of the same level of intellectual refinement and spiritual worth. Whether it was intended as such or not – and both of these positions have their advocates – black writing in the 1770s and early 1780s quickly became seen as part of the broader antislavery movement of the late eighteenth century.

The end of the American Revolutionary War in 1783 generated the conditions in which both abolitionism and black writing flourished in Britain.[49] Not least of these was a marked increase in the black population. British strategies to win the war in America had included offering freedom to any slaves who would fight for them. Many (such as the author Boston King) had taken them up on the offer, and when Royal Navy ships returned in defeat after the Peace of 1783, they brought thousands of black people with them.[50] These black loyalist immigrants tested Britons' self-perception as a humane and charitable people, since there was little opportunity for them to find work, and as foreigners they were ineligible for parish poor relief. This new immigrant group also had ethnic prejudice to contend with. One day labourer who took out an advertisement in the *Morning Herald* in 1792 was clearly aware of what he was up against, and adjusted his expectations accordingly: 'AS FOOT-MAN, or Porter in a Warehouse, a Black man, who lived upwards of three years in his last place ... His colour and appearance not being in

---

[49] The reasons behind this transformation are contested. Christopher Brown, in agreement with earlier work by David Brion Davis, argues that the final loss of the American colonies in 1783 created a sense of shock and a period of national reflection in Britain, leading to widespread support for a number of charitable and humanitarian causes, including abolition. Conversely, Seymour Drescher suggests that British abolitionism only flourished in a moment of 'national optimism', once the uncertainties of war had been resolved. Brown, *Moral Capital*, 105–153; David Brion Davis, *The Problem of Slavery in the Age of Revolution*, (Ithaca, NY: Cornell University Press, 1975), 343–468; Seymour Drescher, 'The Shocking Birth of British Abolitionism', *Slavery & Abolition*, 33:4 (2012), 571–593.

[50] See Alan Gilbert, *Black Patriots and Loyalists: Fighting for Emancipation in the War for Independence* (Chicago, IL: University of Chicago Press, 2012), 116–176; Philip Morgan and Andrew Jackson O'Shaughnessy, 'Arming Slaves in the American Revolution', in Christopher Brown and Philip Morgan (eds.), *Arming Slaves: From Classical Times to the Modern Age* (New Haven, CT: Yale University Press, 2006), 180–208; Cassandra Pybus, *Epic Journeys of Freedom: Runaway Slaves of the American Revolution and Their Global Quest for Liberty* (Boston: Beacon Press, 2006), 3–20; Simon Schama, *Rough Crossings: Britain, the Slaves and the American Revolution* (London: BBC Books, 2005), 26–251. Pybus, *Epic Journeys of Freedom*, 75–121; Stephen Braidwood, *Black Poor and White Philanthropists: London's Blacks and the Foundation of the Sierra Leone Settlement 1786–1791* (Liverpool: Liverpool University Press, 1994), 63–129.

his favour, he would be content with moderate wages.'[51] Matters came to a head over the winter of 1787, and measures were put in place to relocate London's 'black poor' to the new West African settlement of Sierra Leone.[52]

The first Sierra Leone resettlement project coincided with the crystallisation of widespread antislavery sentiment into a formalised abolitionist movement in 1787. That year, the Society for Effecting the Abolition of the Slave Trade (SEAST) was formed. Abolitionism's new, mainstream status precipitated a new wave of black writing. For the first time, black authors began explicitly encouraging popular support for abolishing the slave trade. Ottobah Cugoano published his radical *Thoughts and Sentiments* in 1787, in which he suggested abolishing not only the slave trade but the system of slavery itself. No white author had been so daring. A second, edited-down edition of Cugoano's work appeared in 1791.[53] In the intervening years, another black abolitionist, Olaudah Equiano, had published his own antislavery autobiography, *The Interesting Narrative*. Partly because of Equiano's tireless promotional work, and partly because of its compelling, eloquent and powerful accounts of slavery and freedom, *The Interesting Narrative* was a tremendous commercial success, catapulting its author into celebrity status. By the time of his death in 1797, Equiano had become a reasonably well-heeled man thanks to the popularity of his book. It remains the single best-known work published by a black author in pre-abolition Britain.[54]

---

[51] *Morning Herald*, 10 May 1792. The expatriation of the 'black poor' is dealt with in detail in Braidwood, *Black Poor and White Philanthropists*; see also James Walker, *The Black Loyalists: The Search for a Promised Land in Nova Scotia and Sierra Leone, 1783–1870* (Toronto: University of Toronto Press, 1992).

[52] For Sierra Leone, see Christopher Fyfe, *A History of Sierra Leone* (Oxford: Oxford University Press, 1962); Suzanne Schwarz, 'Commerce, Civilization and Christianity: The Development of the Sierra Leone Company', in David Richardson, Suzanne Schwarz and Anthony Tibbles (eds.), *Liverpool and Transatlantic Slavery* (Liverpool: Liverpool University Press, 2007), 252–277; Suzanne Schwarz, 'Reconstructing the Life Histories of Liberated Africans: Sierra Leone in the Early Nineteenth Century', *History in Africa*, 39:1 (2012), 175–207; Michael Turner, 'The Limits of Abolition: Government, Saints and the "African Question", c. 1780–1820', *English Historical Review*, 112:446 (1997), 319–357.

[53] Ottobah Cugoano, *Thoughts and Sentiments on the Evil and Wicked Traffic of the Slavery and Commerce of the Human* Species (London, 1787); Ottobah Cugoano, *Thoughts and Sentiments on the Evil of Slavery* (London: Kirkby et al., 1791).

[54] Olaudah Equiano, *The Interesting Narrative of the Life of Olaudah Equiano, or Gustavus Vassa, the African* (London, 1789); John Bugg, 'The Other Intersting Narrative: Olaudah Equiano's Public Book Tour', *PMLA*, 121:5, 1424–1442. Equiano's daughter received £950 in his will. Vincent Carretta, *Equiano, the African: Biography of a Self-Made Man* (Athens: University of Georgia Press, 2005), 366.

Equiano's success also owed something to the broader political climate in Britain during the early years of the French Revolution. Through the early 1790s, support for abolition was widespread. Indeed, the ideals of 'liberty, equality and fraternity', adopted enthusiastically in radical British popular politics, for most people extended quite naturally to the enslaved in the West Indies. The moderate-reformist connections of SEAST members including Thomas Clarkson, Thomas Walker and even Granville Sharp, who had championed Somerset's cause in 1772, proved beneficial when enthusiasm for these egalitarian ideals was widespread in Britain. The ideological relationship between radicalism and antislavery was underscored after 1792, when news began to come in from across the Atlantic of a slave-led revolution in the French colony of St Domingue.[55] However, popular zeal for reform did not extend to the Houses of Parliament. When William Wilberforce – both the most politically conservative of the leading British abolitionists and the one most deeply embedded in the Westminster establishment – introduced two motions for abolishing the slave trade in 1791 and 1792, they both proved ultimately unsuccessful.[56]

When the formal antislavery movement stalled between 1794 and 1804, it was in some measure because of its associations with contemporaneous ideas about reforming the British political system. In the context of the anti-Jacobin backlash of the French Revolutionary War years, associations between high-profile abolitionists and domestic radicalism became toxic. After 1794, when reportage from St Domingue began to relay stories of impaled infants and massacres of whites, proslavery arguments that British abolitionism led to violent slave rebellions gained greater traction.[57] During the same year, the National Convention in

---

[55] See, for example, Anon., *A Particular Account of the Insurrection of the Negroes of St. Domingo* (London: Assemblée Générale, 1792).

[56] The 1791 motion was voted down (narrowly) in the Commons. The 1792 motion passed in Commons was stalled in the House of Lords, and in 1793 the Commons voted not to revisit the issue. Stephen Tomkins, *William Wilberforce: A Biography* (London: Lion, 2007), 86–120; William Hague, *William Wilberforce: The Life of the Great Anti-Slave Trade Campaigner* (London: HarperCollins, 2008), 169–198.

[57] John Oldfield, *Transatlantic Abolitionism in the Age of Revolution: An International History of Anti-Slavery, c. 1787–1820* (Cambridge: Cambridge University Press, 2013), 104–109; Robin Blackburn, *The Overthrow of Colonial Slavery, 1776–1848* (London: Verso, 1988), 148–161; David Brion Davis, *The Problem of Slavery in the Age of Emancipation* (New York: Alfred A. Knopf, 2014), 4; Ada Ferrer, 'Haiti, Free Soil, and Antislavery in the Revolutionary Atlantic', *American Historical Review*, 117:1 (2012), 40–66; James Walvin, 'The Impact of Slavery on British Radical Politics: 1787–1838', *Annals of the New York Academy of Sciences*, 292 (1977), 343–355; Mark Philp, *Reforming Ideas in Britain: Politics and Language in the Shadow of the French Revolution, 1789–1815* (Cambridge: Cambridge University Press, 2013), 32–33.

Paris voted to abolish slavery throughout the French Empire. British people began to seriously question exactly which type of liberty the antislavery movement represented. Was it truly British – restrained, moderate and honourable – or was it 'Jacobin' – extravagant, corrupt and bloodthirsty? Even leaving the ideological context aside, in mere practical terms the antiradical Two Acts of 1795 made generating the type of popular support hitherto associated with abolitionism appear tantamount to an act of sedition. The Seditious Meetings Act, limiting public assemblies to fifty people or fewer, prevented mass rallies for non-religious purposes. This included abolitionist mass meetings, like the one Clarkson had organised in Manchester in 1788, which had led to the largest popular petition in parliamentary history. Meanwhile, the Treason Act essentially rendered the language of 'liberty, equality and fraternity', which had played so naturally into abolitionism, subversive and potentially dangerous.

During this period, black writing, by and large, receded back into the pulpits of dissenting Christian groups. Evangelical authors such as Boston King recast their antislavery rhetoric as a part of a broader move toward establishment respectability by divorcing it from calls for abolition. Black writing had returned to its strictly religious roots, shifting away from a confrontational and galvanising mode and back to promoting Christian forbearance and the idea of post-corporeal liberation. Even though the only networks that could safely publish black writing in the paranoiac atmosphere of the late 1790s and early 1800s were religious ones, they were still under pressure from the government (not least by Wilberforce himself) to ensure that their activities were depoliticised.[58] Black writers such as King could only be published in this kind of environment when their visions of freedom were sufficiently divorced from the 'liberty' of radical discourse.

Napoleon Bonaparte's reintroduction of slavery in the French colonies in 1804 helped make abolitionism more palatable to conservative interests in Britain, and the parliamentary abolitionist machine, led by the irreproachably loyal Wilberforce, creaked back into action. But the difficult issue of St Domingue – now independent Haiti – still had to be handled sensitively. Black evangelicals such as King and John Jea continued to restrict themselves to spreading antislavery sentiment, rather than advocating emancipation. They kept their activities to a local scale. It was absolutely essential that their message not be confused with the type of 'black violence' arising from the Haitian revolution. Even after the

---

[58] See, for example, David Hempton, *Methodism and Politics in British Society, 1750–1850* (London: Hutchinson, 1984), 68–69.

Abolition of the Slave Trade Act was passed in 1807, black writers' antislavery rhetoric remained tethered to patriotic identity narratives. Abolishing slavery itself, of course, remained out of the question; it was seen as potentially endangering to Britain's beleaguered wartime economy. Plans for emancipating Britain's slaves were not seriously countenanced until 1823, well after the Napoleonic wars had been won. Wartime antislavery writing instead emphasised the Royal Navy's role in suppressing the slave trade, contrasting Britain's attempts to diminish the horrors of slavery with France's active pursuance of it. This patriotic rhetoric received a blow at the end of the wars in 1815, since one of the conditions of the peace negotiations allowed France to continue transporting slaves to their Caribbean colonies for five years without harassment from the Royal Navy.[59]

There was an outcry. Demobbed sailors and soldiers felt betrayed and let down by their government. Their commitment to the dangerous, terrifying task of waging war had been fostered in part by a belief that Britain was a humane as well as powerful nation that would not tolerate slave-trading. During the War of 1812, they had been joined by thousands of formerly enslaved people, just as they had during the American War of Independence. Allowing Britain's biggest commercial and military rival to continue its slave trade with impunity after the war was seen as a betrayal of these new friends and allies. Haiti once again became an important political bone of contention in British popular politics. During the wars, Britain had reopened trade with independent Haiti, and even officially recognised its neutrality, allowing badly needed commercial revenues to flow into the war effort. Despite this, the 1815 treaty offered no protection whatsoever for Haiti. As one commentator put it, 'for the last ten years we have enjoyed this lucrative branch of trade, and have maintained with the people of St. Domingo the relations of peace and amity ... we have now left them to the exterminating sword of France, without a single provision in their favour.'[60] It seemed that the much-lauded humanitarian principles supposedly embodied in Britain's abolition of the slave trade were being abandoned in an over-generous peace

[59] See Davis, *Age of Emancipation*, 74–82; Oldfield, *Transatlantic Abolitionism*, 251–253; David Turley, 'Antislavery Activists and Officials: "Influence", Lobbying and the Slave Trade, 1807–1850', in Keith Hamilton and Patrick Salmon (eds.), *Slavery, Democracy and Empire: Britain and the Suppression of the Slave Trade, 1807–1975* (Brighton: Sussex University Press, 2009), 81–92; Paul Kielstra, *The Politics of Slave Trade Suppression in Britain and France, 1814–48: Diplomacy, Morality and Economics* (London: Macmillan, 2000), 22–55.

[60] Anon., *Observations on that Part of the Late Treaty of Peace with France, Which Relates to the African Slave Trade* (London: Fillerton and Henderson, 1815), 3.

settlement. In this context, abolitionists from outside the political and social elite again came to embrace notions of political reform, and some black authors were keen to associate themselves with both of these movements.

Wedderburn, whose speech at his sentencing hearing at King's Bench in May 1820 was just one of a long line of anti-establishment stunts, was one of the most charismatic of these new 'radical abolitionists'.[61] In stark contrast to the cautiousness of the evangelical black writers of the preceding ten-year period, he presented uncompromising plans for universal slave emancipation outlined in his periodical *The Axe Laid to the Root*, published in 1817.[62] His descriptions of the day-to-day brutality and sexual abuse inherent in the slave system itself, published as part of his 1824 autobiography, *The Horrors of Slavery*, were similarly shocking.[63] Uniquely for any major British writer, Wedderburn actively encouraged violent slave resistance in his writings and speeches. What made his work particularly concerning for the political elite, and especially for absentee planters and slave-owners, was their timing: his texts were published in the aftermath of the large-scale slave rebellions in 1816 in Barbados ('Bussa's Rebellion') and in 1823 in Demerara.[64]

Wedderburn's calls for immediate emancipation indicated that popular abolitionism had split down the middle when it emerged from the wilderness after the wars with France. On one side were working-class radicals such as Wedderburn, joined by dissenters and Unitarians such as Elizabeth Heyrick.[65] For these people, the only way to prevent further slave insurrections was the total and immediate abolition of slavery. On

---

[61] For ultra-radicalism and antislavery during this period, see Iain McCalman, *Radical Underworld: Prophets Revolutionaries and Pornograhers in London, 1795–1840* (Cambridge: Cambridge University Press, 1988); Iain McCalman, 'Introduction', in Wedderburn, *The Horrors of Slavery and Other Writings*, ed. McCalman, 1–40.

[62] Robert Wedderburn, *The Axe Laid to the Root* (London: A. Seale, 1816), vols. 1–6.

[63] Robert Wedderburn, *The Horrors of Slavery* (London: R. Wedderburn, 1824); Robert Wedderburn, *An Address to the Right Honourable Lord Brougham and Vaux* (London: John Ascham, 1831).

[64] Michael Craton, *Testing the Chains: Resistance to Slavery in the British West Indies* (Ithaca, NY: Cornell University Press, 1982), 254–266; Drescher, *Abolition*, 232–233; Hilary Beckles, 'Emancipation by Law or War? Wilberforce and the 1816 Barbados Slave Rebellion', in David Richardson (ed.), *Abolition and Its Aftermath: The Historical Context* (London: Frank Cass, 1985), 80–104; Peter Linebaugh and Marcus Rediker, *The Many-Headed Hydra: The Hidden History of the Revolutionary Atlantic* (London: Verso, 2000), 302–305.

[65] For Elizabeth Heyrick's radicalism, see Claire Midgley, 'The Dissenting Voice of Elizabeth Heyrick: An Exploration of the Links between Gender, Religious Dissent, and Anti-Slavery Radicalism', in Elizabeth Clapp and Julie Jeffrey (eds.), *Women, Dissent and Anti-Slavery in Britain and America, 1790–1865* (Oxford: Oxford University Press, 2011), 88–110.

the other side stood a new generation of parliamentary gradualists led by Thomas Fowell Buxton, who relied on support and patronage from the respectable old guard of the 1780s and 1790s. These figures sought to gain support in Commons, and thought the only way to achieve this was with a more moderate agenda. The combination (though certainly not cooperation) of parliamentary and grass-roots antislavery activism ultimately succeeded in obtaining a slew of restrictive and ameliorative legislation in the latter half of the 1820s.[66]

At the onset of the 1830s, the gap between the radical and parliamentary abolitionists began to close from both sides at once. Emboldened by their successes (and perhaps impressed by the popularity of a series of sugar and cotton boycotts in the late 1820s), parliamentary activists began pushing for immediate abolition from 1829. Meanwhile, amid a broader move toward respectability, radicals began to reconcile their vision for emancipation to more moderate, 'establishment' views.[67] Even Wedderburn eventually came around to the moderatist agenda – his 1831 plan for emancipation, *An Address to Lord Brougham and Vaux*, was, by his standards, shockingly modest in ambition and scope.[68] Just as in the early 1790s, mass petitions began to flow into parliament, this time demanding the end of slavery itself. Women's antislavery societies resumed their key role in the movement, spurred on in 1831 by Mary Prince's accounts of the torture and sexual abuse of enslaved women in the Caribbean. Parliament, already in crisis over domestic reform, stalled as it had before, passing yet more restriction laws in 1830.

It was the slaves themselves who finally forced the issue. In 1831, the Baptist War – another huge slave uprising, this time in Jamaica – and its brutal suppression stimulated widespread press attention in Britain on the question of slavery.[69] The economic conditions surrounding abolition have been at the centre of historiographical debate for decades, but in any case the social unrest caused by Britain's continuing investment in

[66] For amelioration legislation, see for example the restrictive treaties with Brazil and Sweden in 1827, and the acts in 1824 and 1828 preventing slaves from being forcibly transported between colonies.
[67] See Aruna Krishnamurthy, 'Coffeehouse vs. Alehouse: Notes on the Making of the Eighteenth-Century Working-Class Intellectual', in Aruna Krishnamurthy (ed.), *The Working-Class Intellectual in Eighteenth- and Nineteenth-Century Britain* (London: Ashgate, 2009), 85–108; McCalman, *Radical Underworld*, 181–203.
[68] Robert Wedderburn, *An Address to Lord Brougham and Vaux* (London: J. Ascham, 1831).
[69] For the Baptist War, see Michael Craton, *Testing the Chains: Resistance to Slavery in the British West Indies* (Ithaca, NY: Cornell University Press, 1982), 291–322.

the institution was untenable.[70] By 1833 it was obvious that, in Seymour Drescher's words, slavery 'could no longer be sustained without continuous agitation at home and abroad'.[71] The Slavery Abolition Act was passed that year, and on 1 August 1834, around 800,000 slaves in the British West Indies – and more elsewhere in the British Empire – became, if only nominally, free.

Celebrities, Evangelicals, Radicals

If we are to expand our view of early black British writers beyond these now-familiar histories, we require an in-depth understanding of their relationships and the relationships that influenced the production of their texts. A key task of this book, then, is to map some of the web-like structures of social relations that surrounded black writers and their work. Examining three distinct types of network – those which helped to generate celebrity, those that sought to promote their chosen interpretation of Christianity, and those that fought for radical political change – and how they each affected early black writing allows us to see precisely how these authors fit into British society and culture more broadly. By shifting focus and fully recognising their contributions to areas beyond slavery and race, this approach enables us to see that eighteenth-century black intellectuals were important actors in the development of modern British society.

Why is such a shift in focus necessary? After all, some black authors became famous in eighteenth-century Britain explicitly *because* of their public and near exclusive association with the issues of race, slavery and abolition. Part I of this book investigates how these associations were forged by exploring the networks surrounding 'celebrity' black authors and their texts. Histories of celebrity culture in eighteenth-century Britain have traditionally focussed on either the stage or the page, concerning themselves primarily with the 'art' of promoting and disseminating an essential, authentic 'self' for public consumption through either theatre

---

[70] For the famous historiographical debate over the economics of slave emancipation, see Eric Williams, *Capitalism and Slavery* (Chapel Hill: University of North Carolina Press, 1944); Seymour Drescher, *Econocide: British Slavery in the Era of Abolition* (Pittsburgh, PA: University of Pittsburgh Press, 1977). Recent work has focused on the economics of the compensation paid out to former slave owners. See Catherine Hall et al., *Legacies of British Slave-Ownership: Colonial Slavery and the Formation of Victorian Britain* (Cambridge: Cambridge University Press, 2014). See also David Beck Ryden, *West Indian Slavery and British Abolition, 1783–1807* (Cambridge: Cambridge University Press, 2009).
[71] Drescher, *Abolition*, 263.

or the writing of fiction.[72] Felicity Nussbaum, Tom Mole, Claire Brock
and other scholars have argued that celebrities were important to the
development of personal identity in Britain because they simultaneously
defined and subverted an idealised and essential personal 'self', in a way
that could be widely reproduced and marketed.[73] Whereas these studies
have most often focused on the identitive and performative category of
gender, this book demonstrates that some black authors became famous
through the exploitation (and in some cases subversion) of expectations
about them as being uniquely situated to talk about slavery and racial
prejudice.

Beyond Slavery and Abolition breaks somewhat from convention in suggesting that we consider some black authors celebrities. While they were
well known, and undeniably talented, they were certainly not universally
celebrated, and they were seldom beset by adoring admirers (although, as
Hannah Rose Murray has demonstrated, the African American author
and abolitionist Frederick Douglass was during his visit to Britain in the
mid-1840s).[74] Yet, as the numerous and well-publicised sex scandals of
the period show, celebrity status was as often as not conferred by prurient
interest, controversy or sympathy as it was by breathless adoration.[75]
The precise definition of a celebrity in eighteenth-century Britain is still
the subject of debate, but Mole's model, in which celebrity is substanti-
ated in an individual, an audience and an industry, is certainly a useful
starting point.[76] In the case of black celebrity writers, the 'industry' was
provided by popular print culture; the 'audience' was provided by the rise
in popular antislavery sentiment; and the 'individual' took the form of an
antislavery or abolitionist authorial 'self', generated in negotiation with
each writer's production and distribution networks. Understanding the

[72] A foundational text in the study of historical celebrity is Leo Braudy, *The Frenzy of Renown: Fame and Its History* (Oxford: Oxford University Press, 1986). For the significance of essential 'selfhood' in this period, see Dror Wahrman, *The Making of the Modern Self: Identity and Culture in Eighteenth-Century England* (New Haven, CT: Yale University Press, 2004).
[73] David Worrall, *Celebrity, Performance, Reception: British Georgian Theatre as Social Assemblage* (Cambridge: Cambridge University Press, 2013); Felicity Nussbaum, *Rival Queens: Actresses, Performance, and the Eighteenth-Century British Theater* (Philadelphia: University of Pennsylvania Press, 2010); Tom Mole (ed.), *Romanticism and Celebrity Culture* (Cambridge: Cambridge University Press, 2009); Tom Mole, *Byron's Romantic Celebrity: Industrial Culture and the Hermeneutic of Intimacy* (London: Palgrave Macmillan, 2007); Claire Brook, *The Feminization of Fame, 1750–1830* (Basingstoke: Palgrave 2006).
[74] Hannah-Rose Murray, 'A "Negro Hercules": Frederick Douglass' Celebrity in Britain', *Celebrity Studies*, 7:2 (2016), 264–279.
[75] See Matthew Kinservik, *Sex, Scandal and Celebrity in Late Eighteenth-Century England* (Basingstoke: Palgrave Macmillan, 2007).
[76] Mole, *Byron's Romantic Celebrity*, 3–10.

practicalities of producing a marketable and supposedly 'authentic' identity within such well-defined associative networks allows us to see more clearly the mechanisms of celebrity culture and the role of media in constructing eighteenth-century British political identity – that is, the intersection of politics and popular culture.

For Ignatius Sancho, his fame as an antislavery writer was unintentional, since it mostly came to him after his death. Sancho had been a servant and shopkeeper as well as a masterful letter-writer, but after he died, his former correspondents, editor and biographer took great pains to represent him as an 'extraordinary negro', whose literary skills disproved proslavery arguments for the supposed intellectual inferiority of Africans. In contrast, Olaudah Equiano, the most famous black writer of this period, made himself into a public intellectual by navigating abolitionist networks and promoting his work as part of an emerging canon of antislavery writing. By the time Mary Prince's *Life* was published in 1831, abolitionists recognised the value of celebrity in promoting popular antislavery sentiment. Prince's network, centred on members of the Anti-Slavery Society, deliberately engineered for her a form of celebrity that was contingent on a gendered perception of her victimhood as a female slave. They hoped to create in Prince a representative female victim of the inhumanity of slavery, thus appealing to popular abolitionism's substantial female contingent. In each of these examples, black writing that was marketed as being about slavery or ethnicity became more popular than black writing about anything else. Black authors became famous in proportion to the extent that their work reflected the interests of the abolitionist movement. In modern historical and critical studies, as well as in popular culture, this remains the case.

Yet these were not the only stories black authors in eighteenth-century Britain wanted to tell. For some, faith was the most important thing in their lives, and this sometimes led them into opposition against their antislavery contemporaries. Part II of this book explores how evangelical networks influenced how black writing was written, published, sold and read. Traditionally, Britain has rarely been seen as a part of the black evangelical world of the eighteenth and nineteenth centuries.[77] While historians have taken a renewed interest in the role of black evangelicals in the Atlantic world, they usually restrict their attentions to North

---

[77] See, for example, Cedrick May, *Evangelicalism and Resistance in the Black Atlantic, 1760–1835* (Athens: University of Georgia Press, 2008), which only mentions Britain in passing in the context of the American Revolution.

America and the Caribbean.[78] Meanwhile, scholars of eighteenth- and early nineteenth-century British Protestantism have never taken seriously the role of black preachers in helping to facilitate links between evangelical groups and mainstream political culture.[79] As a result, accepted historiographical narratives of black Atlantic evangelicalism currently lack a British perspective, while accepted narratives of British evangelicalism lack a black perspective.

This is a curious omission, since, as E. P. Thompson famously suggested, evangelicalism (and Methodism in particular) was an essential component in the emergence of new egalitarian discourses in Britain during this period.[80] David Hempton has highlighted that the 'conservative instincts' of the Methodist movement (which Thompson found so obnoxious) actually helped to reconcile leading preachers to the abolitionist cause, generating much-needed platforms for popular support during the anti-radical years of the French Revolutionary and Napoleonic Wars.[81] The role of evangelical movements in promoting proslavery discourse, meanwhile, is evidently a source of discomfort for some historians of popular religion, and it is often dealt with rather perfunctorily.[82] Nevertheless, just as they did in the Americas, black authors provided a crucial link between pro-and antislavery discourses and the evolving cultures of evangelicalism in Britain.[83] They effectively acted

---

[78] See, for example, John Catron, *Embracing Protestantism: Black Identities in the Atlantic World* (Gainesville: University of Florida Press, 2016); Rita Roberts, *Evangelicalism and the Politics of Reform in Northern Black Thought, 1776–1863* (Baton Rouge: Louisiana State University Press, 2010); Joanna Brooks, *American Lazarus: Religion and the Rise of African-American and Native American Literatures* (Oxford: Oxford University Press, 2003); Robert Elder, *The Sacred Mirror: Evangelicalism, Honor, and Identity in the Deep South, 1790–1860* (Chapel Hill: University of North Carolina Press, 2016); Sylvia Frey and Betty Wood, *Come Shouting to Zion: African American Protestantism in the American South and British Caribbean to 1830* (Chapel Hill: University of North Carolina Press, 1998).

[79] See, for example, Joseph Stubenrauch, *The Evangelical Age of Ingenuity in Industrial Britain* (Oxford: Oxford University Press, 2016); James Schwenk, *Catholic Spirit: Wesley, Whitefield, and the Quest for Evangelical Unity in Eighteenth-Century British Methodism* (Plymouth: Scarecrow Press, 2008); Grayson Ditchfield, *The Evangelical Revival* (London: UCL Press, 1998); David Hempton: *The Religion of the People: Methodism and Popular Religion, c. 1750–1900* (London: Routledge, 1996).

[80] E. Thompson, *The Making of the English Working Class* (London: Penguin, 1968), 385–440.

[81] Hempton, *Religion of the People*, 162–179.

[82] See, for example, Alan Harding, *The Countess of Huntingdon's Connexion: A Sect in Action in Eighteenth-Century England* (Oxford: Oxford University Press, 2003), 209n219, the only mention of Hastings's consistent proslavery position.

[83] See Charles F. Irons, *The Origins of Proslavery Christianity: White and Black Evangelicals in Colonial and Antebellum Virginia* (Chapel Hill: University of North Carolina Press, 2008).

as translators between the moral lexicon of the slavery debates and those of the evangelical movements of which they were a part. By focusing on the specific textures of this process and by centring black agency in the spread of evangelical religion in Britain during this period, we arrive at a new understanding of how international nonconforming religious movements reconciled protest with loyalty, ensuring their own survival and expansion well into the nineteenth century.

I have already alluded to how Ukawsaw Gronniosaw's proslavery Calvinist friends contributed to his autobiography, ensuring that his voice be understood as a counter-argument to emerging antislavery rhetoric propagated by their Arminian rivals. In Boston King's case, important Wesleyan Methodists, working in collaboration with Wilberforce, encouraged him to write an autobiography that emphasised the possibilities of evangelical Christianity, while carefully avoiding any criticism of the Pitt administration's foreign or domestic policies, including on slavery. When the African American preacher John Jea came to Britain, he too worked within existing Methodist networks, this time organised spatially around the working-class districts of Liverpool, Bolton, Portsmouth and Winchester. Jea's associations with these networks enabled him to remain sensitive to local identity narratives when he composed and published an autobiography and book of hymns in Portsmouth between 1815 and 1816. Nonconformist evangelical networks thus provided rare and valuable opportunities for black authors to write and publish their life stories during the eighteenth century. However, because of denominational politics, conditional patronage and an increasing desire for establishment respectability, these opportunities often came with strings attached – usually relating to how slavery was represented.

Not so with politically radical networks. As Part III of this book shows, radicalism offered black authors unparalleled autonomy and intellectual freedom. Scholars of working-class culture in this period, notably Emma Griffin, have recently returned to autobiography as a key source on the radical movements.[84] This is related to a broader desire to understand how considerations of class and class consciousness intersected with other identitive categories such as race and gender. Life-writing not only offers arresting and immediate detail about how popular politics affected people at the individual level, but has in many instances also enabled us

---

[84] Emma Griffin, *Liberty's Dawn: A People's History of the Industrial Revolution* (New Haven, CT: Yale University Press, 2013); see also David Vincent, *Bread, Knowledge and Freedom: A Study of Nineteenth-Century Working Class Autobiography* (London: Europa, 1981); David Vincent, *Literacy and Popular Culture: England 1750–1914* (Cambridge: Cambridge University Press, 1989).

to fully 'see' members of the emergent working class who, by dint of their gender or ethnicity, were even more marginalised than their white male peers.[85] Increasingly, studies of working people's autobiographies highlight just how intellectually and personally diverse British plebeian radicalism was during this crucial period in the formation of working-class identity.

What happens to our view of radicalism when we look at it through the lens of black leadership? Iain McCalman's seminal work on Wedderburn and London's 'radical underworld' has demonstrated that black intellectuals were indeed key players in the movements for political reform in Britain.[86] Yet by placing such figures at the very centre of our investigations, we can begin to highlight the interconnectedness of domestic reform and contemporaneous debates over empire, migration and slavery. This reminds us that British radicals were not completely parochial in their concerns; indeed, like all serious political thinkers of the period, they kept a close eye on how British interests unfolded around the globe. Formerly enslaved black radicals represented a crucial link between the struggle for political and personal liberty at home with that of the oppressed in other parts of the globe – principally in Africa and the Americas.[87] This is not to overlook the fact that the domestic reform movements became increasingly nationalist (and indeed racist) from the late 1820s onward.[88] Rather, by centralising black radical perspectives and exploring the networks that influenced and helped to forge them, it encourages us to view working-class culture as encompassing views on global and imperial, as well as national politics.

In Ottobah Cugoano's case, the most influential network for him consisted of the new black immigrant community arriving in Britain after the American Revolutionary War. Cugoano served as a link between black radicalism, which resisted state-sponsored oppression of black people – for example, discouraging compliance with the Sierra Leone

---

[85] Kathryn Gleadle, *Borderline Citizens: Women, Gender, and Political Culture in Britain, 1815–1867* (Oxford: Oxford University Press, 2009); James Epstein, *Scandal of Colonial Rule: Power and Subversion in the British Atlantic during the Age of Revolution* (Cambridge: Cambridge University Press, 2012), 156–184; McCalman, *Radical Underworld*, 50–72; Mike Sanders, *Women and Radicalism in the Nineteenth Century* (London: Routledge, 2001).

[86] McCalman, *Radical Underworld*, and Robert Wedderburn, *The Horrors of Slavery and Other Writings*, ed. Iain McCalman (Princeton, NJ: Marcus Wiener, 1991).

[87] For the 'transatlantic proletariat', see Peter Linebaugh and Marcus Rediker, *The Many-Headed Hydra: The Hidden History of the Revolutionary Atlantic* (London: Verso, 2000), esp. 287–326.

[88] Ryan Hanley, 'Slavery and the Birth of Working-Class Racism in England, 1814–1833', *Transactions of the Royal Historical Society*, 26 (2016), 103–123.

resettlement project of 1787 – and white radicalism, which sought parliamentary reform. This nascent black radicalism was carried forward into the nineteenth century by Robert Wedderburn. Making use of an extensive network of radical collaborators, publishers and conspirators, he was able to produce a visionary rhetoric of global freedom, in which an idealised, post-revolutionary British liberty was inextricably linked to freedom from slavery and tyranny for all enslaved people. While Wedderburn's dependence on his interpersonal network eventually proved to be his downfall, his story epitomises how black writing was produced in eighteenth- and nineteenth-century Britain: as collaborative artefacts that emerged not from individual geniuses but from relationships between several actors.

In concentrating on how these tensions played out, this book examines discourses – constellations of ideas, texts, statements, shared values and assumptions, quirks of language, etc. – as much as it does interpersonal networks. It is no coincidence that discourses of celebrity, evangelicalism and radicalism in particular were undergoing significant shifts just as black writing was first being published in Britain. It rather indicates that black writing helped to constitute these changes. Black intellectuals were, in other words, highly significant actors in the emergence of radically new and persistent discourses of modernity. They were interested in matters well beyond the purview of slavery and abolition, even if that has always been the main frame of reference in which they are read.

Early black authors have been bound to slavery and abolition in this way. But by looking at their other bonds – to family, colleagues, patrons, students, employers, comrades and even, more abstractly, to discourses – we can begin to see the true extent of their contributions to British society and culture. By understanding how and why their work was written, published, sold and read, we can see that they used their own experiences to reach out and make readers care – of course, about the horrors of slavery, but just as much about freedom, faith, equality and friendship. And by revisiting their work mindful of these different types of bonds, we can begin the work of returning these authors to their rightful place, not at the margins but at the centre of British and Atlantic history.

Part I

Black Celebrities

1   Ignatius Sancho and Posthumous Literary Celebrity, 1779–1782

Our study begins at an ending. On 14 December 1780, Ignatius Sancho, a corpulent and splendid man, died at home, in the rooms behind his little grocery at 19 Charles Street, Mayfair. He left behind his wife, Anne, five children (whom he liked to call his 'Sanchonettas'), a dog named Nutts and a wide circle of friends and correspondents from all ranks of London society. Besides a shopkeeper, he had been an actor, a composer, a celebrated epistolarian and a high-ranking servant to one of the most elite families in the country. He was also the first black man that we know of to have voted in a parliamentary election.[1] He was sorely missed by everyone who knew him. A decision was made to publish his correspondence, for the benefit of his widow and children. Letters were collected; a subscription was raised. A short biography was commissioned. Steps were taken to prime the market. His editor, biographer and correspondents were left with a difficult question to answer: how was he to be remembered?

Sancho is routinely described as a 'man of letters'.[2] The phrase is freighted with the connotations of gentility, cultural refinement and social 'politeness' that tend to characterise popular depictions of eighteenth-century British society. Unlike most other black writers of the period, Sancho was raised from an early age in well-to-do and aristocratic London households. Born into slavery in 1729, he came to Britain at the age of two and was given as a gift to 'three maiden sisters, resident at Greenwich'.[3]

---

[1] Vincent Carretta, 'Three West Indian Writers of the 1780s Revisited and Revised', *Research in African Literatures*, 29:4 (1998), 75.

[2] See, for example, the collection of essays published to coincide with the unveiling of his portrait at the National Portrait Gallery, Reyahn King et al. (eds.), *Ignatius Sancho: African Man of Letters* (London: National Portrait Gallery, 1997).

[3] Ann Dingsdale has conjectured that 'these may have been the Legge sisters, three single women, sisters of the earl of Dartmouth, who lived directly opposite Montagu House.' Greenwich Education Services, *Ignatius Sancho (1729–1780): Life and Times* (London, 1998) cited in Brycchan Carey, '"The Extraordinary Negro": Ignatius Sancho, Joseph Jekyll, and the Problem of Biography', *British Journal for Eighteenth Century Studies*, 26 (2003), 2.

Despite his evidently precocious intellect, the sisters tried to keep him in a state of 'African ignorance'. This ultimately led him to flee their household in 1749 to live with Mary Montagu, Duchess of Montagu. He worked as a butler in the Montagu household for two years, until his mistress's death in 1751. Having inherited a small annuity from the Duchess, he left domestic service and, in 1758, married Anne Osborn, a black West Indian woman. When their third daughter, Elizabeth, was born in 1766, the pressures of a growing family meant that Sancho was forced to return to service, this time as valet to George Montagu, first Duke of Montagu of the second creation. Finally, in 1773, Ignatius, Anne, and their children all left the Duke's household to set up a grocer's shop.

Sancho was a prolific letter-writer for his entire adult life. Among his most widely reproduced correspondences is his exchange with the novelist Laurence Sterne between 1766 and 1768. Reprinted several times during his lifetime and immediately after his death, this brush with an established member of the traditional British literary 'elite' is often treated as the most remarkable aspect of Sancho's long and varied career.[4] However, with the dedicated Sancho scholarship undertaken since the late twentieth century, a fuller picture has emerged: one that paints him as a leading figure in the establishment of black British identity, a pioneer of antislavery and antiracist thought and a talented, inventive polymath in his own right.

Throughout his life, he cultivated and maintained meaningful social relationships with a wide range of correspondents, primarily through his mastery of familiar letters. As Clare Brant reminds us, the Habermasian conceptualisation of social arenas – as divisible into two non-porous 'public' and 'private' spheres – is an active hindrance to the reader of the eighteenth-century letter.[5] Social convention, particularly among culturally elite circles, allowed for ostensibly private manuscript letters to be composed and read in company, discussed, reviewed, circulated and even submitted for publication without permission from the original correspondent.[6] Letters might also be written with a view to posterity,

---

[4] See Markman Ellis, *The Politics of Sensibility: Race, Gender and Commerce in the Sentimental Novel* (Cambridge: Cambridge University Press, 1996), 49–128; Lynn Festa, *Sentimental Figures of Empire in Eighteenth-Century Britain and France* (Baltimore, MD: Johns Hopkins University Press, 2006), 85–87; M.-C. Newbould, *Adaptations of Laurence Sterne's Fiction: Sterneana, 1760–1840* (London: Routledge, 2013), 90–94.

[5] Clare Brant, *Eighteenth-Century Letters and British Culture* (London: Palgrave Macmillan, 2006), 5.

[6] The latter happened to Sancho when his letter to John Browne was supposedly 'inserted unknown to Mr. Sancho' into the 13 May 1778 edition of the *Public Advertiser*. Sancho, *Letters*, 191–192. For public letter reading and writing, see Eve Tavor Bannet, *Empire*

since it was not unusual for particularly good epistolary performances, or the correspondence of well-known individuals, to be archived and/or posthumously published. The status of a handwritten letter as neither fully 'private' nor 'public' facilitated (indeed, actively encouraged) the construction of multiple epistolary personae, easing some of the tensions inherent in a social environment that often made contradictory demands of its actors.

To no one was the process of enacting multiple epistolary characters more necessary than Sancho. As a man, he was expected to be world-wise, gallant and carousing; as a Christian, he should display sobriety and devotion to his family. As an educated man of property, he was expected to discourse knowledgably on literature, music, philosophy, art and politics; as a shopkeeper, he needed to display due deference to his customers and social superiors. As a British man, he should be patriotic and dedicated to his country; as a black man, he had to acknowledge his alien status. The only way Sancho could exist in all these different states at once was to emphasise particular aspects of his personality, values and beliefs according to different correspondents and social situations. These epistolary techniques helped Sancho to maintain a precarious social situation as black 'insider' in the rarefied world of aristocratic and bourgeois London society.

Take, for example, his correspondence with a young black man-about-town, Julius Soubise. The son of an enslaved black woman and a white man in St. Kitts, Soubise was brought to England in 1764 at the age of ten and worked as a servant to the Duchess of Queensberry. He 'soon became the subject of satiric engravings as a macaroni or fop', and he and the 'eccentric' Queensberry were 'rumoured to be lovers'.[7] These rumours were clearly circulating by 1773, when a suggestive etching featuring the two of them fencing was produced by William Austin (see Figure 1.1). Sancho's letters to young men of Soubise's age were usually filled with playful curiosity about their sexual adventures and a jocular, world-wise sensibility. For example, when writing to his regular correspondent William Stevenson in 1777, he playfully chided him with a knowing comment on his dissolute habits. 'While thou hast only one mouth to feed – one back to cloath – and one wicked member to indulge – thou

of Letters: Letter Manuals and Transatlantic Correspondence, 1680–1820 (Cambridge: Cambridge University Press, 2005), 225–273.

[7] Vincent Carretta (ed.), Unchained Voices: An Anthology of Black Authors in the English-Speaking World of the 18th Century (Lexington: University Press of Kentucky), 103 n. 3; Nussbaum, The Limits of the Human, 7.

Figure 1.1 William Austin, *The D—— of —————— playing at FOILS with her favorite Lap Dog MUNGO after Expending near £10,000 to make him a ——*, 1773, hand-coloured etching, 273 mm × 376 mm. Courtesy of the Lewis Walpole Library, Yale University.

wilt have no pity from me.'[8] His letters to Soubise, on the other hand, took on an altogether different character.

In a much-cited letter dated 11 October 1772, he advised Soubise to be more cautious and Christian in his lifestyle, deploying, in Ellis's words, a 'tone of pious morality more akin to conduct-book discourse and the reforming language of the sermon' than the libertine mode he favoured with other men:[9]

Happy, happy lad! What a fortune is thine! – Look round upon the miserable fate of almost all our unfortunate colour – superadded to ignorance – see slavery, and the contempt of those very wretches who roll in affluence from our labours superadded to this woeful catalogue – hear the ill-bred and heart-wracking abuse of the foolish vulgar. – You, S[oubis]e, tread as cautiously as the strictest rectitude can guide ye.[10]

---

[8] Sancho, *Letters*, vol. 1, 170–171.
[9] Ellis, 'Sentimental Libertinism and the Politics of Form', 210.
[10] Sancho, *Letters*, vol. 1, 42.

At the time, their social positions were relatively comparable – Sancho was still working as a valet in the Montagu household, while Soubise's position was technically that of valet to Queensberry, who had apparently solicited Sancho's 'intervention' in the first place.[11] Yet Sancho's advice to tread carefully drew its seriousness and authority from another thing they had in common: the likelihood that either of them could have remained in slavery. Whatever the reason, it is clear that he was able to carefully pitch the tenor and content of his writing to suit his readership. This was to become a key ingredient in commercially successful black writing up until at least the abolition of slavery in the British colonies more than half a century later.

Sancho's eye for the changing demands of social convention, his performance of multiple epistolary personae and the consideration he evidently gave to posterity when writing led some late twentieth-century critics to characterise him as 'obsequious' or 'apologetic, complaisant', the 'golden black boy of the English aristocracy and gentry'.[12] Sukhdev Sandhu pithily summed up this tendency when he lamented that 'Sancho has often been condemned by critics and historians for being a ludicrous, preening traitor to his race.'[13] However, a new critical orthodoxy on Sancho has since emerged that positively valorises his 'heterogeneous self-portrayal' as a strategy of survival and even subversion in the constrained social ecosystem of eighteenth-century London's polite *ton*.[14] Many (notably Ellis and Brycchan Carey) have recognised this as a contribution to generating antislavery sentiment among the wider reading public.[15] In particular, his epistolary enactments of sensibility and libertine masculinity, widely celebrated at the time as an example of the

[11] Jekyll, 'Life', in Sancho, *Letters*, v. 1, xiii.

[12] James Walvin, *Black and White: The Negro in English Society, 1550–1945* (London: Allen Lane, 1973), 61. It should be noted that Walvin later modified his opinion of Sancho. Norma Myers, *Reconstructing the Black Past: Blacks in Britain, 1770–1830* (London: Routledge, 1996), 133. Folarin Shyllon, *Black People in Britain, 1555–1833* (Oxford: Oxford University Press, 1977), 33.

[13] Sukhdev Sandhu, 'Ignatius Sancho and Laurence Sterne', *Research in African Literatures*, 29:4 (1998), 88.

[14] See, for example, Soren C. Hammerschmidt, 'Character, Cultural Agency and Abolition: Ignatius Sancho's Published Letters', *Journal for Eighteenth-Century Studies*, 31:2 (2008), 259–274; Francoise Le Jeune, '"Of a Negro, a Butler and a Grocer" (Jekyll, 7) – Ignatius Sancho's Epistolary Contribution to the Abolition Campaign (1766–1780)', *Etudes Anglaises*, 61:4 (2008), 440–445; C. L. Innes, *A History of Black and Asian Writing in Britain* (Cambridge: Cambridge University Press, 2002), 17–55.

[15] Brycchan Carey, '"The Hellish Means of Killing and Kidnapping": Ignatius Sancho and the Campaign against the "Abominable Traffic for Slaves"', in Brycchan Carey, Markman Ellis and Sarah Salih (eds.), *Discourse of Slavery and Abolition: Britain and Its Colonies, 1760–1838* (London: Palgrave Macmillan, 2004), 81–95; Ellis, *Politics of Sensibility*, 49–128.

intellectual potential of African people, have been understood as among the most powerful weapons in his antiracist and antislavery arsenal.[16] Certainly, the way black men were represented in Britain in the context of transatlantic slavery was at issue in his letters to Soubise. Meanwhile, his brushes with some of Britain's leading celebrities – especially his correspondence with Sterne, his portrait by Thomas Gainsborough and his friendship with the actor David Garrick – have provided loci for more widespread popular and scholarly interest than that enjoyed by most black authors of the period.[17] Indeed, the mere fact of his *connectedness* – the magnitude of his social cachet among the established eighteenth-century cultural elite – has drawn far more attention than the process by which it was constructed. As with Equiano, Sancho is often understood as something of a celebrity without a full consideration of how he attained that status.

It has been established, then, that culturally speaking, Sancho had friends in high places and that he knew how to suit his writing for them. Yet he was not widely known and celebrated beyond this immediate social circle until years after his death. Despite the liminal public/private status of the eighteenth-century familiar letter as a form, the transition from essentially private *correspondent* to explicitly public *author* took place posthumously for Sancho. In an effort to raise money for his widow and children and to celebrate his life, his friends consciously made a literary celebrity of him after his death. Sancho's editor, biographer and memorialisers attempted to emphasise his literary achievements by accentuating the sentimental aspects of his character and 'story'. In doing so, they actually shifted focus away from the intrinsic personal characteristics for which he was remembered so fondly by his friends and on to the perceived ethnic differences which were to mark him out as a novelty. By the time his collected *Letters* appeared in 1782, a broad market had heard about the black man who had corresponded with Sterne. With the professed aim of 'shewing that an untutored African may possess abilities equal to an European', the editing and paratext to his correspondence played up to that public perception, ensuring a form of

---

[16] See, for example, Brycchan Carey, *British Abolitionism and the Rhetoric of Sensibility: Writing, Sentiment, and Slavery, 1760–1807* (London: Palgrave Macmillan, 2005), 1–72; Nussbaum, *The Limits of the Human*, 189–212; Markman Ellis, 'Ignatius Sancho's Letters: Sentimental Libertinism and the Politics of Form', in Carretta and Gould (eds.), *Genius in Bondage*, 199–217; Felicity Nussbaum, 'Being a Man: Olaudah Equiano and Ignatius Sancho', in Carretta and Gould (eds.), *Genius in Bondage*, 54–71; Markman Ellis, *Politics of Sensibility*, 49–128.

[17] See, for example, the essays in King et al. (eds.), *Ignatius Sancho, African Man of Letters*.

celebrity contingent on his status as (to quote the very first words of his posthumous biography) 'the extraordinary negro'.[18]

Public Life after Death

Within a few months of his death, one of Sancho's correspondents, Frances Crewe, began contacting their mutual acquaintances to request copies of his letters. At the same time, she began to raise a subscription to publish them. Writing to Sir Martin Holkes on 24 July 1781, Thomas Lord recalled how this process took place:[19]

Miss Crew lately dind here, she patronizes Ignatius Sancho's family, a widow, & three children, one a cripple, Mr. Holkes answered for one of them, Miss Crew hath received already near one hundred pounds by subscription for his Letters, knowing Sancho I threw in my mise [crumb, breadcrumb, *OED*]. I fear as Dr Johnson at present declines the drawing up the Memoirs of Sancho's Life, that the account may not be so entertaining as the subject would bear, some of Sancho's letters being surprising, when known, that he wrote them behind his counter, whilst he was serving in a little retail way to his customers, women and children, at a time that he was in a very bad state of health, labouring under a complication of distempers.[20]

This quotation illuminates a number of the processes that concern this chapter. Above all, as this letter was written by a correspondent not included in the *Letters*, it demonstrated that Sancho was fondly remembered by a larger social network than that represented in his published correspondence. Second, it demonstrates that the colour of Sancho's skin was not the primary measure of his character given by his friends, nor even the most 'surprising' aspect behind the composition of his erudite letters. This might in itself be surprising given the wording of the editor's preface and the biography included with his published correspondence. Third, its phrasing sheds new light on the commissioning of Sancho's biographer by demonstrating that Samuel Johnson was asked first and 'declined' the task, or at least could not find time to complete it to the publication deadline. This contradicts the account of Joseph Jekyll, the man finally commissioned to write the biography, who suggested that Johnson first promised and afterward neglected to write it.[21]

---

[18] Sancho, *Letters*, vol. 1, ii, iii.

[19] This letter confirms William Stevenson's widely accepted identification of Crewe as the editor. See Ignatius Sancho, *Letters of the Late Ignatius Sancho*, ed. Paul Edwards and Polly Rewt (Edinburgh: Edinburgh University Press, 1994), 279–281.

[20] Norfolk Record Office, MC 5D/30/3 503X7, 'Thomas Lord to Sir Martin Holkes, 24 July 1781', ff. 1–2.

[21] See Sancho, *Letters*, ed. Edwards and Rewt, 268.

Finally, Lord's mention of Mr. Holkes 'answering for' one of Sancho's children suggests a wide network of patronage for the family, incorporating and stretching well beyond the subscription to and sale of the *Letters*. This suggests that Sancho was aware of his own impending death and put measures in place to provide for his family once he was gone. All of these circumstances demand a reading of the *Letters* as a purposefully constructed commercial and literary artefact, in which Sancho's self-representations were carefully but not unproblematically manipulated by Crewe and Jekyll to show him in the best light presumed possible and thereby advance an antislavery agenda and maximise income for the support of his family.

While Carey, Ellis and Sandhu have all demonstrated that close readings of Sancho's letters mark him out as a consistent and outspoken attacker of racial prejudice and slavery, less has been done to demonstrate how his status as a black man influenced how his work was edited and then read after publication.[22] Soren Hammerschmidt has suggested that Sancho's blackness overtook his own 'heterogeneous self-portrayal' in the years after his death as the primary arbiter of his identity.[23] White readers beyond Sancho's immediate circle of acquaintance found themselves unable to look beyond the issue of his black skin, leading to a homogenised understanding of his writing in the isolated contexts of race and slavery. A reading of three poems written about Sancho, two during his own lifetime and another shortly after his death, broadly supports Hammerschmidt's assertion but suggests that reductionist readings of his letters began well before Crewe and Jekyll's interventions in the manuscripts.

The first two of these poems, written by Ewan Clark (a stranger to Sancho, as far as we are aware) and published in his *Miscellaneous Poems* in 1779, were a reworking of the exchange of letters between Sancho and Sterne. The text of these letters was reprinted several times during Sancho's lifetime, accruing him a small degree of 'reflected' celebrity as a correspondent of Sterne's and moreover as an oddity because of the combination of his race and level of education and refinement. 'To their contemporaries', observes Ellis, 'such a connection was unusual enough to appear a kind of wonder of the age.'[24] It was certainly worth reprinting. As well as appearing in Sterne's posthumously published

---

[22] See Carey, 'Ignatius Sancho and the Campaign', 81–95; Ellis, 'Sentimental Libertinism and the Politics of Form', 199–219; Sukhdev Sandhu, 'Ignatius Sancho: An African Man of Letters', in Reyahn King et al. (eds.), *Ignatius Sancho: African Man of Letters* (London: National Portrait Gallery, 1997), 45–75.

[23] Hammerschmidt, 'Character, Cultural Agency and Abolition', 270.

[24] Ellis, 'Sentimental Libertinism and the Politics of Form', 199.

correspondence, the exchange appeared in the *Monthly Review*, the *Edinburgh Magazine and Review*, the *Monthly Miscellany* (twice), the *Gentleman's Magazine*, the *Sentimental Magazine* and the *Weekly Miscellany*, all before Sancho's death, with several more republications appearing immediately afterward and another spate after the publication of the *Letters* in 1782.[25] Sancho was identified in various ways in the titles of these reprints, ranging from the specific ('Ignatius Sancho, a free Black in London') to the generalised ('a Black, in the service of the Duke of Montague') to the obliviously 'vulgar and illiberal' ('a NEGROE').[26] In other words, before the publication of his *Letters*, Sancho was known to the public primarily (and often generically) as a 'black' who wrote to Laurence Sterne on the topic of slavery.

Clark's poems, entitled 'From Ignatius Sancho to Mr. Sterne' and 'From Mr. Sterne, to Ignatius Sancho', were fairly literal versifications of the original letters.[27] The chief artistic liberty Clark appears to have taken with the source material is the elevation of Sancho's sentimental rhetoric to a more declarative pitch. For example, Sancho's original letter stated by way of introduction that 'I am one of those people whom the vulgar and illiberal call *"Negurs."* – The first part of my life was rather unlucky, as I was placed in a family who judged ignorance the best and only security for obedience.'[28] In Clark's reworking, this was rephrased to become

> I am from that ill-fated lineage sprung,
> Term'd *Negroe* by the low, illiberal tongue.
> Fate on my youthful years indignant lowr'd,
> And in life's bowl her baneful acids pour'd:
> Plac'd me where unenlighten'd ignorance,
> Was for obedience deem'd the best defence.[29]

While this passage anticipated the coupling of sentimentalism and anti-slavery discourse which was to characterise much abolitionist rhetoric in the following decades, the other major deviation from the original letters undercut the essentially universalising message promoted by Sancho

---

[25] *Monthly Review, or Literary Journal*, 53 (Nov. 1775), 403–413; *Edinburgh Magazine and Review*, 4 (Dec. 1775), 696–698; *Monthly Miscellany*, 3 (Dec. 1775), 561–563; *Monthly Miscellany*, [no number], (Sep. 1776), 405–406; *Gentleman's Magazine*, 46 (Jan. 1776), 27–29; *Sentimental Magazine*, [no number] (Sep. 1776); 405–406; *Weekly Miscellany*, 9 February 1778, 451–452.
[26] *Monthly Miscellany*, [no number], (Sep. 1776), 405; *Edinburgh Magazine and Review*, 4 (Dec. 1775), 696; *Weekly Miscellany*, 9 February 1778, 451.
[27] Ewan Clark, *Miscellaneous Poems* (Whitehaven: J. Ware & Son, 1779), 214–219.
[28] Sancho, *Letters*, vol. 1, 95–96.   [29] Clark, *Miscellaneous Poems*, 214.

when he first reached out to Sterne.[30] Where the original passage read 'the latter part of my life has been – thro' God's blessing, truly fortunate, having spent it in the service of one of the best families in the kingdom', Clark's poem stated that 'Plac'd with the truly good, and nobly great / more mild than freedom seems my servile state'.[31] This transliteration of free domestic service into bonded servility drew attention to Sancho's own supposed lack of agency in his professional capacity as a butler to the Duke of Montagu, and the resonances therein with his infant status as enslaved. In other words, the cardinal marker of Sancho's identity, for Clark, was his ethnic and professional similitude to slaves.

An elegiac poem published in 1782 represented Sancho quite differently. The 'Epistle to Mr. J. H——, on the Death of His Justly Lamented Friend, Ignatius Sancho' focused primarily on his intrinsic personal qualities and interests. Mentions of his profession emphasised his industriousness, as opposed to the comparative modesty of his stations as butler and shopkeeper. For example,

> Look where, his brow ne'er forrow'd by a frown,
> An honest industry his labours crown;
> See him oft listen with attentive ear,
> The calm Revenge, and stifle Censure's sneer:
> Home pac'd Compassion where Detraction came,
> And Anger, as she stalk'd, put out her flame![32]

This poem chiefly lamented the loss of Sancho as a friend, and while it acknowledged the 'sublimer beams' of 'Learning's ever-copious streams', emanating from his conversation, the focus remained on his social status as 'Monitor and Sage' to his friends.[33] Tellingly, the poem made only one oblique reference to Sancho's skin:

> Who judge complexion ere they look for sense;
> And count the heart an atmosphere too dense;
> Ah! pity these, and teach them yet to know,
> Content and truth, superior beauties, flow
> From hidden worth; teach them with joy to scan,
> Those brighter honours that exalt the man.[34]

---

[30] See, for example, Brycchan Carey, 'William Wilberforce's Sentimental Rhetoric: Parliamentary Reportage and the Abolition Speech of 1789', *The Age of Johnson: A Scholarly Annual*, 14 (2003), 281–305.

[31] Sancho, *Letters*, vol. 1, 96; Clark, 'From Ignatius Sancho to Mr. Sterne', 215.

[32] Anon., 'Epistle to Mr. J. H——, on the Death of His Justly Lamented Friend, Ignatius Sancho', in Anon., *A Select Collection of Poems: With Notes, Biographical and Historical* (London: J. Nichols, 1772), vol. 8, 277.

[33] Anon., 'Epistle to Mr. J. H——', 278.   [34] Anon., 'Epistle to Mr. J. H——', 278–279.

Extreme caution must always guide any interpretation of absence in a historical text. However, it noteworthy that the only mention of skin colour, in an eighty-line poem on the subject of a man best known to the public for being black, was a repudiation of racial prejudice.

This is all the more significant when considering that no further mention of his 'complexion' was made in the page of biographical notes that accompanied the 'Epistle'. Rather, Sancho's elite literary, musical and intellectual preferences were highlighted. The chief measure of his character was not his 'complexion' but rather his 'wit and humour', the fact that he was 'conversant with music in its happiest branches', his 'strong inclination for literary pursuits', and his extensive 'knowledge of the Sacred Writings'.[35] The final line of the biographical notes functioned like an advertisement for the forthcoming *Letters* and thus revealed a practical motive behind the publication of the poem, complementing its nominal elegiac function. Sancho's 'correspondences', the editor wrote, 'were chiefly of a literary kind, and are now preparing for the public inspection, in two volumes 8vo. for the benefit of his Widow and four Children, under the auspices of a very respectable subscription.'[36] The dual meaning implied by 'respectable subscription', as referring to a subscription by respectable persons as well as a respectably large sum of money, further reinforced Sancho's public status as an individual whose personal qualities entitled him to posthumous respect and recognition. It appears that Sancho's popularity among his friends inspired them not only to publicly declare his intellectual achievements but also to support his efforts to provide financially for his family after his death.

In Crewe's case, the desire to care for both Sancho's family and his reputation led to the collection, edition and publication of some of his letters. While it seems likely that Sancho himself initiated this process, it is now agreed among academics that Crewe was the editor of the *Letters*.[37] An examination of manuscript versions of some of his letters indicates that Crewe continued the construction of a sentimental epistolary style with the intention of drawing attention to Sancho's intellectual prowess and, especially, his moral sensibilities. Editorial decisions included the elision of details dealing with the unglamorous minutiae of Sancho's daily life as a shopkeeper, such as the removal of a postscript about sausages from an otherwise achingly sentimental letter written to

---

[35] Anon., 'Epistle to Mr. J. H——', 280.   [36] Anon., 'Epistle to Mr. J. H——', 280.

[37] For suggestion of Sancho's involvement, see Carey, 'Ignatius Sancho and the Campaign', 82–93. Consensus on Crewe as the editor has been unilateral since Sancho, *Letters of the Late Ignatius Sancho*, ed. Edwards and Rewt. Manuscript evidence cited above confirms this identification.

Figure 1.2 Ignatius Sancho's Trade Card, c. 1778, engraving on
paper, 620 mm × 970 mm.
Courtesy of the British Museum.

Seth Stevenson on 5 December 1778.[38] More problematic, however, are
Crewe's interventions downplaying or obscuring the ethical ambiguities
of his connection to slave-grown produce such as sugar and tobacco.
While some modern scholars have noted the 'heavy irony' in Sancho's
sale of slave-grown produce, there is no mention of this seeming conflict of interests in the published *Letters*.[39] But Sancho himself never
attempted to conceal his sale of such commodities as sugar or tobacco,
or their links to slavery – indeed, as his trade cards show, slave-grown
products formed a key part of his livelihood, and he was keen to advertise
them for their quality (Figure 1.2).

A letter to Rev. Seth Stevenson, written on 4 January 1779, revealed
Sancho's anxieties over selling sugar to be largely expressed in mercantile, rather than ethical terms:

[38] BL, Add. MSS. 89077, Stevenson Papers: The Letters of Ignatius Sancho, 'Ignatius
Sancho to Seth Stevenson, 5 Dec. 1778'. The published version of this letter appears
without postscript in Sancho, *Letters*, 120–121.
[39] Ellis, *The Politics of Sensibility*, 58.

I have with utmost care & attention strove that the Quality of the Goods (you so kindly commissioned one to send) should be the very best in kind – The Scotch snuff I got at Mr. Arnold's – the Rappee is Harham's best – the tea I hope will meet with approbation – the Sugar, I have doubts of – it doth not please me – in truth, it is a shocking article at present – it will I fear be so for some time – there is a villainy in that business – tamely suffer'd – too gross for patience – I am loseing in the course of the last 12 months – above as many pounds by it – & can not please any of my customers – the lumps I have sent you are at prime last – & indifferent as they are sell usually now at 9d/pr pound – the coffee – is pick'd – & is the very same – as his Majesty (God Bless him) constantly has …[40]

On first reading, this reference to the 'villainy' in the sugar business would seem like an outspoken attack on slavery. However, such an outburst would have been completely self-destructive in what was essentially a courtesy letter accompanying a large and profitable order from a well-respected elderly clergyman. Sancho's concern over his losing money by the 'shocking article' suggests that his concerns are rather more to do with the quality of the product he was able to offer his customer, as also indicated by his protestations of the quality of the rest of the order. It was common in the eighteenth century for importers and wholesalers to mispackage inferior quality produce and claim that it was of a higher standard. As Selwyn Carrington has demonstrated, imports of high-quality sugars into Britain had been falling throughout the American Revolution, leaving the market saturated with 'indifferent' produce.[41] Sancho would have struggled to obtain the top-quality groceries expected by his high-status clientele, and therefore it is not surprising that he would feel the need to apologise for selling inferior sugar.

It is possible that Crewe made the conscious decision not to include this letter when she compiled the published correspondence. The letter formed part of a collection originally owned by Sancho's friend William Stevenson (son of Rev. Seth Stevenson), and most of the other manuscripts from the same bundle made it into the final published *Letters*. As well as the removal of this and other letters primarily dealing with trade, evidence suggesting that Crewe intervened in selecting the content of the published *Letters* may be inferred elsewhere. For example, in October 1777, Sancho wrote to William Stevenson, recounting a conversation about him with a mutual friend, John Meheux. The version published in

---

[40] BL, Add. MSS. 89077, Stevenson Papers: The Letters of Ignatius Sancho, 'Ignatius Sancho to Seth Stevenson, 4 Jan. 1779'.

[41] Selwyn H. H. Carrington, 'The American Revolution and the British West Indies Economy', in Barbara Solow and Stanley Engerman (eds.), *British Capitalism and Caribbean Slavery: The Legacy of Eric Williams* (Cambridge: Cambridge University Press, 1987), 135–162.

the *Letters* read, 'I made him read your letter – and what then? "truly he was not capable – he had no classical education – you write with elegance – ease – propriety." – Tut, quoth I, pr'ythee give not the reins to pride.'[42] By comparison, the original manuscript version included an additional passage: 'I made him read yr. letter – & what then – truly, he was not capable – he had no classical education – you write with elegance – ease propriety – tut Quoth I – my bum in a hat box – man! Prithee – give not the reins to pride.'[43] Crewe removed the reference to Sancho's 'bum' because it undercut the serious tone of the advice he was offering. The result was a rather more sonorous passage which emphasised Sancho's oracular, mentoring role to his younger male friends. The reader was presented with the image of a far more serious exchange of philosophical advice, both in the reported scene and the in report itself, than Sancho had originally intended. While the libertine and sentimental mode of many of his letters led to frequent references to his body (at least one mention of his 'bum' was retained in the published *Letters*), Crewe may have made this particular editorial decision with the intention of emphasising the intellectual gravitas of the author.[44]

Another omitted manuscript letter hints at the extent to which Sancho's original libertine letters were sanitised by Crewe's editorship. Dealing with the potentially thorny issues of domestic politics, ethnicity and debauchery, and written on 1 April 1779, apparently when Sancho was drunk, this extraordinary manuscript justifies reproduction in full:

No – that was your mistake – tho a kind one – I have no Irish stuff – wish I had – but by the folly of our saving every debt in the way of Irish Commerce – the duty is so Extravagantly high – as to preclude every Idea of national profit. – Read the crisis – & blush for the blunders, barbarity, & madness of thy countrymen – Read – the transactions of both houses – & then reply – I am sir an Affrican – with two ffs if you please – & proud am I to be of a country that knows no politicians – nor lawyers – nor [scribbled out] – nor x1x2x3x4x5x [*sic*] nor thieves of my denomination save *natural* for by the pomposity of Ministerial Omnipotence, I do aver that you, aye & Highmore – one of the Douces form a Jametto – mark, I do not mean a Trio – for most exquisite – as I know thy feelings are, I would not wound them by a design'd blunder – no, not for a tenth Aldremediah – but the Macaban is fine – & I thank thee – for thy zeal to serve me – tell Osborne to Love me – as I do him – Give Highmore a drubbing for debaunching – thy room – & wronging the chastity of thy Pembroke table – abuse him – for his naughty poetry – & to conclude maledict him & every soul thou meetest with – in the salt *fish* manner – but beware of connivances – & remember, there is nothing less

---

[42] Sancho, *Letters*, vol. 1, 159–160.
[43] BL, Add. MSS. 89077, Stevenson Papers: The Letters of Ignatius Sancho, 'Ignatius Sancho to William Stevenson, n.d.'
[44] Sancho, *Letters*, vol. 1, 55.

wholesome than the spawn of barble – from which – & the 7 plagues of the Hebrew Talmad.

Pray heaven of his mercy keep us all – now to &c &c.
       Invincibly inexplicable,
       Ign Sancho[45]

In the bottom-right corner of the verso section of the folded sheet, Sancho had scrawled 'Damn'd High' in a bubble, by way of explanation for his 'invincibly inexplicable' prose. The libertine preoccupations of this letter – manly interest in politics, over-indulgence in alcohol, lewd double-entendre – were mixed with tropes and characteristics unique to Sancho's correspondence.[46] While absolving himself of responsibility for the 'blunders, barbarity and madness' of the British political state by avowing himself to be 'an Affrican', he simultaneously reminded Stevenson of the rightfulness of his place within their social circle. His enactment of the libertine mode here, as elsewhere, was dependent on an external locus of sexuality, mastery of literary and arcane texts, intellectual elitism and good humour. Bourgeois cultural pursuits became a surrogate for sex when Highmore 'debauched' the 'chastity' of Stevenson's writing desk with his 'naughty poetry'. Sancho's pride in his origins, meanwhile, was expressed in direct opposition to the British statesmen who, he assumed, embodied masculine characteristics antithetical to his own. British 'lawyers' and 'politicians' thus became synonymous with 'thieves' and other words too foul to write out; their deceitfulness was counterpoised against the honesty and industry he had inherited from his African origins. The now well-known links between literary sentimental libertinism and political radicalism were uniquely reconfigured by Sancho to incorporate a positive image of African ethnicity – one whose 'natural' characteristics were amenable to idealised British masculine social behaviours supposedly neglected by British politicians.[47]

Crewe's probable decision to exclude these manuscripts from the published collection can thus be understood to stem from a desire to

---

[45] BL, Add. MSS. 89077, Stevenson Papers: The Letters of Ignatius Sancho, 'Ignatius Sancho to William Stevenson, 1 Apr 1779'.

[46] Sancho was no stranger to writing about politics. His account of the Gordon riots of 1780, for example, are now among the best-known to historians. See Brycchan Carey, '"The Worse than Negro Barbarity of the Populace": Ignatius Sancho Witnesses the Gordon Riots', in Ian Heywood and John Seed (eds.), *The Gordon Riots: Politics, Culture and Insurrection in Late Eighteenth-Century Britain* (Cambridge: Cambridge University Press, 2012), 141–162.

[47] For libertinism and radicalism, see G. J. Barker-Benfield, *The Culture of Sensibility: Sex and Society in Eighteenth-Century Britain* (Chicago, IL: University of Chicago Press, 1992), 215–287; Ellis, *The Politics of Sensibility*, 190–221.

exalt Sancho's posthumous public reputation as an exemplarily intelligent, respectable black man and minimise opportunities to attack him as anything less than British. Indeed, she explicated her 'desire of shewing that an untutored African may possess abilities equal to an European' in her preface to the text.[48] Deletions of humorous or banal details from Sancho's original letters helped her to heighten their sentimental tone and remind readers of Africans' capacity for higher intellectual and moral reasoning, helping to make the *Letters* resemble, in Carey's words, 'an epistolary novel of sentiment illustrating the immorality of slavery'.[49] However, this process was not unproblematic. Hammerschmidt, for example, has suggested that in Crewe's hands, Sancho was 'turned into the object of abolitionist argument: he became a specimen to illustrate and validate the larger abolitionist discourse, at the expense of his heterogeneous self-portrayal'. Of necessity, Hammerschmidt argues, 'Sancho himself must not figure as anything but black and African, so that his intellectual achievements can assume their full representative function in the service of the abolitionist argument.'[50] While Hammerschmidt's definition of the term 'abolitionist' in this context is debatable, his broader contention is supported by new evidence.

The printed version of Sancho's 16 November 1779 letter to Stevenson linked an exclamation about his poverty to a mention of his ethnic status: 'never poorer since created – but 'tis a general case – blessed times for a poor Blacky grocer to hang or drown in! – Recieved from your good reverend parent (why not honoured father?) a letter.'[51] The mention of the 'poor Blacky grocer' invited the reader to be moved to compassion at the spectacle of another's hardship. This classic characteristic of sentimental literature was actuated, in this instance, by Sancho's deprived social and economic status and, crucially, his ethnic alterity from the assumed reader. However, the manuscript version of the same passage read slightly differently: 'never poorer since created – but tis a general case – receiv'd from your Good revd parent (why not honrd father) a letter.'[52] In this passage the emphasis fell on the fact that financial hardship was *shared* among *all* British people – there was no suggestion that Sancho was suffering more than anyone else because of his position as 'a poor Blacky grocer'. Indeed, there was no mention *at all* of Sancho's being black – this appears to have been an invention on Crewe's part.

[48] Sancho, *Letters*, vol. 1, ii.   [49] Carey, 'Ignatius Sancho and the Campaign', 82.
[50] Hammerschmidt, 'Character, Cultural Agency and Abolition', 259, 270.
[51] Sancho, *Letters*, vol. 2, 116.
[52] BL, Add. MSS. 89077, Stevenson Papers: The Letters of Ignatius Sancho, 'Ignatius Sancho to William Stevenson, 16 Nov 1779'.

In her attempt to inspire sympathetic feelings in the overwhelmingly white readership of the *Letters*, she had actually distanced them from the intended object of sympathy by drawing attention to the perceived *differences* between them. Several scholars have recognised this effect as a recurring limitation of sentimentalist antislavery discourse in general.[53] In attempting to continue Sancho's work of constructing for himself a fully legitimate sentimental authorial persona, and thereby undermine hierarchies of race, Crewe actually generated a spectacle of racial difference.

A similar effect can be observed in the biography Crewe commissioned to preface the edited letters. From its opening words, Joseph Jekyll's biography of Sancho introduced him as, above all, an 'extraordinary negro'.[54] Simultaneously, scenes of affective distress invited sympathy from the reader while recalling stereotypical depictions of personal characteristics supposedly 'innate' to Africans. Carey has characterised many of the details in Jekyll's biography as 'almost certainly untrue'; in particular, he suggests that an episode in which Sancho's father committed suicide bore 'some remarkable similarities' to John Bicknell and Thomas Day's 1773 sentimental poem 'The Dying Negro', as well as other literary sources.[55] Similarly, Jekyll suggested that Sancho left the three sisters to whom he had been given as a child because of the 'dread of constant reproach arising from the detection of an amour, infinitely criminal in the eyes of three Maiden Ladies'.[56] This episode recalled quite clearly the Soubise controversy, of which Jekyll was well aware. Indeed, an oblique reference was made to the fact that Queensberry had 'intrusted to his [Sancho's] reformation a very unworthy favourite of his own complexion' later in the biography.[57] Jekyll's well-meaning attempts to paint Sancho as a victim of circumstances (as per the sentimental mode of his biography as a whole) even threatened to disrupt the antislavery prerogative of the *Letters*. The 'freedom, riches and leisure' Sancho enjoyed from his inclusion in the Duchess of Montagu's will, Jekyll claimed, 'naturally led a disposition of African texture into indulgences; and that which dissipated the mind of Ignatius completely drained his purse'.[58] Here, again, the sympathetic narrative hinged on the supposedly irreconcilable conflict between being African and being free. Just like in 'Ardrah, Whydah, and Benin', where 'a Negro will stake at play his fortune, his children

---

[53] See, for example, Marcus Wood, *Slavery Empathy and Pornography* (Oxford: Oxford University Press, 2002), 12–18; Stephen Ahern, 'Introduction', in Stephen Ahern (ed.), *Affect and Abolition in the Anglo-Atlantic, 1770–1830* (London: Ashgate, 2013), 8.
[54] Sancho, *Letters*, vol. 1, iii.   [55] Carey, 'The Extraordinary Negro', 1–14.
[56] Jekyll, 'Life', in Sancho, *Letters*, vol. 1, vii–viii.
[57] Jekyll, 'Life', in Sancho, *Letters*, vol. 1, xiii.
[58] Jekyll, 'Life', in Sancho, *Letters*, vol. 1, ix.

and his liberty', Sancho was unable to handle his freedom responsibly and fell victim to gambling, or, as Jekyll put it, 'the propensity which appears to be innate among his countrymen'.[59] Thus Jekyll's attempts to remain faithful to Sancho's commitment to the sentimental mode backfired. By framing Sancho as the victim of his own inherited ethnic characteristics, he had inadvertently questioned the capacity of black slaves to live free.

These paratextual editions and additions formed part of a broader attempt to market Sancho's *Letters* as a piece of sentimental literature intended to challenge the morality of slavery and secure his posthumous reputation as a 'man of letters'. Generically, the text was designed to sit alongside posthumous letter collections by well-known libertines and sentimentalists of the time, such as *Letters of the Late Lord Lyttelton* and, of course, *Letters of the Late Rev. Laurence Sterne*.[60] Given that the nominal objective behind publishing Sancho's letters was to support his family, an edited collection after the model of Sterne and Lyttelton's *Letters* was a safe bet. Sterne's expensive three-volume sets of correspondence had gone through at least three major editions in the seven years since they were published, while Lyttelton's slightly cheaper text had gone through no fewer than nine editions in the three years since his death.[61] Recognising the scale of the potential market, Crewe selected John Nichols as the printer and primary seller of Sancho's correspondence. This was another canny choice, since Nichols was a successful publisher of a range of 'serious' literary works of the sort suited to aristocratic and aspirational middle-class readers. During 1782 alone, he produced, in addition to Sancho's *Letters*, translations of Dante and Euripides, reprints of Shakespeare and Henry Fielding's works, biographies of William Hogarth, Latin treatises, Greek and British histories, scientific dissertations and an eight-volume *Bibliotheca Topographica Britannica*.[62]

---

[59] Jekyll, 'Life', in Sancho, *Letters*, vol. 1, ix.

[60] Thomas Lyttelton, *Letters of the Late Lord Lyttelton* (London: J. Bew, 1780); Laurence Sterne, *Letters of the Late Laurence Sterne* (London: T. Beckett, 1775).

[61] Based on ECCO keyword search: 'Author = "Sterne" OR "Lyttelton" AND 'Date = "1768–1782"' [i.e. from the year of Sterne's death until the year of publication of Sancho's Letters]. *Eighteenth Century Collections Online* (Gale Cengage, 2008–2013). Retrieved 09/07/2014.

[62] Dante Alighieri, *The Inferno of Dante*, trans. Charles Rogers; Euripides, *The Nineteen Tragedies and Fragments of Euripides*, trans. Michael Wodhull; William Shakespeare, *Hamlet, Prince of Denmark, a Tragedy*; Henry Fielding, *The History of Tom Jones, a Foundling* (4 vols.); John Nichols, *Biographical Anecdotes of William Hogarth*; George Isaac Huntingford, *Metrika Tina Monostrophika*; Samuel Musgrave, *Two Dissertations*; Anon., *Bibliotheca Topographica Brittannica* (8 vols.), all (London: J. Nichols, 1782).

Nichols's prestige as a publisher and his commitment to bourgeois respectability had been confirmed in 1780, when he took over as editor-in-chief and publisher of the *Gentleman's Magazine*.[63] Evidently, Sancho proved a memorable character for Nichols's clientele: he included an anecdote about him in *Literary Anecdotes of the Eighteenth Century*, which he edited in 1814.[64] Crewe's choice of him as the publisher of the *Letters* ensured that they were directed toward a readership receptive to Sancho's commitment to literary sensibility.

Sancho's *Letters* attest, most overtly of all the primary texts under discussion, to a central contention of this book: that the content of early published writing by black authors was powerfully influenced by the networks surrounding its composition, publication and dissemination. While his letters demonstrated a striking degree of social plasticity, they were also useful as tools to maintain and build on his social position. Rebecca Earle has suggested that letter writing was a practice which 'not only affirmed the authority of the elite, but also provided a means of expression for more marginal members of society'.[65] At times, Sancho's correspondence fulfilled either of these functions separately; in other cases it united them, enabling him to articulate his own marginalisation *while* affirming the authority of his socially elite correspondents. An acknowledgement of this complexity enables a new reading of Sancho's *Letters* as a text fundamentally influenced by social networks.

While his friends remembered him fondly for his personal qualities, those who had not met him in person continued to see the colour of his skin as the primary expression of his person. As his celebrity grew beyond his own social network, thanks largely to the exchange of letters between him and Laurence Sterne, the focus on his blackness narrowed. Through selection, edition, excision and even addition, Frances Crewe took on the project of accommodating him in the sentimental literary tradition after his death, simultaneously drawing attention to his ethnic alterity as an unfortunate circumstance which he had ultimately overcome by his heroic simulation of inherently British values. Jekyll's brief biography underscored this process, painting him as the victim of his own African

[63] Julian Pooley and Robin Myers, 'Nichols family (*per. c.* 1760–1939)', in *ODNB*, available at www.oxforddnb.com/view/article/63494.

[64] John Nichols (ed.), *Literary Anecdotes of the Eighteenth Century* (London: J. Nichols, 1812–1814), vol. 8, 682–683.

[65] Rebecca Earle, 'Introduction', in Rebecca Earle (ed.), *Epistolary Selves: Letters and Letter-Writers, 1600–1945* (London: Ashgate, 1999), 1.

personality traits and hinging the narrative tension of the 'Life' on the obliteration of these characteristics in favour of more agreeable British tendencies.

Any reading of Sancho's *Letters* must be influenced by the knowledge that they were posthumously published to support the author's family. In some respects, Sancho's letters were also originally *written* with this ultimate goal in mind. When his daughter Elizabeth wrote to William Stevenson on 26 May 1818, she thanked him for agreeing to pay her rent of twelve pounds per year. She mentioned that the Duchess of Buccleuch had also given her forty pounds and that John Meheux, now married, was also 'very good' to her.[66] Without the networks of patronage established through Sancho's popularity and social intelligence, Elizabeth, a black shopkeeper's daughter in nineteenth-century London, would simply not have had access to this level of financial help. When on 2 February 1820 she presented Gainsborough's portrait of her father to Stevenson, she ensured that the esteem in which her father was held would be retained in posterity.[67] So, in terms both of ensuring his family was financially well provided for and of his own posthumous reputation as a serious figure in London's literary and culturally elite circles, Sancho succeeded. His careful balancing act in constructing manly libertine and sentimental personae without appealing to stereotypical depictions of black sexual profligacy gave future abolitionists a paragon of black masculinity which powerfully counterpoised racist depictions of Africans as intellectually and morally incapable of managing their own freedom. While this nuanced self-portrayal was somewhat undercut by well-meaning editorial interventions, Sancho was remembered fondly by enough wealthy people to ensure that his daughter enjoyed the protection of a Duchess almost forty years after his death.

[66] BL, Loan 96 RLF 1/583, Miss Elizabeth Sancho, Daughter of Ignatius Sancho, 'Elizabeth Sancho to William Stevenson, 26 May 1818'.
[67] BL, Loan 96 RLF 1/583, Miss Elizabeth Sancho, Daughter of Ignatius Sancho, 'Elizabeth Sancho to William Stevenson, 02 Feb 1820'. This letter was also published anonymously in Anon., 'New Light on the Life of Ignatius Sancho: Some Unpublished Letters', *Slavery & Abolition*, 1:3 (1980), 358.

I then asked him what it was; he told me it was snow: but I could not in anywise understand him. He asked me if we had no such thing in my country; and I told him, No. I then asked who made it; he told me a great man in the heavens, called God: but here again I was to all intents and purposes at a loss to understand him; and the more so, when a little after I saw the air filled with it, in a heavy shower, which fell down on the same day. After this I went to church.[1]

The Oracle was a newspaper that specialised in scandal, rumour and titillation. On 12 August 1789, it ran a story about a 'certain beautiful DUTCHESS', who had supposedly 'exposed to the stolen glances of an Officer, the *contour* of a Venus'. The military officer, apparently, declared that 'the sight of such a model of perfection inspired equal admiration in him (though sensations of a warmer kind) as the first sight of a fall of *snow* did in *Olaudah Equiano*, on his arrival in England!'[2] While Equiano's first experience of snow prefigured the first stirrings of his Christian conversion, the officer's glimpse of the '*contour* of a Venus' stimulated stirrings of an altogether more profane kind.

While the bawdy detail of the *Oracle* story might have somewhat undermined the spiritual significance of its source material, it does demonstrate that Equiano's autobiography, *The Interesting Narrative*, was famous enough by August 1789 to act as a kind of cultural touchstone: an anchor tethering the punchline of a dubious piece of ribaldry to a shared set of experiences. Equiano's fame would continue to grow for years after this point, spurred on by book tours, promotional talks, printed advertisements and public endorsements from some of the country's biggest names in politics and activism. By associating his name and personal identity explicitly and consistently with the abolitionist movement, Equiano became the most famous black man in the eighteenth-century Atlantic world. Since this fame was predicated as much on his

---

[1] Olaudah Equiano, *The Interesting Narrative*, vol. 1, 104–105.
[2] *The Oracle; Bell's New World*, 12 August 1789.

personality as it was on his considerable intrinsic talents and artistic achievements, he also became the biggest black celebrity of the period.

Equiano's reputation – and primacy – has been secured in successive generations of modern scholarship. Both historians and literary critics, from Paul Edwards's pioneering work in the 1960s to Vincent Carretta's more recent extensive biographical studies, have considered him the most significant black political and literary figure active in Britain for the entire period of British involvement in slavery.[3] Interest in Equiano was further stimulated in the early years of the twenty-first century following Carretta's discovery of baptismal records and ships' muster rolls indicating that he was born in South Carolina and not in West Africa as he claimed in *The Interesting Narrative*.[4] These discoveries, along with a number of responses from, for example, Paul Edwards, Catherine Obianuju Acholonu and Dorothy Chinwe Ukaegbu, challenging Carretta's thesis of a Carolina birth, have encouraged ever-more archival research in search of clues about his 'true' natal identity.[5] For a restlessly itinerant former slave, Equiano's life was extraordinarily well documented. Indeed, he has inspired so much archival scholarship in recent years that it seems little remains to be rediscovered about the events of his life.[6]

---

[3] See Olaudah Equiano, *Equiano's Travels: His Autobiography: The Interesting Narrative*, ed. Paul Edwards (London: Heinemman, 1967); Vincent Carretta, *Equiano, the African: Biography of a Self-Made Man* (London: Penguin, 2007). For a review of some of the key studies in the extensive literature on Equiano, see Ryan Hanley, 'The Equiano Effect: Representativeness and Early Black British Migrant Testimony', in Jennifer Craig-Norton, Christhard Hoffmann and Tony Kushner (eds.), *Migrant Britain: Histories from the 17th to the 21st Centuries (Essays in Honour of Colin Holmes)* (London: Routledge, 2018), 262–271.

[4] Vincent Carretta, 'Olaudah Equiano or Gustavus Vassa? New Light on an Eighteenth-Century Question of Identity', *Slavery & Abolition*, 20:3 (1999), 96–105; see also Carretta, *Equiano, the African*, 2–16.

[5] Catherine Obianuju Acholonu, 'The Igbo Roots of Olauadah Equiano', in Chima J. Korieh (ed.), *Olaudah Equiano and the Igbo World* (Trenton, NJ: Africa World Press, 2009), 49–66; Dorothy Chinwe Ukaegbu, 'Status in Eqighteenth-Century Igboland: Perspectives from Olaudah Equiano's *Interesting Narrative*', in Korieh (ed.), *Equiano and the Igbo World*, 93–116; Paul Lovejoy, 'Autobiography and Memory: Gustavus Vassa, alias Olaudah Equiano, the African', *Slavery & Abolition*, 27:3 (2006), 317–347; Paul Lovejoy, 'Construction of Identity: Olaudah Equiano or Gustavus Vassa?', *Historically Speaking*, 7:3 (2006), 9.

[6] Most of the newspaper and manuscript primary sources relating to Equiano (what Carretta calls 'Equiana') that have been discovered so far are now widely available in published form. See, for example, Olaudah Equiano, *The Letters and Other Writings of Gustavus Vass (Olaudah Equiano, the African): Documenting the Abolition of the Slave Trade*, ed. Karlee-Ann Sapoznik (Princeton, NJ: Marcus Wiener, 2013); Vincent Carretta, 'New Equiana', *Early American Literature*, 44:1 (2009), 147–160; Olaudah Equiano, *The Interesting Narrative and Other Writings*, ed. Vincent Carretta (London: Penguin, 1995, repr. 2005), 237–393. Many more primary sources are also published in full in Carretta, *Equiano, the African*. Editors sometimes disagree over how to transcribe certain

A brief summary, therefore, may suffice to frame this study into Equiano's emergence as a celebrity abolitionist in Britain. *The Interesting Narrative* suggested that he was born around 1745 in Igboland in West Africa and enslaved around the age of eleven. After changing hands several times on his way to the coast, he was finally sold to European merchants and transported to Virginia via Barbados. He was bought by a Royal Navy Lieutenant named Michael Pascal around 1754 and given the name Gustavus Vassa, by which he was primarily known for the rest of his life.[7] Accompanying Pascal as a valet around the Atlantic world during the Seven Years' War, Equiano was baptised in London in 1759. Pascal eventually sold Equiano to Captain James Doran, and Doran then sold him to a Philadelphia Quaker named Robert King. By working as an independent trader during his regular travels around the Caribbean and mainland American colonies, Equiano was eventually able to purchase his own freedom from King in 1767. Now free, he continued to travel extensively around the Atlantic and beyond, even participating in an expedition to the Arctic in 1773. After being involved briefly in a project to grow sugar (using slave labour) on the Mosquito Coast in Central America in 1775, Equiano returned to London for much of the American Revolutionary War. While he never stopped travelling, he did become increasingly involved in the British antislavery movement during the 1780s, associating with some of the highest-profile abolitionists in the country. He published his autobiography, *The Interesting Narrative*, in 1789, attaching the name Olaudah Equiano to it, and spent the next five years travelling around Britain and Ireland promoting it. The text was an enormous commercial success, going through nine editions between 1789 and 1794. Equiano remained active in British popular politics until his death in March 1797.

It is clear that Equiano's personal fame was instrumental in making him an influential figure in British political life. However, aside from Carretta and John Bugg's explorations of his national book tours, little is known about *how* he became famous, and how this affected the

---

phrases and words in the primary sources. In this chapter, therefore, I have consulted and cited the original documents wherever possible.

[7] For naming and identity in Equiano, see Peter Jaros, 'Good Names: Olaudah Equiano or Gustavus Vassa', *The Eighteenth Century*, 54:1 (2013), 1–23; Paul Lovejoy, 'Olaudah Equiano or Gustavus Vassa – What's in a Name?', *Atlantic Studies*, 9:2 (2012); Vincent Carretta, 'Response to Paul Lovejoy's "Autobiography and Memory"', *Slavery & Abolition*, 28:1 (2007); Paul Lovejoy, 'Autobiography and Memory: Gustavus Vassa, alias Olaudah Equiano, the African', *Slavery & Abolition*, 27:3 (2006), 317–347. I adhere to convention in referring to the author of *The Interesting Narrative* as Olaudah Equiano in this chapter.

publication, sale and reading of his book.[8] As well as the controversy
surrounding his nativity, scholars have tended to focus instead on Equiano's contributions to transatlantic histories of race, religion, autobiography and of course slavery and emancipation.[9] The overriding question
in much of this scholarship is one of identity: how did he understand
himself, and how was he understood by others? This chapter engages
with these key questions by exploring the mechanisms by which Equiano
made his name(s) known to the British public: newspapers articles,
controversy, activism, self-publicism, networking and charisma. Each of
these mechanisms played into the production of the ultimate commodification of the authorial self: the autobiography of a former slave. Fame,
I argue, profoundly influenced how Equiano wrote, published and promoted himself, and finally enabled him to *embody* popular abolitionism,
both in his charismatic persona and textually in the form of his eminently
saleable life story.

This is not to ascribe a cynical or self-serving motivation to Equiano's
celebrity. On the contrary, an investigation of his tireless public campaigning puts his commitment to the antislavery cause beyond question.
Nevertheless, the specific social conditions of the late 1780s and early
1790s in Britain enabled the emergence of a new type of celebrity. As
Linda Shires puts it, the 'waning influence of established civil authorities and a persistence of class struggle led to the rise of a new host of
public figures ... who gained fame differently than they might have in the
past.'[10] Equiano's close association with key democratic movements of
the period – abolitionism and the movement for domestic reform –
enabled him to accrue a type of individualised fame predicated on his
broad-ranging social connectedness and a well-crafted public image of

[8] Carretta, *Equiano, the African*, 330–368; John Bugg, 'The Other Interesting Narrative:
Olaudah Equiano's Public Book Tour', *PMLA*, 121:5 (2006), 1424–1442.
[9] Recent work on these themes includes Yael Ben-Zvi, 'Equiano's Nativity: Negative
Birthright, Indigenous Ethic, and Universal Human Rights', *Early American Literature*,
48:2 (2013), 399–423; '"I Whitened My Face, That They Might Not Know Me": Race
and Identity in Olaudah Equiano's Slave Narrative', *Journal of Black Studies*, 39:6
(2009), 848–864; Rebecka Fisher, 'The Poetics of Belonging in the Age of Enlight-
enment: Spiritual Metaphors of Being in Olaudah Equiano's *Interesting Narrative*', *Early
American Studies*, 11:1 (2013); Ramesh Mallipeddi, 'Filiation to Affiliation: Kinship and
Sentiment in Equiano's *Interesting Narrative*', *ELH*, 81:3 (2014), 923–954; Andrew
Kopec, 'Collective Commerce and the Problem of Autobiography in Olaudah Equiano's
Narrative', *Eighteenth Century: Theory and Interpretation*, 54:4 (2013), 461–478; Matthew
D. Brown, 'Olaudah Equiano and the Sailor's Telegraph: The *Interesting Narrative* and
the Source of Black Abolitionism', *Callaloo*, 36:1 (2013), 191–201; Vincent Wimbush,
White Men's Magic: Scripturalization as Slavery (Oxford: Oxford University Press, 2012).
[10] Linda Shires, 'The Author as Spectacle and Commodity: E. Barrett Browning and
Thomas Hardy', in Carol Christ and John Jordan (eds.), *Victorian Literature and the
Victorian Visual Imagination* (Berkeley: University of California Press, 1995), 199.

integrity, honesty and self-sufficiency. The relative novelty of this 'demo-cratic' construction of fame – novel because it required widespread 'plebeian' literacy and a mature industrialised publication apparatus to function – underpins a central contention of this chapter: that Equiano not only was an architect of his own celebrity but also was an influential figure in the emergence of British celebrity culture itself.

Before *The Interesting Narrative*

Equiano's early abolitionist activity did not gain him the attention he perhaps deserved. During the early 1780s, he had begun to establish himself as a leading black intellectual in Britain, intervening in several cases on behalf of enslaved Africans. One of the best-known of these was the court case surrounding the *Zong* massacre. Although it was not publically acknowledged at the time, it was Equiano who brought news of the massacre, in which 130 enslaved Africans were needlessly drowned by slave-traders during the middle passage, to the attention of the aboli-tionist lawyer Granville Sharp. The *Zong* would probably never have caused much of a stir in Britain had it not been for the fact that the ship's owners had tried to put in an insurance claim for their lost 'property'. The insurers refused, prompting the owners to take them to court in 1783. Publicised extensively by Sharp, this case was to become an early and major catalyst for widespread moral indignation at the brutality and rapaciousness of the slave trade, and Sharp even made some public declarations that he intended to pursue a charge of murder against the surviving crew members.[11] Because of his exertions in the *Zong* case, Sharp began, in James Walvin's words, 'to take on heroic status' in the public eye, being hailed in the *Gentleman's Magazine* as 'a true patriot' and 'a true Christian'.[12] Equiano, meanwhile, went almost completely unrecognised – and certainly uncongratulated – for his crucial interven-tion in the case.

However, his friendship with Sharp did play a part in bringing him to more widespread public attention. When Equiano returned to London from a voyage to Philadelphia in 1786, he was recommended, almost certainly by Sharp, to the Commissioners of the Royal Navy as Commis-sary for the Black Poor aboard the ill-fated expedition to establish a free black colony in Sierra Leone. The Commissary was to play a vital role in

---

[11] See James Walvin, *The Zong: A Massacre, the Law, and the End of Slavery* (New Haven, CT: Yale University Press, 2011), 102–160.

[12] Walvin, *Zong*, 105.

the expedition. He would be in charge of provisions for those travelling to Sierra Leone, as well as negotiating between the black settlers and the white directors of the expedition aboard ship. This was the most senior government appointment any black man had ever attained in Britain, and it was the subject of a report in the *Morning Herald* for 29 December 1786.[13] The commission, however, proved something of a poisoned chalice. With the ships lying at anchor, the project failed to attract black settlers for the new colony quickly enough. Equiano's relations with the other key officers aboard the ships quickly fell apart, resulting in an acrimonious spat that culminated in a press war in miniature. Equiano complained that Joseph Irwin, the superintendent of the project, was embezzling funds, while Irwin in turn was convinced that Equiano was trying to stir up trouble among the black settlers. Thomas Boulden Thompson, captain of the naval escort assigned to protect the convoy, wrote to the Commissioners of the Royal Navy to complain that both Equiano and Irwin were unsuitable for the positions they had been assigned. To an extent, he corroborated *both* of their complaints about each other: Equiano took 'every means to actuate the minds of the Blacks to discord', while Irwin never took any action 'which might indicate that he had the welfare of the people the least at heart'.[14] Equiano was dismissed from the project shortly afterward. Irwin was not even cautioned.

The fallout from Equiano's dismissal was bitter and public. As we will see in Chapter 7, Equiano's friend and collaborator, Ottobah Cugoano, published a response that likened the expedition to a slave ship. It was probably Cugoano who forwarded a letter from Equiano, complaining bitterly about Irwin and the ship's chaplain, Patrick Fraser, and calling them 'great villains', to the offices of the *Public Advertiser* in April 1787.[15] Irwin's allies fired back a series of published letters, suggesting that Equiano's 'cloven foot' was 'perfectly manifest' in reports of their misconduct and demanding that the public disregard 'more of these *black* reports which have been industriously propagated; for if they are continued, it is rather more probable that most of the dark transactions of a *Black* will be brought to *light*.'[16] Once the voyage had got under way without Equiano, Fraser reiterated Irwin's earlier complaints, accusing Equiano of stirring up trouble and encouraging the black passengers to

---

[13] *Morning Herald*, 29 December 1786.
[14] TNA, T1/643/681, f. 87. 'Letter from Thomas Boulden Thompson, 21 March 1787', repr. in Equiano, *Letters and Other Writings*, ed. Sapoznik, 71.
[15] *Public Advertiser*, 11 April 1787.
[16] *Public Advertiser*, 14 April 1787 [emphasis in original].

'absent themselves purposely' from his sermons, 'for no other reasons whatever than that I am white'.[17]

Equiano did not rise to the bait. His response was fastidiously cool:

An extract of a letter ... having appeared ... in the public papers, wherein injurious reflexions, prejudicial to the character of Vasa, the Black Commissary, were contained, he thinks it necessary to vindicate his character from these misrepresentations, informing the public, that the principal crime which caused his dismission, was an information he laid before the Navy board, accusing the agent of unfaithfulness in his office.[18]

Equiano here negotiated his reply to an instance of public racial prejudice very carefully indeed. He recognised instantly that an angry response, no matter how well justified, would only play into the hands of his antagonists, who were keen to link blackness to primitive emotionality and whiteness to enlightened reason. The calculated sophistication of vocabulary in his 14 July letter, the length and complexity of the single sentence that comprised it, and even the slightly pompous references to himself in the third person: these were all conscious negotiations with the reader about how Equiano's character was to be understood. Here was a man, the letter suggested, who has been driven to lower himself to publicly defend his reputation from the unreasonable depredations of self-interested antagonists. He was educated and literate, but he would depend only on the truth – not on rhetorical flourish – to make his point. When *The Interesting Narrative* was published in 1789, one reviewer called it 'a Round unvarnish'd Tale ... written with much Truth and Simplicity'.[19] Equiano liked the sound of this so much he put it in advertisements for subsequent editions.[20] In 1787, he was already fore-grounding the same values of honestly, integrity and simplicity in his public persona. He was, in other words, beginning to build his brand.

While the Sierra Leone project debacle seemed to end badly for Equiano, being dismissed was probably the best thing that could have happened for him. The project itself ended in tragedy, with almost all the settlers either dying or being re-enslaved within a few months of arriving on the West African coast. In that respect Equiano had a lucky escape. And even though he had been dismissed from the project, he was 'vindi-cated' when his request for his wages was granted by the Admiralty Board late in 1787.[21] Perhaps as a consequence of this, he felt entitled to

---

[17] *Morning Chronicle*, 3 July 1787.   [18] *Public Advertiser*, 14 July 1787.
[19] Anon., *The General Magazine and Impartial Review*, July 1789, repr. in Equiano, *Letters and Other Writings*, ed. Sapoznik, 127.
[20] See Equiano, *The Interesting Narrative and Other Writings*, ed. Carretta, 356–364.
[21] Equiano, *The Interesting Narrative*, vol. 2, 243.

subscribe much of his future published correspondence 'Gustavus Vassa, the Ethiopian and King's Late Commissary for the African Settlement'.[22] Moreover, his involvement in the project, as Carretta has pointed out, had put him in touch with many of his most influential contacts.[23] Indeed, the explosion of popular abolitionist sentiment, in part actuated by these same individuals, was to provide the essential catalyst for Equiano's ascent to nationwide celebrity.

His first act as a public abolitionist was to wade into a running debate between his friend James Ramsay and the proslavery advocate and former planter James Tobin. Ramsay and Tobin had been publishing responses and counter-responses addressed to each other for years, ever since Ramsay's *Essay on the Treatment and Conversion of African Slaves* first appeared in 1784.[24] In January 1788, Equiano joined the fray by publishing a lengthy attack on Tobin's treatises. As well as attacking his description of slave conditions, he also challenged Tobin's lamentation that 'the great numbers of negroes at present in England, the strange propensity shewn for them by the lower orders of women, and the rapid increase of a dark and contaminated breed, are evils which ... call every day more loudly for enquiry and redress.'[25] This was controversial territory, but Equiano refused to compromise his position on 'intermarriage'. He met Tobin head-on:

The mutual commerce of the sexes of both Blacks and Whites, under the restriction of moderation and law, would yield more benefit than prohibition ... Away then with your narrow impolitic notion of preventing by law what will be a national honour, national strength, and productive of national virtue – Intermarriages![26]

This was an extraordinary position to take on this issue in late eighteenth-century England. Ever since hundreds of black loyalists had arrived in London after the American Revolutionary War, commentators had complained in newspapers about the supposed ill-effects of miscegenation among the working classes (see Chapter 7). Occasional, timid defences of mixed marriages as unavoidable surfaced in the press, but no one had ever had the temerity to suggest that they might be actively beneficial to British society. This was of course a sincerely held belief on Equiano's

---

[22] *Public Advertiser*, 28 January 1788; *Public Advertiser*, 5 February 1788.

[23] Carretta, *Equiano, the African*, 236.

[24] James Ramsay, *Essay on the Treatment and Conversion of African Slaves in the British Sugar Colonies* (London: James Phillips, 1784); James Tobin, *Cursory Remarks upon the Reverend Mr. Ramsay's Essay* (London: G. and T. Wilkie, 1785); James Ramsay, *A Letter to James Tobin, Esq.* (London: James Phillips, 1787); James Tobin, *A Short Rejoinder to the Reverend Mr. Ramsay's Reply* (London: G. and T. Wilkie, 1787).

[25] Tobin, *Cursory Remarks*, 118.   [26] *Public Advertiser*, 28 January 1788.

part – his future wife, Susannah Cullen, was white. Nevertheless, he must have been aware that his statements on the issue would have been seen as controversial.

Another public attack on a proslavery polemicist – this time on Gordon Turnbull, author of *An Apology for Negro Slavery* (1786) – was both more personal and made more pointedly in defence of Ramsay and his *Essay*. On 5 February 1788, Equiano struck out at the self-interest and hypocrisy he saw as motivating Turnbull's attack on Ramsay: 'You, I say, apprehensive that the promulgation of truth will be subversive of your infamous craft, and destructive of your iniquitous gain, … attempt to wound the reputation of the reverend Essayist by false calumnies, gross contradictions of well-known facts, and insidious suppression of others.'[27] Equiano began to deploy his personal experiences here as evidence, claiming a long-standing relationship with Ramsay and close knowledge of his 'irreproachable' character.[28] As a rhetorical technique, this was not a particularly innovative strategy – personal vindications, the solicitation and provision of character references and running pamphlet disputes were a peculiar feature of eighteenth-century publishing. However, Equiano's emphasis on directness and simplicity, as much as his reliance on the irrefutable evidence of personal experience of slavery, were becoming consistent enough to be associated readily with the name 'Gustavus Vassa, the Ethiopian'. Moreover, this review of Turnbull's *Apology* sheds light on the process leading up to Equiano's composition of *The Interesting Narrative*. 'Many of the facts [Ramsay] relates I know to be true, and many others still more shocking, if possible, have fallen within my own observation, within my feeling', he wrote, 'for were I to enumerate even my own sufferings in the West Indies, which perhaps I may one day offer to the public, the disgusting catalogue would be almost too great for belief.'[29] Taken in the context of Equiano's earlier published work, *The Interesting Narrative* may be seen as a refutation of the 'falsehoods' expounded in proslavery polemic.

Maintaining a respectable public character became more important to Equiano as he began to think of himself as an abolitionist. His increasing fame in this sphere was bringing him into the orbit of the country's social and political elite. On 21 March 1788, he 'had the honour of presenting the Queen with a petition on behalf of my African brethren, which was received most graciously by her Majesty'.[30] However, almost as soon as he began to think about writing his autobiography, Equiano also came to recognise the need for a network to help him get it published and sold.

---

[27] *Public Advertiser*, 5 February 1788.   [28] *Public Advertiser*, 5 February 1788.
[29] *Public Advertiser*, 5 February 1788.   [30] Equiano, *The Interesting Narrative*, vol. 2, 243.

Luckily for him, the perfect network was ready-made, and he already knew a couple of its key players. SEAST's London Committee was formed in May 1787, and among its founding members was Equiano's old friend Granville Sharp.[31] Reprinting and publicising abolitionist tracts was central to the Committee's efforts: their very first resolution included a provision 'for distributing [Thomas] Clarkson's Essay [*on the Slavery and Commerce of the Human Species*] and such other publications' around the country.[32] Given his intervention in the debate over Ramsay's *Essay*, Equiano was obviously well aware of the widespread appeal of such publications and the effectiveness of SEAST backing. From about the time he declared his intention to write his own abolitionist tract, he began to solicit the attention and favour of more leading abolitionists. On 13 February 1788, for example, he published a letter in several leading London newspapers, exalting Sharp, Ramsay and Bielby Porteus, the Bishop of London who had praised Sharp's work on the *Zong* case and denounced the slave trade in a published sermon in 1783.[33]

During the period, Equiano followed the progress of abolitionism in Parliament closely and sought to publicly align himself with its successes. On 31 March, for example, he published an edited version of a letter he had sent to Lord Hawkesbury, president of the Board of Trade, in which he had outlined the benefits of free trade with Africa.[34] On 18 June 1788, he went to Westminster to attend the third reading of the 'Dolben Act' in Commons. This act, introduced by Sir William Dolben, the MP for Oxford University, merely limited the maximum number of slaves who could be transported according to the tonnage of the ship. Nevertheless, it was widely celebrated for an assumed reduction in slave mortality rates and hailed as the first step toward abolishing the slave trade altogether.[35] Equiano was delighted when the bill passed in Commons. The very same day, he wrote an effusive letter of thanks addressed 'To the Honourable and Worthy Members of the BRITISH SENATE' and published in the

---

[31] John Oldfield, *Popular Politics and British Anti-Slavery: The Mobilisation of Public Opinion against the Slave Trade, 1787–1807* (Manchester: Manchester University Press, 1995), 41–42.

[32] BL Add MSS 21254, 'Fair Minute Books of the Committee for the Abolition of the Slave Trade, 22 May 1787', f. 2.

[33] *Public Advertiser*, 13 February 1788; *Morning Post*, 21 February 1788. See also Bielby Porteus, *A Sermon Preached before the Incorporated Society for the Propagation of the Gospel in Foreign Parts* (London: T. Harrison and S. Brooke, 1783).

[34] *Public Advertiser*, 31 March 1788; see also 'Letter to the Right Honourable Lord Hawkesbury, 13 March 1788', in Equiano, *Letters and Other Writings*, ed. Sapoznik, 24–26.

[35] See Hugh Thomas, *The Slave Trade: The Story of the Atlantic Slave Trade: 1440–1870* (London: Simon & Schuster, 1997), 508–510.

Public Advertiser and the *Morning Chronicle*. The letter also contained a coded reference to 'J.R. and T.C.': clearly a nod to James Ramsay and Thomas Clarkson, Equiano's influential friends in SEAST.[36] After the bill had passed, he and several other 'Sons of Africa' published more letters of thanks addressed to Dolben, the Prime Minister William Pitt, and the leader of the opposition, Charles James Fox.[37]

He did not forget what was owed to the parliamentary opponents of the bill either. On 28 June, he published a disappointed letter to Thomas Townshend, president of the Board of Control, who had spoken out against the act when it was read in the House of Lords. Equiano had little option but to respond to Townshend, given that his opposition to the bill hinged on the disastrous outcome of the Sierra Leone resettlement project from which he had been so unceremoniously removed. Townshend reiterated claims made by Boulden Thompson that 'shortly after their arrival there, some of [the black settlers] embraced the first opportunity of embarking for the West Indies.'[38] Equiano felt that Townshend had been 'misled by your information' and repeated his claims that the project failed because of the 'flagrant abuses' committed by Irwin. He even seized the opportunity to vindicate his own behaviour on the project, reminding Townshend (and the readers of the *Public Advertiser*) that the Commissioners of the Royal Navy were 'satisfied with my conduct'.[39]

By this point, Equiano was very conscious that he had a public image to maintain. On 1 July his public character had essentially been lionized in the *Morning Chronicle*. The *Chronicle* had introduced him to their readers as 'an Ethiopian now resident in the metropolis' with 'an irreproachable moral character' who had 'frequently distinguished himself by occasional essays in the different papers, which manifest a strong and sound understanding'.[40] The abolition debates had renewed public interest in the intellectual and moral capabilities of Africans. As the editors of the *Chronicle* recognised, the new political climate also generated a market for a popular figure who embodied and represented such capabilities.

Certainly, Equiano was well known enough by the summer of 1788 to also become a target for journalistic satire. In a throwaway aside in the *Times*, a reporter mocked his indignation at Townshend's speech in Lords. 'GUSTAVUS VASSA, the black', the report read, 'who has personally attended all the discussions on the Slave Trade in both Houses of Parliament, was asked what became of the prisoners taken in

---

[36] *Public Advertiser*, 19 June 1788; *Morning Chronicle*, 20 June 1788.
[37] *London Advertiser*, 15 July 1788.   [38] *Public Advertiser*, 28 June 1788.
[39] *Public Advertiser*, 28 June 1788.   [40] *Morning Chronicle*, 1 July 1788.

the African wars, who were not sold to the European Merchants? he replied, "That they made of them *Sable Soup*, and *Black Bouille!*"[41] This joke, drawing on the lazy and entrenched myth of African cannibalism, also tastelessly referred to the tragic reality that many of the original Sierra Leone settlers were displaced during conflict between local Temne populations and slave-traders, meaning that some were almost certainly ensnared into the transatlantic slave trade for the second time in their lives. Equiano was furious. He immediately wrote a short letter to the press in response: 'To the author of Sable Soup and Black Bouille, who belied GUSTAVUS VASA in yesterday's paper – thus sayeth the Almighty – "No Lyars, nor *Devourers* of *human* Rights, shall have any Inheritance in the Kingdom of Heaven."'[42] This exchange may have stuck with him. In *The Interesting Narrative*, he brilliantly inverted the myth of African cannibalism in his description of arriving aboard a slave ship for the first time: 'When I looked round the ship too, and saw a large furnace of copper boiling ... I no longer doubted of my fate ... I asked them if we were not to be eaten by those white men with horrible looks, red faces, and long hair?'[43] Scholars often note Equiano's skilful deployment of the trope of cannibalism in this passage.[44] Its origins may well lay in a personal affront. A man like Equiano could not let thoughtless depictions of Africans as cannibalistic savages pass without challenge. He was far too principled – and ambitious – for that.

By the end of summer 1788, Equiano had established himself as one of the leading abolitionist intellectuals in Britain. He had produced multiple reviews of books on slavery, published a number of letters and essays in the main London newspapers and had even been the subject of a satirical piece in the *Times*. He had forged strong connections with several of the leading lights in SEAST and had corresponded with the Queen herself on the subject of abolition. The idea of writing an autobiography of his life under slavery had first occurred to him in February 1788. He had probably encountered the spiritual autobiography produced in 1772 by Ukawsaw Gronniosaw, and he had almost certainly read his friend Ottobah Cugoano's *Thoughts and Sentiments* when it was first published

---

[41] *Times*, 5 July 1788. This was probably a reprint, since Equiano's response appeared in the same day's edition of the *Morning Post*.
[42] *Morning Post*, 5 July 1788.   [43] Equiano, *The Interesting Narrative*, vol. 1, 71–72.
[44] See, for example, Carl Plasa, '"Stained with Spots of Human Blood": Sugar, Abolition and Cannibalism', *Atlantic Studies*, 4:2 (2007), 225–243; Mark Stein, 'Who's Afraid of Cannibals? Some Uses of the Cannibalism Trope in Olaudah Equiano's *Interesting Narrative*', in Brycchan Carey, Markman Ellis and Sara Salih (eds.), *Discourses of Slavery and Abolition: Slavery and Its Colonies, 1760–1838* (London: Palgrave Macmillan, 2004), 96–107; Alan Rice, *Radical Narratives of the Black Atlantic* (London: Continuum, 2003), 120–146.

in 1787.[45] But those had been relatively short publications with limited print runs and quite niche readerships. Equiano saw that the time was right for a first-hand account of slavery with truly widespread popular appeal. He had the talent, and he had already built a platform with his earlier publications and activism. If he could take advantage of the prevailing public mood, a new autobiography, mixing life narrative with abolitionist polemic, could bring many around to the abolitionist interest. In the autumn of 1788, he decided the time was right to produce such an interesting narrative.

Making a Name for Himself: *The Interesting Narrative*

A number of Equiano's decisions about how to publish and promote his work suggest that he sought to accrue a degree of personal fame as an abolitionist, intellectual and spokesperson for black people both free and enslaved. Indeed, the publication of the *Narrative* reflected a radical shift in his public persona. Before November 1788, Equiano had been exclusively known as Gustavus Vassa, an essentially private individual. He had become well known in London because of his public service, intelligent interjections in the abolition debates and leadership of grass-roots black political activism, but he was not (or at least did not consciously try to be) the *embodiment* of anything beyond himself. However, when he began to solicit subscriptions to pay for the publication of his autobiography, a schism in his identity became apparent. On one hand, 'Gustavus Vassa' remained a major player in the abolitionist movement, exercising personal influence and taking a leading role in its networking and petitioning functions. On the other, a new figure emerged: Olaudah Equiano. This figure was charisma as a commodity. Equiano was much more than a brilliant author; he was a figurehead of popular abolitionism, a living demonstration of the moral indefensibility of enslaving fellow human beings and an avatar of the wrongly enslaved. Readers could hear him speak in person, reach out and touch him, and in so doing become a part of the movement – and the art – he represented. In exchange for the price of a book, they could understand and, in a sense, participate in the

---

[45] In addition to Chapters 4 and 7 of this book, see Vincent Carretta, 'Three West African Writers of the 1780s Revisited and Revised', *Research in African Literatures*, 29:4 (1998), 81–83, and Paul Edwards, 'Three West African Writers of the 1780s', in Charles T. Davis and Henry Louis Gates Jr. (eds.), *The Slave's Narrative* (Oxford: Oxford University Press, 1985), 175–198, for possible collaborations between Equiano and Cugoano. For Gronniosaw's influence on Equiano and others, see Henry Louis Gates Jr., *The Signifying Monkey: A Theory of African-American Literary Criticism* (Oxford: Oxford University Press, 1988), 127–170.

life of an enslaved human being. Importantly, by investing financially in Equiano through the purchase of his book, readers could also perform their own 'humanity', proclaiming to the world their emotional and moral sensitivity and their commitment to freedom and equality.

The first and most important step in the creation of this new personality-commodity was to link it to a commercially available product that people could buy, share and talk about. Thus the emergence of Equiano as a celebrity was intrinsically linked to the production of *The Interesting Narrative*. In fact, the very first time Equiano used the name 'Olaudah Equiano' in public was in the printed solicitation for subscriptions he produced in November 1788.[46] The name itself, as Paul Lovejoy points out, 'appears to be derived from Ekwuno, Ekweano, Ekwoanya, or Ekwealo, all common Igbo names'. It was important, in the context of publishing his abolitionist autobiography, to use this African name 'because his authority rested on his African birth'.[47] Indeed, given that the 'abolition' being promoted was of the transatlantic slave trade as against slavery itself, it was crucial that Equiano highlight his (putative) African origins. As he well knew, the gains made in exciting public indignation against slavery, just as in Parliament, thus far had revolved around the horrors of the middle passage. In February 1789, he even published a letter of thanks to the Plymouth abolition society for their role in promoting the famous plan of the *Brookes* slave ship.[48] By highlighting his Africanity from the title page onward, Equiano was consciously asserting the authenticity of his own testimony.

Of course, this did not mean that 'Gustavus Vassa, the Ethiopian/ African' was retired. Indeed, it was important that readers understood that the Olaudah Equiano was the same person as the Gustavus Vassa of whom they may have already heard. Thus, he decided that the full title of his autobiography would be *The Interesting Narrative of the Life of Olaudah Equiano, or Gustavus Vassa, the African*. In published letters and essays in newspapers, Equiano continued to sign himself 'Gustavus Vassa' or occasionally as 'Olaudah Equiano, or Gustavus Vassa'. Newspaper advertisements for *The Interesting Narrative* always bore both

---

[46] 'Solicitation for Subscriptions to *The Interesting Narrative* (Keele University Special Collections, reference 74/12632)', repr. in Equiano, *The Interesting Narrative and Other Writings*, ed. Carretta, 345–347; Vincent Carretta, '"Property of Author": Olaudah Equiano's Place in the History of the Book', in Vincent Carretta and Philip Gould (eds.), *Genius in Bondage: Literature of the Early Black Atlantic* (Lexington: University Press of Kentucky, 2001), 133. For naming and identity in Equiano, see Lovejoy, 'What's in a Name?'

[47] Lovejoy, 'What's in a Name?', 167.

[48] *Public Advertiser*, 14 February 1789. This letter, unconnected to *The Interesting Narrative*, was signed 'Gustavus Vassa'.

names, ensuring that the well-known individual remain linked to his work, and indeed that his work would be linked back to him. However, as Lovejoy and others have observed, he privately preferred to be called Gustavus Vassa.[49] Indeed, as the son of one of his acquaintances later recalled, he 'fell into fits if any one pronounced his real name, which was Olaudah Equiano'.[50] His 'African' name, then, was generally reserved for the hero of his autobiography. It was an integral part of the product, the mark of his celebrity. Perhaps just as significantly, the use of an African name in relation to *The Interesting Narrative* had important ramifications for how it was positioned in the burgeoning marketplace for abolitionist testimony.

As the minutes of SEAST meetings show, personal accounts of the slave trade proved hugely popular in 1788 and 1789. Narratives detailing the horrors that the transatlantic slave trade held for British sailors as well as enslaved Africans had been flying off the shelves. Alexander Falconbridge's *Account of the Slave Trade on the Coast of Africa* and James Stanfield's *Observations on a Guinea Voyage*, for example, were both bought, published and distributed by SEAST.[51] New editions were reprinted every few months by the Society's publisher James Phillips, in ever-increasing numbers.[52] Stanfield's tract, now largely forgotten, was so successful at the time that it even resulted in a (dreary) poetic spin-off in 1789.[53] Members of SEAST's London Committee had to negotiate with the authors for weeks, sometimes months, to procure the copyright for such valuable intellectual property.[54] In this context, Equiano realised that he had a unique selling point: his narrative could give an authentic point of view from the perspective of the enslaved. He was careful, therefore, to hold onto the copyright for his work rather than

---

[49] Lovejoy, 'What's in a Name?'

[50] 'Verso of a Letter to Granville Sharpe Esq.r, In Old Jewry Cheapside, 6 May 1780 (Sierra Leone Collection, box 4, supplement 1, folder 1. University of Illinois at Chicago Library, Special Collections)', in Equiano, *Letters and Other Writings*, ed. Sapoznik, 194–195.

[51] Alexander Falconbridge, *An Account of the Slave Trade on the Coast of Africa* (London: J. Phillips, 1788); James Stanfield, *Observations on a Guinea Voyage* (London: J. Phillips, 1788).

[52] Between 1787 and 1789, Phillips's quarterly retainer from SEAST grew from £100 to £400. BL Add MSS 21254–21255, 'Fair Minute Books of the Committee for the Abolition of the Slave Trade, 1787–1789'.

[53] James Stanfield, *The Guinea Voyage: A Poem in Three Books* (London: J. Phillips, 1789).

[54] For example, the Committee agreed to publish 3,000 copies of Falconbridge's *Account* 'as expeditiously as possible' on 22 February 1788, but Thomas Clarkson was still negotiating the contract with him in May. BL Add MSS 21254, 'Fair Minute Books of the Committee for the Abolition of the Slave Trade, 5 Feb 1788', f. 34; BL Add MSS 21255, 'Fair Minute Books of the Committee for the Abolition of the Slave Trade, 22 May 1788', f. 20.

selling it to his friends in SEAST.[55] Even though they could guarantee him a decent distribution network, he would not be able to retain the profits from the sale of the work. More importantly, perhaps recalling the Sierra Leone debacle, he wanted to remain in control of how he and his work were publicly represented. He would have to do the job himself.

Going it alone, however, did necessitate some extra effort. First and foremost, he needed to finance the publication itself. Equiano's exceptionally wide and diverse network of friends and patrons once again came in handy here. In November, with the manuscript well under way, he produced and distributed a flyleaf to a targeted group, soliciting subscriptions for his book. The specificity with which he imagined the finished product indicates that he was already thinking carefully about his marketing strategy by this point. The work would be printed in two volumes, duodecimo format. It would cost seven shillings (or six shillings unbound), and subscribers would be asked to pay half that amount up front to cover printing expenses. For very discerning readers, a few copies would be printed 'on Fine Paper, at a moderate advance of Price': what Carretta refers to as a 'deluxe edition'.[56] One of the recipients of this solicitation was Josiah Wedgwood, by then a member of SEAST and the designer of the famous 'Am I not a man and a brother?' cameo. Equiano knew Wedgwood already, but he was careful not to overstep the bounds of politeness when he was asking, essentially, for help in crowd-funding his new venture. 'I Pray you to Pardon this freedom I have taken', he wrote on the back of the flyleaf he sent to Wedgwood, 'in beging your favour, or the apperence of your Name amongst others of my Worthy friends.'[57]

These were no behind-the-scenes machinations. They were rather to become a significant aspect of his allure as a celebrity. Equiano consciously marketed himself as a well-connected man. This is most obvious in the prefatory material to *The Interesting Narrative* itself. When the text was first published in March 1789, for example, it was prefaced by a complete list of all 311 subscribers, which was reprinted and expanded

---

[55] Carretta discusses the importance of Equiano's retaining copyright over his own work at length in Carretta, *Equiano, the African*, 270–302.

[56] 'Solicitation for Subscriptions to *The Interesting Narrative* (Keele University Special Collections, reference 74/12632)', repr. in Equiano, *The Interesting Narrative and Other Writings*, ed. Carretta, 345–347; Vincent Carretta, '"Property of Author": Olaudah Equiano's Place in the History of the Book', in Carretta and Gould (eds.), *Genius in Bondage*, 133.

[57] 'Holograph letter from Gustavus Vassa to Josiah Wedgwood written on the printed solicitation for subscriptions to *The Interesting Narrative*, dated November 1788 (Keele University Special Collections, reference 74/12632)', repr. in Equiano, *The Interesting Narrative and Other Writings*, ed. Carretta, 347.

with each of the eight succeeding editions printed in Equiano's life-time.[58] This read like the guest list for an exclusive but rather conservative formal ball. In large typeface at the very head of the list were Equiano's most influential patrons: the Prince of Wales and the Duke of York. The rest of the subscribers followed in alphabetical groupings, ordered internally by social seniority. For example, under 'B', the Duke of Bedford and Duchess of Buccleuch sat at the top of the list, followed by the Lord Bishop of Bangor and Lord Belgrave, with the untitled subscribers whose surnames began with the letter 'B' listed alphabetically thereafter.[59] Even a casual reader skimming this list would not be able to miss the quality of the subscribers. Owning this book, potential buyers were to understand, put one in company with some of the wealthiest and most fashionable, honoured and important people in Britain; it was a status symbol. Of course, leading abolitionists including Clarkson, Ramsay and Wedgwood had all subscribed for multiple copies. A number of black men had also helped fund the publication, including Cugoano and 'William, the Son of Ignatius Sancho'.[60] This varied but self-consciously respectable subscription list again helped to guide the reader toward a particular set of conclusions about Equiano and his social status.

Having managed to pay for the book to be printed through pre-sales subscriptions alone, Equiano now sought widespread acclaim and exerted ever-greater control over his public image. The distribution model for the first edition of *The Interesting Narrative* is a case in point. He remained the main vendor for the *Narrative*, but made sure that it was available from no fewer than twelve major London booksellers.[61] As Carretta has pointed out, the appearance of many of these sellers on the subscription lists suggests that Equiano paid for their services with free copies of *The Interesting Narrative*.[62] This was a mutually beneficial arrangement: the booksellers got to keep all the profits from binding and selling the text, while Equiano got free marketing and distribution. There were significant fringe benefits, too, of which he was surely aware when selecting his business partners. For example, one of what Carretta calls the 'subscriber-distributors' of *The Interesting Narrative*, Joseph Johnson, was also the editor of the monthly *Analytical Review*.[63] It was of course in Johnson's own financial interests to promote the book, and it was through his influence that the text received its first literary review, written

---

[58] Carretta discusses the subscription lists at length in Carretta, *Equiano, the African*, 294–300.
[59] Equiano, *The Interesting Narrative*, vol. 1, vi.
[60] Equiano, *The Interesting Narrative*, vol. 1, viii, xiii.
[61] Equiano, *The Interesting Narrative*, vol. 1, i.
[62] Carretta, *Equiano, the African*, 290–294.   [63] Carretta, *Equiano, the African*, 331.

by a young, as-yet-unknown critic named Mary Wollstonecraft. That Johnson saw this review as a marketing opportunity is clear: the header text for the review only mentioned that the *Narrative* was sold 'by the Author, No. 10, Union-street, Middlesex Hospital; and J. Johnson', omitting mention of the other eleven sellers.[64] Similarly, John Murray, another of the subscriber-distributors, appears to have supplied the review copy to the *General Magazine* for its July 1789 issue in exchange for being the only listed seller.[65] The editor of the *General Magazine* was the abolitionist playwright Thomas Bellamy – another of Equiano's subscribers.[66]

The reviews themselves were influenced by the editorial stance of the publications in which they appeared. Wollstonecraft's was the longest and most balanced. She instantly identified the aspects of the text which would be of most interest to readers. She deemed the 'whole account of his unwearied endeavours to obtain his freedom' as 'very interesting', but thought that the 'narrative should have closed when he once more became his own master.' This was not least because the 'long account of his religious sentiments and conversion to methodism' that made up much of the second volume was 'rather tiresome'. More useful from a marketing perspective was the extract 'from the part descriptive of the national manners' of the Igbo that followed Wollstonecraft's review.[67] The review in Bellamy's *General Magazine*, meanwhile, was something of a 'puff piece': a glowing endorsement of the book's abolitionist message with little engagement with the text itself.[68] The *Gentleman's Magazine*, always rather sympathetic toward the West Indies interest (and significantly with no known editorial connection to Equiano) ran a much more critical review, stating that the literary performance placed 'the writer on a par with the general mass of men in the subordinate stations of civilized society, and prove[d] that there is no general rule without an exception'.[69] Despite this apparent dismissiveness of the literary abilities of black people, the editor John Nichols did not miss the opportunity to try and shift a few back copies of Ignatius Sancho's *Letters*, which he himself had published in 1782, by directing readers to the review of the *Letters* published six years earlier.[70]

---

[64] *Analytical Review*, 4 (May 1789), 27–29.
[65] *General Magazine and Impartial Review*, (July 1789), 315.
[66] Equiano, *The Interesting Narrative*, vol. 1, vii.
[67] *Analytical Review*, 4 (May 1789), 27–29.
[68] *General Magazine and Impartial Review*, (July 1789), 315.
[69] *Gentleman's Magazine*, (June 1789), 539.
[70] *Gentleman's Magazine*, (June 1789), 539.

One slightly hostile review from a partisan source was never going to seriously harm sales. In any case, Equiano was discovering a consummate talent for promotion and salesmanship. Between March and May 1789, Equiano placed numerous advertisements for the first edition of the *Narrative* in the *World*, the *Morning Star* and the *Star*.[71] He also began to explore the marketing opportunities presented by public speaking. On 9 May, he was one of the invited speakers at a public debate on the abolition question held at Capel Court on Bartholomew Lane, London. The advertisement for the debate also helped to promote *The Interesting Narrative*; he was billed as 'the celebrated Oubladah Equiano, [*sic*] or Gustavus Vassa, who has lately published his Memoirs'.[72] This celebrity status helped to motivate people to buy the text; sales of the first edition were healthy, if not particularly spectacular. The original print run – probably of the standard 500 copies – sold out after about nine months, prompting Equiano to publish a second edition in December 1789. During this time, he largely restricted his promotional activities to London and its immediate surroundings, as implied by the promise on the title page that it was available from 'all the Booksellers in town and country'.[73] He soon realised that he was limiting himself.

A short foray into Cambridge in July 1789 had proven successful, in terms of both networking with local abolitionists and selling a few extra copies of his *Narrative*.[74] Thomas Clarkson, a former star student at the University, had facilitated his introduction to sympathetic locals, including Thomas Jones, Master of Trinity College and a corresponding member of SEAST.[75] This had been a memorable trip for Equiano. He most likely met his future wife, Susannah Cullen, while he was there – something to which he referred in a letter published in the 1 August edition of the *Cambridge Chronicle*. 'Nor have even the fair-sex refused to countenance the sooty African,' he noted coyly.[76] It was to be, of course, a celebrity wedding. In April 1792, the *Morning Herald* reported on the marriage of 'the celebrated GUSTAVUS VASSA' and Susannah Cullen, noting that 'an immense crowd of people' were in attendance to celebrate the happy day.[77]

Perhaps falling in love inspired him to be more ambitious. When he published the second edition in December that year, he set his sights on a

---

[71] Carretta, 'New Equiana', 150.   [72] *Gazeteer and New Daily Advertiser*, 9 May 1789.
[73] Equiano, *The Interesting Narrative*, i.   [74] See Carretta, *Equiano, the African*, 335.
[75] 'Thomas Clarkson to Thomas Jones, 9 July 1789', cited in Carretta, *Equiano, the African*, 335.
[76] Cambridge Chronicle, 1 August 1789, cited in Bugg, 'The Other Interesting Narrative', 1435.
[77] *Morning Herald*, 21 April 1792.

full-fledged national book tour. The market in London remained the largest in the country, but it was far more saturated than elsewhere. Moreover, he stood a better chance of getting good attendance and local press coverage if he gave public lectures and readings from the *Narrative* in large provincial towns, especially where he could link to pre-existing abolition societies through his friends in SEAST. From 1790 to 1794, Equiano travelled near-continuously around the country, promoting and selling his book. As both Carretta and John Bugg have explored in detail, this itineracy enabled Equiano to manifest his celebrity status and embody his abolitionist credentials for a much broader and more diverse audience than for the first edition.[78] By appearing in person around the country to promote his text, Equiano shifted the focus away from 'the London literati' and toward the much larger market occupied by 'the anonymous workers of the industrial north'.[79] Hannah-Rose Murray has explored how, fifty years later, Frederick Douglass's widespread celebrity in Britain would emerge from 'the desire not only to hear him speak, but to physically touch him and to witness a formerly enslaved individual in the flesh'.[80] As early as 1790, Equiano recognised the same desires in his potential readers and made an effort to reach out and come within touching distance.

Over the next four years, Equiano travelled to every major urban settlement in Britain, always collecting more subscriptions for new editions of *The Interesting Narrative* and promoting sales. Equiano published new editions wherever he could raise enough local subscriptions. His first tour, from summer to autumn 1790, took in Birmingham, Manchester and Sheffield. His second, from February 1791 to February 1792, led him to Derby, Nottingham, Halifax, Leeds, York, Dublin, Belfast, Carrickfergus and back to London via the Scottish borders. After his wedding in April that year, he toured again, this time travelling to Glasgow, Edinburgh, Aberdeen, Dundee, Perth, Newcastle, Durham and William Wilberforce's home town of Hull. In 1793, he targeted the West Country, touring Shrewsbury, Sharp's home town of Gloucester, and Bristol. East Anglia came next: in 1794, he spent three months in Norwich. All the while, Equiano was publishing new editions.[81] There was both an egalitarian and commercial impetus driving this restless itineracy: Equiano wanted to share his antislavery identity and political

---

[78] Carretta, *Equiano, the African*, 330–368; Bugg, 'The Other Interesting Narrative', 1424–1442.

[79] Bugg, 'The Other Interesting Narrative', 1427.

[80] Hannah-Rose Murray, 'A "Negro Hercules": Frederick Douglass' Celebrity in Britain', *Celebrity Studies*, 7:2 (2016), 264.

[81] Carretta, *Equiano, the African*, 337–358.

ideology with as many people as possible. By reframing his assumed readership – the consumers of the identity he had bound to *The Interesting Narrative* – as broad-based rather than exclusively elite or metropolitan, he came to embody both textually and literally the egalitarian principles underpinning the abolitionist movement of the early 1790s.

Equiano was a charismatic synecdoche of abolition in particular, but also of a more general air of change in the British political atmosphere. The optimism and egalitarian spirit of the early years of the French Revolution inspired a new wave of cosmopolitan popular radicalism in Britain. Unlike later waves of radicalism (see Chapter 8), domestic reformers felt themselves comfortable bedfellows with the abolitionists in the early 1790s. Sharp, for example, was a long-standing member of the moderate and highly respectable reformist organisation the Society for Constitutional Information.[82] Clarkson was highly sympathetic to the revolutionary cause, spending five months in Paris in 1789–1790 working toward the abolition of slavery in the French colonies.[83] Equiano, meanwhile, became deeply enmeshed in the radical scene. In 1792, for example, he was lodging with Thomas Hardy, Secretary of the London Corresponding Society, the most significant and organised reformist group in the country.[84] After Hardy and two others were prosecuted for treason and acquitted in a widely celebrated trial in 1794, Equiano paid into a collection to help defray their expenses.[85] He made a point of travelling to the so-called Jacobin city of Norwich to promote his book, publishing the eighth edition there in 1794. This was no cynical attempt at self-promotion by piggybacking on the prevailing political zeitgeist. In 1796, two years after he had stopped promoting and selling his *Narrative*, Equiano was reported as taking the chair at a feast celebrating the anniversary of Hardy's acquittal.[86] By this point, repressive government legislation had kicked in, and the wave of popular reforming sentiment in Britain had crested. Equiano's public association with Hardy and the London Corresponding Society continued to draw antiradical censure even after his death in March 1797. In a satire appearing in the *Anti-Jacobin* in December that year, he was represented as being prevented

---

[82] See Christopher Brown, *Moral Capital: Foundations of British Abolitionism* (Chapel Hill: University of North Carolina Press, 2006), 189.

[83] See John Oldfield, *Transatlantic Abolitionism in the Age of Revolution: An International History of Anti-Slavery* (Cambridge: Cambridge University Press, 2013), 85–90.

[84] TNA, Treasury Papers, TS 24/12/2, 'Gustavus Vassa, the African to [Thomas Hardy] 28 May 1792'.

[85] *Morning Post*, 19 May 1795.

[86] *London Packet or Lloyd's Evening Post*, 7 November 1796.

from speaking at a radical feast, as 'it appeared that [he was] entering upon a subject which would have entirely altered the complexion of the Meeting'.[87]

Even before he began publicly associating with popular radicals, Equiano was already well aware that life in the public eye often brings malicious gossip along with it. While it rapidly became popular in the late 1780s and early 1790s, the abolition movement still had powerful enemies, keen to discredit their testimony and harm the reputation of their spokespeople. Equiano learned this the hard way in April 1792. An anonymous letter appeared in the 25 April edition of the *Oracle*, claiming that he had never been to Africa 'but was born and bred in the Danish Island of Santa Cruz in the West Indies'.[88] This complete fabrication was transparently intended to harm the abolitionist cause. 'What, we will ask any man of plain understanding', the article asked, 'must that cause be, which can lean for support on falsehoods as audaciously propagated as they are easily detected?'[89] The *Star* reprinted the allegations two days later, without the more overt anti-abolitionist passages.[90] Equiano, who was touring Scotland with Susannah at the time, did not hear about the stories for several weeks. He no sooner found out than took steps to rescue his reputation. He obtained a copy of the offending *Oracle* article, and on 28 May wrote to Hardy in London, asking him to get hold of the relevant issue of the *Star*.[91] By this point in his career, Equiano had built enough of an independent platform to publicly defend himself without recourse to the traditional press. He would deal with the allegations head-on. When the fifth edition of *The Interesting Narrative* was published in August that year, it was headed with a new note to the reader. Equiano described the *Oracle* story as 'an invidious falsehood' designed 'to hurt my character, and to discredit and prevent the sale of my Narrative'.[92]

To counter these allegations, Equiano needed only ask his friends to vouch for him. His extensive travels and tireless campaigning over the years had put him in touch with some of the most respectable people in Britain, and he was sufficiently well liked for many to advocate on his behalf. One of his associates in Glasgow, John Montieth, wrote an angry letter to Alexander Tillock, the editor of the *Star*, on 30 May 1792, possibly threatening legal action. Tillock responded by quickly climbing down; the article had been lifted from the one in the *Oracle*, he claimed, therefore '[i]f it be erroneous, you will see it had not its origin with us.'[93]

[87] *Anti-Jacobin or Weekly Examiner*, 4 December 1797.   [88] *The Oracle*, 25 April 1792.
[89] *The Oracle*, 25 April 1792.   [90] *The Star*, 27 April 1792.
[91] TNA, Treasury Solicitor's Papers, TS/24/12/2, 'Olaudah Equiano to Thomas Hardy, 28 May 1792'.
[92] Equiano, *Interesting Narrative and Other Writings*, ed. Carretta, 5.
[93] Equiano, *Interesting Narrative and Other Writings*, ed. Carretta, 6.

He went further, speculating that the original *Oracle* story 'respecting G. V. may have been fabricated by some of the advocates for continuing the Slave Trade, for the purpose of weakening the force of evidence brought against that trade; for, I believe, if they could, they would stifle the evidence altogether.'[94] At the same time, Equiano's associate, the Rev. Dr Baker at Mayfair, went after Buchanan Millan, the editor of the *Oracle*, visiting his home with a demand that an official apology be made to Equiano. While no such apology was actually printed, it is clear that the interventions had been effective: the would-be scandal lived and died with the two short paragraphs in the *Oracle* and the *Star*, and nobody ever publicly attempted to substantiate the allegations. Triumphant, Equiano reprinted Tillock's retraction and a letter from Baker dismissing the claims made in the *Oracle* at the head of the prefatory material in every subsequent edition of *The Interesting Narrative*.[95]

This vindication of Equiano's character, much like his commercial success, depended on his extraordinary ability to make friends in high places. In the absence of any truly national-scale mass media, fame in the late eighteenth century depended more heavily on word of mouth and quality of social associations in a local or regional context. Fanning out from his London-based abolitionist contacts, Equiano was able to add respectable people from all over the country to his list of allies and character references. With each new edition of *The Interesting Narrative*, he could add new letters of recommendation from local advocates to the beginning of the text. Provincial readers could open the book and see that their minister, mayor or another local worthy was willing to put their name to it, alongside some of the better-known London abolitionists. In Hull, for instance, local readers could be reassured that Peter Sykes, the Lord Mayor, vouched for the text's authenticity and Equiano's good character.[96]

While Equiano made good use of these letters of recommendation as advertising, even restating his character references in letters of thanks in local newspapers, they also served a practical function. These letters were the principal means by which Equiano found places to stay, and premises from which to sell his text, in each of the new towns he visited. They were his 'in', not only to local abolitionist networks, but also to local publishing and bookselling infrastructures. When the Devonshire author and economist William Langworthy wrote to his friend William Hughes in Devizes in 1794, he mentioned that Equiano's part 'in bringing about the motion for a repeal of the Slave Act, has given him much celebrity as

[94] Equiano, *Interesting Narrative and Other Writings*, ed. Carretta, 6.
[95] Equiano, *Interesting Narrative and Other Writings*, ed. Carretta, 6–7.
[96] Equiano, *Interesting Narrative and Other Writings*, ed. Carretta, 11.

a public man'. But Langworthy himself became a functionary of this celebrity status when he stated that Equiano's '*business* in this part of the world is to promote the sale of his book, and is a part of *my business*, as a friend to the cause of humanity, to do all the little service that is in my poor power to a man who is engaged in so noble a cause'.[97] This is how Equiano became a national celebrity in the late eighteenth century. The fight against slavery, in which he was so indefatigably and consistently engaged, provided a locus of influence and a moral foundation for his publicity-generating activities in provincial Britain. He was a celebrity abolitionist.

Plaisterer's Hall, on Addle Street, a few hundred yards from what would become the offices of the Anti-Slavery Society at 18 Aldermanbury, represented salubrious accommodations for any self-made businessman. A 'substantial brick premises', it contained 'numerous convenient apartments' and 'a spacious hall, upwards of forty feet in length, with a music gallery'. It had 'a store-cellar capable of holding 100 butts', perfect for storing excess stock or conducting business from home.[98] That was, at least, what Equiano used it for: the inventory in his will listed 'Sundry Household Goods and Furniture wearing Apparel and printed Books at present on the premises at Plaisterers Hall,' as well as £300 secured on the lease.[99] Equiano may have only been a tenant (as the name suggests, the hall was owned by the Plasterers' Company), but these were both practical premises and fitting accommodation for a well-known and respectable public man of Equiano's standing. Even though he downsized shortly after June 1796, he retained the lease of Plaisterer's Hall until his death.[100]

Equiano had gone from slavery to celebrity and financial security entirely through his own effort. To an extent, he embodied the transformation of the abolitionist movement from an evangelical or niche political interest into an enterprise that bore some resemblance to a commercial cultural industry. The apparatus of industrialised print culture, alongside coeval developments in the formation of the capitalist subject (such as renewed emphases on individual genius, creative originality and economic self-sufficiency), allowed for Equiano's emergence as the commodified 'self' of the abolitionist movement.[101] Studies into

---

[97] Equiano, *Interesting Narrative and Other Writings*, ed. Carretta, 12.

[98] *Times*, 1 January 1798.

[99] TNA, Records of the Prerogative Court of Canterbury, PROB 11/1289/78, 'Will of Gustavus Vassa'.

[100] Carretta, *Equiano, the African*, 365.

[101] On the immutability of the eighteenth-century self, see Dror Wahrman, *The Making of the Modern Self: Identity and Culture in Eighteenth-Century England* (New Haven, CT: Yale University Press, 2004), 265–311.

the formation of celebrity culture in this period often emphasise the commodification of personhood via the reproduction and dissemination of the visual and/or textual image of a given individual.[102] Of course, as a former slave Equiano understood perfectly how industrial capitalism could convert personality into commodity. His experiences as both enslaved subject and independent trader equipped him to recognise that his personhood possessed economic as well as intrinsic value. In the act of writing his autobiography he converted his life into a saleable product while simultaneously asserting his right to self-determination by fixing the meanings of his social interactions – if not in stone then in paper and ink. It may well be for this reason that he adopted his 'African' name near-exclusively in relation to his autobiography, rather than, say, in his holograph correspondence. Olaudah Equiano was the subject of *The Interesting Narrative*; Gustavus Vassa was merely its author.

In any case, as Bugg has shown, the text itself was merely one part of a larger form of personality commodity that Equiano was keen to promote and sell.[103] The other constituents of this 'product' – charisma, influential connections, popular 'moderate' radicalism and a meta-narrative of upward social and economic mobility – were enacted in personal appearances, self-promotion, networking and published correspondence. The antislavery movement generated a set of cultural and popular-political conditions in which Equiano was uniquely qualified to promote and sell an ideology through the commodification of an essential, representative and apparently authentic abolitionist 'self'. Like Sancho, he was 'extraordinary' and unique, yet also to be understood as an avatar for all enslaved people and all abolitionists. Unlike Sancho, he himself was the primary actor in creating this personality commodity, generating a market for it and exploiting his abolitionist contacts to sustain that market. It is this alignment of historical circumstances – individual, audience and industry, to fit it to Tom Mole's model – that qualifies Equiano as an early example and proponent of British celebrity culture.[104]

---

[102] See, for example, Laura Engel, *Fashioning Celebrity: 18th-Century British Actresses and Strategies for Image Making* (Columbus: Ohio State University Press, 2011), 2; Tom Mole, *Byron's Romantic Celebrity: Industrial Culture and the Hermeneutic of Intimacy* (Basingstoke: Palgrave Macmillan, 2007), 1–27; Claire Brock, *The Feminization of Fame, 1750–1830* (Basingstoke: Palgrave Macmillan, 2006).
[103] Bugg, 'The Other Interesting Narrative', 1424–1442.
[104] Mole, *Byron's Romantic Celebrity*, 1–27.

3   Mary Prince and the Infamy of Victimhood,
      1828–1833

If Equiano fulfilled the role of the 'representative' of enslaved men during the first major wave of abolitionism in the late 1780s and early 1790s, then enslaved women were to remain signally *un*represented until the 'final push' of the early 1830s. Mary Prince, the first black woman to publish an autobiography in Britain, was in much the same sense as Equiano an antislavery author, and her text was if anything even more carefully marketed to meet the ends of the formal abolitionist movement. However, her autobiography, *The History of Mary Prince*, was a far more mediated and collaborative text than either Sancho's *Letters* or *The Interesting Narrative*.

Born into slavery in Bermuda around 1788, Prince was separated from her family at the age of ten. Over the next three decades, she was repeatedly sold into various different types of work in Bermuda, Turks Island and Antigua. Around December 1826, she joined the Moravian Church and married a free black carpenter named Daniel James. In 1828, she came with her abusive 'owners', John and Margaret Wood, to London. Aware that under the terms of the Somerset ruling of 1772 she could not be forcibly re-enslaved, and unwilling to submit to any more abuse, she left the Woods' house later that year and found her way to the offices of the Anti-Slavery Society. Eventually, she entered into domestic service in the home of Thomas Pringle, the Society's secretary.[1] It was here, in January 1831, that she dictated her autobiography to Susannah Strickland, an ambitious young author from Suffolk, who was staying with the Pringles at the time.[2] With the help of Joseph Phillips, the Clerk of the Anti-Slavery Society, Pringle then edited Strickland's manuscript version of Prince's testimony, cross-examining Prince

[1] Biographical details are all from Mary Prince, *The History of Mary Prince, a West Indian Slave, Related by Herself*, 3rd edn. (London: F. Westley and A. H. David, 1831), and Moira Ferguson, *Subject to Others: British Women Writers and Colonial Slavery, 1670–1834* (London: Routledge, 1992), 281–298.
[2] January 1831: see Susannah Moodie, *Letters of a Lifetime*, ed. Carl Bastadt, Elizabeth Hopkins and Michael Peterman (Toronto: University of Toronto Press, 1985), 57.

on the details as he went along. Pringle paid for it to be published 'with a view to provide a little fund for [Prince's] benefit'.[3] The result was a gruelling and visceral account of the horrors of plantation slavery, the most graphic that had ever been published. Nevertheless, a number of key details about Prince's life – those that Pringle felt would undermine the cause – were edited out somewhere between recitation and publication.

These processes of transcription, edition, mediation, intercession and interception have formed the basis of much of the existing scholarship – especially literary criticism – on the *History*. A number of critics (perhaps most influentially Gillian Whitlock, Moira Ferguson and Jessica Allen) have sought to elucidate the interplay of Prince, Pringle and Strickland's competing authorities in the production of meaning and identity in the text. Most, however, concede the impossibility of completely retrieving Prince's essential 'authentic voice' from the narrative, since the published version is the only one to have survived.[4] Historians, meanwhile, have tended to think about it more straightforwardly in relation to the abolitionist movement.[5] The extent of its influence on the broader anti-slavery movements, and as a cultural touchstone in British life more generally, has been explored somewhat less frequently. Beyond its inherent significance as the first prose text by a black woman to be published in Britain, and the earliest full-length autobiography of an enslaved woman, Prince's *History* is not always seen as significant beyond the very

[3] Prince, *History*, iv.

[4] A. M. Rauwerda, 'Naming, Agency, and "A Tissue of Falsehoods" in *The History of Mary Prince*', *Victorian Literature and Culture*, (2001), 397–411; K. Merinda Simmons, 'Beyond "Authenticity": Migration and the Epistemology of "Voice" in Mary Prince's "History of Mary Prince" and Maryse Conde's "I, Tituba"', *College Literature*, 36:4 (2009), 75–99; Moira Ferguson, *Subject to Others: British Women Writers and Colonial Slavery, 1670–1834* (London: Routledge, 1992), 281–298; Sue Thomas, *Telling West Indian Lives: Life Narrative and the Reform of Plantation Slavery Cultures 1804–1834* (London: Routledge, 2014), 119–166; Gillian Whitlock, *The Intimate Empire: Reading Women's Autobiography* (London: Continuum, 2000), 8–37; Michelle Gadpaille, 'Trans-Colonial Collaboration and Slave Narrative: *Mary Prince* Revisited', *English Language Overseas Perspectives and Enquiries*, 8 (2011), 63–77; Barbara Baumgartner, 'The Body as Evidence: Resistance, Collaboration, and Appropriation in *The History of Mary Prince*', *Callaloo*, 24:1 (2001), 253–275. Jessica Allen takes a contrasting approach, using the postcolonial theory of Gayatri Chakravorty Spivak to examine the 'negative spaces' in the *History* for evidence of Prince's 'Creole' vernacular. Jessica L. Allen, 'Pringle's Pruning of Prince: *The History of Mary Prince* and the Question of Repetition', *Callaloo*, 35:2 (2012), 509–519.

[5] See, for example, Manisha Sinha, *The Slave's Cause: A History of Abolition* (New Haven, CT: Yale University Press, 2016), 213–214; Clare Midgley, *Women against Slavery: The British Campaigns, 1780–1870* (London: Routledge, 1992), 87–88; Robin Blackburn, *The Overthrow of Colonial Slavery, 1776–1848* (London: Verso, 1988), 142–144. A notable exception to this tendency is Sue Thomas's discussion of Prince's Moravianism in Thomas, *Telling West Indian Lives*, 119–166.

specific political contexts in which it was composed and published. In other words, while its usefulness for the antislavery campaign is routinely invoked, Prince's *History* is not always recognised as having been culturally significant in any broader sense. Obviously, this is related to the story of the text's production – it was, after all, intended as abolitionist propaganda. However, the success of the text on abolitionist terms should not obscure other, unintended consequences of its personalisation of the gendered violence inherent in slavery. Somewhat like Equiano, Prince became something of a 'brand ambassador' for the antislavery movement. In time, her personhood and moral and intellectual character were also contested by pro- and antislavery interests.

In her seminal *Women Against Slavery*, Clare Midgley alludes to the particular function of Prince's narrative that this chapter seeks to explore: 'The *History* was … a contribution to the anti-slavery campaign written by a black woman in her role as a representative of that vast mass of enslaved people in the British West Indies who had no opportunity to tell their stories to the British public.'[6] The key word here is *representative*. Prince's experiences were published on the understanding that they be read as representative of the horrors of slavery as they related especially to women. She herself was marketed as *the* representative of the millions of innocent enslaved women it victimised. The text, and the woman whose life story it commodified, thus had to pull off a difficult balancing act: Prince needed to be morally degraded by her enslavement yet, despite this, morally upright enough to fulfil the representative function of the innocent victim deserving of relief.[7] With this in mind, the purpose of Pringle and Strickland's editorial heavy-handedness begins to come into clearer focus. Their interventions – whether edition, elision, expansion or intercession – were intended to affect not only the way in which the *History* was read but the way in which Prince herself was 'read' as a public persona. Thus, 'Mary Prince' as a representative of all female victims of slavery was (like all public figures) something of an artificial construct. Subsequent libel trials over criticisms of the narrative and controversies hinging on Prince's sexual history demonstrate that this construct was sufficiently public and important enough to be worth contesting.

This chapter explores how Prince's abolitionist network edited and marketed her and her work, deliberately engineering a gendered perception of

---

[6] Midgley, *Women against Slavery*, 87–88.
[7] See Henrice Altink, 'Deviant and Dangerous: Proslavery Representations of Jamaican Slave Women's Sexuality, ca. 1780–1834', in Gwyn Campbell, Suzanne Miers and Joseph Miller (eds.), *Women and Slavery: The Modern Atlantic* (Athens: Ohio University Press, 2008), 210.

her as a passive victim of abuse and exploitation. Ironically, this artificial version of Prince, echoing contemporaneous celebrity culture, hinged on its claims to candour and authenticity.[8] Pringle and his circle recognised the value of women's contributions to the abolitionist movement, as demonstrated by the reinvigoration of ladies' antislavery societies around the country. It was to this key demographic that he marketed Prince, as a representative female victim of the avariciousness and sexual exploitation inherent in slavery. He thus marshalled and reinforced women's support for abolition by appealing to a gendered form of moral outrage. This resulted in a focus as much on a highly visible 'celebrity victim' of slavery as on her text itself.

Editing Mary Prince

Prince's authority over her own autobiography was more complicated than that of any other black writer of the period. Anticipating later nineteenth-century African American slave narratives, white abolitionist editors intervened in the narrative to such an extent that her authorial voice was at risk of being drowned out by an unwieldy paratextual apparatus. The first edition, published in March or April 1831, included a preface and lengthy supplement, both written by Pringle, detailing the circumstances leading to the text's publication. Pringle also attached a second, unrelated narrative, of the life of another former slave named Louis Asa-Asa.[9] The second and third editions, published later that year, also contained a postscript to the preface and a corroborating appendix in which four female witnesses testified to having seen the whip-marks on Prince's back.[10] Like most autobiographies by former slaves, Prince's *History* was produced with the help of an amanuensis, in this case the author Susannah Strickland. In his preface, Pringle was more open than most editors about his and Strickland's role in the production of the final, published piece:

The narrative was taken down from Mary's own lips by a lady … It was written out fully, with all the narrator's repetitions and prolixities, and afterwards pruned into its present shape … No fact of importance has been omitted, and not a single circumstance or sentiment has been added. It is essentially her own, without any

[8] See Laura Engels, *Fashioning Celebrity: 18th-Century British Actresses and Strategies for Image Making* (Columbus: Ohio State University Press, 2011), 2.
[9] Mary Prince, *The History of Mary Prince, a West Indian Slave, Related by Herself*, 1st edn. (London: F. Westley and A. H. Davis, 1831), iii–iv, 24–49.
[10] Prince, *History*, iv, 40. (This and all subsequent citations are from the third edition.)

material alteration farther than was requisite to exclude redundancies and gross grammatical errors, so as to render it clearly intelligible.[11]

Since Strickland's manuscript version of the text has either not survived or has yet to be rediscovered, the only version of Prince's authorial voice left to us is that mediated and approved by Pringle: one that is only 'essentially her own'.

Even taking into account his openly interventionist approach, Pringle's intrusions into the text itself were occasionally quite obnoxious. His footnotes ranged from the explicatory (telling the reader that fifty-seven Bermuda pounds was worth 'about £38 sterling') to the translational (informing the reader that 'Buckra' was a 'Negro term for white people') to the outright intercessional ('She means West Indians').[12] At other times, he used his footnotes to remind the reader of the role he and Strickland had played in the production of the text. After a simple simile in the main body of the text comparing slave-owners' hearts to stone, Pringle added a footnote declaring, 'These strong sentiments, and all of a similar character in this little narrative, are given verbatim as uttered by Mary Prince.'[13] The most overtly polemical paragraph of the text, attacking the position that slavery could ever be beneficial to the enslaved, was accompanied by a footnote declaring that 'this paragraph especially, is given as nearly as was possible in Mary's precise words.'[14] It seems that Pringle was keen to ensure that the passages in the *History* which most directly corroborated the claims of the Anti-Slavery Society were also seen as the most authentic and unmediated. Ironically, the result of such interventions was to undermine the 'authenticity' of the rest of the narrative by implication, foregrounding not the voice of the enslaved subject, but those of her abolitionist allies.

Aside from their undoubtedly sincere charitable intentions, both Strickland and Pringle had their own reasons to promote their own voices through Prince's narrative. In early 1831, Strickland was a young, ambitious author, trying to break into the London literary scene. An established children's author, she had since at least 1826 also been submitting poetry to literary journals intended for both the specialist women's market and a mainstream mixed readership.[15] By 1830, she had set her sights on the most prestigious literary journals, including Frederic

---

[11] Prince, *History*, iii.   [12] Prince, *History*, 4, 13, 22.   [13] Prince, *History*, 5.
[14] Prince, *History*, 22.
[15] For a comprehensive list of publications by Strickland, see John Thurston, *The Work of Words: The Writings of Susanna Strickland Moodie* (Montreal: McGill-Queen's University Press, 1996), 228–242.

Shoberl's hugely popular annual *Forget Me Not*.[16] While she would go on to achieve the widespread literary success she craved with *Roughing It in the Bush* (published under her married name of Susannah Moodie in 1852), she was desperate in the early 1830s to impress London's literary *ton*.[17] It was this desire that first encouraged her to stay with the Pringles in their Pentonville home in north London for much of 1830 and 1831. Even without Prince's *History*, Strickland's time with Pringle undoubtedly enhanced her professional and personal life. As a well-connected literary man himself, he introduced her to 'a variety of well-known literary and artistic figures' including the artists John Martin and George Cruikshank and (presumably through his abolitionist contacts) the 'writer-editor' Thomas Roscoe, son of the famous Liverpool anti-slavery activist William Roscoe. Pringle also 'had an editorial hand' in the literary journal the *Athenaeum*, in which several of Strickland's poems were published in 1830.[18] It was also through Pringle that she met her husband, Lt. John Wedderburn Dunbar Moodie.

Prince was working in the Pringle household during this crucial phase of Strickland's literary ascendancy, and the two women were close. In a letter dated 9 April 1831, Strickland recalled Prince making a special effort to attend her wedding in style: 'Mr. Pringle "gave me" away, and Black Mary, who had treated herself with a complete new suit upon the occasion, went on the coach box, to see her dear Missie and Biographer wed.'[19] Strickland's characterisation of herself here as Prince's 'biographer', as opposed to amanuensis, reflected an awareness of the extensive editorial aspect of her role, and perhaps even her attitude toward the authorship of the text itself. When she was working with Prince and Pringle in January that year, she wrote of the *History* in a similar vein:

I have been writing Mr. Pringle's black Mary's life from her own dictation and for her benefit adhering to her own simple story and language without deviating to the paths of flourish or romance. It is a pathetic little history and is now printing in the form of a pamphlet to be laid before the Houses of Parliament. Of course my name does not appear.[20]

Strickland's evident difficulty in restraining from 'flourish or romance' while 'writing Mr. Pringle's Black Mary's life' underscores the instability of the final product as both a literary and historic source, especially with regard to authorship and authority. While her apparent insistence on her own anonymity might indicate rather a self-effacing propriety for a

---

[16] Moodie, *Letters*, 54.
[17] For the sake of clarity, I refer to Susannah Strickland Moodie by her maiden name throughout this chapter, since she was not married when she transcribed Prince's text.
[18] Moodie, *Letters*, 11–12.   [19] Moodie, *Letters*, 60.   [20] Moodie, *Letters*, 57.

charitable cause, it also reflected her own attitudes toward what consti-
tuted true literary value.[21] In any case, her anonymity was not preserved
for long. Pringle unveiled her as the amanuensis in the third edition of
the *History*, published mere months after the transcription was first
completed.[22]

Strickland continued to draw creative inspiration from working with
Prince for many years after they parted company. As Rauwerda has
pointed out, an exchange in Strickland's 1851 'Rachel, or Trifles from
the Burthen of a Life', in which the eponymous heroine argues with the
wife of a 'West Indian' slave-owner about 'The History of Mary P – '
contains 'one of the very few references ... to the actual transcription of
The History'.[23] In 1854, Strickland edited and expanded this passage for
inclusion in her novel *Flora Lyndsay*:

'By-the-bye, my dear Madam, have you read a tract published lately by this
disinterested [Anti-Slavery] society, called the History of Mary P.? It is set
forth to be an authentic narrative, while I know enough of the West Indies, to
pronounce it a tissue of falsehoods from beginning to end.'

'Did you know Mary P.?'

'I wonder who does. It is an imaginary tale got up for party purposes.'

'You are mistaken,' said Flora quietly. 'That narrative is strictly true. I was
staying the winter before last, with her mistress in London, and I wrote it myself
from the woman's own lips.'

'You!' and Mrs. Dalton started from the ground as though she had been bitten
by a serpent – 'and I have been talking all this time to the author of Mary P. From
this moment, Madam, we must regard ourselves as strangers. No West Indian
could for a moment tolerate the writer of that odious pamphlet.'[24]

As we will see, Strickland was recalling, with the benefit of more than
twenty years' hindsight, a bitter controversy that surrounded the publication of Prince's *History*. Both the *History* itself, and planters' hatred of it
as an effective abolitionist tool, were sufficiently high-profile that they
served as a satirical cultural reference point for Strickland's readers as
late as the 1850s.

Strickland may have forborn writing specifically about Prince until the
fallout from the controversy had subsided. She did, however, begin
introducing antislavery tropes into her fiction almost as soon as she met
her. For example, much like Prince's *History*, Strickland's 1831 children's story 'The Vanquished Lion' occasionally lapsed into outright
abolitionist polemic. In one scene, the young hero, Lewis Fenwick, asked

[21] See Thurston, *The Work of Words*, 3.   [22] Prince, *History*, 41.
[23] Rauwerda, 'Naming', 405.
[24] Susannah Moodie, *Flora Lyndsay; or, Passages in an Eventful Life* (London: Richard
Bentley, 1854), vol. 1, 217–218.

his mother why his uncle, despite being 'such a kind man', persisted in keeping slaves. His mother's response could have come straight from an antislavery pamphlet:

'Because, my dear, like many of his countrymen, he has never rightly considered the subject. He is not aware that, in following the customs of the land, he is committing a great national crime. I trust, Lewis, the time is at hand, when your uncle will break the yoke from off the neck of his slaves, and that the British government will restore to the wronged and degraded African his rights as a man.'[25]

This exchange is one of several in the story on the themes of slavery and prejudice. In another, young Lewis, while travelling around the Cape Coast, 'felt the prejudices of colour operating very forcibly upon his mind against the natives of the country', especially Charka, one of his uncle's slaves.[26] This prejudice is not fully removed until Charka rescues Lewis from a giant snake, at which point Lewis, fulfilling the moralising function of the story, sees the error of his ways. Charka's response reveals him to be both a mawkish caricature of the grateful slave and an object of abolitionist wish-fulfilment: 'The eyes of the black glistened with joy as he pressed the fair youth to his dark bosom. "Dear young massa, think no ill of black man – look no dark upon him. Black man have a large heart – black man love all that treat him well."'[27]

John Oldfield has noted that the association between organised anti-slavery campaigning and the appearance of abolitionist polemic in children's literature strengthened after the formation of the Anti-Slavery Society in 1823.[28] Strickland's insertion of outright abolitionist polemic into children's literature, written during or just after her stay with the Secretary of the Anti-Slavery Society and a formerly enslaved woman, sheds light on the confluence of social and cultural forms of abolitionist labour undertaken by women in the early nineteenth century. Her desire to include a heroic black character as an illustration of the irrationality of racial prejudice may conceivably have stemmed from her friendship with Prince. Her patronising depiction of the same character's servile gratitude, however, serves to highlight white abolitionists' utter dependence on black authors to provide anything approaching an 'authentic' first-hand account of slavery.

[25] Susannah Moodie, *Voyages: Short Narratives of Susannah Moodie*, ed. John Thurston (Ottowa: University of Ottowa Press, 1991), 37.

[26] Moodie, *Voyages*, 36.   [27] Moodie, *Voyages*, 39.

[28] John Oldfield, 'Anti-Slavery Sentiment in Children's Literature, 1750–1850', *Slavery & Abolition*, 10:1 (1989), 50–54.

Prince's *History* occasionally hinted toward a quiet, but powerfully articulate anger that gave the lie to the effusiveness of characters like Charka. In some passages, this anger threatened to break through the smooth sentimental mode favoured by Pringle, troubling his careful marketing of Prince as the archetypical helpless female victim of slavery. It is here that the contest between author and editor over precisely what Prince was supposed to represent emerges most clearly. In the passage where Prince was taken from her mother and sold at Hamilton, Bermuda, the narrating voice becomes positively schizophrenic:

My heart throbbed with grief and terror so violently, that I pressed my hands quite tightly across my breast, but I could not keep it still, and it continued to leap as though it would burst out of my body. But who cared for that? Did one of the many by-standers, who are looking at us so carelessly, think of the pain that wrong the hearts of the Negro woman and her young ones? No, no! They were not all bad, I dare say, but slavery hardens white people's hearts against the blacks.[29]

The phenomenological detail in this passage – Prince's sense that her heart would burst out of her body – provided exactly the type of visceral, affecting, personal perspective Pringle needed to illustrate the terror and pain of slavery. This is an example of Prince, to borrow Ferguson's phrase, 'simultaneously conforming and subversively erupting (consciously and unconsciously) out of that conformity'.[30] Just as her heart had threatened to erupt from her ribcage, Prince's anger seemed about to burst from the confines of Pringle's editorial control. Yet, as A. M. Rauwerda has noted, her indignation at the refusal of the 'by-standers' to help her seemed to be checked by an external intervention in mid-flow, prompting her to concede that, perhaps, 'they were not all bad' after all.[31] Post-hoc, Pringle secured his control over this portion of the narrative even further by reiterating its function as evidence to support *his* abolitionist work. He inserted a lengthy footnote at the end of the passage: 'Let the reader compare the above affecting account,' it read, 'with the following description of a vendue of slaves at the Cape of Good Hope, published by me in 1826.'[32]

Prince's ability to contradict Pringle, tonally or substantively, was of course severely limited by the effects of both gender and racial hierarchies in British society. Pragmatically speaking, she could ill-afford to upset Pringle, since she depended on him for her home and employment. They

[29] Prince, *History*, 4.   [30] Ferguson, *Subject to Others*, 298.
[31] Rauwerda, 'Naming', 403.   [32] Prince, *History*, 4.

had first met in November 1828, shortly after Prince left the Woods' house.[33] At that time Prince, alone, dangerously ill from the Woods' abuses and all but destitute, was lodging with a local shoe-black named Mash. Though she had received a little help from the Moravians, she was struggling to survive in London. Making matters worse was the fact that she knew she could not return to her husband in Antigua. While the provisions of the Somerset ruling prevented her from being forced to return to slavery for as long as she remained in England, she was still, technically speaking, a slave. This much had been confirmed in 1827 by Lord Stowell's ruling in the case of Grace Jones.[34] As soon as she set foot back in Antigua, she could be forced back into bonded servitude and severely punished or killed with near-impunity for having absconded in London. She was, essentially, trapped in England.

Fortunately, Prince later noted, 'a woman of the name of Hill told me of the Anti-Slavery Society, and went with me to their office, to inquire if they could do any thing to get me my freedom.'[35] This may have been Emma Hill, a laundress who had worked with Prince at the Woods' house and later testified to the veracity of the History.[36] Another possibility is that this was Jane Hill, sister to the black abolitionist Richard Hill. Richard brought Jane with him when he came to London in 1827 and left her there when he was commissioned by the Anti-Slavery Society to gather information in Haiti early in 1830.[37] Richard Hill was on good professional terms with Pringle especially, and he worked with him directly during his time in Haiti. He and Jane were also evidently aware of the Society's role in supporting black women in London. In April 1830 Richard formally applied through Pringle to the Society for 'an allowance of £5 a month' to support Jane 'during the time of her continuance in England'.[38] The Hills, two black, West Indian–born intellectuals, both well acquainted with the work of the Anti-Slavery Society and with Pringle's philanthropic activities in particular, were well situated to link Prince with her (eventual) publication network.

Whoever facilitated the introduction between them, it is clear that publishing the History was neither Prince nor Pringle's first choice to

---

[33] Prince, History, 21.
[34] See Peter Fryer, Staying Power: The History of Black People in Britain (London: Pluto Press, 1984), 130–132.
[35] Prince, History, 21.   [36] Times, 1 March 1833.
[37] Frank Cundall, 'Richard Hill', Journal of Negro History, 5:1 (1920), 38. See also Marlene Manderson-Jones, 'Richard Hill of Jamaica, His Life and Times, 1795–1872', PhD thesis, University of the West Indies, Mona (1973).
[38] Bodleian Library, MSS Brit. Emp., 5/18/C1/71, 'Richard Hill to Thomas Pringle, 5 Apr. 1830 and Thomas Pringle to Richard Hill, 6 Apr. 1830'.

provide for her financial relief. When Prince first came to the Society's office after leaving the Woods' house in November 1828, Pringle took her to George Stephen, their solicitor. They established that Prince could not be manumitted except by private settlement with her legal 'owner' John Wood. With this in mind, according to the *History*, 'they offered him ... a large sum for my freedom', but found that he 'would not consent to let me go free'.[39] Frustrated, the Society petitioned Parliament on Prince's behalf, but, as Pringle recalled in 1831, Wood 'dexterously contrived to neutralise all our efforts, until the close of the [parliamentary] Session of 1829; soon after which he embarked with his family for the West Indies'.[40] With Wood unavailable to answer the case, Parliament could do little. Prince's hopes of manumission were extinguished for the time being. Unable to return to her husband or family, she would need to find a way to survive independently in London. She became a domestic servant in Pringle's house.

Pringle's experience with Wood encouraged him to try to settle similar cases in the future as privately and quickly as possible. In October 1831, he and the chair of the Anti-Slavery Society, Zachary Macaulay, were approached by a black woman named Nancy Morgan. Like Prince, Morgan was still technically enslaved but wanted to return to the West Indies to be reunited with her husband and child in Tobago. However, she could not afford to purchase her own freedom. Pringle and Macaulay acted quickly and perhaps rashly, paying £60 sterling from their own pockets for Morgan's freedom on the assumption that they could claim the money back from the Society's coffers. Their unilateral decision to expend such a large sum ruffled a few feathers at the next Society meeting on 2 November. When they requested reimbursement, another of the leading members, Joseph Sturge, objected to their actions and made a remarkable motion that, in the future, it be considered 'out of the province of the Anti-Slavery Society to employ any part of their funds in the emancipation of slaves'.[41] This presented something of an embarrassment for the chair and secretary; Sturge's motion was postponed until the next meeting and quietly dropped.[42] Pringle was, however, able to recoup some of his costs by applying to the Birmingham Ladies' Negro's Friend Society, who donated £20 toward Morgan's cause.[43]

---

[39] Prince, *History*, 21.   [40] Prince, *History*, 26.
[41] Bodleian Library, MSS Brit. Emp. 5/20/E5/2, 'Rough Minutes of the Anti-Slavery Society, 2 Nov. 1831'.
[42] Bodleian Library, MSS Brit. Emp. 5/20/E5/2, 'Rough Minutes of the Anti-Slavery Society, 23 Nov. 1831'.
[43] Anon., *The Seventh Report of the Ladies' Negro's Friend Society, for Birmingham* (Birmingham: B. Hudson, 1832), 38–39.

Like Strickland, Pringle appears to have been affected both personally and professionally by his relationship with Prince. The ramifications of these relationships on the overall progress of British abolitionism were relatively minor: while Strickland became a lifelong abolitionist after her time with Prince and Pringle, she was never able to produce a convincing black character in her antislavery fiction. Pringle's subsequent attempts to manumit enslaved women on an individual basis, meanwhile, were quietly shelved by the Anti-Slavery Society. Yet in itself the *History* became a major contribution to the abolitionist corpus of the early nineteenth century. This is largely because Prince was seen to personify the horrors that plantation slavery held for women in particular, and in Britain women were fast becoming the key demographic in the abolitionist propaganda war. Pringle and Strickland's interventions in the autobiography and their negotiations with Prince over how her suffering and agency were depicted were fundamental to the transformation of Prince from anonymous to representative victim. So, too, was the means by which the *History* was marketed and distributed.

Marketing Mary Prince

Pringle was not a particularly wealthy man; when he became ill with a respiratory complaint in 1834, the surgeon and physician's bills nearly ruined him, and he was forced to apply for relief from the Committee of the Literary Fund.[44] His decisions first to employ Prince as a domestic servant in 1829 and then to personally fund the *History*'s publication in 1831, bypassing the Society's usual channels, could not have been taken lightly.[45] Like his involvement in obtaining financial relief for Jane Hill, and Nancy Morgan's manumission, the extraordinary lengths he went to in order to help Prince fit with a pattern of mixing official and personal intervention in individual cases. In his preface to Prince's *History*, he was keen to point out that 'the Anti-Slavery Society have no concern whatever with this publication, nor are they in any degree responsible for the statements it contains.'[46] His statement anticipated later charges that Prince was merely a 'tool' of the Society, used by them to promote abolitionism through false autobiographical testimony. However, it also intentionally obfuscated the extent to which the Society had, in fact, supported the distribution and sale of the text. It is true that a small number of copies of the *History* were distributed through Strickland and

---

[44] BL, Western MSS, Loan 96 RLF 1/797/24, 'Thomas Pringle to Mr. Duncan, 7 Oct. 1834', ff. 1–3.
[45] 'personally fund the publication': see Prince, *History*, iv.   [46] Prince, *History*, iv.

Pringle's personal networks without going through the Society. For example, in April 1831, Strickland sent twenty copies to her friend, the Suffolk poet James Bird, asking if he could 'in the way of trade dispose them'.[47] However, by far the largest number of copies were distributed by Pringle's close friend and clerk of the Anti-Slavery Society, Joseph Phillips. Having assisted Pringle in the editing and verification process, it was Phillips who acted as the principle agent for distributing the *History*.

Close attention to the distribution model for Prince's autobiography suggests that the distinction between an 'official' Anti-Slavery Society tract and an 'independent' abolitionist tract could become blurred. Some authors actively sought an official Anti-Slavery Society affiliation as a means to extend their existing publications' reach. This could be an effective marketing tool. For example, when the Rev. S. C. Wilks wrote to the Society to request an endorsement for his sermon on *The Duty of Prompt and Complete Abolition of Colonial Slavery*, they not only agreed 'to insert the "Antislavery Office" in conjunction with the name of his publisher, as a place at which it may be purchased', but also advertised it at length in their periodical, the *Anti-Slavery Monthly Reporter*.[48] The Society were happy to assent to such requests. Like their predecessor organisation SEAST, they were keen to promote as much print-based activity as possible, especially beyond London. On 1 June 1830 the Society established two special subcommittees: one 'to acquire some influence over the daily press' and another 'to avail themselves of the co-operation of other friends of the Society for the purpose of engaging agents to be employed in diffusing information throughout the country on the subject of slavery'.[49] Writers such as Wilks could make use of the Society's prestige, contacts and distribution networks to give their work truly national reach, even if they had originally produced their works independently.

Prince was in just the opposite situation. The *History* was produced very much with the support of key members of the Society, yet it was self-consciously marketed as an independent co-production of Prince, Pringle and the putatively anonymous amanuensis Strickland. It was distributed unofficially using official channels, with Phillips coordinating sales through provincial antislavery associations – especially ladies' associations. The *History*'s affiliation with the Anti-Slavery Society was

---

[47] Moodie, *Letters of a Lifetime*, 61.
[47] Moodie, *Letters of a Lifetime*, 61.
[48] Bodleian Library, MSS Brit. Emp. 5/20/E5/2, 'Rough Minutes of the Anti-Slavery Society, 6 Oct 1830'; *Anti-Slavery Reporter*, 3:21 (October 1830), 447.
[49] Bodleian Library, MSS Brit. Emp. 5/20/E5/2, 'Rough Minutes of the Anti-Slavery Society, 1 Jun. 1830.'

made yet more ambiguous by the fact that Phillips used the Society's office at 18 Aldermanbury as a distribution centre, inviting bulk orders from the same address on the title page. However, unlike most of the other texts available from the office, the costs of publishing the *History* were underwritten not by the Society but by Pringle himself. He was keen to minimise risk and maximise the return on his investment for Prince – after all, he could not afford to keep her in work forever. Phillips thus supplied the tract 'at trade price to Anti-Slavery Associations', rather than simply claiming the profits back after sale.[50] He also pushed the *History* to ladies' associations on a 'sale or return' basis, such as with the Bristol Ladies' Antislavery Society in June 1831.[51] Pringle need not have worried about his investment; the *History* was a commercial success and went through at least three editions within months.

Several factors help to explain why Pringle did not publish the *History* straightforwardly through the Society. First, one of the main functions of the text was to generate a small fund for Prince's relief. As underscored when he tried to claim back the money for Morgan's manumission in 1831, expending the Society's funds on individual charity cases could generate tension. Second, the Society had already overreached itself with its publishing output. In March 1830, it was forced to apply to the Quakers for a loan of £1,000 'to relieve the Committee from the pecuniary claims now urgently pressing upon them, arising chiefly from the greatly increased exertions that have been made in publishing & diffusing information on the subject of slavery'.[52] They could not afford to finance a pamphlet like the *History* unless they, not the author, would receive the profits.

A third factor may also have persuaded Pringle to pursue the publication as an independent venture rather than an 'official' Anti-Slavery Society tract: it was simply too radical. The unflinching portrayals of violence in the *History* could have been seen as morally inappropriate for the respectable ladies to whom Pringle hoped to market it. Midgley has explored in detail the delicate balancing act between 'feminine respectability' and political and humanitarian intervention that female abolitionists were obliged to strike in the early nineteenth century.[53]

[50] Prince, *History*, i.
[51] Bodleian Library, MSS Brit. Emp., 5/18/C1/20, 'M. K. Draper to Thomas Pringle, 24 Jun. 1831.'
[52] Bodleian Library, MSS Brit. Emp. 5/20/E5/2, 'Rough Minutes of the Anti-Slavery Society, 16 Mar. 1830.'
[53] In particular, Midgley identifies the emergence of separate 'radical' and 'philanthropic' strands of female antislavery activism in this period. Midgley, *Women against Slavery*, 91–116.

Especially for women who saw antislavery activism as a philanthropic, rather than political issue, the question of respectability was paramount. Some male abolitionists, including William Wilberforce, opposed women's involvement in the movement altogether. Pringle, as secretary of the Society, was well aware of this. In February 1831, for example, Daniel Hack of the Brighton Antislavery Association wrote to him on behalf of a concerned friend:

> We are a little looking towards the establishment of a Ladies Association amongst us, but as some doubt has arisen in the mind of one of our warmest & most influential friends as to the propriety of such a step, & whether our female friends are not in taking a very active part in such Associations moving a little out of their province, I particularly wish to obtain all the information that can easily be given us, upon the subject.[54]

The anxieties of the Brighton Association were more forcefully articulated in 1833 by an 'Englishwoman' in her *Address to the Females of Great Britain on the Propriety of Their Petitioning Parliament for the Abolition of Negro Slavery*. In it, the anonymous author associated female abolitionism with Wollstonecraftian 'fanaticism' and insisted that English women *'must never outstep propriety to serve the best cause, nor sacrifice a positive duty at the shrine of a problematic obligation.'*[55]

Compromise is an inescapable fact of leadership, and Pringle knew he had to remain sensitive to the reservations of such parties if he was to ensure the widest possible support for emancipation. He could never seriously consider turning away the support of women – they were far too valuable to the cause. As Seymour Drescher puts it, after 1823 'the direct participation of women became massive and decisive' in securing progressive abolitionist victories in popular opinion and legislature.[56] Pringle knew what he had on his hands with Prince's *History*: an authentic first-hand account of slavery, told from a woman's perspective, including accounts of moral degradation and the destruction of families. It would be a potent tool in galvanising this crucial demographic for the abolitionist cause. On the other hand, he also knew that it might be considered too graphic for a self-styled 'official' group such as the Society to be seen peddling to respectable ladies – at least officially. The endless depictions of women being stripped naked and hung up by the wrists, of flesh

---

[54] Bodleian Library, MSS Brit. Emp., 5/18/C1/28, 'Daniel P. Hack to Thomas Pringle, 2 Feb 1831.'

[55] Anon, *Address to the Females of Great Britain on the Propriety of Their Petitioning Parliament for the Abolition of Negro Slavery* (London: J. G. & F. Rivington, 1833), 7, 5. Emphasis in original.

[56] Seymour Drescher, *Abolition: A History of Slavery and Antislavery* (Cambridge: Cambridge University Press, 2009), 250.

'lain open' with the cow-skin, of 'blood streaming' from wounds in pregnant bellies, and of female bodies 'raw with gashes' that make up so much of Prince's narrative were at once too shocking for ladies to read and too shocking for them to ignore. While some official Society pamphlets had included white testimony that, under slavery 'the unhappy females are ... equally liable with the men to have their persons ... shamelessly exposed and barbarously tortured', such accounts had never before been marketed explicitly toward women.[57] The distribution model finally settled on, in which the Society's infrastructure could be used to distribute, market and sell Prince's shocking text directly to women, but any official association was strenuously denied and no Society money was directly allocated to fund it, allowed Pringle to have it both ways.

This does not mean that he was willing to completely disregard concerns over the polite sensibilities of his female readership. As Sue Thomas and others have shown, Pringle and Strickland edited out all mention of Prince's consensual premarital sexual relations from the *History*.[58] Yet, significantly, he chose to retain episodes where sexual *violence* was heavily implied. He recognised that such depictions were precisely what was needed to marshal and extend British women's support for the abolition of slavery in the early 1830s. Indeed, as Henrice Altink has demonstrated, depictions of male-on-female violence, including implications of rape and sexual abuse, were commonplace in non-affiliated abolitionist literature from the 1820s onward.[59] Abolitionist depictions of slavery also commonly featured scenes in which enslaved women's bodies were exposed during the act of whipping or flogging, appealing to multivalent notions of decency. Henry Whiteley's *Three Months in Jamaica in 1832*, for example, made this association explicit: 'Two young women ... were, one after the other, then laid down and held by four men, their back parts most indecently uncovered, and thirty-nine lashes of the blood-stained whip inflicted on each poor creature's posteriors.'[60] Prince's narrative, despite being marketed toward ladies, abounded with similar scenes.

---

[57] Society for the Abolition of Slavery, *A Brief View of the Nature and Effects of Negro Slavery* (London: S. Bagster, 1830), 1–2.

[58] See Sue Thomas, 'Pringle v. Cadell and Wood v. Pringle: The Libel Cases over *The History of Mary Prince*', *Journal of Commonwealth Literature*, 40:1 (2005), 113–135.

[59] Henrice Altink, *Representations of Slave Women in Discourses on Slavery and Abolition, 1780–1838* (London: Routledge, 2007), 131–139.

[60] Henry Whiteley, *Three Months in Jamaica in 1832; Comprising a Residence of Seven Weeks on a Sugar Plantation* (London: J. Hatchard and Son, 1833).

The most direct appeal to feminine notions of sexual decency in the *History*, however, revolved around the exposure of not the female but the male body. Prince complained that one of her former owners, Mr. D—, 'had an ugly fashion of stripping himself quite naked, and ordering me then to wash him in a tub of water', an imposition that was, to Prince, 'worse ... than all the licks'.[61] Modern readers will instantly identify Mr. D—'s coercive demand as sexual abuse, but it would not necessarily have been parsed as such by its intended readership of middle-class women in the 1830s. It may very well have been intended to allude to a more physically violent sexual assault – the implication being that if Mr. D— was indecent enough to strip himself naked and demand to be washed by a female slave then he would be indecent enough to rape her. Yet Prince's characterisation of this 'habit' as 'ugly', rather than, for example, 'barbarous' or 'terrifying', implied an appeal to moral outrage on the grounds of decorum and proper social relations between the sexes, rather than moral repulsion at violent sexual assault.

Compare this with the moral argument of the Anti-Slavery Society as expressed in *A Brief View of the Nature and Effects of Negro Slavery*: 'The effect of ... the general absence of the marriage tie, is that the most unrestrained licentiousness (exhibited in a degrading, disgusting and depopulating promiscuous intercourse,) prevails almost universally among the Slaves; and is encouraged no less universally, by the example of their superiors the Whites.'[62] The Society's line on the effects of slavery on normative gender relations was crystal clear: slavery degraded the morals of both master and slave; it assaulted the sanctity of marriage; and licentiousness and sexual abuse abounded in slave societies. As Midgley has suggested, the philanthropic, evangelical tradition in women's anti-slavery activism during this period was linked to an 'idealisation' of traditional gender relations in Britain.[63] Prince's *History* appealed to these associations by providing first-hand evidence of not only the violence but the *impropriety*, in gendered terms, attendant on slave-holding.

The notion of sexual propriety was later used to undermine Prince's credibility, even as it boosted her public visibility. Altink has explored how both pro- and antislavery rhetoric during this period encouraged an existing popular conception of enslaved women as sexually licentious. Proslavery representations linked such assumptions to the racialized notion that black women were sexually voracious and prone to marital inconstancy.[64] These were precisely the preconceptions mobilized against

---

[61] Prince, *History*, 13.   [62] Society for the Abolition of Slavery, *A Brief View*, 2.
[63] Midgley, *Women against Slavery*, 91.
[64] Altink, *Representations of Slave Women*, 67–87.

Prince by leading proslavery advocate James MacQueen in a series of articles seeking to undermine her, Pringle and the *History*. In an article for the *Glasgow Courier* published on 26 July 1831, MacQueen argued that Pringle had been duped by Prince's story and that he saw 'nothing but purity in a prostitute, because she knew how and when to utter the name of the Deity, to turn up the whites of her eyes, and to make a perfect mockery of religion'.[65] In another, longer article printed in *Blackwood's Magazine* for November 1831, he set about attacking Prince's moral character by quoting hostile letters about her, written by her enemies and the friends of the Wood family in Antigua. For example, he reproduced one letter by Martha Wilcox, a free black woman the Woods had hired to take on Prince's duties when she was seriously ill and whom Prince had described in the *History* as 'a saucy woman'.[66] In her letter, Wilcox repeated MacQueen's allegations that Prince was a prostitute, claiming that 'she took in washing, and made money by it. She also made money, *many, many* other ways by her badness; I mean, by allowing men to visit her, and by selling ★ ★ ★ ★ ★ to worthless men," &c.'[67] While other testimonials MacQueen had acquired focused on the Woods' supposedly humane treatment of their slaves, those dealing with Prince's character were geared toward undermining not her reliability as a witness against slavery but her right – her moral ability – to give evidence in the first place.

The *Blackwood's* article gave rise to a libel suit by Pringle – not for the attacks on Prince's character but for the attacks on his.[68] He was incensed. 'Have you seen how I am abused in Blackwood's Magazine', he wrote to Strickland in December 1831, 'about poor Mary Prince? I am prosecuting Blackwood for libel.'[69] MacQueen had insinuated that Pringle and Prince were having an affair and that by having her in the house, he was degrading the morals of the (white) women in his family:

[T]he delicacy and modesty 'of the females of his family' cannot be of the most exalted character. [Pringle's] continued labour … is to call for and to nestle amidst all kinds of colonial immorality and uncleanliness – every falsehood and

---

[65] *Glasgow Courier*, 26 July 1831, cited in Sue Thomas, 'New Information on Mary Prince in London', *Notes and Queries*, 58:1 (2011), 83.

[66] Prince, *History*, 14.

[67] James MacQueen, 'The Colonial Empire of Great Britain', *Blackwood's Magazine*, 30 (November 1831), 749.

[68] Sue Thomas has examined the events and contexts of the libel trials in depth in Thomas, 'Pringle v. Cadell and Wood v. Pringle', 113–135; Thomas, *Telling West Indian Lives*, 152–165.

[69] 'Thomas Pringle to Susannah Moodie, 20 December 1831', in Thomas Pringle, *Additional Letters to the South African Letters of Thomas Pringle* (n.p.: Van Riebeeck Society, 2011), 16.

every lie that is told or can be invented – every thing that is grovelling, despicable, and low, in the vices of semi-barbarians – and on every occasion to lay all these before the eyes, and impress them upon the minds, of the females of his family![70]

When Pringle's libel action for these passages was brought against Thomas Cadell, the London publisher of *Blackwood's* on 21 February 1833, he had his solicitor, Mr. Wilde, again assert that the *History* 'had been so published by him, not as connected with the association [the Anti-Slavery Society], but on his own individual judgement and responsibility'. Wilde also called Prince to the stand and invited Cadell's solicitor to cross-examine her on her behaviour in the Pringle household.[71] Wilde had called their bluff; Cadell's counsel chose not to cross-examine Prince and admitted that 'the plaintiff was entitled to a verdict; but he contended that under the circumstance nominal damages would satisfy the justice of the case.'[72] The judge, it seems, agreed. When the jury returned a verdict in favour of Pringle, he was awarded a mere five pounds, plus the costs of the suit.

In addition to the original offending articles by MacQueen, reports of this trial helped to boost the public visibility of Prince and the *History*. Having long railed against 'the poison contain'd from time to time in Blackwood's, on the Question of Slavery', Pringle's allies were now 'jubilant' that the jury had found against it.[73] There was, perhaps, a personal aspect to the feud; Pringle had been one of the founding editors of *Blackwood's* when it launched as the *Edinburgh Monthly Magazine* in 1817 but was soon dismissed by then-publisher William Blackwood over poor sales.[74] Perhaps, thanks to the efforts of the Anti-Slavery Society's subcommittee dedicated to influencing the daily press, Pringle's victory in court was reported in the *Times, Morning Chronicle, Morning Post, Standard*, and the *Examiner*, as well as in provincial papers across the country including the *Bury and Norwich Post, Caledonian Mercury, Barrow's Winchester Journal, Leeds Mercury*, and *Essex Standard*.[75] Of course, Prince's silence in the dock did little to enhance her public profile as an individual, except perhaps to emphasise her own

[70] MacQueen, 'The Colonial Empire of Great Britain', 751.
[71] *Times*, 21 February 1833.   [72] *Times*, 21 February 1833.
[73] Bodleian Library, MSS Brit. Emp., 5/18/C1/49, 'Thomas Mounsey to Thomas Pringle, 5 May 1831; Thomas, 'Pringle v. Cadell and Wood v. Pringle', 126.
[74] David Finkelstein, 'Pringle, Thomas (1789–1834)', in *ODNB*, available at http://ezproxy-prd.bodleian.ox.ac.uk:2167/view/article/22807.
[75] *Morning Chronicle*, 22 February 1833; *Morning Post*, 22 February 1833; *The Standard*, 22 February 1833; *Examiner*, 24 February 1833; *Bury and Norwich Post*, 27 February 1833; *Caledonian Mercury*, 28 February 1833; *Barrow's Worcester Journal*, 28 February 1833; *Leeds Mercury*, 2 March 1833; *Essex Standard*, 2 March 1833.

feminine restraint and thus undermine the accusations of lewdness levelled at her by MacQueen, Wood and her Antiguan enemies.

In any case, neither Pringle nor Prince could enjoy their victory for long. On 27 February 1833, they were in court for another libel case, this time brought *against* Pringle by one of Prince's former owners, John Wood. He claimed that the representation given of him in *The History* was unfair and that he had always treated Prince 'with kindness'.[76] More specifically, he objected to the suggestions made by Pringle in his paratext that he (Wood) had incited Prince to be unfaithful to her husband 'in order that that circumstance might be made use of against her as an instance of depravity'.[77] Once again, the anti-abolitionist's case hinged ultimately on undermining Prince's 'moral character' with a view to discrediting her testimony as a textual witness of slavery. Unlike in the *Pringle v. Cadell* case, Prince was aggressively cross-examined by the prosecution about the details of her personal life, especially her sexual history. The report of the trial in the *Times* did not shrink from the details, nor the jury's evident titillation:

She had lived seven years before with Captain Abbot. She did not live in the house with him, but slept with him sometimes in another hut … One night she found another woman in bed with the Captain in her house. The woman had pretended to be a friend of witness. (Laughter.) Witness licked her, and she was obliged to get out of bed. (A laugh.)[78]

This public shaming of Prince was not in and of itself damaging to Pringle's defence. After all, he had overseen the Anti-Slavery Society during a period when it explicitly concentrated on producing ever-more shocking printed depictions of the moral degradation inherent in slavery. Much more harmful to Pringle's case was Prince's admission that she 'told all this to Miss Strickland when the lady took down her narrative. These statements were not in the narrative published by the defendant.'[79] The Woods had sought to establish that the *History* was a fabricated libel, partly through trying to establish that Prince herself had been misrepresented. Here they had found evidence that Pringle and Strickland had directly intervened in how Prince had put herself, and her life under slavery, forward to public view. Prince herself had never tried to withhold these aspects of her past. It was Pringle who, aiming to court the support of British women by painting Prince as a thwarted paragon of conjugal virtue, had spelled his own defeat. The jury found

---

[76] *Times*, 1 March 1833.
[77] Thomas, 'Pringle v. Cadell and Wood v. Pringle', 127; *Times*, 1 March 1833.
[78] *Times*, 1 March 1833.   [79] *Times*, 1 March 1833.

against him and he was ordered to pay £25 in damages, along with Wood's substantial legal costs.

Prince's appearance at the Court of King's Bench in February 1833 was the last time she was known to appear in public. Her deposition at the hearing is, in fact, the latest known record of her, though Thomas has speculated that she could have returned to her husband in Antigua after the Slavery Abolition Act came into force in August 1834.[80] The Society's press office obviously did not want to publicise Pringle's loss as it had with his victory over *Blackwood's* the preceding week. Reports of the second trial appeared only in the *Times* and the *Christian Advocate*.[81] After producing a successful autobiography; after having her messy, complex life story 'pruned' and 'shaped' to fit an abolitionist narrative; after being presented as a model of feminine virtue and victimhood; after having her intimate relationships held up to ridicule and public scrutiny; after being painted in the press as a prostitute; after being put on trial for someone else's libels; after, in short, having endured life in the prurient British public eye as a formerly enslaved black woman, Prince slipped once again into obscurity.

The libel trials were, in a sense, an extension of the *History* itself. They were ultimately less concerned with the factual bases of Prince's narrative than how her character was represented. Pringle, Phillips and Strickland had very carefully edited Prince's words to present her as an archetypical female victim of slavery, a form of personality commodity that could be successfully marketed to women to encourage their much-needed support for abolitionism. Prince herself, it seems, was more interested in telling her story than in her image. Her indignation and unflinching honestly erupted through Pringle's control at points, forcing him to intervene in the text in footnotes and through an unwieldy framing apparatus. To be safe, he avoided officially affiliating the Anti-Slavery Society with the *History*, even while he used their infrastructure to promote and distribute it. The controversy that resulted ultimately from Prince's account actually had less to do with the text and more to do with who she was, and what she was held to represent. As Strickland's mid-century novels attest, Prince's fearless honesty, Pringle's attempts to mould her and the impact of her *History* were such that they were felt decades later.

---

[80] Antigua was one of the British colonies that did not institute the apprenticeship system after abolition.

[81] Thomas, *Telling West Indian Lives*, 164.

Part II

Black Evangelicals

4   Ukawsaw Gronniosaw and British Calvinism, 1765–1779

A Narrative of the Most Remarkable Particulars in the Life of James Albert Ukawsaw Gronniosaw, the first text ever published in Britain by a black author, begins with a religious conflict. Around 1727, in Borno, now part of Nigeria, the young prince Gronniosaw disclosed to his parents that 'I was, at times, very unhappy in myself, it being strongly impressed on my mind that there was some GREAT MAN of power which resided above the sun, moon and stars, the objects of our worship.'[1] The implication in the *Narrative* was that Borno culture did not recognise Abrahamic religions, though as Jennifer Harris has pointed out, the area was predominately Muslim.[2] Supposedly, Gronniosaw's mother 'was apprehensive that my senses were impaired, or that I was foolish' because of his insistence on believing in a single God.[3] Like so many paragons from the canon of the Christian faith, he was persecuted for his beliefs; his siblings 'disliked' him and 'supposed that I was either foolish, or insane'. His father 'was exceedingly angry', saying that 'he would punish me severely if ever I was so troublesome again.'[4]

All of this led the young prince into such a state of consternation that when some traders from the Gold Coast arrived in Borno and offered to take him away with them, he accepted the offer immediately. 'I was the more willing', Gronniosaw stated in the *Narrative*, 'as my brothers and sisters despised me, and looked upon me with contempt on account of my unhappy disposition; and even my servants slighted me, and disregarded all I said to them.'[5] Gronniosaw felt that in going to the Gold Coast he was answering a spiritual call: 'I seemed sensible of a secret impulse upon my mind which I could not resist that seemed to tell me I must go.'[6] His instinctive adherence to Christianity, the *Narrative*

---

[1] Ukawsaw Gronniosaw, *A Narrative of the Most Remarkable Particulars in the Life of James Albert Ukawsaw Gronniosaw* (Bath: W. Gye and T. Mills, [1772]), 1.
[2] Jennifer Harris, 'Seeing the Light: Re-Reading James Albert Ukawsaw Gronniosaw', *English Language Notes*, 42:4 (2004), 43–57.
[3] Gronniosaw, *Narrative*, 4.   [4] Gronniosaw, *Narrative*, 2, 4.
[5] Gronniosaw, *Narrative*, 5.   [6] Gronniosaw, *Narrative*, 5.

implied, incentivised his movement away from his family in the African interior and toward the Gold Coast, and ultimately to his enslavement and transportation to Barbados and then to New York. Importantly, Gronniosaw's prescient knowledge of a God foreshadowed his eventual conversion to Calvinism – a Christian denomination whose leadership were largely proslavery at the time of his autobiography's publication.[7]

After about forty years working as a house slave in influential Dutch Reformed households in New York, he gained his freedom in his purchaser's will and enlisted as a sailor.[8] He first came to Britain in the 1760s, when he met his wife, a weaver named Betty. After a brief period working as a butler in Amsterdam for another Dutch Reformed family, Gronniosaw returned to London to marry Betty and raise a family. The Spitalfields Riots of 1769 meant that Betty was no longer able to work as a weaver in London, and the family were forced to move to the country in search of work. After periods in Colchester, Norwich and Kidderminster, they moved once more to Chester, where Gronniosaw died on 5 October 1775.[9] Almost all of the events and decisions in his life had been influenced by Calvinism or individual Calvinists.

Studies into the relationship between dissenting Christian groups and the transatlantic slave trade during this period have tended to focus on the abolitionist efforts of the Quakers and Arminian Methodists, while histories of British Calvinism have downplayed the scale to which key members of the organisation were involved in the transatlantic slave trade.[10] Where these implications are acknowledged, historians have

---

[7] See, for example, Boyd Schlenther, *Queen of the Methodists: The Countess of Huntingdon and the Eighteenth-Century Crisis of Faith and Society* (Bishop Auckland: Durham Academic Press, 1997), 83–95; Frank Lambert, *Pedlar in Divinity: George Whitefield and the Transatlantic Revivals, 1737–1770* (Princeton, NJ: Princeton University Press, 1993), 204–214.

[8] For the influential nature of the families for whom Gronniosaw worked, see below and C. S. Williams, *Cornelius Van Horne and His Descendants* (New York: C. S. Williams, 1912), 7–12; Joel Beeke and Cornelis Pronk, 'Biographical Introduction', in Theodorus Frelinghuysen, *Forerunner of the Great Awakening: The Sermons of Theodorus Jacobus Frelinghuysen*, ed. and trans. Joel Beeke (Grand Rapids, MI: William Eerdman, 2000), vii–xxxviii.

[9] Gronniosaw, *Narrative*, 10–39; *London Evening Post*, 10 October 1775, 1.

[10] See Brycchan Carey, *From Peace to Freedom: Quaker Rhetoric and the Birth of American Antislavery, 1657–1761* (New Haven, CT: Yale University Press, 2012); Maurice Jackson, *Let This Voice Be Heard: Anthony Benezet, Father of Atlantic Abolitionism* (Philadelphia: University of Pennsylvania Press, 2008); Judith Jennings, *The Business of Abolishing the British Slave Trade 1783–1807* (London: Frank Cass, 1997); Christopher Brown, *Moral Capital: Foundations of British Abolitionism* (Chapel Hill: University of North Carolina Press, 2006), esp. 333–450. Alan Harding's history, *The Countess of Huntingdon's Connexion*, demonstrates the tendency to minimise the denomination's involvement in slavery. The word 'slave' appears twice in the text – once in relation to nineteenth-century antislavery work and once in a footnote which states that 'There is no

been quick to point out that Calvinist theology itself 'hindered' a move against slavery, since it required no corporeal freedom to achieve salvation.[11] While such equivocations take into account the important effects of theology on slave-ownership, they also downplay the effects of slavery on the administration of Calvinist evangelism.

This hesitance to acknowledge Calvinist support for slavery may explain the lack of attention paid to Gronniosaw's *Narrative* in its specific denominational context. Literary studies on the text have tended to focus on Gronniosaw's construction of black identity. Such studies (notably Henry Louis Gates Jr.'s highly influential reading of the 'trope of the talking book') tend to understand Gronniosaw as interacting with a monolithic and theologically undifferentiated 'Christianity', which acted as both synecdoche and symptom of white hegemony as a whole.[12] Jennifer Harris, meanwhile, has considered the *Narrative* through the lens of Gronniosaw's likely childhood interaction with Islam, considering it as a text 'which manipulates Western suppositions and challenges Western superiority', though she understates the extent to which his authorial agency was compromised by his financial circumstances and poor literacy in English.[13] Again, this approach tends to homogenise many complex and often competing iterations of Christian supremacy into a singular notion of 'Western superiority'. In general, academics have struggled to reconcile Gronniosaw's status as a former slave with his embracing of quite a pronouncedly proslavery religious sect.

How, then, did British Calvinists influence the *Narrative*'s interactions with the issues of slavery? How was Gronniosaw's authority over his own life story compromised by a social network of individuals with interests in both the expansion of Calvinism and the continuation of the slave trade? The *Narrative* was used to posit a doctrinal agenda in response to the increasing popularity of John Wesley's rival sect, the Arminian Methodists, whose antislavery and egalitarian hermeneutics were gaining popularity and posing a serious challenge to Calvinism in its strongholds in south-west England and Wales.[14] Gronniosaw's

---

evidence that LH had any serious doubts about the morality of keeping slaves.' Alan Harding, *The Countess of Huntingdon's Connexion: A Sect in Action in Eighteenth-Century England* (Oxford: Oxford University Press, 2003), 14, 209 n. 219.

[11] See, for example, Schlenther, *Queen of the Methodists*, 91.

[12] See Henry Louis Gates Jr., *The Signifying Monkey: A Theory of African-American Literary Criticism* (Oxford: Oxford University Press, 1988), 127–170; Helena Woodard, *African-British Writings in the Eighteenth Century: The Politics of Race and Reason* (Westport, CT: Greenwood Press, 1999), 33–42.

[13] Harris, 'Seeing the Light', 43–57.

[14] David Hempton, *Methodism: Empire of the Spirit* (New Haven, CT: Yale University Press, 2005), 11–31.

Narrative formed part of a pamphlet war in which the critical differences between Arminian Methodism and Calvinism, including their respective stances on the slave trade, were publicly debated. It was produced in support of a view of slavery as a route to conversion for Africans. A number of leading Calvinists defended slavery on these grounds, but the key figures in the production of the *Narrative* stand out as particularly recalcitrant proslavery advocates.

Ukawsaw Gronniosaw and British Calvinism

Gronniosaw's association with Calvinism and its prominent ministers, along with his introduction to several leading proslavery advocates, began long before his own emancipation from slavery. His 'master', Theodorus Frelinghuysen, an influential Dutch Reformed minister in New York, was central to the first 'Great Awakening' of evangelical Christianity on the East Coast during the 1740s and 1750s and a supporter of slavery. Up to his death around 1757, Frelinghuysen was 'a particular friend' to leading Calvinist George Whitefield.[15] Whitefield visited Frelinghuysen numerous times while Gronniosaw was serving as a house slave, during both his tours of the East Coast in 1739–1740 and 1744–1748.[16] Since Gronniosaw was not treated excessively harshly during his bondage under Frelinghuysen, Whitefield's Calvinism did not demand that his enslavement should be terminated. On the contrary, his slavery could be viewed as a kindness, since Frelinghuysen had been at pains to ensure the boy's conversion to a specifically Calvinistic form of Christianity.[17] In fact, Frelinghuysen's attitude toward slavery was not dissimilar to Whitefield's own.

In 1740, Whitefield had established an orphanage at Bethesda, Georgia. To fund it, he took up shares in the neighbouring Providence Plantation, staffed by over a hundred slaves.[18] Whitefield lent his considerable celebrity to the proslavery cause in Georgia while its legality was being debated during the 1740s and began purchasing slaves for his Bethesda orphanage as soon as the trustees of Georgia definitively approved slavery

[15] Gronniosaw, *Narrative*, 20.
[16] Boyd Schlenther, 'Whitefield, George (1714–1770)', in *ODNB*, available at www.oxford dnb.com/view/article/29281.
[17] For example: 'He [Frelinghuysen] took me home with him, and made me kneel down, and put my two hands together, and pray'd for me, and every night he did the same.' Gronniosaw, *Narrative*, 12.
[18] See George Whitefield, *An Account of the Money Received and Disbursed for the Orphan-House in Georgia* (London: W. Strahan, 1741), 5.

in 1750.[19] 'It is plain to a demonstration, that hot countries cannot be cultivated without negroes,' he wrote in 1751. 'What a flourishing country might *Georgia* have been, had the use of them been permitted years ago?'[20] He expressed his stance on the enslavement of Africans in terms of a biblical precedent: 'As for the lawfulness of keeping slaves, I have no doubt, since I hear that some that were bought with *Abraham's* money, and some that were born in his house.'[21] While his keenness to incorporate slavery into his Calvinist fundraising portfolio marked him out as, to borrow Boyd Schlenther's phrase, 'perhaps the most energetic, and conspicuous, evangelical defender and practitioner of slavery', Whitefield did not assume any inequality between the spiritual potential of black and white people, though he did consider non-Christian Africans to be spiritually 'wretched'.[22] 'Blacks are just as much, and no more, conceived and born in sin, as white men are', he wrote in 1740. 'Both, if born and bred up here, I am persuaded, are naturally capable of the same improvement.'[23] Whitefield would have been pleased with the pains Frelinghuysen had taken to ensure Gronniosaw's conversion, having preached with mixed success to a number of black slave congregations during his visits to America.[24]

Indeed, Whitefield's interest in the spiritual condition of slaves was one of his top priorities, to the extent that 'this consideration, as to us, swallows up all temporal inconveniencies whatsoever.'[25] His defence of American slavery was predicated on the common 'benevolist' viewpoint favoured by religious slave-owners keen to reconcile their involvement in slavery with their Christian faith. This belief maintained that corporeal bondage was a positive benefit to slaves, since it often led to their conversion.[26] Whitefield's apologism went a step further, prioritising the conversion of African slaves to Christianity not only over their freedom but over every aspect of their physical well-being. While censuring the harsh treatment of slaves, Whitefield conceded that degradation, subjection and even bodily mutilation were potentially conducive to the slaves' ultimate salvation. On 23 January 1739, for example, he wrote an open

[19] For a detailed examination of Georgian slavery legislation during the 1740s, see Betty Wood, *Slavery in Colonial Georgia, 1730–1775* (Athens: University of Georgia Press, 1984), 74–88.
[20] George Whitefield, *Works of George Whitefield* (London: Edward and Charles Dilly, 1771–1772), vol. 2, 404.
[21] Whitefield, *Works*, vol. 2, 404.   [22] Schlenther, 'Whitefield, George (1714–1770)'.
[23] George Whitefield, *A Collection of Papers, Lately Printed in the Daily Advertiser* (London: J. Oswald et al., 1740), 9.
[24] Lambert, *Pedlar in Divinity*, 134–168.   [25] Whitefield, *Works*, vol. 2, 405.
[26] For a more detailed examination of Whitefield's views on slavery, see Lambert, *Pedlar in Divinity*, 205–215.

letter addressed 'to the inhabitants of Maryland, Virginia, North and South Carolina', later reprinted in the *Daily Advertiser* in London, and again in Philadelphia in 1740 as a stand-alone volume.[27] After chiding slave-owners for torturing their slaves with knives and pitchforks, White-field mitigated such behaviour on the basis that it engendered depend-ence on God for comfort, and thus facilitated spiritual conversion:

> Your present and past bad usage of them, however ill-designed, may thus far do them good, as to break their wills, increase the sense of their natural misery, and consequently better dispose their minds to accept the redemption wrought out for them, by the death and obedience of Jesus Christ.[28]

Despite this seemingly contradictory stance on the treatment of slaves, it is clear that Whitefield maintained an interest in what he perceived as the spiritual well-being of both free and unfree black people in America well into the 1740s, and by the time Gronniosaw left America around 1762, he 'had heard him [Whitefield] preach often at New York'.[29] This, along with his presence at Whitefield's meetings with Frelinghuysen, formed the basis of a relationship characterised by 'very friendly' but infrequent encounters between the two men until Whitefield's death in 1770.[30] According to his will, Whitefield's property at Bethesda, and around fifty slaves there, passed into the hands of his friend and fellow Calvinist, and Gronniosaw's future patron, Selina Hastings, Countess of Huntingdon, who was by that time already a leading figure in British Calvinism.

When he came to relate the *Narrative* in 1771 or 1772, Gronniosaw was forthcoming about his dependence on George Whitefield and other Calvinist ministers when he first arrived in London. Having been conned out of almost all of his money by an unscrupulous publican in Portsmouth, he appeared at Whitefield's tabernacle in Moorfields, stating that the minister was 'the only living soul I knew in England'.[31] It was Whitefield, according to the *Narrative*, who 'directed me to a proper place to board and lodge in Petticoat-Lane, till he could think of some way to settle me in, and paid for my lodging, and all my expences'.[32] Through Whitefield, Gronniosaw met a number of prom-inent dissenting ministers in London, including the Baptist Dr. Andrew Gifford, whose meetings Gronniosaw attended regularly.[33]

It is important to note here that, even though relatively minor hermen-eutical disagreements became highly divisive among senior dissenting

[27] George Whitefield, *Three Letters from the Reverend Mr. G. Whitefield* (Philadelphia: B. Franklyn, 1740); Whitefield, *A Collection of Papers*, 5–11.
[28] Whitefield, *A Collection of Papers*, 9.   [29] Gronniosaw, *Narrative*, 23.
[30] Gronniosaw, *Narrative*, 26.   [31] Gronniosaw, *Narrative*, 26.
[32] Gronniosaw, *Narrative*, 26.   [33] Gronniosaw, *Narrative*, 27.

ministers during the 1760s, common parishioners such as Gronniosaw rarely became involved in interdenominational politics. Therefore Gronniosaw's attendance at a Baptist meeting house, or indeed his subsequent baptism by Gifford, does not necessarily imply a partisan allegiance to a Baptist ministry at the expense of Calvinism or indeed any other form of Christianity. Moreover, Baptist theology was by the 1750s so diverse that it encompassed ministers with Calvinist sympathies as well as those who identified more with Wesley's Arminianism.[34] An examination of Gifford's published works reveals him to fall into the former category; in 1771 he even edited a collection of Whitefield's *Eighteen Sermons*.[35] As Edwin Cannan and Roger Hayden suggest, Gifford's 'unusual combination of a Calvinist theology with evangelical passion' marked him out as a preacher whose discourse was certainly influenced by his friend Whitefield's 'flaming evangelicalism'.[36] The sermons Gronniosaw heard at Gifford's meetings in London would have been distinctly Calvinist in character.

It was also through Whitefield's influence that Gronniosaw met his wife, Betty, who worked as a weaver in the house procured for his lodgings, on Petticoat Lane, and was 'a member of Mr. Allen's [Calvinist] meeting'.[37] His 'strict' style of preaching does not appear to have been to Gronniosaw's tastes, since he and Betty 'often went together to hear Dr. Gifford', despite Allen's meeting-house being situated on their home street.[38] Their decision to favour Gifford's Baptist meeting over Allen's could also have been related to the popular misconception that baptism offered protection from re-enslavement.[39]

While personal incompatibility or uncertainty as to his personal security in London may account for Allen's relatively small presence in Gronniosaw's life, other factors may help to explain his minor status in

---

[34] Baptism and Calvinism were by no means mutually exclusive. For an introduction to this vast area of scholarship, see William Brackney, *A Genetic History of Baptist Thought* (Macon, GA: Mercer University Press, 2004).

[35] See Andrew Gifford, *A Sermon in Commemoration of the Great Storm, Commonly Called the High Wind, in the Year 1703* (London: A. Ward, 1733); George Whitefield, *Eighteen Sermons* (London: J. Gurney, 1771).

[36] Edwin Cannan, 'Gifford, Andrew (1700–1784)', rev. Roger Hayden, in *ODNB*, available at www.oxforddnb.com/view/article/10657.

[37] Gronniosaw, *Narrative*, 26.

[38] Vincent Carretta (ed.), *Unchained Voices: An Anthology of Black Authors in the English-Speaking World of the 18th Century* (Lexington: University of Kentucky Press, 1996), 57 n. 95. A sample of Allen's style can be found in John Allen, *The Destruction of Sodom Improved, as a Warning to Great Britain* (London: A. Millar, 1756); Gronniosaw, *Narrative*, 27.

[39] See Seymour Drescher, *Abolition: A History of Slavery and Antislavery* (Cambridge: Cambridge University Press, 2009), 98.

the *Narrative*. After the period of his acquaintance with Gronniosaw drew to a close, John Allen became a staunch supporter of American Independence, publishing extensively on the subject under the pseudonyms 'Junius Junior' and 'British Bostonian' between 1767 and 1776.[40] Either his acquaintance with Gronniosaw in London, his experiences of slave plantations following his relocation to America in 1770, or a combination of both, inspired Allen to write *The Watchman's Alarm* in 1774. In it, he pointed out the inconsistency of the colonists' demands for liberty while they insisted on trading in enslaved Africans. In particular, Allen rejected precisely the benevolist justification for slavery, predicated on the conversion of the African slaves, that Whitefield so energetically propounded. '[A]ny among you, professing Christianity', he harangued slave-owning Americans, 'at the same time are guilty of so glaring a trespass on the laws of society and humanity, may inconsistently gloss over [slaves'] detestable usage with the idle pretence of christianizing them.'[41] The incompatibility of Allen's views on slavery with those of Whitefield and Gronniosaw's patron, Selina Hastings, may account for the scant mention of Allen's name in the *Narrative*. Allen's antislavery credentials, particularly his scoffing at the 'pretence' of converting African slaves to Christianity, would have alienated him from the two individuals key to bringing Gronniosaw's *Narrative* to press, both of whom attempted to use conversion to justify increasing their ownership of slaves at Bethesda. By the time the biography was published in 1772, Allen's well-known criticisms of George III and the North administration, along with allegations of banknote forgery in 1768, had hardly made his name an asset to a respectable 'old Whig' aristocrat such as Gronniosaw's patron Hastings.[42]

In any case, Gronniosaw's *Narrative* did not share with *The Watchman's Alarm* the sentiment that Christianising slaves was a mere 'pretence'. Rather, it explicitly propounded 'predestination', a tenet of Calvinist hermeneutics which had long been used to support Calvinist proslavery discourse. The question of predestination (that is, the pre-ordination of a spiritual 'elect' to divine grace) also formed a major bone of contention between the Countess of Huntingdon's Calvinist Connexion and their main rivals outside the established church, the Arminians. Predestination held that divine grace, for some, was irresistible, thereby circumscribing the question of free will and, by extension, bodily enslavement. In other

[40] See, for example, John Allen, *The American Alarm, or The Bostonian Plea, for the Rights, and Liberties, of the People* (Boston: D. Kneeland, 1773).
[41] John Allen, *The Watchman's Alarm to Lord N—h* (Salem, MA: E. Russell, 1774), 25–26.
[42] Jim Benedict, 'Allen, John (d. 1783x8)', in *ODNB*, available at www.oxforddnb.com/view/article/380.

words, a person's corporeal freedom in life had no bearing on their ability to enter God's kingdom upon death.[43] Applied to the question of American slavery, this doctrine demanded precisely the type of missionary work being carried out by Whitefield and later Hastings among the slaves at Bethesda, without requiring their emancipation.

The view expressed in the *Narrative* attempted to balance the doctrine of predestination with the author's suffering under chattel slavery:

> Though the Grandson of a King, I have wanted bread, and should have been glad of the hardest crust I ever saw. I who, at home, was surrounded by slaves, so that no indifferent person might approach me, and clothed with gold, have been inhumanly threatened with death; and frequently wanted clothing to defend me from the inclemency of the weather; yet I never murmured, nor was I discontented. – I am willing, and even desirous to be counted as nothing, a stranger in the world, and a pilgrim here, for 'I know that my REDEEMER liveth,' and I'm thankful for every trial and trouble that I've met with, as I am not without hope that they have all been sanctified to me.[44]

This passage began with what appeared to be an appeal to tragic pathos by highlighting the depth of Gronniosaw's fall in social status, the irony of his once having been waited on by slaves before becoming one himself. However, to realise this appeal to sentiment, the corporeal and emotional suffering inherent in the condition of slavery had to be highlighted. To do so would have been severely at odds with the crucial tenet of predestination, and so a description of American slavery was supplanted by a non-specific threat of death and a metaphor for suffering in general (the inclement weather). The evasion of Gronniosaw's own suffering under slavery in this passage resulted in a transplant of responsibility from the individuals involved in the buying of slaves (such as Whitefield and Hastings) to the will of God. Simultaneously, this metaphor legitimised enslavement by likening it to something as inevitable and blameless as the vagaries of the weather. Moreover, Gronniosaw was represented as being actively grateful for his own political and social nullification through enslavement: he was 'desirous to be counted as nothing, a stranger in the world', since 'every trial and trouble', just like his own pre-ordination to divine grace, were all 'sanctified' in advance.

The biblical quotations in the *Narrative* were also carefully selected to reinforce a Calvinist view on predestination. For example, when Gronniosaw found comfort in prayer, the sentiment was supplemented by a quote from Hebrews, chapter 10:

---

[43] David Carter, 'Calvinist Methodism', in *DMBI*, available at www.wesleyhistorical society.org.uk/dmbi/index.php?do=app.entry&id=526.

[44] Gronniosaw, *Narrative*, 28.

The Lord was pleas'd to comfort me by the application of many gracious promises at times when I was ready to sink under my trouble. *Wherefore He is able also to save them to the uttermost that come unto God by Him seeing He ever liveth to make intercession for them.* Hebrews x. ver. 14. *For by one offering He hath perfected for ever them that are sanctified.*[45]

In this passage, it was unclear as to whose voice was quoting the scripture, though the quote was embedded into the text in such a way that it seemed to be Gronniosaw speaking directly to the reader. The choice of quotation was particularly important, as it was actually a composite of two separate verses from separate chapters of Hebrews. The last part, from Hebrews 10:14, is cited in the text, unlike many of the other biblical quotations that litter the *Narrative*. This citation emphasised the authority of the succeeding copy as unanswerable, acting as a kind of semiotic 'nod' to the informed Calvinist reader. Read in conjunction with the uncited quotation from Hebrews 7:25 immediately preceding it, the passage seems to specifically refute the Arminian doctrine of perfection through the imitation of Christ as redundant, since '*by one offering He hath perfected for ever them that are sanctified*' already. Moreover, little interpretation is needed to understand that in this context 'He is able also to save them to the uttermost who come unto God' referred to the conversion of slaves as practised by Whitefield, Frelinghuysen and Hastings. These two passages, when placed together as though they represented a single lesson from a biblical source, underscored the broad theological position of the *Narrative* and its patrons.

If this position seems counterintuitive for a man who had suffered enslavement and slavery first-hand, it should be remembered that the circumstances related to the production of the *Narrative* cast serious doubts over Gronniosaw's authority over the published text. Many of the individuals on whom he relied for money and sustenance espoused precisely this Calvinistic view of slavery. As such he was likely to have been influenced toward such an outlook. This was not limited to the friends and acquaintances he made through Whitefield and Hastings. For example, he worked for some time in Amsterdam as a butler in the household of a Dutch Reformed family, having been recommended by 'some of my late Master Freelandhouse's [Frelinghuysen's] acquaintance, who had heard him speak frequently of me'.[46] To all intents and purposes, Dutch Reformed theology held the same beliefs on predestination and slavery to the British Calvinism practised by Selina Hastings

---

[45] Gronniosaw, *Narrative*, 19.   [46] Gronniosaw, *Narrative*, 27.

and her circle, which was precisely why Gronniosaw could be purchased by Frelinghuysen as a child.

After his return to Britain in the late 1760s, Gronniosaw sought out Benjamin Fawcett, whose edition of John Baxter's *Saints' Everlasting Rest* had helped to spark Gronniosaw's own religious awakening.[47] This puritan text influenced Calvinist theology at large, and Gronniosaw would have likely first read it while still living with Frelinghuysen. But this was not the only influence Fawcett had on Gronniosaw's life. It was through Fawcett, then ministering from Kidderminster, that he was able to find a job in the area and support his family. They settled for three or four years in Kidderminster, owing Fawcett their livelihood and only source of income.[48]

Fawcett had taken a personal interest in the spiritual lives of the enslaved since at least 1756, when he wrote *A Compassionate Address to the Christian Negroes in Virginia*.[49] This text explicitly exhorted black slaves to reconcile themselves to their enslavement on the grounds that it had no bearing on their spiritual freedom. 'Blessed be *God*,' he wrote, 'your slavery is, I hope, by no means so dangerous to your immortal souls. And the freedom of the soul for eternity is infinitely preferable to the greatest freedom of the body in its outward condition upon Earth.'[50] Fawcett consistently encouraged black slaves to remain passive victims of their mistreatment at the hands of slave-owners and overseers, 'to submit, yea conscientiously and cheerfully to submit', to 'be always faithful and obedient to your earthly masters', to 'be patient, be submissive and obedient, be faithful and true, even when some of your masters are most unkind'.[51] This anti-insurrectionary tract shared much in common with Whitefield's contemporaneous works on the subject, in that it attempted to justify the abuse of slaves on the grounds that it made them more inclined to seek solace in Christian faith. This ideology necessarily invoked hierarchical, racialized discourse in an attempt to justify itself. For example, in an appendix apparently not intended for 'Christian Negroes', Fawcett explained:

The Inhabitants of *Negroland* are, either devoted to the delusions of *Mahomet*, or to the grossest *Pagan idolatry*. And therefore we cannot but consider them, both in their *civil* and *religious* capacity, as unspeakably wretched, even while they are at

---

[47] Gronniosaw, *Narrative*, 38.
[48] Brian Kirk, 'Fawcett, Benjamin (1715–1780)', in *ODNB*, available at www.oxforddnb.com/view/article/9217.
[49] Benjamin Fawcett, *A Compassionate Address to the Christian Negroes in Virginia* (London: J. Eddowes and J. Cotton, 1756).
[50] Fawcett, *Compassionate Address*, 11–12.
[51] Fawcett, *Compassionate Address*, 16, 15, 18.

Liberty in their own native huts: this not a little softens the dreadful idea which we are ready to form of their *Slavery* in *America*, where the real interest for their present life (if they fall into the hands of humane masters) is much promoted by inuring them to wholesome labour, and their best interest for the life to come may be secured by the glorious light of the Gospel, which, it is hoped, is shining around them.[52]

For Fawcett as much as Whitefield, the enslavement and exploitation of Africans' labour was a benevolent activity, since it ultimately led to their salvation.

While it is clear that Fawcett was by no means opposed to slavery, his desire to support black slaves and former slaves in turning to Christian faith, like Whitefield's, manifested itself in the use of social influence to help Gronniosaw improve his financial situation. In 1771, Fawcett recommended him to 'Mr. Watson', who employed him 'in twisting silk and worsted together'.[53] Considering that Fawcett 'invited the Countess of Huntingdon to establish the chapel she opened in Kidderminster in 1774', he may have also introduced Gronniosaw to the local Calvinists who became instrumental in the production of the text of his life story.[54] In any case, it is clear from the *Narrative* that Fawcett stood alongside Whitefield as a key influence in Gronniosaw's spiritual and social life. Both Calvinists had published on the topic of slavery, and both had supported it as a means of bringing Africans to Christian salvation. More importantly for Gronniosaw, both were operating under the same Calvinist ideology when they assisted him in Britain. It was ultimately through the interventions of Whitefield and Fawcett that Gronniosaw was in a position to relate his experiences in the *Narrative*.

While these influences suggest a partial explanation for the *Narrative*'s apparent proslavery stance, a more significant factor was Gronniosaw's limited literacy in English. Indeed, Helena Woodard attributes his repeatedly falling prey to British con artists, in part, to his inability to read the language.[55] His second language at Frelinghuysen's house would have been Dutch, and his understanding of spoken English would have been picked up from visitors and during his time as a free man in New York. By around 1770, while he was working in Norwich, Gronniosaw was still unable to read English and 'was obliged to appeal to some one

---

[52] Fawcett, *Compassionate Address*, 32.
[53] Gronniosaw, *Narrative*, 38. 'Mr. Watson' was possibly Brook Watson, a merchant who presented Phillis Wheatley – another black author patronised by Selina Hastings – with a folio edition of Milton's *Paradise Lost* while she was on a visit to London in 1773. E. M. Lloyd, 'Watson, Sir Brook, first baronet (1735–1807)', rev. John C. Shields, in *ODNB*, available at www.oxforddnb.com/view/article/28829.
[54] Carretta, *Unchained Voices*, 58 n. 129.   [55] Woodard, *African-British Writings*, 33–42.

to read the letter [he] received' when news of his wife's condition arrived from London.[56] Certainly, when the *Narrative* was written in 1772, he was still too unfamiliar with written English to compose a publishable auto-biography. Instead, the story was 'taken from his own mouth and commit-ted to paper by the elegant pen of a young lady of the town of Leominster'.[57]

The question of Gronniosaw's amanuensis deserves further attention, since it profoundly influences how the *Narrative* can be read, particularly in the context of Calvinist social networks of the period. As Carretta points out, the 'young lady' was identified, 'probably inaccurately', in the 1809 Salem, New York, edition of the *Narrative* as Hannah More.[58] More harboured a lifelong 'hostility towards Calvinists', and as such would have been unlikely to enter Gronniosaw's social circle.[59] The publisher of the Salem edition probably intended to boost sales by associating the *Narrative* with a well-known abolitionist writer, recognis-ing the currency of stories of emancipation in the climate following the abolition of the American slave trade in 1808. Again, Gronniosaw's relationship to Calvinist networks suggests a more plausible scenario. In a letter to Selina Hastings in January 1772, he mentioned that he had been visiting Leominster and had gone 'to Mrs. Marlowe's, were [*sic*] I was shewed kindness to from my Christian friends'.[60] Mary Marlow was a fellow correspondent of Hastings and was probably introduced to Gronniosaw by Fawcett. The 'young lady' amanuensis, who wrote the story down 'for her own satisfaction, without any intention at first that it should be made public', was therefore most likely a daughter or family friend of hers at Leominster.[61]

It was almost certainly through either Fawcett or Marlow that Gronniosaw was brought to the attention of Selina Hastings, and it is clear from Gronniosaw's exclamation that 'Dear Maddam I hope Shall have Happiness to see you and Convers With you before I go Home [i.e. to heaven]' that they had not yet held a conversation in person prior to 1772.[62] Hastings sent Gronniosaw a 'favour', probably a letter and a charitable donation, over the Christmas period of 1771, 'a time of

---

[56] Gronniosaw, *Narrative*, 32.   [57] Gronniosaw, *Narrative*, iv.
[58] Carretta, *Unchained Voices*, 54 n. 4; Vincent Caretta, 'Gronniosaw, Ukawsaw (*b*. 1710x14, *d*. after 1772)', in *ODNB*, available at www.oxforddnb.com/view/article/71634.
[59] S. J. Skedd, 'More, Hannah (1745–1833)', in *ODNB*, available at www.oxforddnb.com/view/article/19179.
[60] Ch.F., F/1:1574, 'James Albate to Selina Hastings, 3 January 1772'. This is the only known surviving manuscript letter written by Gronniosaw.
[61] Gronniosaw, *Narrative*, iii.
[62] Ch.F., F/1:1574, 'James Albate to Selina Hastings, 3 January 1772'. There is no evidence to suggest that they ever met in person.

necesity' for Gronniosaw and his family, via Mr. Newben, one of the students at Hastings's training college at Trevecca in Brecknockshire, South Wales. Hastings was staying at Trevecca at the time, preparing her students for an ill-fated mission to convert Whitefield's old orphanage at Bethesda into a training college and base of operations for expanding the Connexion in the Americas. During her stay at Trevecca, much to the dismay of the tutor, Walter Churchy, Hastings regularly sent the students out on such errands across the country.[63] For example, Newben was still attending to Connexional business in January 1773 when Hastings unceremoniously interrupted his studies with an order scrawled on the back of a used letter-wrapper: 'I must request you to go to London as a student is there.'[64] With a missionary enterprise under way in America, as well as the continuing expansion of her Connexion, it does not appear that Hastings had time to personally attend to Gronniosaw's situation.

However, her associates in Kidderminster and Leominster were able to recommend Gronniosaw's *Narrative* to Walter Shirley, her cousin and lieutenant in the Connexion. Shirley wrote a preface to the text and recommended it to print, 'with a view to serve ALBERT and his distressed family, who have the sole profits arising from the sale of it'.[65] The income Gronniosaw received from the publication of the *Narrative* after 1772 enabled him and his family to remain in Kidderminster for at least another two years. During their time there, Gronniosaw and his wife Betty attended the Old Independent Meeting House, continuing their lifelong association with dissenting worship.[66]

The family had been confirmed in their distaste for other denominations during their time in Norwich during the late 1760s. When their infant daughter died, Gronniosaw, detached from Calvinist organisations, was unable to convince the local Baptist church to bury her, 'because we were not members'.[67] Similarly, the local parson of the Anglican Church refused to bury her because she had never been baptised. Even the Quakers, with whom Gronniosaw had associated in the past, would not bury his daughter. Eventually, when Gronniosaw was at the point of digging a grave in his own garden, the local Anglican parson agreed to bury the child but not to read a funeral sermon.[68]

---

[63] JRL, Methodist Collections, Selina Hastings, Countess of Huntingdon Papers, 1977/504 'Selina Hastings to Walter Churchy, n.d. 1772'.

[64] JRL, Selina Hastings, Countess of Huntingdon Papers, 1977/504, 'Selina Hastings to Mr. Newben, 3 January 1773'.

[65] Gronniosaw, *Narrative*, iv.

[66] TNA, Parish Records, RG 4/3374, 'Worcestershire: Kidderminster, Old Meeting House (Independent): Births & Baptisms'.

[67] Gronniosaw, *Narrative*, 37.   [68] Gronniosaw, *Narrative*, 38.

Woodard, reasonably, attributes this remarkably un-Christian behaviour to racist disapproval of Gronniosaw and his children.[69] It is also important to recognise that such a traumatic event, 'one of the greatest trials I ever met with', would have likely prejudiced Gronniosaw against the Baptist and Anglican Churches and further strengthened his affinity for (and dependence on) the Calvinist Connexion.

Another consequence of this traumatic episode was that Gronniosaw became very conscientious in having his remaining children baptised. Very shortly after arriving in Kidderminster in 1771, Gronniosaw's children, Mary, Edward and Samuel, were all baptised together.[70] However, when his youngest child, James, was born in 1774, Gronniosaw appears to have been unable to support the family, even with money beginning to come in from the second edition of the *Narrative*, published by Samuel Hazard in Bath during the same year. At some point after this the family moved to Chester. The Countess's Connexion was expanding there, and Gronniosaw may have been offered work or invited by a Calvinist friend.[71] The exact nature of the family's circumstances between 1774 and 1775 remain unclear, but he was well regarded enough by the time of his death on 5 October 1775 for an obituary to appear in the *London Evening Post*: 'Died, This Thursday se'nnight, at Chester, aged 70, James Albert Ukawsaw Gronniosa, an African Prince of Zaara'.[72] After that, Gronniosaw's legacy developed through posthumous changes to his autobiography.

The Publication and Sale of Gronniosaw's *Narrative*

By the time Hastings came into contact with Gronniosaw, her Connexion was in the midst of an acrimonious pamphlet war with the Wesley brothers' Arminian Methodists. Gronniosaw's *Narrative* represented a textual response to Wesley's public censure of Hastings's trading in slaves. The rift between Wesley's Arminian followers and Hastings's circle ostensibly originated over a question of doctrine. On one hand, Calvinist predestination held the notion of irresistible grace, while on the other, Wesley's Arminian doctrine held the notion of 'Christian perfection', by which any individual could achieve grace through perfecting

---

[69] Woodard, *African-British Writings*, 39–40.
[70] TNA, Parish Records, RG 4/3374, 'Worcestershire: Kidderminster, Old Meeting House (Independent): Births & Baptisms'.
[71] The head of the Countess of Huntingdon's college at Trevecca, for example, was the former curate of Coddington, near Chester. Harding, *The Countess of Huntingdon's Connexion*, 230.
[72] *London Evening Post*, 10 October 1775, 1.

their moral behaviour in imitation of Christ.[73] As has already been discussed, this influenced each denomination's official stance on the question of slavery. During the 1760s and early 1770s, the disagreement between Hastings and Wesley became personal, and the rivalry between the two denominations developed in animosity, particularly with regard to the issue of slavery.

It was John Wesley who first converted Hastings from Anglicanism to Methodism in the late 1730s, making an exception to his egalitarian religious principles and affording her a private pew in his chapel at Donnington, near Shrewsbury.[74] Through Wesley, Hastings met Whitefield, who introduced her to older Calvinistic notions of predestination. The hierarchical implications of predestination chimed with her old Whig politics and social experiences as an aristocrat. By late 1744, the Countess's interest in predestination had overtaken her enthusiasm for Wesley's notion of Christian perfection, and over the course of the following twenty years, correspondence between Hastings and Wesley became infrequent and stilted.

A letter from John Wesley on 8 January 1764 signalled the start of a period of mutual hostility between them. He was incensed that she had invited Whitefield and others to preach at her Brighthempston chapel, '& as much notice taken of my Brother [Charles] & me, as of a couple of Postillians'. He jealously attacked what he saw as snobbery on her part. 'It only confirmed to me in the judgement I had formed for many years, I am too rough a preacher for tender ears.' Clearly, Wesley saw Hastings's slight as a personal attack and emphatically rejected the possibility that he was left uninvited because of a disagreement over doctrine:

'No, that is not it; but you preach perfection' What: without why or wherefore? Among the unawaken'd? Among Babes in Christ? No. To these I say not a word about it. I have two or three grains of common sense. If I do not know how to suit my Discourse to my audience at these years, I ought never to preach more.[75]

Meanwhile, Hastings's relationship with Whitefield grew stronger, and he bequeathed the orphanage at Bethesda to her in 1770, along with around fifty slaves.[76] Even while she and her cousin Shirley were arranging for the publication of Gronniosaw's *Narrative* and, a year later, of Phillis Wheatley's *Poems on Various Subjects*, Hastings increased the

---

[73] David Carter, 'Christian Perfection', in *DMBI*, available at www.wesleyhistorical society.org.uk/dmbi/index.php?do=app.entry&id=611.

[74] Schlenther, *Queen of the Methodists*, 86.

[75] JRL, John Wesley, Copy Letters, 1977/607, 'John Wesley to Selina Hastings, 8 January 1764'.

[76] Schlenther, *Queen of the Methodists*, 91.

number of slaves at Bethesda. By 1780 she owned more than a hundred.[77] This drew censure from early abolitionists including the Philadelphia Quaker Anthony Benezet, who wrote to her in 1774, describing the slave trade as an 'Iniquitous Traffick'.[78] Even before this, Wesley had taken exception to Hastings's dealings in the slave trade, and he made his opinions on the matter public in early 1774 with the publication of his *Thoughts upon Slavery*, in which he declared, 'I absolutely deny all Slave-holding to be consistent with any degree of even natural justice.'[79] Given the nature of the rivalry between Wesley and Hastings, such public censure helped set her in her course of extending her investments, both ideological and financial, in slavery.

Hastings was not the only individual involved in the *Narrative*'s publication who took a personal interest in refuting John Wesley. Shirley, who wrote the preface to the text, held a particular grudge against Wesley and the Arminians. Under orders from Hastings, Shirley had organised a mass protest against the Arminian conference in Bristol in 1771, to 'insist on the recantation' of the resolutions made during the previous year's conference in London.[80] The protest turned out to be a disaster, and Shirley and Hastings were humiliated while Wesley celebrated his conference with record attendance, and again resolved upon the doctrines of Christian perfection and antinomianism which the Calvinists found so obnoxious.[81] This hardened Shirley's opinion of the Arminians, and his correspondence with Hastings over the following four years revealed a determination to check its success. He suggested a number of times, for example, that Calvinist churches be built in areas where Wesley's preaching-houses appeared to be popular.[82] Shirley even wrote to Hastings in February 1772 to suggest that she expel all those with Arminian sympathies from her college at Trevecca, warning her that she 'must never expect peace there unless the College consists wholly of Arminians or wholly of Calvinists'.[83]

Shirley's hard-line anti-Arminianism was manifested also in his preface to Gronniosaw's *Narrative*. The short piece firmly established the *Narrative* as proof of the doctrine of predestination:

---

[77] Schlenther, *Queen of the Methodists*, 94 n. 46, 48.
[78] Ch.F., A3/1/33, 'Anthony Benezet to Selina Hastings, 25 May 1774'.
[79] John Wesley, *Thoughts upon Slavery* (London: R. Hawes, 1774), 31.
[80] Walter Shirley, *A Narrative of the Principal Circumstances Relative to the Rev. Mr. Wesley's Late Conference* (Bath: W. Gye and T. Mills, 1771), 7. Note that this pamphlet refuting Wesley's doctrine was printed by the same publishers as Gronniosaw's *Narrative*.
[81] For a detailed examination of the Bristol Conference affair, see Harding, *The Countess of Huntingdon's Connexion*, 266–278.
[82] See Ch.F., E4/1/12, 'Walter Shirley to Selina Hastings, 14 May 1772'.
[83] Ch.F., E4/1/8, 'Walter Shirley to Selina Hastings, 17 February 1772'.

Now it appears from the experience of this remarkable person, that God does not save without knowledge of the truth; but, with respect to those whom He hath fore-known, though born under every outward disadvantage, and in regions of the grossest darkness and ignorance, he most amazingly acts upon their minds.[84]

Like Fawcett, Shirley took the spiritual (and by extension moral) deprivation of non-Christian Africans for granted. However, he was explicit in positing Gronniosaw's early awareness of monotheism as proof that he was one of God's predestined individuals, one of 'those whom He hath fore-known'. Shirley used the 'Preface' as an opportunity to specifically refute Arminian doctrine, arguing that 'Whatever *Infidels* and *Deists* may think; I trust the Christian Reader will easily discern an All-wise and omnipotent Appointment and Direction in these movements.'[85] The reference here to 'deists' (those who believe in divine creationism but not in God's direct intervention in earthly matters) was intended to be read as meaning those who held the Arminian doctrine of perfection, since they emphasised the need for human action in attaining a state of grace.

Shirley's gibe at Wesley and the Arminians may seem a rather opaque reference to be made in a general preface, but Gronniosaw's *Narrative* was never intended for a general readership. An examination of the publishing patterns of the various editions of the text show that it was primarily marketed toward, printed for and distributed among an informed Calvinist readership who would have been acutely aware of the political tensions between Hastings's and Wesley's social circles. What becomes clear from an examination of the various destinations of Gronniosaw's *Narrative* during his lifetime is that its increasingly broad geographical distribution was not matched by diversification in its readership. Before the author's death in 1775, in Britain at least, the *Narrative* was a Calvinist text for Calvinist readers.[86] This may have something to do with the nominally charitable motive behind its publication: it would after all have been impossible to ensure that the proceeds from the sale of the text found their way back to 'serve Albert and his distressed family' if distribution moved outside of the control of Calvinist social and professional networks. This would account for the first American edition of the text appearing in 1774 at the Rhode Island printing house of 'S. Southwick', the Baptist-Calvinist publisher who first printed Phillis

---

[84] Gronniosaw, *Narrative*, iv.   [85] Gronniosaw, *Narrative*, iv.
[86] See Ryan Hanley, 'Calvinism, Proslavery and James Albert Ukawsaw Gronniosaw', *Slavery & Abolition*, 36:2 (2015), 360–381.

Wheatley's elegiac poem *On the Death of . . . George Whitefield* in 1771.[87] But the practical difficulties inherent in all transatlantic financial proceedings (exacerbated in the mid-1770s by the increasingly turbulent Anglo-American political atmosphere) rendered the type of direct charity 'arising from the sale' of the *Narrative* as advertised in Shirley's preface virtually impracticable. The title page of the Southwick 1774 edition proclaimed the *Narrative* to have originated in Bath but to have been 'reprinted and sold' in Newport, Rhode Island. This indicates that the interpersonal printing and distribution network of the *Narrative* as established by Hazard, and later expanded by Hastings's preferred publishers William Gye and Thomas Mills, had not been entirely circumvented by Southwick's reproduction, though precisely what this meant for Gronniosaw's financial situation is impossible to tell. In any case, it seems unlikely that he benefitted directly from the sale of the Rhode Island reprint.

After Gronniosaw's death, the notion of charity no longer bound publishers to strictly Calvinist distribution networks. Neither did it morally obligate Calvinist publishers to sell the text, though Hazard for example was still selling back issues of his edition of the *Narrative* as late as 1800.[88] During the decade following Gronniosaw's death, only one new edition of the *Narrative* was printed. This was a translation of the text into Welsh, appearing in 1779. Here the influence of Hastings's circle was obvious: her college at Trevecca was in Brecknockshire, only a few miles from Aberhonddu (Brecon), where the *Narrative* was reprinted.[89] As one English observer discovered in 1772, most of the parishioners and many of the students at Trevecca spoke only Welsh.[90] Hastings was not unaware of this nor of the potential problems it could pose to the expansion of her church in Britain and Anglophone America. While in Bath in August 1772, she began personally teaching one of her Welsh-speaking students English and wrote to one of the Masters at Trevecca to express her intentions to teach others:

---

[87] Ukawsaw Gronniosaw, *A Narrative of the Most Remarkable Particulars in the Life of James Albert Ukawsaw Gronniosaw* (Newport, RI: S. Southwick, [1774]). Phillis Wheatley, *An Elegiac Poem: On the Death of . . . George Whitefield* (Newport, RI: S. Southwick, [1771]). Wheatley included a conciliatory postscript in verse addressed to Hastings.

[88] Samuel Hazard, 'Advertisement', in Henry Venn, *The Complete Duty of Man: or, a System of Doctrinal and Practical Christianity* (Bath: S. Hazard, 1800), 393.

[89] Ukawsaw Gronniosaw, *Berr Hanes o'r pethau mwyaf hynod ym mywyd James Albert Ukawsaw Groniosaw, tywysog o Affrica: fel yr adroddwyd ganddo ef ei hun* (Aberhhondu: W. Williams and E. Evans, 1779).

[90] Anon., *Some Account of the Proceedings at the College of the Right Hon. the Countess of Huntingdon, in Wales, Relative to Those Students called to go to her Ladyship's College in Georgia* (London, 1772), 17.

Roberts quickly improves in his English he will in another month quite master all difficulty and be as well understood as any minister of this nation. If I succeed with him I intend to have one of the Welsh students in their turn with me for this purpose till they all are masters & have it made easy to them in both languages.[91]

The translation of the *Narrative* itself was undertaken by William Williams Pantycelyn, the eminent Welsh Calvinist hymn-writer, described by Derec Llwyd Morgan as 'an author of great vision, brilliance, and pertinence', and one of the most famous and influential hymn-writers in the history of Welsh Calvinism.[92] Pantycelyn was a member of Huntingdon's circle and often visited Trevecca College, regularly working with senior students and masters there. The publication of Pantycelyn's translation indicates that there was a predominately Welsh-speaking market for the text, most likely among the parishioners of the well-established Welsh Calvinist churches, fostered by the palpable presence of Trevecca nearby. Moreover, the fact that an individual of Pantycelyn's popularity translated the text indicates how important it was perceived to be by those primarily concerned with Calvinist preaching.

By the end of the 1770s then, Gronniosaw's *Narrative* had been exclusively printed by publishers with Calvinist sympathies, and predominately marketed toward and read by practising Calvinists. However, subsequent publication patterns for the text demonstrate a move away from a Calvinist readership and toward one more concerned with the growing debate surrounding the abolition of the slave trade. In 1786, the year before the inauguration of SEAST, a heavily edited version of Gronniosaw's text was issued, probably without permission, in Clonmel, Ireland.[93] The publisher, Thomas Lord, had no pre-existing connections with Hastings or her Calvinist social or professional network. Prior to Lord's version of the text, editions had only varied from Gye and Mills's first in as far as they corrected spelling errors and updated archaic language choices – i.e. 'display'd' in the first edition became 'displayed' in the second – and similar minor alterations. The relative care with which the text was preserved prior to Lord's edition reflects the desire as much to preserve the Calvinist moral of the story as to faithfully recount the principal events of Gronniosaw's life.[94]

[91] JRL, Methodist Collections, 1977/504, Box 2, 'Selina Hastings to Thomas Jones, 3 August 1772'.

[92] Derec Llwyd Morgan, 'Williams, William (1717–1791)', in *ODNB*, available at www .oxforddnb.com/view/article/29556.

[93] Ukawsaw Gronniosaw, *The Life and Conversion of James Albert Ukawsaw Gronniosaw, an African Prince. Giving an Account of the Religion, Customs, Manners, &c. of the Natives of Zaara, in Africa* (Clonmel: Thomas Lord, 1786).

[94] For a detailed discussion of unauthorised editions of Gronniosaw's *Narrative* published after 1779, see Ryan Hanley, 'Black Writing in Britain, 1770–1830', PhD thesis, University of Hull (2015), 72–80.

It was only after 1786 that Gronniosaw became read primarily through the lens of the antislavery movement.

There is a dearth of historical and literary studies of Gronniosaw's *Narrative*, but those that exist emphasise the intelligence and agency of the author.[95] There can be no doubting Gronniosaw's intelligence; his text was littered with more scriptural references than his amanuensis and various editors combined could identify; he was conversant in at least three languages; and he was sufficiently impressive to 'stand before 38 ministers' of the Dutch Reformed Church 'for seven weeks together' discussing theology during his time in Amsterdam.[96] However, an examination of his personal circumstances at the time of the *Narrative*'s composition, taken alongside a close reading of the text in the light of the proslavery oeuvre of those individuals most intimately involved in its publication, reveals that his authorial agency was severely compromised. This accounts for the passages in the text which seem to be intended to directly refute the theology of Hastings's Arminian rivals and may well account for what Woodard describes as Gronniosaw's 'subdued treatment of incidents which can be attributed to racial prejudice', as well as his apparent hesitance to condemn the slave trade.[97]

This is not to depict the *Narrative* as a fabrication of a group of proslavery Calvinists, nor Gronniosaw as a passive victim of misrepresentation: he managed, without precedent, to authentically depict his life in Africa from an African perspective. In so doing, he refuted many long-held British suppositions about the lack of civilisation in traditional African life. 'It is a generally received opinion, in *England*, that the natives of *Africa* go entirely uncloth'd', the *Narrative* noted with indignation, 'but this supposition is very unjust: they have a kind of dress to appear decent.'[98] However, the impact of such a depiction was limited by the manner in which the text was published and marketed, further distorting its meaning to suit Calvinist interests. As the Methodist preacher and autobiographer Boston King would learn during his time in Britain in the 1790s, this type of post-composition alteration became commonplace in evangelical black writing. Ultimately, while the history of the composition and publication of Gronniosaw's *Narrative* during the eighteenth century details a repeated misrepresentation of the author, the first black voice in British print culture persisted for decades, generating an original framework for successive generations of evangelical writers to come.

---

[95] See, for example, Harris, 'Seeing the Light', 43–57.   [96] Gronniosaw, *Narrative*, 28.
[97] Woodard, *African-British Writings*, 35.   [98] Gronniosaw, *Narrative*, 2.

5   Boston King, Kingswood School and British Methodism, 1794–1798

> I doubt not but the day will arrive, when Negro-preachers may be found, that will carry the gospel into the Negro-land.[1]

Thomas Coke's prediction, published as part of a report on his 1789 missionary tour of the British West Indies, was to be fulfilled very quickly indeed. To take the Methodist word into Africa had been the ambition of a number of black itinerant preachers, and one of the first to achieve it in 1791 was a man who later became known personally to Coke: Boston King.[2] Coke had, by that time, personally ordained more than one black preacher, acting in his capacity as one of the two appointed superintendents for the Methodist connexion in America.[3] However, opportunities for preachers to travel from America to Africa were limited, and during this period missionary funds were more often directed toward evangelising in the New World than to free people born in Africa.[4] However, the second attempt at creating a settlement in Sierra Leone in 1791 provided an opportunity for former black Loyalists in Nova Scotia to return to Africa. Among the first wave of these black emigrants was Boston King, an ordained Methodist minister.

King was born into slavery in Charleston, South Carolina, in the late 1760s. In about 1779, he absconded from his master Richard Waring and joined the British colonial forces. After the final defeat of the British

---

[1] Thomas Coke, *To the Benevolent Subscribers for the Support of the Missions Carried on by Voluntary Contributions in the British Islands* (London: [Epworth Press], 1789), 17.

[2] King's missionary activity formed one arm of a 'pan-evangelical' effort to spread Christianity through Africa from Sierra Leone. See Suzanne Schwarz, 'The Legacy of Melvill Horne', *International Bulletin of Missionary Research*, 31:2 (2007), 88–94.

[3] John Wigger, *American Saint: Francis Asbury and the Methodists* (Oxford: Oxford University Press, 2009), 139–158.

[4] Missions to convert black people in the Americas began in Nova Scotia in 1784. The first concerted Methodist mission to West Africa was in 1811, well after King travelled alone to preach to the Sherbro people between 1798 and 1802. David Hempton, *Methodism: Empire of the Spirit* (New Haven, CT: Yale University Press, 2005), 151.

in 1783, he and his wife Violet escaped to Nova Scotia.[5] He converted to Methodism on 5 January 1784 and started preaching in 1785. By 1791 he was placed in charge of a Methodist meeting in Preston, Nova Scotia, about eleven miles northwest of Halifax. On 16 January 1792, he led his congregation across the Atlantic to join the new settlement on the West African Coast. After teaching schoolchildren and preaching the gospel at Sierra Leone for two years, he was offered the opportunity to come to Britain to further his education at the Methodist School at Kingswood, near Bristol.[6] During his time at Kingswood between 1794 and 1796, he wrote an autobiography, 'Memoirs of the Life of Boston King', which was published in instalments in the *Methodist Magazine* between March and June 1798.

Coke and his Methodist network profoundly affected the contents of King's final published 'Memoirs'. These individuals shared a common agenda for the international future of the movement and shared an idea of how to ensure its survival and continuing expansion in the turbulent decade following the death of their leader, John Wesley, in 1791. Coke, as head of the Methodist missions and one of the most influential figures in the movement, had the means and motive to ensure that King's 'Memoirs' espoused the particular political and doctrinal stances that he believed were central to the survival of the Methodist movement during the 1790s.

While the Methodist networks of the 1790s have been mapped by both political and ecclesiastical historians alike, British Methodist abolitionism – particularly the work of black Methodist preachers in Britain – has perhaps not received as much attention as it deserves.[7] Much of our

---

[5] In 1783, King was recorded as being twenty-three years old in 'the Book of Negroes', a record of the black Loyalist soldiers fleeing to Canada after the American Revolution. The book also states that he left his master 'about four years ago'. However, King's *Memoirs* state that he was twelve years old when he absconded, putting his year of birth at 1768. TNA, Dorchester Papers, 'Book of Negroes', [1783], 30/55/100/10427, ff. 70–71; Boston King, 'Memoirs of Boston King', *Methodist Magazine*, 21 (1798), 107.

[6] Boston King, 'Memoirs of the Life of Boston King', in Anon., *The Methodist Magazine, for the Year 1798; Being a Continuation of the Arminian Magazine* (London: G. Whitfield, [1799]), 157–161, 209–213, 261–265.

[7] For work on Methodist social networks, see Hempton, *Empire of the Spirit*; David Hempton, *Methodism and Politics in British Society, 1750–1850* (London: Hutchinson, 1984); David Hempton, *Religion and Political Culture in Britain and Ireland: From the Glorious Revolution to the Decline of Empire* (Cambridge: Cambridge University Press, 1996), 25–49; John Turner, *Conflict and Reconciliation: Studies in Methodism and Ecumenism in England 1740–1982* (London: Epworth Press 1985); Bernard Semmel, *The Methodist Revolution* (London: Heinemann, 1974). For Methodism in Sierra Leone, see Suzanne Schwarz, '"Our Mad Methodists": Methodism, Missions and Abolitionism in Sierra Leone in the Late Eighteenth Century', *Journal of Wesley and Methodist Studies*, 3 (2011), 121–133.

understanding of the movement has been coloured by E. P. Thompson's appraisal of it as having profoundly conservative instincts, as 'serving *simultaneously* as the religion of the industrial bourgeoisie ... and of wide sections of the proletariat' in the interests of social conservatism.[8] More recently, scholars such as David Hempton have painted a rather more complex picture, demonstrating that the movement was besieged by internal conflict, especially during the 1790s. Consequently, to attribute any particular political ideology to the connexion as a whole is problematic, and a more flexible model, factoring in geographic and social specificities, is required to understand the political sentiments of any particular Methodist group of circuit. Hempton goes as far as to suggest that 'Methodism forged a symbiotic relationship with its host environments.'[9] The protean nature of Methodist political sentiment, along with the uncertain position of black preachers within it, may explain the lack of any sustained historical or literary study of Boston King's 'Memoirs' or the specific social or cultural contexts surrounding their production and publication. Wherever King has been mentioned or anthologized, his 'Memoirs' have been discussed only in relation to his personal status as a former slave or migrant to Nova Scotia and/or Sierra Leone.[10]

However, his relationships with other Methodists had a direct influence on his career as a preacher. He relied on Coke as his superintendent and a potential means of returning to preach in Africa. While he was living at Kingswood School, he was financially dependent on Joseph Bradford, the governor there. Even after his studies at Kingswood were complete, King's extant correspondence shows that his standard of written English was nowhere near as high as that in the 'Memoirs'. It is safe to assume, therefore, that he was assisted in the composition of his text by someone at the school. While King was studying at Kingswood, the school was governed by a committee almost exclusively populated by men who shared Coke's vision for the future of Arminian Methodism. These men wanted the connexion to be more respectable, more hierarchical in structure, and to have a closer relationship to the established church and government policymakers. They were also central to the composition and edition of King's 'Memoirs'.

---

[8] E. Thompson, *The Making of the English Working Class* (London: Random House, 1963), 355.

[9] Hempton, *Empire of the Spirit*, 7.

[10] See, for example, Henry Louis Gates Jr. and Evelyn Brooks Higginbotham (eds.), *African American Lives* (Oxford: Oxford University Press, 2004), 498–499; Suzanna Ashton (ed.), *I Belong to South Carolina: South Carolina Slave Narratives* (Columbia: University of South Carolina Press, 2010), 14–39.

The 'Memoirs', as a piece of black autobiography, also lent additional legitimacy to Coke's avowed support for the abolition of the slave trade – a gesture that helped to ingratiate the Methodists to the Tory cabinet through William Wilberforce. This was not simply a case of Coke attempting to catch the attention of a potential ally for the Methodists in the House of Commons. Wilberforce and Coke were in sustained written communication with one another, discussing precisely these issues, during the two years between the completion of the manuscript in 1796 and its publication in 1798. King had left Britain by August 1796, and thus his authorial control over the text was severely compromised during the editing process. King's 'Memoirs' formed part of a demonstrative dialogue between Coke and Wilberforce, in which political support for abolition and avowals of constitutional loyalty were bartered for a leavening of legislation that many Arminians felt to be repressive.[11] A close reading of the text in this light reveals it to espouse precisely those political ideologies which would have been most useful to Coke and his circle in ensuring good relations between Methodism and Wilberforce's parliamentary abolitionism and, by extension, the Tory administration.

Boston King, Kingswood School and the Writing of the 'Memoirs', 1794–1796

King arrived in Britain at Plymouth on 16 May 1794. He had sailed aboard the *Harpy*, which set off from Freetown on 26 April, making the crossing in fifty-one days.[12] He travelled to London a couple of days later, spending six weeks there and occasionally preaching at Methodist meeting-houses across the city, including the New Chapel at City-Road and Snowsfield Chapel, two of the largest in the entire connexion.[13] While he was in London, he travelled upriver to visit an old friend from Sierra Leone: the settlement's first governor, John Clarkson. It is easy to see why King was keen to pay him a visit. Clarkson led the exodus of Nova Scotian black Loyalists to Africa in 1791/1792, proving so popular among the former soldiers that he became known as 'Moses' during the voyage.[14]

---

[11] Hempton has pointed out that, in a letter to Wilberforce, Wesley had 'bemoaned the fact that Methodists were neither accepted as Anglicans nor afforded relief as dissenters under the Act of Toleration'. For this reason, they were afforded no protection from anti-dissenter mobs, though these were uncommon by the late 1790s. David Hempton, *The Religion of the People: Methodism and Popular Religion, 1750–1900* (London: Routledge, 1996), 88.

[12] *Lloyd's Evening Post*, 19 May 1794.   [13] King, 'Memoirs', 264.

[14] James Walker, *The Black Loyalists: The Search for a Promised Land in Nova Scotia and Sierra Leone 1783–1870* (Toronto: University of Toronto Press, 1976), 157.

He vigorously supported their rights during the turbulent first year of the settlement, even when this approach brought him into conflict with other members of the board. Hugh Brogan suggests that the well-documented spat between Clarkson and the Sierra Leone Company's Chairman, Henry Thornton, came about 'above all because Clarkson insisted on putting the views and interests of the Nova Scotians first', even before the economic imperatives laid down by the board of directors.[15] King's personal association with Clarkson, and his 1794 visit in particular, was to contribute to his increasing financial dependence on the Methodist network centred on Kingswood School. He also met a number of other important figures in London, including the moderately pro-reform MP Samuel Whitbread at his home at 17 Grosvenor Street.[16] In August 1794, King moved to Bristol, where he met Coke, who was there to act as secretary to the Methodist conference. Coke took King to Kingswood School, where he spent the next two years and wrote his 'Memoirs'.

The exact nature of King's daily experience of Kingswood school is uncertain, since his status there was never clearly defined. Although he was a schoolteacher back in Sierra Leone, he had only ever taught young children 'the Alphabet, and to spell words of two syllables, and likewise the Lord's Prayer'.[17] The curriculum at Kingswood, as laid out by John Wesley in 1749, was designed to give boys between the ages of six and twelve a grounding in key works of ecclesiastical literature as well as a grasp of the classical languages. Classes covered 'Reading, Writing, Arithmetick, English, French, Latin, Greek, Hebrew, History, Geography, Chronology, Rhetorick, Logick, Ethicks, Geometry, Algebra, Physicks, Musick'.[18] The staple academic texts for the boys included English and Latin grammar textbooks, William Cave's *Primitive Christianity*, and dialogues of Erasmus, Phoedrus and Sallust. The emphasis in most of the classes was on translation between English and another language.[19] While it is safe to assume that some of the specific texts to be taught were updated between 1749 and King's arrival in 1794 (probably to include one or more of Wesley's tracts after his death in 1791), it is clear from the nature of the syllabus that King lacked the language skills and experience to act as a teacher at Kingswood.

---

[15] Hugh Brogan, 'Clarkson, Thomas, 1760–1846', in *ODNB*, available at www.oxford dnb.com/view/article/5545.

[16] Patrick Boyle, *The Fashionable Court Guide* (London: Patrick Boyle, 1794), lists Whitbread's address.

[17] King, 'Memoirs', 263.

[18] John Wesley, *A Short Account of the School, in Kingswood, near Bristol* (Bristol: William Pine, 1768), 1.

[19] Wesley, *Short Account of the School*, 3–5.

However, he could not have attended as a pupil, either. Obviously, age was an issue – the school syllabus had been designed for boys 'between the years of six and twelve', and King was in his late twenties by the time he arrived at Kingswood.[20] Moreover, the ethos of the school relied on a gruelling disciplinarian regime which would not have been applicable to an adult learner. In particular, King might have resented the expectation of daily supervised field labour, having witnessed the horrors of plantation slavery from a young age in South Carolina.[21] There was a two-year course of 'academical learning' for older boys available at Kingswood, designed as a more theologically focused alternative to the courses on offer at Oxford and Cambridge. But this would have been far too advanced for King, since again they relied on an accepted level of preliminary reading in French, Latin and Greek as well as a wide-ranging knowledge of classic tracts such as Bunyan's *Pilgrim's Progress* and even Hume's *History of England*.[22] Since his purpose in coming to Kingswood was that he 'might be better qualified to teach the natives' in Sierra Leone 'not only to learn the English language, but also [to] attain some knowledge of the way of salvation thro' faith in the Lord Jesus Christ', it seems unlikely that he would have invested his limited time in learning the classical languages.[23] Frankly, he had more important matters to attend. Moreover, extant manuscript letters written by King show that his standard of written communication in English was not up to the standard of his verbal skills, even after his time at Kingswood, and he certainly would not have been qualified to write academic essays. For example, when he wrote to Clarkson from Freetown in 1798 to request financial support, his spelling and grammar actively obscured his meaning: 'And many other Familys is thinking of going when the Rin id over & it appire that their cheif reason is because the Company enquire quit rent for their Lands a yea ago but the people will not compy with it I should wonder if one half of the Colony should [undecipherable].'[24] Because of the disparity between his deep theological knowledge and his less practiced academic skills, King likely occupied an interstitial academic position in the school, occasionally sitting in on classes, discussing theological

---

[20] See Vincent Carretta, 'Explanatory Notes', in Vincent Carretta (ed.), *Unchained Voices: An Anthology of Black Authors in the English-Speaking World of the 18th Century* (Lexington: University of Kentucky Press, 1996), 366 n. 1, 368 n. 40; Wesley, *A Short Account of the School*, 3.
[21] King, 'Memoirs', 105.   [22] Wesley, *A Short Account of the School*, 9–11.
[23] King, 'Memoirs', 264–65.
[24] Boston King, 'Boston King to Thomas Clarkson, 16 January, 1798', in Christopher Fyfe (ed.), *'Our Children Free and Happy': Letters from Black Settlers in Africa in the 1790s* (Edinburgh: Edinburgh University Press, 1991), 54.

matters with the masters (quite possibly including the prospect of a mission to Sierra Leone, attempted unsuccessfully by Coke in 1796) and studying independently in the school's considerable library.[25]

King was financially dependent on the school's governing body during his time at Kingswood. As well as paying for his food, lodging and tuition (valued normally, at child's rations, at £12 per annum), the school also allowed him free use of their library. This privilege was denied to the students on the 'course of academical learning', who had to supply their own textbooks in addition to their fees.[26] The account books for the school show that the parents of the boarders almost always received the invoice for additional or unforeseen expenses incurred by their children, such as damage to property or medical bills.[27] They also show that, uniquely, the cost of King's clothes and boots was defrayed by the school: on 25 September 1795, £6. 11s. was paid out to 'Mr. [William] Hunt, for Boston King's clothes'.[28] However, unlike the masters at the school, and its governor, Joseph Bradford, King was not given a salary. There was a portion of the budget set aside for the boys' spending money, which they received each month, but it is not clear from the accounts whether King was allotted any of this for his own personal use. If he was, the amount would have been very small indeed, since the total 'pocket-money' for twenty-five boys for the year of 1796 was only £6. 13s.[29]

Nevertheless, King's education evidently amounted to a noticeable financial investment, even though Kingswood was still a comparatively buoyant part of the Methodists' fundraising portfolio. Coke's motivations in bringing him to Kingswood in 1794, therefore, needed to be compelling, since he would need to convince the Kingswood Committee and the national Arminian conference to release the funding. As the superintendent of Methodism's overseas missions, he had a long-standing ideological interest in the 'salvation' of black slaves through their conversion. Indeed, it was Coke who finally convinced Wesley to establish Methodist missions in America, and between 1784 and 1793 he

---

[25] For Coke's 'disastrous' Sierra Leone mission, see Schwarz, 'Our Mad Methodists', 121–133.

[26] Wesley, *A Short Account of the School*, 9.

[27] See, for example, Kingswood School Archives, 'Account books for 1796'.

[28] Kingswood School Archives, 'Account books for 1795', f. 3. The only clothier named 'Mr. Hunt' advertising in Bristol newspapers between 1780 and 1800 was 'William Hunt Junr. Woollen-Draper, Taylor, and Salesman, Wine-Street'. Hunt also gave 'generous discounts' for business clients, so it would seem likely that Kingswood would have preferred him. *Felix Farley's Bristol Journal*, 30 August 1783, 4.

[29] Anon., *History of Kingswood School by Three Old Boys* (London: Charles Kelly, 1898), 86.

had personally undertaken four missions the British West Indies.[30] In 1789, he wrote publicly to the subscribers to the Methodist missionary fund, reassuring them of his personal commitment to evangelising the slaves: 'I confess, the interests of this work, particularly that part of it which relates to the myriads of poor Negroes who inhabit the British Isles in that great Archipelago, possess a large portion of my heart.'[31] After he had set up the Methodist Episcopal Church in America in 1784, Coke ordained the first two black Methodist preachers, Absolom Jones and Richard Allen.[32] He ordained another, William Black, at the Baltimore Conference in 1789 and asked him to superintend the mission in Nova Scotia, where more than 10,000 of the black Loyalists had settled following the American Revolution.[33] It was Black who appointed King to his first ministry in Preston, Nova Scotia, in 1791.[34]

It may have been that Coke's investment in King was simply an extension of his missionary activities. However, it should be kept in mind that his influence at Kingswood was deeply affected by the paranoid political environment of the late 1790s, both among the Arminian Methodists and in the broader context of British religious society. He had been busy establishing himself as Wesley's spiritual successor as *primus inter pares* in the Methodist conference since the founder's death in 1791. In order to shake off the reputation he had acquired as something of a dissenter following his establishment of the separatist Episcopal Church in America, Coke took an increasingly conservative approach as the 1790s went on. In terms of his stance on slavery, for example, this meant that he recommended evangelising unfree black people without directly agitating for their emancipation, even in the very early 1790s when abolitionism enjoyed broad support in Britain.[35] Moreover, rising pressure for separation from the Church of England from the lower ranks of the movement drew unwelcome attention from the Pitt administration, especially after 1794.[36] Coke's solution was to attempt to consolidate the power base of British Methodism within a more rigidly hierarchical structure, while simultaneously reasserting the Methodists' loyalty to the

---

[30] See Thomas Coke, *A Journal, of the Rev. Dr. Coke's Fourth Tour on the Continent of America* (London: G. Paramore, 1793).

[31] Thomas Coke, *To the Benevolent Subscribers*, 17.

[32] Wigger, *American Saint*, 244–248.

[33] Alan Gilbert, *Black Patriots and Loyalists: Fighting for Emancipation in the War for Independence* (Chicago, IL: University of Chicago Press, 2012), 208.

[34] King, 'Memoirs', 213.

[35] See, for example, Coke's mention of the 'necessity of the New Birth' at a sermon for enslaved people in Montego Bay in 1791. Thomas Coke, *A Continuation of the Rev. Dr. Coke's Third Tour through the West Indies* (London: G. Paramore, 1791), 5.

[36] Hempton, *Methodism and Politics*, 68–69.

Crown and the established Church. Relations with the Tory administration were helped by the association between Coke and Wilberforce, based on a mutually beneficial arrangement in which government scrutiny was allayed in exchange for renewed Methodist support for the abolition of the slave trade. Kingswood School's governing body, the Kingswood Committee, was central to Coke's plan to quash dissenting voices within the Methodist movement itself. Since these events came to their crisis during King's stay at the school (and during the composition of his 'Memoirs'), it is to this period that we must turn first.

The year of King's arrival at Kingswood, 1794, was a turbulent one for the Methodist movement, and consequently a difficult time for the school's management. The long-serving headmaster, Thomas McGeary, a personal friend of Wesley, resigned his position in 1794 because of a dispute over the administration of the sacrament at Kingswood chapel without the official sanction of Anglican authorities – one of Coke's key initiatives in the Methodist Conference.[37] His replacement, Andrew Mayer, an itinerant preacher who had worked the difficult Liverpool circuit the previous year, had no such reservations.[38] At the same time, Kingswood was becoming a considerable source of income – the connexion's Reading Room even borrowed £600 from the school's coffers in 1796.[39] The school was operating at maximum capacity, and in 1795 it closed its doors to all but the sons of Methodist preachers.[40] Even with this proviso in place, demand for places still outstripped supply, though the school was financially stable enough to make allowances for the sons of preachers who could not be accommodated onsite.[41] The demands of Kingswood as a lucrative institution competed for administrative attention with the superintendence of the boys' education. The Kingswood Committee decided that the school needed executive as well as academic direction. Thus the office of school governor was created, and filled by Bradford.[42] He was given a modest salary at the school of £6 per month, most likely indicating that the work at the school was part-time and could be undertaken alongside his normal itinerancy.[43] Like McGeary, Bradford had been a close personal companion of Wesley. Unlike McGeary,

---

[37] Ives, *Kingswood School*, 107–108.

[38] Anon., *Minutes of Several Conversations, between the Preachers Late in Connection, with the Rev. Mr. Wesley* (Bristol: W. Pine, 1794), 9.

[39] Anon., *An Extract of the Minutes of Several Conversations Held at Leeds, July 31, &c. 1797* (London: G. Whitfield, 1797), 41.

[40] Anon., *Extract of the Minutes . . . 1797*, 41.

[41] Anon., *Extract of the Minutes . . . 1797*, 40.

[42] Gary Best, *Continuity and Change: A History of Kingswood School, 1748–1998* (Bath: Kingswood School, 1998), 46–47.

[43] Kingswood School Archives, 'Account books for 1795', f. 12.

however, he was another proven ally, helping to push through Coke's plan for the administration of the sacrament. He had also sided with Coke during a row with George Whitehead over the publication of Wesley's official biography, co-signing a letter of disapproval addressed to Whitehead on 9 September 1791.[44] Kingswood's academic and administrative arms were now within the locus of Coke's influence.

Coke's influence over the increasingly important Kingswood School is significant to our study of King's writing because his manuscript letters show that he could not have produced his autobiography without a significant editing process. He himself acknowledged that he was 'well aware of my inability for such an undertaking, having only a slight acquaintance with the language in which I write'.[45] Certainly, he was put under pressure from without to write his 'Memoirs', complaining that it was 'by no means an agreeable task to write an account of my Life', but he had agreed because of 'the importunity of many respectable friends, whom I highly esteem'.[46] Moreover, King was at great pains to 'acknowledge the obligations I am under to Dr. Coke, Mr. Bradford and all the Preachers and people' in his narrative.[47] The special notice of Coke may have been in reference to his introducing him into Kingswood, although as a lay-preacher with a self-professed desire 'spreading the knowledge of Christianity' among 'my poor brethren in Africa', it would have been in King's own interests to maintain a positive relationship with the Superintendent for Foreign Missions.[48] But considering Bradford's comparatively minor presence in the academic affairs of Kingswood School, King's mention of him at the exclusion of any of the other masters may be significant. Although Bradford did occasionally interact with the boys at Kingswood, he did not teach any of the lessons, and his role was essentially administrative rather than academic. Bradford, having ministered to some black people during his time in Bristol, may have felt himself particularly well qualified to assist King in his studies in English, or even in the composition of his life story.[49]

Whoever had assisted him, once King had finished writing his 'Memoirs', he left Kingswood School and returned to London. The school paid for his transportation, and the record books show an invoice for £7. 14s. 6d.

---

[44] John Annesley Colet, *A Letter to the Rev. Thomas Coke LLD. and Mr. Henry Moore* (London: J. Luffman, 1792).
[45] King, 'Memoirs', 105.   [46] King, 'Memoirs', 105.   [47] King, 'Memoirs', 265.
[48] King, 'Memoirs', 261, 210.
[49] For the high proportion of free black people in Bristol during the 1790s, see Madge Dresser, *Slavery Obscured: The Social History of the Slave Trade in an English Provincial Port* (London: Continuum, 2001). For the historically high proportion of black Methodists, see Hempton, *Religion and Political Culture*, 158–159.

'for removal of Mr. Bradford, B. King' and several of the older boys 'to London with boxes' on 19 July 1796.[50] According to a letter to Clarkson on 16 January 1798, Thornton had promised King free passage back to Sierra Leone.[51] Yet King had underestimated how divisive popular politics had become since his visit to London two years previously, and in particular the potentially damaging effects of his personal association with the Clarkson brothers, who by this point were under intense scrutiny for their supposedly Jacobinal tendencies.[52] For his part, John Clarkson had no patience for the 'insistent evangelicalism' and profit-driven focus of Thornton's direction of the Company, and the two had clashed during Clarkson's stint as Governor of Sierra Leone between 1791 and 1792.[53] Thornton, a member of the Clapham sect and supporter of Pitt and Wilberforce, was evidently unimpressed by the news that King had visited Clarkson on his first visit to London, and reneged on his offer of free transportation. King called this to Clarkson's attention on his return to Sierra Leone: 'Do you know Dear Sir that Mr Thornton after promous me my passag if I wantd work And only because I came don the river to see you that time He desired Cappin Smith to charge 15 Ginny but Sir I regardeth not because I know I shall able to Pay them and I do ashoure it will only serve To attach my love more to you because I know it was only out of spite.'[54]

King may have been bending the truth slightly in this letter to Clarkson. He had other connections in Britain who were willing to help him financially. Through Bradford, Coke or the Kingswood Committee, the school was able to pay a significant amount toward his passage back to Sierra Leone, although they did need to hide the payment among some of the additional expenses so as not to arouse too much attention at the conference. Under the heading 'What Sons of Preachers, who were not admitted into Kingswood School, have an allowance for their education', in the school's annual financial report to the conference, ten pounds and ten shillings were allocated to 'Boston King, for his conveyance to Africa'.[55] While this is not the fifteen guineas that King specified as the asking price for his transport costs, £10. 10s (or 10 guineas) was a reasonable rate for the cost of a voyage to the West African coast. It is likely that Kingswood School covered the complete costs of King's travel

[50] Kingswood School Archives, 'Account books for 1796'.
[51] King, 'Boston King to John Clarkson, 16 January 1798', 55–56.
[52] See John Oldfield, *Transatlantic Abolitionism in the Age of Revolution: An International History of Anti-Slavery, c. 1787–1820* (Cambridge: Cambridge University Press, 2014), 108–109.
[53] Brogan, 'Clarkson, Thomas (1760–1846)'.
[54] King, 'Boston King to Thomas Clarkson, 16 January 1798', 55–56.
[55] Anon., *Extract of the Minutes . . . 1797*, 40.

and that the fifteen guineas he was initially quoted after his row with Thornton was an intentionally prohibitive price for such a journey. Another possibility, though impossible to prove or disprove, is that Coke requested the funds to be released as part of his planned mission to the Fula people in Sierra Leone, due to start late in 1796.[56] This plan proved itself to be unworkable at around the time King was in transit to Sierra Leone, so there is no way to tell if his journey was paid for through Coke's influence or for simple charitable reasons by Bradford.

From the moment King arrived in Britain, throughout his studies and the composition of his 'Memoirs', he was financially and socially dependent on a relatively small network of individuals within the Methodist connexion. His home and place of study were managed by a committee and governor, all of whom had a close political, professional or personal relationship to the man who took ultimate responsibility for King's career as a preacher and missionary in Africa. It is clear that he was aided in writing his 'Memoirs' while he was at the school, and the content of the narrative seems to suggest that he felt more indebted to Coke and Bradford than most. However, during his stay in Britain, political and personal differences divided even fellow abolitionists to the extent that the paternalist vision of evangelising in Africa was subordinated to partisan squabbling. When he fell afoul of such squabbles, King turned once again to his brethren in the Methodist movement – specifically, to Kingswood – for support. They were happy to oblige. Vincent Carretta has ascertained that King returned to Sierra Leone, worked as a schoolteacher briefly, and then travelled as a preacher to the Sherbro people, around a hundred miles south of Free Town, where he died in 1802.[57] Research carried out by Christopher Fyfe shows that he maintained contact with John Clarkson until at least 1798.[58] However, when King returned to Sierra Leone, he left his memoirs, in manuscript form, behind him.

Thomas Coke, William Wilberforce and the Publication of the 'Memoirs', 1796–1798

There is a gap in the history of the production of King's 'Memoirs', between the completion of the manuscript in 1796 and the publication of

---

[56] John Pritchard, 'Sierra Leone', in *DMBI*, available at http://wesleyhistoricalsociety .org.uk/dmbi/index.php?do=app.entry&id=2484.
[57] Carretta, 'Explanatory Notes', 368 n. 41.
[58] King, 'Boston King to Thomas Clarkson, 16 January 1798', in Fyfe (ed.), *Our Children Free and Happy*, 55–56.

the first section in the *Methodist Magazine* for March 1798. This cannot be accounted for by the publication process alone. Common difficulties in distributing a monthly periodical, which might have otherwise slowed the production process, were essentially circumvented by the ready-made readership, root-and-branch structure and the roving nature of the Methodist itinerancy.[59] The manuscript 'Memoirs' most likely either remained at Kingswood under Bradford's care or Coke arranged to have them sent to his friend and ally George Whitfield in London to be filed away.[60] What can be said with some certainty is that the publication dates, between March and July 1798, were specifically chosen by those involved in publishing it. To understand why, it is necessary to explore Methodist politics in the early 1790s in more detail.

Before 1794, when support for parliamentary reform was widespread, Coke had been trying to maintain the relationship between the state and the Methodist connexion. He was keen to demonstrate to the government, as well as his fellow clergymen, that his vision for the future of British Methodism was in keeping with Wesley's own. The fact that Wesley had evidently kept Coke close during the final years of his life granted this contention the appearance of legitimacy. Coke designated himself and his followers as the 'true' Wesleyan Methodists. His faction tended toward reconciling some of the more 'enthusiastic' evangelical characteristics of the movement with 'establishment' politics, particularly through their open denunciation of domestic political radicalism.[61] By reassuring Anglican authorities that they did not desire a break from the established church, Coke and his circle reaffirmed their reliability and the respectable nature of Methodism, aping Wesley's 'conservative tendencies'.[62] Indeed, during the first few years after Wesley's death, Coke began to style himself and his allies as 'the preachers late in connexion with the Rev. Mr. Wesley'.[63]

His main opposition within the Methodist movement came from Alexander Kilham. While the high regard for Wesley's memory common

[59] John Feather, *A History of British Publishing* (London: Croom Helm, 1988), 110.
[60] George Whitfield, not to be confused with the Calvinist minister George Whitefield, ran the Epworth Press, the official publishing house for the Methodist connexion.
[61] See, for example, Thomas Coke, *Four Discourses on the Duties of a Minister of the Gospel* (London: G. Whitfield, 1798), 1–19.
[62] Hempton, *Methodism and Politics in British Society*, 59.
[63] See, for example, Anon., *Vindex to Verax. Or, Remarks upon 'A Letter to the Rev. Thomas Coke, LL.D. and Mr. Henry Moore'* (London: J. Moore, 1792). Coke retained this appellation for his group well into the conservative period of the 1800s, even when the term 'Wesleyan Methodists' was in common parlance. See, for example, JRL, Methodist Collections, 1977/473, MAW Ms 326, 'Coke to Viscount Erskine, 1806'.

to all Methodists required him to pay lip-service to the founder's opinions on the matter, Kilham attempted to garner support for a formal separation from the Anglican Church months before Coke's Plan of Pacification was ratified in April 1795. Moreover, his nascent political radicalism manifested itself in his unerring support for more democratic government of the Methodist connexion, and particularly for the appointment of unordained lay-preachers to the annual conferences.[64] Yet, even in the early 1790s, Kilham's reformist sentiments did not take serious hold among mainstream Methodists, in part because of the continuing popularity of Wesley and his conservative habits.

In general, support for Kilham's plans within the connexion was muted. However, the sudden intensification of government suspicion of religious dissent prompted Coke and his circle to take action against him in 1795. It was always against the ordained preachers' interests to support Kilham's plans for more democratic representation at the conferences, but they were not galvanised into action against him until 'gentlemen of rank' in London made it known that Pitt's government was, as Hempton puts it, 'concerned about the constitutional loyalty of provincial preachers'. In particular, Wilberforce, keen to preserve evangelical diversity, 'delivered timely hints of government intentions to nervous London preachers', apprising them of the potential consequences if they allowed a politically radicalised element to grow within the connexion.[65] The solution was obvious. Kilham was brought before regional disciplinary court in 1795 and was formally expelled from the connexion in 1796.

Wilberforce's communication with prominent London preachers in 1795 (doubtless including Whitfield) opened a crucial dialogue between senior Methodists – primarily Coke – and the Tory government. Considering his background in missionary activity in the West Indies, and his support of free black people, Wilberforce must have seen Coke as a potential ally in his abolitionist campaign. For his part, Coke recognised the need to reassert the mainstream Methodists' allegiance to the crown and the government, particularly given Kilham's recent reformist agitation. A key outcome of this dialogue was that Coke drafted a letter of allegiance to the House of Hanover, in which he declared that the

[64] For evidence of Kilham's political radicalism, see his attack on 'Civis', an antiradical polemicist, in Alexander Kilham, *The Hypocrite Detected and Exposed; and the True Christian Vindicated and Supported* (Aberdeen: J. Chalmers, 1794). For Kilham's plan to restructure the Methodist church, see Alexander Kilham, *The Progress of Liberty, amongst the People Called Methodists. To Which Is Added, the Out-lines of a Constitution* (Alnwick: J. Catnach, 1795).
[65] Hempton, *Methodism and Politics*, 68–69.

monarchy would be sustained by a 'cloud of incense', meaning the prayers of Methodists.[66]

More importantly, perhaps, Coke and Bradburn's public denunciation of Kilham and his secessionist movement, the Methodist New Connexion (MNC), helped to allay some of the fears that Wilberforce had communicated. In truth, Coke's personal view of the situation in 1797 was of a connexion more politically divided than was actually the case. In a somewhat melodramatic letter to his fellow preacher Charles Atmore on 15 May 1797, he wrote, 'I pity you all exceedingly. You are in an awful state. The spirit of sedition stalks with Giant-like strides: and the professors of Christianity, yea of vital religion among you, are devouring each other. What will this come to?'[67] Yet this was not the official line. Publicly, Coke was keen to show that the expulsion of Kilham and his associates was 'a fatal blow to Methodist Jacobinism'.[68] Still, elements of the Tory government went unconvinced, and the Methodists were watched closely as potential radical sympathisers.

This was where Wilberforce became indispensable to Coke's circle. A close friend of Pitt, he was of course above suspicions of Jacobinism, and he was keen to support evangelicalism, particularly where it could be properly controlled through a formal connection to the Anglican Church. In addition, Wilberforce's support for the abolition of the slave trade could always be depended on and took precedence over other politically sensitive matters. For example, he organised a collection for Thomas Clarkson following his retirement from public life, despite the fact that the retirement came about largely because of suspicions over his 'enthusiasm for the French Revolution'.[69] It was probably because of Wesley's early support for abolition (see Chapter 4) that Wilberforce was well disposed toward Wesleyan Methodism, rather than any new personal regard for Coke or anyone else. Indeed, Wesley's last letter, written to Wilberforce in 1791, mentioned that he had read 'a tract wrote by a poor African', probably Cugoano or Equiano, and urged him to 'go on, in the name of God, & in the power of his might! Till even American slavery (the vilest that ever saw the sun) shall vanish away before it.'[70] Coke, of

---

[66] Hempton, *Methodism and Politics*, 68–69.

[67] JRL, Methodist Collections, 1977/489, 'Thomas Coke to Charles Atmore, 15th May 1797'.

[68] Hempton, *Methodism and Politics*, 69.

[69] John Oldfield, *Popular Politics and British Anti-Slavery: The Mobilisation of Public Opinion against the Slave Trade, 1787–1807* (Manchester: Manchester University Press, 1995), 80–81.

[70] JRL, Methodist Collections, 1977/609, 'John Wesley to William Wilberforce, February 26th 1791'.

all people, would have recognised the potential common ground between the political establishment (or at least one member of it) and his own circle within the Methodist connexion. Specifically, the conformity to Wesleyan ideals which he had been at such pains to demonstrate, as well as his long-standing commitment to the conversion of the enslaved, could have helped to strengthen relations between himself and Wilberforce. Coke knew also that Wilberforce and Wesley had bonded specifically on the issue of abolition and, in particular, that they were both supporters of black authors.

It was into this political and social environment that King's autobiography was published in the official Wesleyan *Methodist Magazine*. The renaming of the magazine from the *Arminian Magazine* in early 1798 was significant in that it represented an assumption of Coke's Wesleyan Methodism as the definitive incarnation of the movement, over and against Kilham's fledgling MNC. Whitfield was the printer and bookseller for the mainstream Methodists throughout the turbulent 1790s. He also edited and printed the *Arminian Magazine*, both before and after it changed its name. This means that Whitfield was the only named individual who definitely edited King's 'Memoirs' prior to their publication. One of his unofficial functions in the connexion was to act as Coke's agent in London when he was travelling in America. At the conference in 1796, for example, it was resolved that every preacher in the connexion should make a collection for Coke's missions, 'and let the money so collected, be deposited into the hands of Mr. Whitfield'.[71] Whitfield had also been a minor actor in Coke's public dispute with Whitehead in 1791 and was one of Coke and Bradford's co-signatories on a letter condemning Whitehead's behaviour. Coke's influence within the Methodists, therefore, clearly extended to the machinations of its publishing output during the period.

While the majority of the *Methodist Magazine*'s output was ostensibly depoliticised, it is fruitful to examine some of the ideologies at play in King's contribution. Eschewing the more outspoken denunciation of conditions on plantations that characterised, for example, Cugoano's work, the first part of King's narrative focused instead on his life as a Loyalist soldier during the American Revolution. To escape the cruelty of his American owner, King 'determined to go to Charles-town, and throw myself into the hands of the English. They received me readily, and I began to feel the happiness of liberty, of which I knew nothing before.'[72] The 'establishment' arm of the British abolitionist movement

[71] JRL, Methodist Collections, 1977/483, 'Papers relating to Dr. Coke'.
[72] King, 'Memoirs', 107.

had been making a virtue out of this particular necessity for quite some time, and in the long shadow of the French and Haitian Revolutions it was a timely reminder that abolitionism and loyalty to the British government were not mutually exclusive. While the connotations of the word 'liberty' had been associated with Painite political radicalism during the first half of the 1790s, there had been a concerted effort to reclaim it for counterrevolutionary purposes after 1794.[73] In the case of King's narrative, the binary was simple: British liberty or the tyranny – indeed the *slavery* – represented by revolutionary insurrectionism.

King's 'Memoirs' went on to show that his conduct in fighting for the British army was conspicuously meritorious. After foiling a defector's plot to steal horses, he managed to infiltrate American lines to raise support for the besieged forces at Nelson's Ferry.[74] This type of detail, in attesting simultaneously to King's unshakeable loyalty to the Crown and natural bravery, emphasised the continuing usefulness (both economic and political) of freed slaves at the same time as reinforcing their humanity and nobility. Equally important was the representation of the benefits arising from evangelising black people, something which both Wilberforce and Coke had long advocated. For example, when King was recaptured by the Americans and put back into slavery, his suffering was ameliorated only by the fact that 'many of the masters send their slaves to school at night so that they may learn to read the scriptures. This is a privilege indeed.'[75] However, King granted no concessions to the ameliorationist anti-abolition lobby who opposed Wilberforce's abolitionist bills in Parliament, and he was quick to point out that 'all these enjoyments could not satisfy me without liberty!'[76] Indeed, King's narrative fits best into the tradition of earlier evangelical black autobiography – particularly Gronniosaw's *Narrative* – in that the protagonist displays an almost supernatural affinity with Christian religiosity with little or no external influence. Whereas Gronniosaw's narrative was designed to construe the Calvinist message of predestination, King's conversion – the commencement of his quest for Christly perfection – was reliant on his corporeal freedom.

King's narrative struck a balance between sensitivity to the need for an economically and ethically workable alternative to the transatlantic slave trade and giving a forceful argument for its discontinuation. Some of the best-known black abolitionist writing published before 1798 had been associated with radical politics. Following the famous treason trials of

---

[73] Mark Philp, *Reforming Ideas in Britain: Politics and Language in the Shadow of the French Revolution, 1789–1815* (Cambridge: Cambridge University Press, 2013), 294.
[74] King, 'Memoirs', 108–110.   [75] King, 'Memoirs', 110.   [76] King, 'Memoirs', 110.

John Horne Tooke and Thomas Hardy in 1794, this association become deleterious for the British abolitionist movement. Even worse, the conservative establishment began to view the types of popular political activity that had hitherto characterised British abolitionism – particularly mass petitions and public meetings – as potentially insurrectionary and dangerous. The British government took the example of the revolution in Saint Domingue, with its scenes of shocking black-on-white violence, as one of the potential consequences of seditious meetings.[77] Meanwhile, poor relations between white directors and prominent black settlers in Sierra Leone were being communicated back to a British readership that was largely unsympathetic to the complaints of the black people there.[78] What was important for the publishers of the *Methodist Magazine* was that King's antislavery views did not stray into the category of 'radical' abolitionism.

Some British readers of King's 'Memoirs' may have been relieved, then, to hear that Methodism acted as a means by which a former slave became reconciled to his white peers.

[O]ne Sunday, while I was preaching at Snowsfield-Chapel, the Lord blessed me abundantly, and I found a more cordial love to the White People than I had ever experienced before. In the former part of my life I had suffered greatly from the cruelty and injustice of the Whites, which induced me to look upon them, in general, as our enemies: And even after the Lord had manifested his forgiving mercy to me, I still felt at times an uneasy distrust and shyness towards them; but on that day the Lord removed all my prejudices.[79]

This dispelled any image of the vengeful slave rising up in violence against his former master, effectively defusing what some saw as a potentially explosive association between evangelicalism and slave revolts. This passage explicated the central role that evangelicalism was supposed to play in the peaceful emancipation of the slave. King did not claim to have been self-emancipated, as was actually the case, but rather that his freedom came about as a manifestation of God's 'forgiving mercy'. The lines between evangelisation and emancipation were blurred – freedom of the spirit and freedom of the body became one and the same thing. This was the shared central tenet of both Wesley and Wilberforce's

---

[77] A recent discussion of conservative reactions to the Haitian Revolution can be found in Srividhya Swaminathan, *Debating the Slave Trade: Rhetoric of British National Identity* (Farnham: Ashgate, 2009), 28–29. See also David Brion Davis, 'Impact of the French and Haitian Revolutions', in David Geggus (ed.), *The Impact of the Haitian Revolution in the Atlantic World* (Columbia: University of South Carolina Press, 2001), 3–9.

[78] See, for example, Christopher Fyfe, *A History of Sierra Leone* (London: Longmans, 1962), 59–87.

[79] King, 'Memoirs', 264.

evangelical abolitionism. King's uncoupling of the concepts of personal emancipation and political abolitionism enabled him to denounce the slave trade without a whisper of support for the forms of popular protest which had linked the abolition movement to other forms of political unrest in the past.

The text's final word on abolition was both conciliatory and congratulatory to British abolitionists. 'I have great cause to be thankful that I came to England', it stated, 'for I am now fully convinced, that many of the White People, instead of being enemies and oppressors of us poor Blacks, are our friends, and deliverers from slavery, as far as their ability and circumstances will admit.'[80] The final part of this passage offered a proviso to the reconciliation of the Christian African to the Briton. It would certainly have been naive of King to imagine that there were no white proslavery advocates in British politics. Indeed, Wilberforce's defeated bills for abolition had already proved that there were. But the characterisation of British people, in canonical language, as the 'deliverers from slavery', echoed Wilberforce's own speeches given in the House of Commons, in which he encouraged his fellow Members of Parliament to 'withdraw from temptation' by 'diffusing our beneficence' in abolishing the Slave Trade.[81] King's 'Memoirs' represented an appropriately grateful and emphatically non-violent black voice in which the dividends of the virtuous economic self-denial represented by abolition were paid in the form of interracial harmony. The fact this text was published in the *Methodist Magazine* served as a reminder of the compatibility between Methodist abolitionism and political loyalism.

These protestations of loyalty echoed those expressed by Coke in some of his direct correspondence with Wilberforce. Indeed, in a letter written around the time of Kilham's secession from the Methodists, Coke had written to Wilberforce, outlining a formal 'plan in respect of the union between the Establishment and the Methodists'. Coke recognised that Wilberforce was keen to preserve the loyalty of the hugely popular Methodist movement from the potentially radicalised influence of the MNC, which was by this point beginning to gain ground among the working-class laity. After all, if certain Methodists became disillusioned with the Tory government, they may have broken ranks and joined with Kilham's more overtly reformist MNC. Such new democratic institutions were threatening for Pitt's government as well as the Anglican Church, since they drew popular allegiance away from both. 'I would just observe', wrote Coke, 'that division among us, would not at all serve

[80] King, 'Memoirs', 264.
[81] William Wilberforce, *The Speech of William Wilberforce Esq. ... on the Question of the Abolition of the Slave Trade* (London: Logographic Press, 1791), 49.

the establishment; for the present seceding parts are gathering large congregations.' Coke had yet to mention this plan to the Methodist conference, since he first needed to deal with opposition from within the Anglican Church. Coke perceived Wilberforce as a crucial ally if 'this probably last chance to save the Methodists to Church and state' was to succeed. However, his confidence in his own power within the connexion was telling. 'I am nearly certain, if the Dean [of Carlisle, who opposed the plan] knew the minds of the leading preachers members [sic] of the Conference as well as I do & my present influence among them, he would not think my plan impracticable as far as it respects us.'[82]

While it is clear from these letters that Coke's epistolary style had little in common with King's, the 'Memoirs' espoused a very similar political ideology to the one Coke was keen to demonstrate to Wilberforce. They also owed something of a stylistic debt to Coke's earlier published writing, as well as the earlier output of the *Methodist Magazine* edited by Whitfield. King's 'Memoirs' were, after all, written in the tradition of the Methodist spiritual conversion narrative. The fact that their subject was a black man was perhaps intended to convey the universality of the power of Methodist spiritual enlightenment, but the timing of their publication suggests that more pragmatic motivations were at work.

Coke himself was no stranger to the spiritual conversion format, having written and published two biographies of converted sinners during the 1790s. In *A Sermon ... on the Death of the Rev. John Richardson*, he demonstrated his famously vehement preaching style, sharply contrasting the everlasting fate of the righteous with that of the atheist:

Behold the placid countenance of the dying saint! See the crowns of glory and the palms of victory! Smiling angels minister unto him, and long to tune their golden harps, and shout him welcome to the skies! ... Behold the miserable wretch, that is dying without an interest in Christ! Does he look upward, the wrath of Christ lowers down upon him. Does he look downward? Tophet opens to receive him. Does he look within? Mountains of guilt separate him from the only Being that can reverse his doom. Does he look around him? Devils await to lead him to their own habitation. Such as they have themselves, they will give to him.[83]

The hectoring evangelical style in this passage is a sample of the kind of preaching Coke perceived to be vital to the continuing expansion of Methodism. In 1798, he exhorted his fellow preachers to do the same:

[82] Huntingdon Library, California, Letters of William Wilberforce, 'Thomas Coke to William Wilberforce, n.d.', vol. 17, f. 129.
[83] Thomas Coke, *A Sermon Preached at the New Chapel, in the City-Road, London, Feb. 19, 1792, on the Death of the Rev. John Richardson, A.B* (London: G. Paramore, 1792), 10–11.

It is my desire, above all things, that you my brethren, and myself should, in the highest spiritual sense, be FLAMES OF FIRE: then ... all opposition would fall before us; and we should, with our evangelical brethren of other parties, become principal instruments of bringing all mankind to the unity of the knowledge of the son of God.[84]

Aside from Coke's apparent subordination of sectarian interests to the more important objective of Christian evangelicalism (something he was keen to demonstrate that he shared in common with Wilberforce), this passage represented a direct instruction to his fellow Methodist preachers (whose membership included King) regarding their mode of delivering the gospel.

An instance of such 'flaming' evangelicalism could be seen in King's 'Memoirs', in the passage where he attempts to have the African 'pagans' send their children to his Christian school in Sierra Leone. It shared an apocalyptic tone with Coke's funeral sermon for the Rev. John Richardson, particularly in the way it drew a contrast between the fates of the righteous and the atheists:

[I]f you will obey [God's] commandments he will make you happy in this world, and in that which is to come; where you will live with him in heaven; – and all pain and wretchedness will be at an end; – and you shall enjoy peace without bitterness, and happiness for all eternity ... He likewise gives you an opportunity of having your children instructed in the Christian Religion. But if you neglect to send them, you must be answerable to GOD for it.[85]

It is conceivable that King had based his own preaching style on Coke's. However, it is important to remember that King's 'Memoirs' were intended as a demonstrative account, to be held up as an example for other Methodists, and that Coke likely had a hand in their composition. Moreover, this method of preaching was shown in the 'Memoirs' to be extraordinarily effective for King, quintupling his African scholars of Christianity from four to twenty in the space of a few days.[86] This gave additional gravity to the exhortation Coke had published for Methodist preachers to be 'FLAMES OF FIRE' during the same year and simultaneously attested to the effectiveness of missionary activity being carried out in association with the Sierra Leone company. With this in mind, it is worth pointing out here that Wilberforce was a member of the board of directors of the Sierra Leone company at the time the 'Memoirs' were published.

---

[84] Coke, *Four Discourses*, iv.   [85] King, 'Memoirs', 263.   [86] King, 'Memoirs', 263.

Structurally, the 'Memoirs' have much in common with another of Coke's biographical accounts. The sermon he delivered at the funeral of Mrs. Hester Ann Rogers at Spitalfields on 26 October 1794 celebrates Rogers's pious life but emphasises the role of her conversion to Methodism in the creation of her godly character. Considering that the primary focus of both the sermon and the 'Memoirs' is the spiritual conversion of the subject, it is worth examining the points of congruence between the two, especially since the experiences of the black slave-born King and the white middling-class Rogers differed so widely in every other respect.

Following the death of their respective fathers during their childhoods, both King and Rogers described dreams or nightmares about the wrath of God being visited upon them, and for both this marked the beginning of their journey of religious enlightenment.[87] They both next experienced deep feelings of guilt or inadequacy during a religious sermon, King identifying himself as a 'miserable wretched sinner' and Rogers considering herself as 'a lost, perishing sinner'.[88] After a long period of self-doubt, both found comfort in Methodism and became finally confirmed in their belief. Both subsequently began to guide others toward God, though unlike King, Rogers 'never indeed assumed the authority of teaching in the church'.[89] What is remarkable (and unusual) in both of these narratives is that as the commitment of the subjects to their newfound religion increased, so too did their sense of inadequacy and resolve to turn from sin.

Of course, the notion of Christly perfection was always a central tenet of Wesleyan Methodism and was to be expected in any Methodist conversion narrative. But the narrative structure of Rogers's conversion story was closely echoed in King's 'Memoirs'. The 'evangelical' element of his text – that is, the element extolling the virtues of Methodism – had much in common, in terms of both content and form, with other conversion narratives written by Coke. It is possible that King was keenly following the published output of Coke during the composition of the 'Memoirs' and attempting to emulate his style. However, it is more likely that Coke, who was politically invested in the way that Methodism was represented in the text, had some hand in the composition of the sections of the narrative dealing with spiritual conversion.

---

[87] King, 'Memoirs', 106; Thomas Coke, *A Funeral Sermon Preached in Spitalfields-Chapel, London on Sunday Oct 26, 1794 on the Death of Mrs. Hester Ann Rogers* (Birmingham: J. Belcher, 1795), 15.
[88] King, 'Memoirs', 158; Coke, *A Funeral Sermon*, 16.   [89] Coke, *A Funeral Sermon*, 32.

Boston King's 'Memoirs' were written at the end of a period of widespread popular support for both reform of British Parliament and the abolition of the slave trade, but they were published during a time when oppressive government measures had, to some extent, muted both. His friends among the Methodists, on whom he financially relied while he was in Britain, all shared a formalised, hierarchical vision for the future of the connexion. Led in the conference by Thomas Coke, key figures such as Thomas Pawson, Alexander Mather and Joseph Bradford managed to minimise secessions from the connexion without budging on the issue of separation from the Church of England. These figures were also directly involved in the management of Kingswood School, where King wrote his 'Memoirs'. Coke's close friend George Whitfield ran the Epworth Press, the publishing house that produced the magazine in which King's memoirs was published. Coke himself had written more than one spiritual conversion narrative during the 1790s, and the similarities between these and King's 'Memoirs' suggest an authorial or editorial connection.

A close reading of King's narrative shows it to espouse precisely the political opinions, relating to both loyalty to the Crown and abolitionism, with which Coke and his circle were most keen to publicly associate. The most obvious explanation for this is that King's political and doctrinal stance was influenced by Coke and his circle during his time in Britain. However, King had left Britain by the time issues surrounding separation from the Anglican Church and suggestions of political radicalism within the Methodist connexion became critical for Coke to address. Indeed, the view expressed in the 'Memoirs', that the freeing of slaves was a matter for the attention of the evangelical elite, was at odds with King's own act of self-emancipation. Nevertheless, the illustrative message of King's story – that emancipated slaves would remain loyal to the British state when its sovereignty was under question – was a political view welcomed by Coke's correspondent Wilberforce.

It is clear from the verifiability of the content of the 'Memoirs', such as the specificity of the shipping dates, that King himself originally composed his story. However, given his financial dependence on the elite in charge of Kingswood School, as well as his own limited literacy, it seems likely that he was assisted in writing it and that his assistant held a particular view on the management of the Methodist connexion at large which they hoped to further. When King left Britain in 1796, he left his 'Memoirs' in the hands of the same social network which had financially supported him at Kingswood. Their appearance in 1798 coincided with a point of crisis in relations between Methodism and the British state. A reading of their religious and political ideologies finds them to express precisely the same views of conversion and abolition which Wilberforce and Coke held in common. Either Boston King was remarkably prescient in his understanding of the political climate of a country he visited only once or his narrative went through a process of edition and revision by those who stood to gain from so doing. Whatever the cause, it is clear that King's 'Memoirs' formed an important part of a dialogue intended to attest to the compatibility of Wesleyan Methodism and political loyalty to the Crown in the wake of the extensive religious and political disunity that characterised the early 1790s.

King had always operated well within the 'mainstream' of the Methodist
movement in Britain and as a result had been rather dependent on a
relatively small network of individuals centred on Coke. However, as
demonstrated by the Alexander Kilham controversy, a number of rup-
tures were beginning to make themselves felt throughout the connexion.
A substantial element wanted to break away and form their own movements, ones that were more representative of their local memberships,
more closely linked with the democratic and radical societies emerging
in provincial centres around the country. Indeed, from the turn of the
nineteenth century, Methodist politics – along with the character of
Methodist evangelism in general – were increasingly differentiated by
concerns at the regional, rather than national, level. By the time King left
for Sierra Leone in 1796, these fractures were already making themselves
manifest. Five years later, another black Methodist arrived in Britain to
preach against slavery and spread the gospel. He instantly recognised that
these were profoundly local questions.

John Jea 'was born in the town of Old Callabar, in Africa, in the year
1773'. He was enslaved at the age of two along with his family and sold
into slavery in New York.[1] By around 1790 he had emancipated himself
and became an itinerant Methodist preacher. A true 'citizen of the world',
over the next three decades he travelled and preached in various parts of
the British Isles, the United States, the West Indies and Argentina, as
well as a short stay in the port of 'Venneleia, in the East Indies'.[2] His
autobiography, *The Life, History and Unparalleled Sufferings of John Jea,
the African Preacher*, was written between June 1815 and October 1816,

---

[1] John Jea, *The Life, History and Unparalleled Sufferings of John Jea, the African Preacher*
(Portsea: John Williams, [1815/16]), 3. For the role of Old Calabar in the slave trade of
the early 1770s, see Randy Sparks, *The Two Princes of Calabar: An Eighteenth-Century
Atlantic Odyssey* (Cambridge, MA: Harvard University Press, 2004), 33–69.
[2] Jea, *Life*, 78.

in Portsea, a working-class town very near to Portsmouth.[3] In 1816 he also selected and compiled *A Collection of Hymns*, some of which were of his own composition, from the same location.[4] Little is known about Jea's movements after these two publications, but he was still travelling at least as late as October 1817, when he was to be found preaching on the Grand Parade in St. Helier on the island of Jersey.[5] This chapter focuses on Jea's experiences in Britain, specifically during his visits to the two port cities of Liverpool and Portsmouth and their hinterlands, between 1801 and 1817. It examines the effect of local social and political concerns, specifically those related to the primary subjects of Jea's writing: the slave trade and Methodist theology.

The differing demographics, political environments and perceived spiritual needs of Liverpool, Portsmouth and Jersey coalesced with their developing relationships to the transatlantic slave trade to produce unique political environments and congregational needs. Jea's texts and sermons, in attending to these needs, were not uncomplicatedly representative of his own opinion of slavery and antislavery. By using specific local contexts to reconstruct Jea's experiences in these settings, we can reread the *Life* for evidence of competing interests, particularly with regard to local evangelical and pro- and antislavery attitudes. Equally, by highlighting these differences, we can begin to get a sense of the changing range of experiences – economic, social and spiritual – available to black people in non-metropolitan Britain across the crucial two decades framing the abolition of the slave trade.

Jea visited Lancashire twice: once in 1801–1802 and again around 1804–1805. During this period, Liverpool's involvement in the transatlantic slave trade generated employment for many of his working-class parishioners.[6] At the same time, secessionism began to unsettle Wesleyan

---

[3] 'between June 1815 and October 1816': Jea described coming to Portsmouth from being held as a prisoner of war in France when 'peace was proclaimed between France and Great Britain', presumably after the Battle of Waterloo in June 1815 but before the Second Treaty of Paris in October 1815. He mentions that his third wife, Mary, was 'well' at the time of the text's publication, but he married a fourth time in October 1816. Therefore the text was almost certainly in print before this date. Jea, *Life*, 92, 95; *Hampshire Telegraph*, 28 October 1816, 3. Jea also felt compelled to publish a short vindication of his autobiography, though as I became aware of it shortly before publication, this pamphlet has not been discussed here. John Jea, *An Explanation of that part of The Life and Unparalleled Sufferings of the Reverend John Jea ... Respecting his Learning to Read: Intended to Convince Those who Disbelieve it* (Portsea, J. Williams, [1816]).

[4] John Jea (ed.), *A Collection of Hymns* (Portsea: James Williams, 1816).

[5] *La Chronique de Jersey*, 4 October 1817, 2.

[6] Jane Longmore has suggested that approximately one in eight Liverpool families were dependent on the slave trade by 1801. Jane Longmore, '"Cemented by the Blood of

Methodists in the large manufacturing towns of the region. On the other hand, when Jea came to Portsmouth in 1815, the town served as a key administrative centre and home port for the Royal Navy's role in the suppression of the slave trade.[7] Here, Wesleyan Methodism was relatively (though not completely) untroubled by the new secessionist groups gaining popularity across the north of England. Congregations in Hampshire in 1816, by and large, felt differently about the slave trade and Methodism from those in Lancashire in 1801. Jea emphasised different elements of his Methodist-antislavery ideology according to what he perceived were the needs of local Wesleyan networks and working-class congregations in each of these locations.

This 'local' focus raises a number of methodological challenges for the historian. The local historiographies of these regions, understandably, tend to focus on the historical events and contexts which are perceived to have impacted most significantly on the social, political and cultural makeup of their given areas. Numerous accounts of Liverpool's relationship with the slave trade exist, for example, with several more published since the 2007 bicentenary of the passing of the Abolition of the Slave Trade Act.[8] This has coincided with a greater (though still not great) degree of scholarly attention being paid to the history of the city's black community.[9] The historiography of Portsmouth and Portsea, on the other hand, largely focuses on its naval heritage.[10] Little has been said of local attitudes to suppression of the slave trade, and still less about

a Negro"? The Impact of the Slave Trade on Eighteenth-Century Liverpool', in Richardson, Schwarz and Tibbles (eds.), *Liverpool and Transatlantic Slavery*, 243.

[7] See, for example, Anon., *Steel's Original and Correct List of the Royal Navy and Hon. East-India Company's Shipping* (London: Steel and Co., 1814); Anon., *The Navy List: Corrected to the End of June, 1818* ([London], John Murray, 1818), 54, 65; National Royal Navy Museum, Portsmouth, Admiralty Library, Selected Parliamentary Papers for 1818, 'Return of all Vessels Engaged in the Slave Trade', ff. 59–61.

[8] See, for example, Katie Donington, Ryan Hanley and Jessica Moody (eds.), *Britain's History and Memory of Transatlantic Slavery: Local Nuances of a 'National Sin'* (Liverpool: Liverpool University Press, 2016); Franca Dellarosa, *Talking Revolution: Edward Rushton's Rebellious Poetics, 1782–1814* (Liverpool: Liverpool University Press, 2014); Arline Wilson, *William Roscoe: Commerce and Culture* (Liverpool: Liverpool University Press, 2008); Hugh Crow, *The Memoirs of Captain Hugh Crow: The Life and Times of a Slave Trade Captain*, ed. John Pinfold (Oxford: Bodleian Library, 2007); David Richardson, Suzanne Schwarz and Anthony Tibbles (eds.), *Liverpool and Transatlantic Slavery* (Liverpool: Liverpool University Press, 2007); Gail Cameron, *Liverpool: Capital of the Slave Trade* (Liverpool: Picton Press, 1992); Roger Anstey and E. H. Hair (eds.), *Liverpool, the African Slave Trade, and Abolition: Essays to Illustrate Current Knowledge and Research* (Liverpool: Historic Society of Lancashire and Cheshire, 1976).

[9] See, for example, Ray Costello, *Black Liverpool: The Early History of Britain's Oldest Black Community, 1730–1918* (Liverpool: Picton, 2001).

[10] See John Field, *Portsmouth Dockyard and Its Workers 1815–1875* (Portsmouth: Portsmouth City Council, 1994); J. G. Coad, *The Portsmouth Block Mills: Bentham,*

the history of the local black community.[11] Meanwhile, despite David Hempton's call for more localised studies of British Methodism, no significant contributions have been made in the study of Methodist networks in either Lancashire or Hampshire since John Vickers' PhD thesis on central southern England in 1986.[12] There is also a noticeable lack of modern Anglophone scholarly historiography of any focus taking Jersey as its primary subject matter.[13] As such, parts of this chapter draw on nineteenth-century local histories, which tended to give greater attention to the task of constructing prosopographies of ecclesiastical and evangelical movements than those published more recently.

The difficulties posed by the comparative paucity of historiography are compounded by a lack of clarity in the primary texts over the processes of authorship. The *Hymns*, for example, were accompanied by a preface in which Jea set out his motivation (being 'importuned by a number of respectable and religious friends'), and to some extent the means by which he selected the hymns, but did not explicate who had written each one.[14] Similarly, like most of the autobiography in this study, the *Life* contained a caveat regarding the author's literacy. 'My dear reader, I would now inform you,' the final page of text read,

that I have stated this in the best manner I am able, for I cannot write, therefore it is not quite so correct as if I had been able to have written it myself; not being able to notice the time and date when I left several places, in my travels from time to time, as many do when they are travelling; nor would I allow alterations to be made by the person whom I employed to print this Narrative.[15]

Brunel and the Start of the Royal Navy's Industrial Revolution (Swindon: English Heritage, 2005).

[11] Some of these aspects of Portsmouth's past are mentioned in James Thomas, *Portsmouth and the East India Company in the Eighteenth Century* (Portsmouth: Portsmouth City Council, 1993); James Thomas, *The Seaborne Trade of Portsmouth, 1650–1800* (Portsmouth: Portsmouth City Council, 1984).

[12] W. Donald Cooper, *Methodism in Portsmouth, 1750–1932* (Portsmouth: Portsmouth City Council, 1973); D. A. Gowland., *Methodist Secessions: The Origins of Free Methodism in Three Lancashire Towns: Manchester, Rochdale, Liverpool* (Manchester: Chetham Society, 1979); John Vickers, 'Methodism and Society in Central Southern England 1740–1851', PhD thesis, University of Southampton (1986).

[13] A rare Anglophone counterexample is Godfrey Le Quesne, *Jersey and Whitehall in the Mid-Nineteenth Century* (St. Helier: Société Jersiaise, 1992). A classic local history of Jersey is George Balleine, *A History of the Island of Jersey from the Cave Men to the German Occupation and After* (London: Staples Press, 1950).

[14] Those referred to in this chapter as being written by Jea are those identified as such by Graham Russell Hodges in his edited collection of Jea's works. Page numbers in citations of Jea's *Hymns* refer to the original 1816 edition. Hymns not identified by Hodges as being written by Jea are listed as 'Anon.' Graham Russell Hodges (ed.), *Black Itinerants of the Gospel: The Narratives of John Jea and George White* (London: Palgrave, 2002), 165–178.

[15] Jea, *Life*, 95.

This statement presented a contradiction: Jea could not write, yet he claimed authority over the means of the text's transmission from spoken testimony to printed artefact. Jea relegated his publisher to a mere employee – and elided his amanuensis altogether – with deceptive off-handedness. In fact, no other black devotional autobiography had yet been published in Britain with such a direct statement of editorial control. Yet such control was circumscribed, quite literally, by the invisible influence of the amanuensis. Unlike Gronniosaw and King, Jea was able to oversee the production and distribution of his autobiography and thereby claim a degree of personal authenticity or immediacy in the text. Yet, like his evangelical predecessors, his inability to write it down for himself required his words to be represented, at some stage, by an outside party.

Jea's refusal of editorial alterations demands a very specific methodology in the recovery of his movements. Anecdotal asides, such as his childhood memory of 'a day of fasting, prayer and thanksgiving ... commanded by General Washington', allow a fairly accurate chronology of events to be constructed and used as a framework in which to understand the text.[16] In this case, Jea was alluding to the day of national humiliation ordered by Congress on 6 May 1779, during which 'all recreations and unnecessary labour' were strictly forbidden, though Jea and his family were still forced to work.[17] However, the processes of dictation and transcription, subject to two separate processes of interpretation, render the reconstruction of other details more difficult. Nowhere in the *Life* is this more evident than in the relation of events occurring in Lancashire. Since Jea's amanuensis was from (or at least *in*) Portsmouth, these sections had been through a *triple* process of inflection. When Jea heard any proper noun during his time in Lancashire, it was usually enunciated in a Lancashire accent. Since he could not write, he then verbally related this word as he remembered hearing it (i.e. in Lancashire dialect) in his own New England accent, to his Portsmouth amanuensis. The amanuensis then wrote the noun down as well as they were able, using their own cultural knowledge to correct the text where they could.

For example, the *Life* stated that Jea travelled to 'Baudley Mores, about fourteen miles from Liverpool' in 1801, where he met with 'Mr. Cooper' and 'Christopher Hooper'.[18] Here the influence of a Lancashire dialect

---

[16] Jea, *Life*, 7.

[17] George Washington, *The Writings of George Washington*, ed. John Fitzpatrick (Washington, DC: United States Government Printing Office, 1936), vol. xiv, 369.

[18] Jea, *Life*, 57.

was palpable in the translation of 'Bolton-le-Moors' into 'Baudley Mores', while Jea's referral to Wesleyan Methodist preacher Christopher Hopper as 'Hooper' might be evidence of misread handwriting, mishearing or simple misremembering. A certain amount of logical deduction is therefore required to reconstruct the contexts to which Jea alluded in his text. In this case, a keyword search for 'Cooper' and 'Hooper' in the *Methodist Magazine* produced a funeral sermon for Hopper given by Thomas Cooper in 1802, which mentioned that Hopper, an eminent preacher credited with leading Methodist evangelism in the newly industrialised north-west of England during John Wesley's premiership, was living in Bolton at the time Jea was in the area.[19] A consultation of the placements of the Methodist preachers, detailed annually in the same publication, confirmed that Cooper was also on the Bolton circuit during that time.[20] Using these methods, it is possible to deduce Jea's itinerary in Britain with a reasonable degree of accuracy. Hereafter, such deductions have been explicated in the notes.

Lancashire, 1801–1805

According to the *Life*, Jea converted to Thomas Coke and Francis Asbury's Methodist Episcopal Church around 1790, was baptised and subsequently absconded from slavery.[21] When his former owner tried to have him re-enslaved, he demonstrated his knowledge of the Gospel to the New York magistrates, who consequently told him that he was 'at liberty to leave'.[22] Jea's experience was unusual; while a law abolishing the importing and exporting of slaves was passed in New York in 1788, the same act, in David Gellman's words, 'confirm[ed] the long-established legal principle that Christian baptism did not change a slave's status' and 'highly restricted use of slave testimony' in emancipation proceedings.[23] Jea's assertion that

[i]t was a law of the state of the city of New York, that if any slave could give a satisfactory account of what he knew of the work of the Lord on his soul he was free from slavery, by the Act of Congress, that was governed by the good people the Quakers, who were made the happy instruments, in the hands of God, of releasing some thousands of us poor black slaves from the galling chains of slavery

---

[19] *Methodist Magazine*, 25 (1802), 395–402; *Methodist Magazine*, 26 (1803), 389–397, 456–465; Thomas Jackson, *The Lives of the Early Methodist Preachers* (London: William Nichols, 1865), vol. 1, 179–240.
[20] *Methodist Magazine*, 25 (1802), 395–402.   [21] Jea, *Life*, 32   [22] Jea, *Life*, 33.
[23] David Gellman, *Emancipating New York: The Politics of Slavery and Freedom, 1777–1827* (Baton Rouge: Louisiana State University Press, 2006), 68.

was therefore entirely erroneous.[24] It is far more likely that Jea absconded. This would explain why, apparently apropos of nothing, 'it pleased God to put it into [Jea's] mind to cross the Atlantic main' and come to Britain, where the Mansfield ruling of 1772 ensured that he could not be forcibly deported back to slavery.[25] His decision to misinform his readership about this technically illegal escape stemmed, like the publication of his autobiography, from a desire to link evangelical Christianity with personal and spiritual freedom.

The emancipating power of the church remained with Jea for the rest of his life. When he eventually recrossed the Atlantic, arriving in Liverpool aboard the *Superb* on 25 June 1801, his first concern was to enquire 'for the people that were followers of the Lord Jesus Christ, seeing that the place was large and populous, I believed in my heart, that God had a people there'.[26] His intuition proved correct. The Liverpool Wesleyan circuit was the second largest in the Chester district after Manchester and served as an administrative hub for local connexional affairs. Among other factors, the above-average proportion of committed Roman Catholics (many of them Irish immigrants) in Liverpool produced a tough environment for an expansionist church such as Wesleyan Methodism, which was steadily reconciling itself to the approach and character of the Anglican Church.[27] The working-class community (around 25 per cent of the total population) was transient in Liverpool, as it was comprised chiefly of casual dock workers and sailors.[28] This prevented the Wesleyans from establishing and maintaining large and committed working-class congregations of the sort seen in Lancashire's manufacturing towns, such as Manchester and Bolton, at around the same time.[29] The Wesleyan conference's response was simple: they sent more preachers to Liverpool than any other nearby circuit and stationed both district superintendents Adam Clarke and James Wood there to oversee operations.[30] Jea's offer to preach 'unto the people in Liverpool' the key Methodist tenets of

---

[24] Jea, *Life*, 39.   [25] Jea, *Life*, 49.

[26] Jea, *Life*, 49, 54–55; *Lancaster Gazetteer*, 27 June 1801, 3; Jea rendered the Captain's name 'Able Stovey' – the *Superb* only docked in Liverpool once prior to 1807, when Jea was in South America. The captain's name was Abel Storey.

[27] John Belchem has estimated that the number of Irish Catholics in Liverpool in 1800 was 4,950, or about 10 per cent of the total population. John Belcham, *Irish, Catholic and Scouse: The History of the Liverpool-Irish* (Liverpool: Liverpool University Press, 2007), 7; David Hemption, *Methodism: Empire of the Spirit* (New Haven, CT: Yale University Press, 2005), 188.

[28] John Langton and Paul Laxton, 'Parish Registers and Urban Structure: The Example of Late-Eighteenth Century Liverpool', *Urban History*, 5 (1978), 80.

[29] Hempton, *Empire of the Spirit*, 90, 104.

[30] *Methodist Magazine*, 24 (1801), 562; *Methodist Magazine*, 25 (1802), 478.

'faith, repentance, and remission of sin by Jesus Christ' would have been welcomed by Clarke and Wood.[31]

Jea's sermons proved popular locally, and 'the report of [his] preaching and exhorting spread all through Liverpool, and in the country'.[32] While for reasons to be discussed shortly he was careful to avoid denouncing the slave trade too rigorously during his time in Liverpool, his experiences as both a slave and sailor tethered his old-fashioned revivalist theology to concrete experiences shared by many among his congregation. He spoke with a tendency toward sensationalism when describing miraculous occurrences, in a style reminiscent of the 'flaming evangelicalism' Coke was so keen to encourage in the Methodist Episcopal itinerants then travelling between plantations in North America. In other words, Jea brought something of the spiritual experience of the plantations to the very heart of Britain's slave-trading infrastructure.[33]

Since the secession of the MNC in 1796, the Wesleyans in Britain had become increasingly authoritarian and loyalist, losing some of their appeal to (especially radicalised) working-class laymen in the process. Hempton suggests that 'Methodism became more centralised, more bureaucratic, more clerical and more respectable' and thus 'less attractive to the increasingly class-conscious proletariat' during the course of the nineteenth century, but the Wesleyans' focus was already shifting away from working-class populism by 1801.[34] The emergence of many secessionist groups during the first decade of the nineteenth century, all of whom emphasised expansion into working-class communities, attests to widespread dissatisfaction with the Wesleyans' lurch toward 'respectability'. The solidifying of hierarchical structures and reiteration of loyalty to the state church under Coke's influence (see Chapter 5) saw a greater dependence on ordained ministers at the expense of lay preachers like Jea. In Liverpool, the Kilham controversy had already led to the establishment of a small MNC circuit, but it floundered after 1797.[35] The town was seen as such a difficult place to preach in the first years of the nineteenth century that the Wesleyan Conference stationed exclusively senior preachers there.[36] Jea's low-status credentials,

---

[31] Jea, *Life*, 56.   [32] Jea, *Life*, 56.
[33] For a detailed reading of Jea's spectacular evangelicalism, see Ryan Hanley, '"There to Sing the Song of Moses": John Jea's Methodism and Working-Class Attitudes to Slavery in Liverpool and Portsmouth, 1801–1817', in Donington, Hanley and Moody (eds.), *Britain's History and Memory of Transatlantic Slavery*, 39–59.
[34] David Hempton, *The Religion of the People: Methodism and Popular Religion, 1750–1900* (London: Routledge, 1996), 17.
[35] See Gowland, *Methodist Secessions*, 20–21.
[36] *Methodist Magazine*, 24 (1801), 562; *Methodist Magazine*, 25 (1802), 478.

sensationalist narratives and revivalist zeal, in truth suited better to the new secessionist groups including the MNC, actually addressed a deficiency in the local Wesleyan circuit.

For similar reasons, Jea held a unique appeal for the growing black community of Liverpool, which was, proportional to the total local population, the largest in Britain outside London. The actual *size* of this population should not be overstated, however. The total number of black people in Liverpool in 1801 was around 500, or 1.5–2 per cent of the population, and this figure is inflated by the fluctuating numbers of Asian 'Lascar' sailors recorded simply as 'black'.[37] Nevertheless, a significant number of former slaves and their children had settled in the town, particularly Loyalist soldiers who were freed by British forces during the American Revolution.[38] Jea's appeal to these former slaves went beyond shared skin colour or even shared experiences of slavery. His experience and training as a preacher had tailored his repertoire and style to the needs and spiritual desires of enslaved and formerly enslaved people. Jea lamented the practice of denying slaves spirituality in his hymn 'Confession':

> When we were carried 'cross the main
> to great America
> There we were sold, and then were told
> That we had not a soul.[39]

The Methodist Episcopal emphasis on miraculous rebirth and reinvention of the spiritual self, inherited from older, Wesley-era British Arminianism, appealed to people whose enslavement was supposedly justified by their erstwhile spiritual wretchedness. Even while the mainstream Wesleyan Methodist movement in Britain increasingly distanced itself from revivalist 'enthusiasm' in pursuit of greater state approval, across the Atlantic the Episcopal Church was at the forefront of the evangelical 'Second Great Awakening'. Revivalist elements of Methodist Episcopal sermons were especially popular with black churchgoers, and when the African Methodist Episcopal Church was established in America in 1816 to cater specifically to black congregations, greater emphasis was placed on revivalism.[40] While Jea was trained in the Methodist Episcopal tradition prior to the African Methodist Episcopal secession,

---

[37] Norma Myers, *Reconstructing the Black Past: Blacks in Britain, 1780–1830* (London: Routledge, 1996), 22.

[38] See Myers, *Reconstructing the Black Past*, 73–74.

[39] John Jea, 'Confession', in Jea (ed.), *Hymns*, 202–203.

[40] See James Campbell, *Songs of Zion: The African Methodist Episcopal Church in the United States and South Africa* (Oxford: Oxford University Press, 1995), 3–31.

he was used to preaching to majority-black congregations comprised largely of slaves, former slaves and their immediate descendants. He understood how to effectively deploy the imagery of slavery in his sermons.

The language of slavery, emancipation and rebirth peppered Jea's sermons at Liverpool. He recounted a number of them in the *Life*. For example, he presented an anecdote about a crew-mate being struck by lightning after talking blasphemously with a commentary from Psalm 107: 'He brought them out of darkness and the shadow of death, and brake their bands in sunder.'[41] Other sermons frequently made use of the story of Moses, who led his people out of slavery.[42] Yet the sermons Jea delivered in Liverpool, for all their antislavery evocations, did not amount to abolitionist agitation. True to the early Methodist heritage, they emphasised forgiveness, stoicism and the universality of salvation over direct action and self-emancipation of the sort that Jea himself had achieved. 'I could not forget', he preached to a Liverpool congregation in 1805, 'God's promises to his people if they were obedient, that he would send blessings upon them,' before quoting some thirty-one verses from Leviticus detailing the apocalyptic consequences of disobedience to the Lord.[43]

This reluctance to preach the virtues of abolitionism and self-emancipation did not only reflect Jea's faith. The concentration of wealth from the slave trade in Liverpool meant that the local infrastructure, including the jobs of many black people in the area, was dependent on the institution.[44] This, in combination with the 'successful mobilization of the pro-slavery lobby', made it a difficult place to be an abolitionist in the first years of the nineteenth century. As Brian Howman puts it, 'for reasons of self-preservation (physical and economic), abolitionists were perhaps keen to avoid attracting attention to themselves in a town with such a numerous, active and potentially violent pro-slavery lobby.'[45] True, the local antislavery circle headed by William Roscoe and William Rathbone had been active in the late 1780s and early 1790s. But Roscoe and his circle were bourgeois reformists whose abolitionism was bound up with their sympathies for the ideals of the French Revolution.[46] After the onset of war with France in 1793, local resistance to abolition only hardened, and Liverpool, in F. E. Sanderson's appraisal, 'was not to experience any significant local agitation on the subject until 1804' when

---

[41] Jea, *Life*, 53.   [42] See Hanley, 'There to Sing the Song of Moses', 47–49.
[43] Jea, *Life*, 68–71.   [44] See Longmore, '"Cemented by the Blood of a Negro"?', 243.
[45] Brian Howman, 'Abolitionism in Liverpool', in Richardson, Schwarz and Tibbles (eds.), *Liverpool and Transatlantic Slavery*, 279.
[46] Wilson, *William Roscoe*, 133–154.

slavery was reintroduced in the French colonies after a ten-year hiatus.[47]
However, agitation did not denote popularity, and unemployed sailors
rioted in Liverpool's streets when Roscoe spoke for Catholic emancipation and against the transatlantic slave trade in the House of Commons
in 1807.[48] The riots were ostensibly in protest against 'popery', but proslavery interests were also clearly at issue. It was not a coincidence that
the only other riots in the country following Roscoe's speech took place
in Bristol, Britain's second-largest provincial slaving port. Keen to focus
on the town's interest in the slave trade, the *Morning Chronicle* wryly
described the Liverpool rioters as 'a set of wretches more savage a
thousand times than the Coromantyn negroes, or the most savage tribes
of Africa'.[49]

While this tumultuous political environment was not especially unkind
to Jea – he preached at a chapel in Byrom Street, Liverpool, for five
months in around 1805 – it might have contributed to his decision to
leave the city and tour other towns in Lancashire during the winter of
1801–2.[50] Jea first moved to 'Baudley Mores, about fourteen miles from
Liverpool, where [he] met with Mr. Christopher Hooper [i.e. Hopper],
who had travelled in the time of Mr. Wesley. [He] also met with Mr.
Cooper, a Methodist preacher.'[51] Hopper was long retired and too
elderly and frail to continue in his preaching duties by the time Jea
arrived. A reading of Cooper and Hopper's sermons yields clear evidence
of their influence on Jea's attitude toward religion and class. A veteran
from the early days of Methodist expansion in the 1740s, Hopper was like
Jea in that he prided himself on engaging those he saw as belonging to the
'lower orders' in religion. In a 1766 sermon he declared that 'I have done
with flattering titles, bare names, and empty sounds; therefore I do not
ask whether thou art a king, or a subject; a rich man, or a beggar.'[52]
Cooper had less time for working people but praised Hopper for his
heroic commitment to evangelising them. In a funeral sermon published
in 1803, he described how

the lower orders of the inhabitants, especially, were sunk into such a degree of
ignorance, superstition, bigotry, immorality, and brutality as, perhaps, had not
before been known since the first dawn of the glorious Reformation to that time.
Finding them in a condition so truly deplorable, it was natural for the preachers
who were supposed to have no right to legal protection, to expect the most

---

[47] F. E. Sanderson, 'The Liverpool Abolitionists', in Anstey and Hair (eds.), *Liverpool, the African Slave Trade, and Abolition*, 220.
[48] Sanderson, 'The Liverpool Abolitionists', 226.   [49] *Morning Chronicle*, 9 May 1807, 3.
[50] Jea, *Life*, 71.   [51] Jea, *Life*, 57.
[52] Christopher Hopper, *The Plain Man's Epistle to Every Child of Adam* (Newcastle: J. White and T. Saint, 1766), ii.

determined and abusive opposition ... Among the honoured instruments of this extraordinary work, Mr. Hopper deservedly held a distinguished place.[53]

Jea was already in the habit of preaching to low-status congregations by the time he met Hopper, but it was not until afterward, at Portsmouth, that he began to address himself directly to 'those rebellious children' at the fringes of legal society.[54]

He emulated Hopper and Cooper in more than approach and target congregations. The language of redemption through obedience which resonated through Hopper's earlier work found similar utility (though pregnant with far more politicised subtext) in the sermons of a former slave. For example, Hopper's 1770 *Discourse on Haggai* conflated the languages of rebellion and sin: 'Only let the sinner know, that he is a rebel against God, that he has taken up arms against his rightful Sovereign, his Lord and maker.'[55] Jea's sermons were more forgiving, but deployed similar rhetoric: 'My young friends, I would intreat [*sic*] of you, by the grace of God, to examine yourselves, and search the bottom of your heart, to know if you are one of those rebellious children.'[56] The notion of obedience ran through much of Jea's work – including a hymn edited (and possibly written) by him entitled 'Obedience Is Better than Sacrifice', in which the voice of God demanded 'thy thankful lips declare / the honour due to me'.[57] Jea's use of this language took on quite a different character in Bolton to when he had used it in Liverpool. Demographically, the most obvious difference between his congregations was the fact that Bolton, unlike Liverpool, had no especially high proportion of black people. And despite the fact that the local infrastructure revolved around a cotton mill, regional support for abolition was high.[58] Bolton echoed other Lancashire cities with large working-class communities (like Manchester, where Jea also preached) in this respect.

Wesleyan Methodist congregations at Bolton and Manchester were comprised largely of factory workers in the first five or so years of the nineteenth century. Over the succeeding decades, which saw both towns become centres for working-class radicalism, MNC, Primitive and Independent Methodists made greater gains locally than the Wesleyans,

[53] *Methodist Magazine*, 26 (1803), 395–398.   [54] Jea, *Life*, 73.
[55] Christopher Hopper, *Substance of a Discourse, on Haggai* (Leeds: Griffith Wright, 1770), 14.
[56] Jea, *Life*, 73.
[57] Anon., 'Obedience Is Better than Sacrifice', in Jea (ed.), *Hymns*, 189.
[58] See, for example, Seymour Drescher, *Capitalism and Antislavery: British Popular Mobilization in Comparative Perspective* (Oxford: Oxford University Press, 1986), 131.

filling the vacuum left behind by the latter's move toward establishment 'respectability'.[59] When Jea was preaching in Bolton and Manchester in around 1802–1803, the only established secessionist form of Methodism was the MNC, which was still in its infancy. And since the individuals who led the later secessions were still members of the Wesleyan conference when Jea was in Lancashire, the character of preaching within the mainstream connexion was still very diverse. Jea's revivalist, accessible style could be accommodated wherever there was a perceived demand for a working-class (or black) lay preacher.

However, when Jea left Britain in around 1805, a charismatic young preacher with some definite ideas about the trajectory of the Wesleyan Methodists was stationed in Manchester.[60] Jabez Bunting's rise to prominence within the connexion, and his emphasis on respectability, left no place for undignified revivalism and rough congregations. When Jea left Liverpool to tour the Americas, he was part of the Methodist mainstream, mixing with some of its most august figures. When he returned to settle in Portsmouth in 1815, he found himself at the very fringes of the movement. His preaching had not changed; Methodism had.

Hampshire, 1815–1817

By the time Jea returned to mainland Britain around 1815, he had experienced a great deal. From Liverpool he travelled to Boston by way of Newburyport, Massachusetts.[61] After about three months, he went on to 'Venneliea, in the East Indies' to preach, but his ship was not permitted to dock there, and after a fortnight he received orders to travel to Buenos Aires.[62] Here, between February and September 1807, he preached until 'all the vessels that were there, were ordered to the different ports to which they belonged'.[63] After disembarking in Boston, Jea travelled the West Indies, Virginia and Baltimore, where 'I was put in prison, and they strove to make me a slave, (for it was a slave country).'[64] This may have contributed to his decision to travel to Limerick in Ireland

<hr />

[59] Gowland, *Methodist Secessions*, 42–67; Hempton, *Religion of the People*, 115–116.
[60] *Methodist Magazine*, 28 (1805), 421.
[61] Jea, *Life*, 75. 'Newburyport': rendered 'Newberry Port' in the text.
[62] Jea, *Life*, 77. 'Venneleia': I have yet to identify this location.
[63] Jea, *Life*, 78–79. 'Between February and September 1807': Jea refers to preaching in 'Buonos Ayres' at 'the period that General Achmet took Monte Video, and General Whitelock came to assist him with his army'. Samuel Auchmuty took Montevideo, in modern-day Uruguay, from Spanish colonial forces on 3 February 1807 and was relieved by John Whitelocke shortly afterward. The city was retaken by the Spanish on 2 September 1807, when Whitelocke ordered the evacuation of friendly forces.
[64] Jea, *Life*, 79.

at the end of the winter of 1807–1808, where he contended with Calvinist and Catholic ministers for two years and married a local woman named Mary.[65] In 1810, they travelled together through the Cove of Cork to Portsmouth, with the intention of joining the Methodist mission to St. John's in Halifax, Nova Scotia. But on arrival in Portsmouth, Mary was taken ill and forced to stay with their Methodist friends there. Jea went on toward St. John's aboard the *Izette* of Liverpool, but the ship was captured off Torbay by the French privateer *Le Petit Charles* on 22 August 1811 and taken to Paimpol in north-west France.[66] The prisoners were then marched across the country to a prison in Cambria, where Jea continued to preach the gospel for eighteen months. After around eighteen months, 'orders came from the minister of Paris, that all who were called Americans, were to go away; we were accordingly marched away to Brest'.[67] Here Jea was ordered aboard a French corvette under American colours and told to fight against the British, but he refused and was thrown into Morlaix prison, about thirty-five miles from Brest. He was released shortly afterward, and he preached around the town of Morlaix for the remainder of the Napoleonic Wars and returned to Portsmouth via Guernsey and Southampton, arriving near the end of 1815.[68]

All these events inflected Jea's practice and outlook as a preacher. Most importantly, they introduced him to an aspect of Methodist preaching which was to become his speciality, in Portsmouth and beyond. Between 1805 and 1815, he preached almost exclusively to sailors and soldiers. This was as true during his time Britain as it was during his time in South America, since even military men who were not stationed in port cities tended to gravitate around them, where they were likely to gain employment suited to their skills and experience. The work undertaken by Methodist preachers in Buenos Aires during the siege of Montevideo was reflected in a few conversions among the British soldiers. One such convert spoke to the Methodist missionary James Bell in the Cove of Cork, Ireland. Bell related the conversation in a letter to Thomas Coke, who had it published in the *Methodist Magazine* in October 1808. 'I was conversing', wrote Bell, 'with the quarter-master of the Horse Royal Artillery, about to sail immediately to Portsmouth. I find he was converted to God lately, when on the Monte Video expedition.'[69] The

---

[65] Jea, *Life*, 80–87.
[66] Jea, *Life*, 88. '*Izette*': Jea stated that 'our vessel was the brig Iscet of Liverpool, HENRY PATTERSON, Master.' In September 1811, the *Liverpool Mercury* recorded that the 'Izette, Patterson, of this port, from Portsmouth for St John's New Brunswick, was taken on the 22d ult. off the Start, by the Little Charles, French privateer, and carried into Paimpol.' *Liverpool Mercury*, 20 September 1811, 2.
[67] Jea, *Life*, 88.   [68] Jea, *Life*, 90–95.   [69] *Methodist Magazine*, 31 (1808), 478.

geographical trajectories of Jea and this unnamed soldier were remarkably similar, given the distances being covered. Both were at Buenos Aires, then the Cove of Cork, and then Portsmouth at the same times. Jea could well have been the one responsible for the quartermaster's conversion.

This is less surprising when one considers both the Methodist practice of preaching to soldiers while they were stationed abroad and the extent of Methodist evangelical ambition in Ireland. And because many of the soldiers and sailors from the South American campaigns returned to mainland Britain via ports in Ireland, there was a considerable degree of crossover between overseas missionary activity and the 'Irish mission', reinforced by the fact that both were superintended by Coke.[70] Rough-and-ready preachers with experience of tending to soldiers' spiritual needs – men like Jea – found a renewed demand for their skills in Irish ports due to the influx of returning sailors who had little time for the gentility of the local Wesleyan ministers. Jea, however, seasoned in the tough atmosphere of plantations – where slave-owners and overseers were often reticent to allow slaves to engage with Christianity – and latterly aboard military vessels, found it far easier to build a rapport with sailors. These specialist preaching skills were only reinforced during Jea's time as a prisoner of war in France between 1811 and 1815.

When Jea published his *Life* in around 1816, he continued to build on these relationships. It was for this reason that he chose to settle in Portsmouth – more specifically in a suburb adjacent to the harbour, Portsea. Despite, or perhaps because, of the increasingly 'respectable' character of the mainstream Wesleyan church during Bunting's primacy, alongside an increase in population of 117 per cent in Portsea (17 per cent higher than the national average), there was a special and growing need for preachers with Jea's kind of experience.[71] Yet the nature of his relationship to the Wesleyan connexion is not clear. No evidence has emerged to suggest any formal link between Jea and any denomination – though it is clear from his work and evidence from the *Life* that he preached Methodist doctrine and associated primarily with Wesleyan Methodists. Graham Russell Hodges suggests that Jea was a member of the Primitive Methodist church, on the basis that the Primitives' emphases on 'visions, glossolalia, constant reference to the Bible' and hymn-singing suited the content of Jea's *Life*.[72] It is true that the

---

[70] John A. Vickers, 'Coke, Thomas (1747–1814)', in *ODNB*, available at www.oxford dnb.com/view/article/5830.
[71] Vickers, 'Methodism and Society', 169.
[72] Hodges (ed.), *Black Itinerants of the Gospel*, 32.

spectacular and visionary nature of Jea's discourses was at odds with general trends in Wesleyan preaching, especially as Bunting consolidated his control after 1810. Indeed, a Wesleyan preacher stationed in Portsea praised the local congregations for their restraint, exclaiming that 'here is no ... extravagance, no dreams, visions, revelations, and lying miracles, but good common sense & decorum.'[73] As Hodges suggests, Jea's preaching was better suited to one of the new secessionist Methodist bodies, particularly the Primitive Methodists. But Hodges overestimates the reach of the Primitive Methodist movement in Britain by the time Jea published his *Life* in 1816. They were based largely in the urban centres of the North Midlands and Yorkshire, and even by the time of the first formal general meeting for the movement in 1819, only four circuits existed: Tunstall, Nottingham, Loughborough and Hull.[74] W. Donald Cooper has stated that Primitive Methodists 'first appeared in Portsmouth in 1849,' well after Jea had left.[75] The only other possible secessionist body to which Jea could have belonged was the MNC. By 1828 there was a small MNC chapel established 'behind the walls of the Dock-yard at Portsea', but in 1816 the organisation was 'weak in the large cities', especially in southern England.[76] Even while he was in Lancashire, where the MNC *had* made significant gains in popularity, Jea never recorded socialising with even remotely 'radical' members of the Wesleyan church, much less open secessionists. He simply had no opportunity to meet them. Even if he had, there is no reason to expect him to have been sympathetic to their goals.

Wesleyan Methodism, on the other hand, not only had provided Jea with a network to facilitate his preaching in Lancashire but was also making strident progress in Portsmouth at the time he arrived. In 1811, at a cost of around £7,000, a new Wesleyan chapel was erected in Green Row, large enough to 'contain two thousand persons'. Two more large preaching-houses in Gosport and Portsea were bought for the connexion over the next fifteen years, though Jea was unlikely to have been able to use them before he left for Jersey in October 1817.[77] The Wesleyans were the only Methodist organisation with either the access to funding or the local support needed to keep pace with the rate at which the

[73] JRL, Methodist Collections, Preachers Letters, 1977/655, 'John Aikenhead to Isaac Keeling, 21 May 1814'.
[74] Anon., *Minutes of a Meeting ... Primitive Methodists* (Hull: John Hutchinson, 1819), 2.
[75] Cooper, *Methodism in Portsmouth 1750–1932*, 3.
[76] Henry Slight and Julian Slight, *Chronicles of Portsmouth* (London: S. and R. Bentley, 1828), 94; E. Alan Rose, 'Methodist New Connexion', in *DMBI*, available at www .wesleyhistoricalsociety.org.uk/dmbi/index.php?do=app.entry&id=1909.
[77] Slight and Slight, *Chronicles of Portsmouth*, 93.

working-class community in Portsmouth grew during the wars with France and America. Even by 1824, the 'Gospel Church' and MNC chapels 'near the streets behind the walls of the Dock-yard at Portsea' barely warranted a footnote in one local history, while the Wesleyan meeting-houses, Green Row and St. Peter's, each received a lengthy description and praise for their 'handsome parapet[s]' and 'peculiar beauty'.[78] Despite the connexion's increasing tilt toward 'respectability', the area in which Wesleyans grew their churches' capacity fastest was Portsea, and it was here that Jea lived and published his two books.

The strength of Wesleyan Methodism in Portsea also suggests that these networks were involved in the transcription of Jea's *Life* and his original hymns. In the short preface to his published *Hymns*, Jea stated that 'I have been importuned by a number of respectable and religious friends, to publish such a collection.'[79] The mention that these 'friends' were specifically 'religious' implies that his connection to them was through his organised preaching activity, and his overt characterisation of them as 'respectable' places them as more likely to be involved (if only informally) in Wesleyan Methodism than one of the more rustic secessionist movements. Indeed, many of the hymns he had collected were originally written by Charles Wesley. However, as we have seen, the Wesleyans had their own print and distribution networks established through the Epworth Press in London, with a far greater reach than John Williams, the Portsea publisher who produced the *Hymns*. Moreover, the perfect spelling and grammar of most of the printed text indicates that an educated amanuensis was employed in its production. The constant misspelling of proper nouns (and the noticeable impact of dialect and phonetics in these mistakes) implies that the amanuensis transcribed Jea's speech relatively faithfully. That these issues were accentuated when describing places in northern England and France might suggest that the amanuensis was from southern England – most likely Portsea or Portsmouth – and was not particularly well travelled. They had also never heard of Christopher Hopper, revered in Lancashire as a grandee of the Methodist movement. All this suggests that the amanuensis, while educated and religious-minded, was like Jea himself not involved formally with the Wesleyan Methodist movement and was less concerned with national connexional politics than the religious affairs of their local area.

By the time Jea published his *Life*, Portsea was already larger and more populous than Portsmouth itself. The centrality of the military base to

---

[78] Slight and Slight, *Chronicles of Portsmouth*, 93–94.   [79] Jea, *Hymns*, 1.

Table 6.1 *Methodist circuits, preachers and members in Central Southern England, 1825*

Circuit	Local Preachers	Preaching Places	Members	Members per Preacher[a]	Members per Preaching Place[a]
Southampton	21	23	486	23	21
Salisbury	27	29	615	23	21
Poole	21	22	530	25	24
Weymouth	13	19	420	32	22
Shaftesbury	13	22	500	38	23
Portsmouth	**14**	**13**	**1,040**	**74**	**80**

[a] Columns 'Members per Preacher' and 'Members per Preaching Place' do not appear in the original source.
Source: Vickers, 'Methodism and Society', 154.

the local economy gave the area a distinctly working-class character, even in comparison with the rest of Portsmouth.[80] There is no doubt that the core of Methodist support in Portsmouth came from the military presence in these economically deprived areas. In May 1814, for example, one of the local Wesleyan preachers, John Aikenhead, expressed his 'fear, that as the Peace will diminish the number of our inhabitants, we shall lose a portion of our society'.[81] While Aikenhead's prediction proved correct – Methodist congregations in Portsmouth and Portsea declined in line with the local population after 1815 – the Portsmouth circuit remained the largest in the area. The individual congregations were also the largest in central southern England. As Table 6.1 shows, by 1825, preachers in Portsmouth needed to attend to congregations more than triple the size of those in the region's second-largest circuit of Salisbury. For Jea, this meant preaching to constantly shifting congregations of between 70 and 100 soldiers, dockers, publicans, prostitutes, landladies and servers in tumble-down back rooms within earshot of the bars and brothels on the west-end of Queen Street, the heart of Portsmouth's sailor town. Thomas Rowlandson's 1814 print 'Portsmouth Point' gives an impression of how this part of the town was perceived in the early

---

[80] John Langston Field, 'Bourgeois Portsmouth: Social Relations in a Victorian Dockyard Town, 1815–75', PhD thesis, University of Warwick (1979), 6–9.
[81] JRL, Methodist Collections, Preachers' Letters, 1977/655, 'John Aikenhead to Isaac Keeling, 21 May 1814'.

Figure 6.1 Thomas Rowlandson, *Portsmouth Point*, 1814, hand-coloured print, 247 mm × 345 mm.
Courtesy of the Lewis Walpole Library, Yale University.

nineteenth century (Figure 6.1). His sermons needed to be loud, engaging and emotionally evocative to hold the attention of his congregation in such an environment.

One of Jea's most shrewd tactics was to invoke nationalist ideology in his sermons, utilising his own ethnic status to compound anti-French, anti-American and antislavery sentiment within a paradigm of patriotic, soldierly fraternity. In 'Works of Creation', for example, Jea reified the British suppression of the slave trade, compounding physical and spiritual liberation from slavery:

> Africa nations, great and small,
> Upon this earthly ball,
> Give glory to the God above,
> And crown him Lord of all.
> 'Tis God above, who did in love
> Your souls and bodies free,
> By British men with life in hand,
> The gospel did decree.
> By God's free grace they run the race,
> And did his glory see,

To preach the gospel to our race,
The gospel Liberty.[82]

Evangelistic fervour and lionisation of British sailors' role in abolishing the slave trade were fairly conventional features of post-1807 poetry
on the subject, but Jea attempted to contain this ideological couplet within
the framework of Methodist theology.[83] Significantly, he was specific
about the fact that the 'captain of an English ship of war' initiated his
extradition from France, transferring him to Guernsey to preach on the
way back to Britain.[84] At the same time, his devotional verse consistently
reinforced two notions: first, that God controlled the seas, and second,
that the Methodist doctrine of Christian perfection through the imitation of Christ (see Chapter 4) was the only route to freedom from slavery.
The first of these notions was expressed most explicitly in hymns such
as 'God's Dominion over the Sea', 'It Is God That Rules the Sea'
and 'For Mariners'.[85] The second notion was expressed explicitly in
'Encouragement':

> Hark! poor slave, it is the Lord,
> It is the Saviour, hear his word . . .
> Thou dost say 'I'm not a slave,
> 'I was born on British ground';
> O remember when thou wast
> In chains of sin and mis'ry bound . . .
> Can a man so hardened be,
> As not to remember me [the Lord]?
> Yes, he may forgetful be,
> Yet I will remember thee.[86]

Jea bound British pride in antislavery ideology to Methodist perfection.
The sinner's insistence that he was not a slave because he was 'born on
British ground' echoed not only the protestations of a number of free
black people across the world during the period of abolition, but also the
refrain of British patriotism itself. Just as being enslaved to tyranny and
being British were incompatible in James Thompson's 'Rule, Britannia!',
Jea reminded his reader that, since 1807, British liberty extended as far as
the nation was able to enforce it.[87]

---

[82] John Jea, 'Works of Creation', in Jea (ed.), *Hymns*, 182.
[83] For a local example, see the celebratory poem by 'J.H.' of 'George's Row, Portsea',
Hampshire Telegraph and Sussex Chronicle, 22 June 1807, 1.
[84] Jea, *Life*, 93.   [85] See Jea (ed.), *Hymns*, 215–218.
[86] John Jea, 'Encouragement', in Jea (ed.), *Hymns*, 209.
[87] While the question of abolishing slavery in the British colonies was under discussion by
other black authors such as Robert Wedderburn at the same time (see Chapter 8), Jea
did not enter into any such discussion.

In this way, Jea appealed not only to the sailors in Portsmouth but also to his black congregants. Portsmouth's black community, while not on the scale of Liverpool's, was larger than most provincial towns. Their engagement with religious life is well documented. Whole groups of black sailors had themselves baptised within short spans of time. Between 28 October and 17 November 1799, for example, five black sailors were baptised at St. Thomas's church alone.[88] In neighbouring Gosport, on 12 June 1816, eight black seamen from the HMS *Venerable*, including one 'Blackman born in Africa', were baptised on the same day.[89] But the black community in and around Portsmouth was not comprised entirely of sailors and soldiers. In its role as a military port, Portsmouth often received African men who had been liberated from illegal slaving voyages and impressed into the Royal Navy. Numerous baptism and burial records exist for African people coming to settle in the area after being freed in this manner. For example, on 6 June 1813, in Exbury near Southampton, 'Irby Amelia Frederick, aged 9 or 10, a native of Poppoe near Whidah, Africa, who was stolen as a slave, but rescued at sea on the way to Brazil, by HMS Amelia' was baptised.[90] Similarly, in September 1818, two African ordinary seamen of the Royal Navy were baptised in Gosport – either slaves liberated during the War of 1812 or during illegal slaving voyages or free Kru sailors recruited on the West Coast of Africa by the West Africa Squadron.[91] What all of these individuals shared in common was first-hand experience of the Royal Navy's opposition to the transatlantic slave trade. If Jea wanted to appeal to this varied and vibrant demographic in his preaching – his hymns about life on a plantation suggest that he did – then his valorisation of British antislavery efforts would have likely brought him a degree of success.

Yet for all his patriotism, Jea may have come into conflict with establishment authority figures. On 23 March 1817, an unnamed black itinerant preacher was threatened with prosecution for preaching outside proper licensed premises by the Magistrates of Winchester, about thirty miles from Portsmouth. While the preacher stood on a stool and exhorted an 'immence crowd of people' who had gathered 'in a large space of ground near the center of the city where the fair is generally holden', one of the local magistrates, the 'Reverend Doctor Sewbell', was summoned. When informed by Sewbell that 'he was acting very illegally in preaching in the aforesaid street', the black preacher 'very civilly'

---

[88] HRO, Fiche 248, 'Copy of Portsea St Thomas Parish Register'.
[89] HRO, Fiche 11, 100–101, 'Gosport Holy Trinity Parish Register'.
[90] HRO, Exbury Parish Register, 50M80/PR1, 'Register of Baptisms'.
[91] HRO, Fiche 12, 'Copy of Gosport Holy Trinity Parish Register'.

descended and stopped his sermon. The congregation, however, reacted violently, becoming 'very riotous' and setting upon Sewbell, who had to make his escape 'thro' the premises of a neighbouring gentleman'. Determined to prevent this type of mass public gathering again, the magistrates enquired of the Law Officers if they had grounds to prosecute the preacher under the Toleration Act of 1812, which prevented dissenting meetings from taking place outside licensed chapels and meeting-houses. The Law Officer, Albert Pell, responded that the case could be tried under the Toleration Act, unless the preacher was not licensed, in which case he could be tried for the more serious crime of organising an unlawful assembly.[92]

Even though black people were increasingly engaged in church life in Hampshire during the first decades of the nineteenth century, it is unlikely that more than one black itinerant preacher was touring the county in 1817. Jea was certainly the only individual fitting such a description to be documented, and as such the above case almost definitely referred to him. Nevertheless, he was ultimately never prosecuted for his meeting in Winchester, possibly because the magistrates did not know his name or did not know where to find him.

In fact, he was based nearby, in Portsea, until October 1817. His third wife, Mary, who was 'well' when the *Life* was published, died there, shortly afterward. On 28 October 1816 he married again, to Miss Jemima Davis in High Wycombe.[93] They returned to Portsea, and on 25 September 1817 their daughter Hephzahbah was baptised in St. John's, an Anglican church which had been built there in 1788.[94] It is not clear why Jea chose to have his child baptised in an Anglican church when there were so many Methodist churches available locally. It may have had something to do with the fact that Jea was in a hurry – ten days later he was preaching 'on the Grand-Parade' in St. Helier, Jersey.[95] Given his avowed fear of drowning and the repeated threats of repatriation and re-enslavement he had endured, it made sense for him to witness his daughter's baptism before travelling south by sea, regardless of whether or not she accompanied him.

Beyond the fact that he preached there on 5 October 1817, little is known about Jea's time in Jersey. As during his time in mainland Britain,

[92] HRO, Opinions of Law Officers, W/D6/14, 'Case and Opinion of Albert Pell, Counsel, 21 April 1817'.
[93] *Hampshire Telegraph*, 28 October 1816, 3.
[94] Portsmouth City Record Office, 'Baptisms Solemnised in the St. John's Chapel in the Parish of Portsea in the County of Southampton, in the Year 1817,' 268. Cited in Hodges (ed.), *Black Itinerants of the Gospel*, 48–49 n. 119.
[95] *La Chronique de Jersey*, 4 October 1817, 2.

he received no financial support from any of the local Methodist circuits, and he was never mentioned in any of the twice-yearly meetings of Wesleyan preachers stationed in the Guernsey area.[96] The latest evidence of Jea's religious activity was an advertisement for one of his meetings in the 4 October 1817 issue of *La Chronique de Jersey*.[97] It is likely that he continued travelling and preaching, but in Hodges's words, 'by the time history swallowed Jea, he was an old man by standards of his time and profession'.[98]

Jea's connection to the local Wesleyan Methodist networks in Hampshire and Lancashire went unremarked in the official literature of the movement. Since he was a lay preacher and not an ordained minister, he could never hope to gain an annuity or financial remuneration for his preaching beyond his bed and board. Almost from the time he first arrived in Britain in June 1801, Jea's style of preaching, cultivated in the emotionally charged atmosphere of the slave plantations of America's East Coast, left him at the margins of an increasingly moderate Wesleyan Methodist connexion. By the time he left mainland Britain in 1817, there was little room in Bunting's new, hierarchical vision of Methodism for Jea's religious 'enthusiasm'.

Yet the intricate relationships between local identities and international politics allowed Jea to alter the content of his sermons, songs and writings, according to his location, to excite the greatest reaction from his working-class congregations. In terms of his engagement with the slave trade, Jea was flexible enough to preach the virtues of passive slave obedience in pre-abolition Liverpool and populist nationalism in suppression-era Portsmouth. He was sensitive to the relationship between the spiritual, material and political needs of his audience. Crucially, he recognised that popular engagement in a political issue as large as abolition was bound to be inflected by its impact on local economics and politics, and like John Wesley himself, he knew how to suit his discourse to his audience.

Jea's approach to preaching was steeped in the missionary tradition from which the Methodist Episcopal Church in America had stemmed. Fiery, millenarian, and with an emphasis on spiritual metamorphosis, this approach proved popular among the dispossessed of society. On one

---

[96] JRL, Methodist Collections, 1977/398, 'Wesleyan Methodist Conference Minutes for the Guernsey District, 1808–1818'; JRL, Methodist Collections, 1977/398, 'Wesleyan Methodist Conference Minutes for the Guernsey District, 1819–1830'.
[97] *Le Chronique de Jersey*, 4 October 1817, 2.
[98] Hodges (ed.), *Black Itinerants of the Gospel*, 34.

Part III

Black Radicals

7   Ottobah Cugoano and the 'Black Poor',
       1786–1791

Ottobah Cugoano's 1787 text, *Thoughts and Sentiments on the Evil and Wicked Traffic of the Slavery and Commerce of Human Species*, was the first piece of black writing published in Britain which can be considered as both unequivocally political and unequivocally abolitionist. An altered and abridged version, *Thoughts and Sentiments on the Evil of Slavery*, followed in 1791, addressed explicitly to his 'Countrymen and brother Sufferers'.[1] As we will see, these were as much radical articulations of black political engagement as they were attacks on the slave trade and colonial slavery. During these years, Cugoano was personally involved in two manifestations of black resistance in London. The first was participation in radical politics through rioting, resisting arrest and letter-writing. The second took the form of disrupting, delaying and protesting against the execution of a plan designed to expatriate black people from Britain.

Cugoano was born around 1757 'in the city of Agimaque, on the coast of Fantyn' in present-day Ghana.[2] He was kidnapped and sold into slavery in 1770, being transported at first to Grenada and then to various other parts of the West Indies in the service of Alexander Campbell. In late 1772, he was brought to Britain, where he could not be legally compelled to return to slavery abroad due to the recent Somerset case, though it is not clear whether he left Campbell's service with or without his blessing.[3] By 1784, Cugoano was working as a domestic servant to the painters Richard and Maria Cosway, and he was depicted in Richard

---

[1] Cugoano's two texts have similar titles, but the subtle differences between them are material to the argument presented in this chapter. For the sake of clarity, the original 1787 text will hereafter be referred to as *Thoughts and Sentiments*, while the shorter 1791 text will be referred to as *Evil of Slavery*. This also applies to short-form citations. Ottobah Cugoano, *Thoughts and Sentiments on the Evil and Wicked Traffic of the Slavery and Commerce of the Human Species* (London, 1787); Ottobah Cugoano, *Thoughts and Sentiments on the Evil of Slavery* (London: Kirkby et al., 1791).

[2] Cugoano, *Thoughts and Sentiments*, 6.

[3] Ottobah Cugoano, 'Advertisement for *Thoughts and Sentiments on the Evil and Wicked Traffic of the Slavery and Commerce of the Human Species*' (London, 1787?), 4.

Figure 7.1 Richard Cosway, *Mr. and Mrs. Cosway*, 1784,
monochrome etching on paper, 293 mm × 362 mm.
© National Portrait Gallery, London.

Cosway's 1784 etching, *Mr. and Mrs. Cosway* (Figure 7.1).[4] He did not
become involved in political campaigning until around 1786, when an
influx of former slaves, freed in exchange for military service for Loyalist
forces in the American Revolutionary War, settled in London.[5]

Black people in eighteenth-century Britain were excluded, sometimes
deliberately, from positions of political authority.[6] Among all black

---

[4] Vincent Carretta, 'Introduction', in Ottobah Cugoano, *Thoughts and Sentiments on the Evil of Slavery*, ed. Vincent Carretta (London: Penguin, 1999), xv.

[5] The historiography of the 'black poor' in London and the establishment of the Sierra Leone colony is discussed below. See also Cassandra Pybus, *Epic Journeys of Freedom: Runaway Slaves of the American Revolution and their Global Quest for Liberty* (Boston: Beacon Press, 2006), 75–121; Gretchen Gerzina, 'Black Loyalists in London after the American Revolution', in John Pulis (ed.), *Moving On: Black Loyalists in the Afro-Atlantic World* (London: Taylor and Francis, 1999), 85–102.

[6] See, for example, the story of a black sugar cooper who was at first admitted to 'the freedom of London'. When the Court of Aldermen realised this, they passed an ordinance that 'no Black should ever again be admitted to the freedom of London'. *Morning Post and Daily Advertiser*, 29 December 1786, 2.

people in eighteenth-century Britain, only Sancho has been identified as being eligible to vote in parliamentary elections.[7] In common with the majority of the population, black people were therefore disenfranchised completely from participating in the political process. However, between 1786 and 1792, London's demography and political landscape both began to change. The black Loyalist migrants met with mixed treatment when they arrived in the metropolis. Many had been injured in the war, and begging was widespread among the black community in Britain.[8] But the loss of America, as Seymour Drescher has demonstrated, led to an increase in popular support for a broad range of humanitarian causes, and in January 1786, a committee was established to provide for the relief of the 'black poor'.[9] This coincided with the emergence of a new popular movement for domestic political reform, later spurred on by the French Revolution and reaching an apogee with the establishment of radical corresponding societies across the country between 1790 and 1792.[10] It was through black intellectuals such as Cugoano that the formerly enslaved were able to participate in these political debates, without having to limit their concerns solely to the transatlantic slave trade.

Before embarking on an investigation of the political activities of London's 'black poor', it is necessary to acknowledge that there is some disagreement among historians as to the cohesiveness of eighteenth-century London's black population. Peter Fryer and James Walvin, for example, take the existence of a unified black community with a shared social and ideological (if not strictly political) perspective for granted,

---

[7] Vincent Carretta, 'Introduction', in Ignatius Sancho, *Letters of the Late Ignatius Sancho, an African*, ed. Vincent Carretta (London: Penguin, 1998), xiv.

[8] Perhaps the best-known black Loyalist beggar in London was Shadrack Furman, who lost his sight and one leg because of the torture he endured after being captured by Patriot forces. When he got to London, he was reduced to playing the fiddle to support himself and his wife. He was eventually granted a lifetime pension of eighteen pounds per year from the Loyalist Claims Commission. See Pybus, *Epic Journeys of Freedom*, 79–80.

[9] Seymour Drescher, 'The Shocking Birth of British Abolitionism', *Slavery & Abolition*, 33:4 (2012), 571–593. For the establishment of the Committee for the Relief of the Black Poor, see Stephen Braidwood, *Black Poor and White Philanthropists: London's Blacks and the Foundation of the Sierra Leone Settlement 1786–1791* (Liverpool: Liverpool University Press, 1994), 63–129.

[10] There is a wealth of scholarship on the establishment and activities of the various radical corresponding societies of the 1790s. Influential edited collections on the topic include Pamela Clemit (ed.), *The Cambridge Companion to British Literature of the French Revolution in the 1790s* (Cambridge: Cambridge University Press, 2011); Michael T. Davis and Paul Pickering (eds.), *Unrespectable Radicals? Popular Politics in the Age of Reform* (London: Ashgate, 2008); Mark Philp (ed.), *The French Revolution and British Popular Politics* (Cambridge: Cambridge University Press, 2004); Robert Maniquis (ed.), *British Radical Culture of the 1790s* (San Marino, CA: Huntingdon Library Press, 2002).

from the mid-eighteenth century onward.[11] Fryer even goes as far as to suggest that 'London had by the 1760s become a centre of black resistance'.[12] More recent studies have understood the black experience in Britain during the 1780s as socially fragmented.[13] However, while we must remain mindful of Norma Myers's criticism that 'historians tend to perceive the black population as comprising an undifferentiated "Black Poor"', Cugoano's experience indicates that black people *did* in fact socialise with one another and joined together in support of political and social causes which overwhelmed their differences in social strata or professional background.[14] Neither were these exchanges between members of a socially undifferentiated underclass of beggars and charity cases. Comparatively well-heeled black intellectuals like Cugoano (and indeed Equiano) represented the interests of their less connected peers to established political networks, acting as a conduit between 'grass roots' forms of political activism and more formalised attempts to obtain changes in government policy.

These established political networks were not limited to elected parliamentary representatives and their circles, though some of Cugoano's most public interactions were with such figures. In fact, while he was keen to publicise his approval of 'establishment' moves toward limiting or abolishing the slave trade, certain elements of Cugoano's work share much in common with contemporaneous radical tracts. In terms of his abolitionism, his work drew heavily on that of white abolitionists more associated with 'radical' than 'establishment' politics. Even the title of his first work, *Thoughts and Sentiments on the Evil and Wicked Traffic of the Slavery and Commerce of the Human Species*, consciously evoked Thomas Clarkson's *Essay on the Slavery and Commerce of the Human Species*. But Cugoano's politics were unique in that they deployed the language of the new political radicalism to combat racialized discrimination in Britain. His occasional adoption of the radical vernacular was a necessary reaction to the marginalisation of the black political voice. This is not to say

[11] Peter Fryer, Staying Power: *The History of Black People in Britain* (London: Pluto Press, 1984), 67–88; James Walvin, *Black and White: The Negro in English Society, 1555–1945* (London: Allen Lane, 1973), 46–79.
[12] Fryer, *Staying Power*, 72.
[13] Norma Myers, *Reconstructing the Black Past: Blacks in Britain, 1780–1830* (London: Routledge, 1996), 56–81; Kathleen Chater, *Untold Histories: Black People in England and Wales during the Period of the British Slave Trade, c. 1660–1807* (Manchester: Manchester University Press, 2009), 35–73. Cassandra Pybus has reconstructed some of the individual stories of black survival in London's streets following the American Revolution but does not explore in depth how they came together in furtherance of common political or social objectives. Pybus, *Epic Journeys of Freedom*, 75–121.
[14] Myers, *Reconstructing the Black Past*, 56.

that all black people in London shared a homogenous political perspective – rather, Cugoano wrote in reaction against a set of social grievances specific to London's black community in the late 1780s.

Cugoano's radical spirit, as well as his dim view of the government's continuing toleration of transatlantic slavery, could be seen in his reaction to the two phases of the Sierra Leone resettlement project in 1786/ 1787 and 1791. The project, once derided as a proto-racist attempt to 'rid Britain of her black population and make Britain a white man's country', has since been reappraised (most substantially by Stephen Braidwood) as a well-intentioned if ill-fated and ill-executed charitable undertaking.[15] But while Braidwood's assertion that the black community were involved in the planning of the first Sierra Leone voyage is well founded, his analysis of the motives and ideology behind government involvement in the project overstates the level of consultation undertaken by the Committee for the Relief of the Black Poor. Consequently the relationship between the Committee and the black people involved in the project is represented as being far more collaborative than was actually the case. Cugoano's writings on the Sierra Leone resettlement project demonstrate that, far from a harmonious partnership, government involvement was seen by the black Loyalists as an opportunistic and cynical attempt to transport a social problem out of sight.

Much like his famous friend and collaborator Equiano, Cugoano used his education and position of relative financial security to further the interests of a network of politically active black people in the metropolis. In this respect he might be best understood as a progenitor of black British radicalism. At the same time, he sought to extend his own social capital and the reach of his work by constructing an authorial persona which emphasised his respectability and gentility in personal correspondence, written to promote his work to respectable statesmen. As well as providing a template for Equiano's more commercially successful work, Cugoano laid the foundations for organised black political engagement in Britain. In doing so, he changed the face of popular radicalism.

---

[15] Walvin, *Black and White*, 144–159; James Walker, *The Black Loyalists: The Search for a Promised Land in Nova Scotia and Sierra Leone 1783–1870* (Toronto: University of Toronto Press, 1976), 94–145; Folarin Shyllon, *Black People in Britain 1555–1833* (London: Oxford University Press, 1977), 117–158. Quotation: Shyllon, *Black People in Britain*, 117. Stephen Braidwood, 'Initiatives and Organisation of the Black Poor', *Slavery & Abolition* 3:3 (1982), 211–227; Braidwood, *Black Poor and White Philanthropists*; Suzanne Schwarz, 'Commerce, Civilization and Christianity: The Development of the Sierra Leone Company', in David Richardson, Suzanne Schwarz and Anthony Tibbles (eds.), *Liverpool and Transatlantic Slavery* (Liverpool: Liverpool University Press, 2007), 252–276.

Ottobah Cugoano and London's Black Radicals

On 28 July 1786, Cugoano took his first decisive action against slavery. Along with his friend, another black man named William Green, he approached the famous abolitionist lawyer Granville Sharp and asked for his help. Samuel Jeffries, owner of the huge Windsor Estate in Westmoreland, Jamaica, had 'trepanned his Negro servant Harry [Demaine] and sent him on ship board,' intending to take him back to slavery in the Americas against his will.[16] Sharp acted swiftly. Three days later, Jeffries received a visit from his former servant Demaine, not only free but accompanied by law officers and demanding restitution.[17]

At the time, Cugoano worked as a servant for Richard Cosway, the official portrait-painter to the Prince of Wales.[18] Vincent Carretta suggests that Cugoano met Sharp through Cosway.[19] It is equally likely, though, that they met through Equiano, who in 1781 had petitioned Sharp for redress following the infamous *Zong* massacre.[20] Certainly, Cugoano and Equiano knew each other well enough by 1788 to be collaborating on public abolitionist letters.[21] Paul Edwards has even suggested that Cugoano's published tracts emerged as a 'collaboration between him and Equiano', since the former's holograph letters contained poor spelling and grammar.[22] Edwards's suggestion is predicated on the comparatively 'elevated rhetorical manner' of Cugoano's published work, but as he acknowledges, frequent grammatical mistakes persist throughout both *Thoughts and Sentiments* and *Evil of Slavery*.[23] Chief among these was a 'failure of agreement' between subject and verb, producing, for example 'exertions . . . has' and 'every slave holder . . . do'.[24] These reflected the grammar of Cugoano's manuscript correspondence.

---

[16] GRO, Granville Sharp Papers, D/3549/13/4/2, 'Extracts from Diary of Granville Sharp, 1783–1792', f. 36; 'Samuel Jeffries': 'Diary' only states 'Mr. Jeffries', but Samuel Jeffries was the only former owner identified in the Legacies of British Slave-Ownership database with this surname. See Legacies of British Slave-Ownership, 'Samuel Jeffries, 1745–19th Dec 1819', available at www.ucl.ac.uk/lbs/person/view/1301937073.

[17] GRO, Granville Sharp Papers, D/3549/13/4/2, 'Extracts from Diary of Granville Sharp, 1783–1792', f. 36.

[18] See Vincent Carretta, 'Three West African Writers of the 1780s Revisited and Revised', *Research in African Literatures*, 29:4 (1998), 81–83.

[19] Vincent Carretta, 'Introduction', in Cugoano, *Thoughts and Sentiments*, ed. Carretta, xv.

[20] For a detailed overview of the *Zong* massacre, see James Walvin, *The Zong: A Massacre, the Law and the End of Slavery* (New Haven, CT: Yale University Press, 2011).

[21] See, for example, *The Diary: or Woodfall's Register*, 25 April 1788, 2.

[22] Paul Edwards, 'Three West African Writers of the 1780s', in Charles T. Davis and Henry Louis Gates, Jr. (eds.), *The Slave's Narrative* (Oxford: Oxford University Press, 1985), 183–187.

[23] Edwards, 'Three West African Writers', 182–184.

[24] Edwards, 'Three West African Writers', 182–184.

For example, in a letter to Granville Sharp in 1791, his habit of confusing the plural and singular forms of the verb 'to be' resurfaced: 'as there is several ships now going to New Brunswick'.[25] Edwards accommodates the notion of an external 'reviser' and 'probably, an expander' with these 'characteristic grammatical errors' by suggesting that 'the reviser, while having better control of English', may not have been 'a native speaker of the language'. This leads him to nominate Equiano as the reviser and/or expander.[26] However, as Carretta points out, Cugoano's holograph letters 'are not significantly less polished than those by Equiano'.[27] Moreover, the grammatical errors identified by Edwards appeared in *Thoughts and Sentiments* and *Evil of Slavery* but did not feature in Equiano's *Interesting Narrative* or published letters.[28] As Carretta suggests, 'many of the formal qualities of Cugoano's *Thoughts and Sentiments* that strike readers as ungrammatical' can be explained by understanding the work to have emerged from the tradition of the '*jeremiad* or *political sermon*', but again none of these featured extensively in Equiano's published work.[29] All of this implies that Equiano did not in fact co-author the tracts produced under Cugoano's name as Edwards has suggested, though he may have had a hand in editing them. In any case, by the time *Thoughts and Sentiments* was published in 1787, Cugoano could draw on an entire network of articulate and organised black people, who were mobilising not just against slavery but also against the poverty and discrimination they encountered as free men in Britain.

Two shifts in the British political landscape had recently taken place to enable him to participate safely in public conversations about domestic and international reform. The first was demographic rather than ideological. The arrival of black Loyalists into Britain after 1783 was one of the many consequences of defeat in the American Revolutionary War. Arming slaves had been an act of desperation on the British generals' part; their manumission of around 10,000 in return for their military support had no basis in colonial policy whatsoever.[30] As Philip Morgan

---

[25] GRO, Granville Sharp Papers, D3549/13/1/S36, 'John Stuart to Granville Sharp, [1791]'.
[26] Edwards, 'Three West African Writers', 185.
[27] Carretta, 'Revisited and Revised', 83.
[28] Edwards, 'Three West African Writers', 184.
[29] Carretta, 'Revised and Revisited', 83 (emphasis in original).
[30] Walker concedes that 'there is considerable difficulty in establishing the total number of Black Loyalists', but the 'Book of Negroes', detailing every black Loyalist wishing to leave New York in November 1783 alone, records more than 3,000 names. Alan Gilbert estimates the number at 'between 9,100 and 10,400 free blacks.' Walker, *The Black Loyalists*, 12; Alan Gilbert, *Black Patriots and Loyalists: Fighting for Emancipation in the War for Independence* (Chicago, IL: University of Chicago Press, 2012), 208.

and Andrew O'Shaughnessy argue, 'British policy, insofar as there was such a thing, was an untidy sequence of advances and retreats, with no simple forward movement, with respect to the idea of arming slaves.'[31] As a result, when the several hundred black Loyalists who had chosen to migrate to Britain arrived after the Peace of 1783, there were no social structures in place to help them find work or relieve them from poverty.

Myers has estimated the number of black people resident in London between 1785 and 1789 at 4,290, or 0.5 per cent of the capital's total population, based on an analysis of Old Bailey Session Papers. Yet, as she acknowledges, this calculation is made on the assumption that black and white people were equally likely to be indicted for a crime, and as such her data should not be used as 'direct, decisive estimates of blacks but to seek indications of numbers'.[32] Even setting aside the possibility of racial prejudice in the eighteenth-century British legal system, a number of circumstances meant that black people were far more likely to appear at the Old Bailey indicted for a crime than their white peers.

First, due perhaps to the prerequisite of military service for emancipation, the vast majority of the former slaves coming to Britain in the 1770s and 1780s were young and male, and therefore statistically more likely to be indicted for a crime.[33] Second, since they had only recently arrived in Britain, none of the Loyalists was eligible for charity relief under the poor laws, again increasing the likelihood of their being indicted for theft.[34] Finally, the post-war economic recession reduced employment opportunities for unskilled labourers and ordinary seamen just as the influx of former slaves was arriving. Coupled with hardening discriminatory attitudes toward the employment of black people, this environment essentially circumscribed any form of economic opportunity for members of the new immigrant community.[35] While a small minority of London's black community, including Cugoano, had trained as domestic servants,

---

[31] Philip D. Morgan and Andrew Jackson O'Shaughnessy, 'Arming Slaves during the American Revolution', in Christopher Leslie Brown and Philip D. Morgan (eds.), *Arming Slaves: From Classical Times to the Modern Age* (London: Yale University Press, 2006), 190–191. The role of black Loyalist soldiers in the American Revolution is covered in more detail in Gilbert, *Black Patriots and Loyalists*, 116–206.

[32] Myers, *Reconstructing the Black Past*, 29–30.

[33] See Deirdre Palk, *Gender, Crime and Judicial Discretion, 1780–1830* (London: Boydell Press, 2006), 21–37.

[34] Anne Winter and Thijs Lambrecht, 'Migration, Poor Relief and Local Autonomy: Settlement Policies in England and the Southern Low Countries in the Eighteenth Century', *Past and Present*, 218:1 (2013), 91–126; Anne-Marie Kilday, '"Criminally Poor?" Investigating the Link between Crime and Poverty in Eighteenth Century England', *Cultural and Social History*, 11:4 (2014), 507–526.

[35] For discriminatory attitudes toward employing black people, see Walvin, *Black and White*, 57–58.

the fashion for black butlers and waiting-boys had largely passed. In any case, supply far outstripped demand for these jobs. Cassandra Pybus has demonstrated that many black men 'who had come to England as servants to officers, and then lost their employment when the officers resigned their commissions, were in dire straits'.[36] In newspapers, advertisements placed by black men trained as barbers, butlers and chambermen seeking employment far outnumbered those placed by houses specifically seeking black servants. According to the *Public Advertiser*, by 1791 the mere sight of a black man in a well-to-do social space was enough to leave some local dandies sniggering behind their hands: 'A black man, in white cloaths, mounted on a black horse, with a white face, caused much pleasantry amongst the fashionable wits last Thursday in Hyde-park'.[37]

By 1786, then, a significant black presence was established in London, characterised by underemployment, poverty and consequently over-representation in criminal indictments. For this reason, Cugoano, much like Equiano, was at pains to demonstrate not only the intellectual faculties of black people but their good taste and respect for eminent establishment figures. The emerging campaign for the abolition of the slave trade provided a natural platform from which to demonstrate black intellectual and political engagement. In 1786, Cugoano wrote to the Prince of Wales, recommending a 'few little tracts' against slavery – probably including James Ramsay's *Essay on the Treatment and Conversion of Slaves*, which he defended in print the following year – for his perusal.[38] This was not the last letter Cugoano wrote to the Prince. When *Thoughts and Sentiments* was published in 1787, he sent a copy to him directly, as well as to other establishment policymakers such as Edmund Burke.[39] In his letter to the Prince, Cugoano gently pointed out the disparity in political means between black and white people: 'and whereas we have no institution of Ambassadors to demand restitution for the injuries which the Europeans have pursued against us we can no where lay our case more fitly than at the feet of your Highness.'[40] He was ostensibly referring to the case of all African people injured by the transatlantic slave system. However, his pseudo-litigious language of laying a 'case' to 'demand restitution for the injuries which the Europeans have pursued', along with his use of the first-person collective

---

[36] Pybus, *Epic Journeys of Freedom*, 81.   [37] *Public Advertiser*, 21 May 1791, 2.

[38] GRO, Granville Sharp Papers, D/3549/13/1/S36, 'John Stuart to Prince of Wales, 1786'.

[39] GRO, Granville Sharp Papers, D/3549/13/1/S36, 'John Stuart to Prince of Wales, 1787'; Sheffield Archives, Papers of Edmund Burke, WWM/Bk/P/1/2105 'Letter from John Stuart [1787]'.

[40] GRO, Granville Sharp Papers, D/3549/13/1/S36, 'John Stuart to Prince of Wales, 1787'.

pronoun, hinted at a more narrowly and formally defined collective identity – one which represented pragmatic political goals.

Of course, by December 1787 Cugoano was indeed part of an all-black political organisation – the first of its kind in Britain. The 'Sons of Africa', as they became known, were a corresponding society writing public and private letters to prominent figures in support of their efforts toward abolition.[41] Along with Equiano and nine others, Cugoano co-signed a letter to Sharp thanking him for his 'humane commiseration of our brethren and countrymen unlawfully held in slavery'.[42] After the passing of the Dolben Act in 1788 limited the overcrowding of slaves aboard ships during the middle passage, the Sons of Africa published separate letters of thanks in the *Morning Chronicle* to three of the bill's highest-profile proponents, William Dolben, William Pitt and Charles James Fox.[43] In total, twenty correspondents identified themselves as members of the Sons of Africa. These letters further contributed to Cugoano's efforts to demonstrate the politeness and respectability of black people, specifically addressing prejudices that supposed licentious behaviour to be natural to them. For example, the letter to Dolben specifically stated that 'we are not ignorant, ... Sir, that the best return we can make [for your efforts against the slave trade] is, to behave with sobriety, fidelity and diligence in our different stations.' Dolben was not ignorant of the implications of this promise, and his reply recognised that 'showing their gratitude by their future conduct in steadiness and sobriety, fidelity and diligence, will undoubtedly recommend them to the British Government, and he trusts, to other Christian powers, as most worthy of their further care and attention.'[44] In a similar vein, at some point during the same year, the Sons of Africa wrote another private letter to Sharp, reassuring him that 'humbleness and sobriety, we are sensible, will best become our condition.'[45] These letters connected the black presence to the mainstream abolitionist campaign by directly repudiating prevailing racialized notions that sought to link black political involvement with moral degeneracy.

[41] The group published letters under this name. See *London Advertiser*, 15 July 1788, 3.
[42] Prince Hoare, *Memoirs of Granville Sharp* (London: Lilerton and Henderson, 1820), 274–375, cited in Cugoano, *Thoughts and Sentiments*, ed. Carretta, 187–188. The other nine cosignatories were George Robert Mandeville, William Stevens, Joseph Almaze, Boughwa Gegansmel, Jasper Goree, James Bailey, Thomas Oxford, John Adams and George Wallace.
[43] *Morning Chronicle and London Advertiser*, 15 July 1788, 3.
[44] *Morning Chronicle and London Advertiser*, 15 July 1788, 3.
[45] 'Letter to Granville Sharp, esq. [Undated]', reprinted in Cugoano, *Thoughts and Sentiments*, ed. Carretta, 189–190 [no source cited].

Other organised forms of black resistance to prejudice in London did not seek to attain the same forms of establishment approval. In September 1786, for example, more than a hundred black men, drawing on their military experience, came together to violently resist one of their number being arrested. An account of the incident appeared in the *General Evening Post* on 9 September:

> Mr. Drawwater, Sheriff's Officer, and two of his men, went to the White Raven, in Mile-End road, to arrest one John Pegg, a black man, and commonly called one of the Corporals, who receive the charity-money . . . After he was arrested, the blackmen, to the number of about one hundred, insisted, that the Officer should not take him away; and hallooed out to their comrades, 'shut the gates!' . . . But Mr. Drawwater, and his men, being resolute, they got the prisoner, with difficulty, on the outside of the gates . . . Several of [the black men] instantly armed themselves with sticks &c. and came on a second time; and after a desperate onset, in Mile-End road, in which Mr. Drawwater's cloaths were torn off, and he was terribly bruised on the head, and almost every part of his body, they rescued the prisoner, and carried him off in triumph.[46]

By 1788, some of London's black people were participating in more mainstream, though not necessarily more respectable, forms of popular radicalism. On 22 July, the last day of voting for one of the City of Westminster's MPs, a 'desperate mob' led by Charles James Fox assembled in Covent Garden. They were supporting the Foxite Whig Lord John Townshend's bid against the incumbent Tory Lord Samuel Hood in an extremely close-run contest when a fracas broke out. When it became clear that the Bow-Street Runners were unable to suppress the riot, local magistrate Sir Sampson Wright called in the support of the militia.[47] Fox, incensed at this 'violation of an existing statute', confronted the magistrate on Bow Street. 'During the altercation between them', reported the *General Evening Post*, 'one of the soldiers aimed a stroke at Mr. Fox with his bayonet; which Thomas Carlisle, a black man, observing, he threw himself between Mr. Fox and the soldier, and received a dangerous wound in his head.'[48] The scene was parodied shortly afterward in an etching by James Gillray (Figure 7.2). In it, the Whig playwright and MP Richard Brinsley Sheridan could be seen threatening a kneeling Sampson Wright while Fox and Edmund Burke are stabbed in the breeches by guardsmen. Tellingly, while Burke was inserted into this scene despite not actually being present, there was no sign of Carlisle or his dramatic personal intervention.

---

[46] *General Evening Post*, 9 September 1786, 2.   [47] *Times*, 24 July 1788, 2.
[48] *General Evening Post*, 24 July 1788, 3.

Figure 7.2 James Gillray, *The Battle of Bow Street*, 1788, hand-coloured
etching and aquatint, 248 mm × 358 mm.
Courtesy of the Lewis Walpole Library, Yale University.

It might seem difficult to see how a figure as committed to courting
respectable patrons as Cugoano could have fit in with London's fledgling black radical scene. Yet links existed. Carlisle, for example, was a
member of the Sons of Africa, and co-signed a private letter to Sharp
along with Cugoano the same year as the Covent Garden riot.[49] John
Pegg, the man whose arrest sparked the riot at the White Raven in 1786,
was a 'Corporal of the black poor', meaning that he was given charity
money for distribution to a 'division' of London's black people by the
Committee for the Relief of the Black Poor.[50] Another of these 'Corporals' was William Green, who was with Cugoano when they applied
to Sharp in July the same year to assist Harry Demaine.[51] Several more

[49] 'Letter to Granville Sharp, esq. [Undated]', reprinted in Cugoano, *Thoughts and
Sentiments*, ed. Carretta, 189–190 [no source cited].
[50] *General Evening Post*, 9 September 1786, 2.
[51] TNA, Treasury Papers, T1/632, 'Proceedings of the Society for the Relief of the Black
Poor, 7 June 1786'.

of the 'black poor' who received the money had co-signed the Sons of Africa letters.[52] Additionally, Cugoano could claim links with leading white radicals through his abolitionist connections.[53] As we have seen, Sharp was a long-standing member of the Society for Constitutional Information, which had been pushing for parliamentary reform since 1780.[54] By 1792, Cugoano's correspondent and friend Equiano was lodging with Thomas Hardy, secretary of 'by far the most important of the new radical societies', the London Corresponding Society.[55] Thus, figures such as Cugoano and Equiano provided a link between the street-level, direct action of London's poor black community and the pamphleteering and corresponding societies which came to characterise British radicalism in the early 1790s.

Similarly, Cugoano's print and distribution networks linked his text with revolutionary ideology. Of his two texts, the only one to list booksellers was *Evil of Slavery*. Of the four named sellers on the title page to this 1791 tract, two were committed and consistent publishers of reformist and pro-French Revolution polemics. As well as selling Cugoano and Equiano's texts and a few other abolitionist pamphlets, Taylor and Company at South Arch, Royal Exchange, kept their customers up to date with the latest happenings from across the Channel. For example, in 1790, the anonymous *Account of the Escape of the French King*, detailing Louis Capet's flight to Varennes and accompanied by a literal translation of some 'effusions of a patriotic annalist' on the subject, could be bought alongside Cugoano's tract.[56] Another of his booksellers, H. Symonds, specialised in polemics relating directly to parliamentary reform in Britain, printing reports of sedition trials and, in 1793, Thomas Erskine's *Declaration of the Friends of the Liberty of the Press*.[57] Symonds also

---

[52] James Bailey and Jonathan Adams are recorded as receiving money from the Committee, as well as 'Joseph Allambazi', who may have been Joseph Almaze. TNA, Treasury Solicitors' Papers for 1786, T1/638, 'An Alphabetical List of the Black People Who Have Received the Bounty from Government'.

[53] For connections between political radicals and abolition before 1794, see John Oldfield, *Popular Politics and British Anti-Slavery: The Mobilisation of Public Opinion against the Slave Trade, 1787–1807* (Manchester: Manchester University Press, 1995), 42–43; James Walvin, 'The Impact of Slavery on British Radical Politics: 1787–1838', *Annals of the New York Academy of Sciences* 292:1 (1977), 343–355; David Brion Davis, *The Problem of Slavery in the Age of Revolution 1770–1823* (Oxford: Oxford University Press, 1999), 343–468.

[54] Society for Constitutional Information, *To the Public: The Address of the Society for Constitutional Information* (London: Society for Constitutional Information, [1780]).

[55] H. T. Dickinson, *British Radicalism and the French Revolution 1789–1815* (Oxford: Blackwell, 1985), 9.

[56] Anon., *An Account of the Escape of the French King* (London: Symonds et al., 1790).

[57] Anon., *The Patriot: Addressed to the Electors of Great Britain, by a Member of the House of Commons. Containing a Dissertation on the Proposed Reform of Parliamentary Election*

published a number of provocative pro–French Revolutionary tracts during the period.[58]

These were not the only links Cugoano's text had to revolutionary France. In 1788, a translation of *Thoughts and Sentiments* appeared in Paris under the title *Reflexions sur la traite et l'esclavage des Negres*.[59] The text's translator, Antoine Diannyere, an abolitionist and political economist, went on to become a founding member of the Class of Moral and Political Sciences (CMPS) in 1795.[60] A pan-disciplinary intellectual institute born from the ashes of the French royal societies, the CMPS was founded on 'true principles of republican equality'; members swore a formal oath of 'hatred to royalty' on admittance, and no hierarchy was recognised.[61] Diannyere's translation of the text's title suggests something of its intended readership. The original English title consciously paraphrased Clarkson's *Essay on the Slavery and Commerce of the Human Species*, implying both Cugoano's literacy and political leanings. In the same spirit, the title of Diannyere's translation paraphrased Nicolas de Condorcet's 1781 antislavery pamphlet *Reflexions sur l'esclavage des Negres*. Like Clarkson in Britain, Condorcet was considered a radical figure in France during the 1780s and in 1791 was elected as a Paris representative in the Assemblée Nationale.[62] In both cases, an association was purposefully formed between Cugoano's ideas and those of high-profile abolitionists known to support domestic political reform. This technique helped booksellers to market writing by a black author to an audience broadly sympathetic to either abolitionism, political radicalism or both.

At points, Cugoano's antislavery writing became intertwined with a politically radical message, though his domestic politics were vague in

---

(London: G. Bourne and H. Symonds, 1790); Thomas Muir, *An Account of the Trial of Thomas Muir ... for Sedition* (London: J. Robertson et al., 1793); Thomas Briellat, *The Trial of Thomas Briellat for Seditious Words* (London: H. Simonds et al., 1794).

[58] Anon., *Flower of the Jacobins: Containing Biographical Sketches of the Leading Men at Present at the Head of Affairs in France* (London: J. Owen and H. Symonds, 1792); Charles James, *An Extenuation of the Conduct of the French Revolutionists* (London: H. Symonds, 1792).

[59] Ottobah Cugoano, *Reflexions sur la traite et l'esclavage des Negres*, trans. Antoine Diannyere (Paris: Royez, 1788).

[60] For the attribution to Diannyere, see Gregory Pierrot, 'Insights on "Lord Hoth" and Ottobah Cugoano', *Notes and Queries*, 59:3 (2012), 367–368.

[61] See Martin S. Staum, 'The Class of Moral and Political Sciences, 1795–1803', *French Historical Studies*, 11:3 (1980), 371–397.

[62] For Condorcet's radicalism in the 1780s, see Nicolas de Condorcet, *Writings on the United States*, ed. and trans. Guillaume Ansart (Philadelphia: University of Pennsylvania Press, 2012); for Clarkson's radicalism, see, for example, Oldfield, *Popular Politics*, 70–95.

comparison with the publications of the corresponding societies. For example, he suggested that any form of justice in government was impossible to realise while an amoral economic elite was able to influence policy in its own favour:

But it so happens in general, that men of activity and affluence, by whatever way they are possessed of such riches, or have acquired a greatness of such property, they are always preferred to take the lead in matters of government, so that the greatest depredators, warriors, contracting companies of merchants, and rich slave-holders, always endeavour to push themselves on to get power and interest in their favour; that whatever crimes any of them commit they are seldom brought to any just punishment.[63]

For Cugoano, participation in the slave trade was such a corrupt enterprise that slave-holders sitting in Parliament invalidated its moral authority to govern. By the 'magnetic influence' of a powerful and wealthy slave-owning political class, 'there [was] a general support given to despotism, oppression and cruelty.'[64] Though expressed in abstract terms, this rhetoric blurred or disregarded the distinctions between the despotism of slavery and that of a corrupt British government, anticipating the anti-slavery radicalism of, for example, Robert Wedderburn (see Chapter 8).

Cugoano's synthesis of antislavery and radical rhetoric blurred not only the lines between the different forms of tyranny permitted by the British government but also those between the revolutionary movements that challenged them. 'History affords us many examples of severe retaliations, revolutions and dreadful overthrows', he warned, 'and of many crying under the heavy load of subjection and oppression, seeking for deliverance.'[65] In the context of his extended attack on chattel slavery, the references to 'subjection and oppression' would seem like an obvious reference to the withholding of physical freedom inherent in the transatlantic system. Yet, coupled with the mentions of historical 'retaliations, revolutions and dreadful overthrows', these generic terms took on lowering radical overtones. Gesturing toward the American Revolution, still fresh in the popular consciousness, Cugoano picked his words from the lexicon of radical polemic. A couple of pages later, he even went as far as to invoke the Painite refrain of 'the natural rights and liberties of men' in his declamation of the evils of slavery:

What revolution the end of that predominant evil of slavery and oppression may produce ... is not for me to determine ... And nothing else can be expected for

---

[63] Cugoano, *Thoughts and Sentiments*, 89–90.   [64] Cugoano, *Thoughts and Sentiments*, 90.
[65] Cugoano, *Thoughts and Sentiments*, 75.

such violations of taking away the natural rights and liberties of men, but those who are the doers of it will meet with some awful visitation of the righteous judgement of God[.][66]

For Cugoano, the language of revolutionary politics, blended with religious millenarianism, best articulated the urgency and necessity of abolishing slavery.

Even the changing use of pronouns in *Thoughts and Sentiments* bore noticeable political connotations. Babacar M'Baye has discussed the use of the collective first person in Cugoano and Equiano's work as signifiers of developing social and political senses of diasporic selfhood.[67] The identifying marker 'we' thus referred variously to 'we the Africans', 'we the enslaved', 'we the black poor', 'we the Christians' and 'we the British people'. Cugoano's authorial perspective demonstrated a startling degree of plasticity, which only avoided destabilising the text's argument thanks precisely to the socially dislocating experiences of kidnap, enslavement, renaming, forced transportation, sale, resale, emancipation, and finally employment in bourgeois domestic service. The constant disruptions in his social status enabled him to view British and slave societies from both within and without at the same time, in much the same way as Ignatius Sancho had.[68] This was how the suggestion that 'you might seek grace and repentance' for 'the horrible iniquity of making merchandize of us' could be coherently followed a few pages later by the patriotic assertion that 'we would wish to have the grandeur and fame of the British empire to extend far and wide'.[69]

Of course, it should be remembered that Cugoano's intended readership was not exclusively white nor British-born. As with other radical corresponding societies, the Sons of Africa supported their members' published tracts. While poverty was a pressing issue for most black people in eighteenth-century London, a few found the money to buy

---

[66] Cugoano, *Thoughts and Sentiments*, 76–77.

[67] Babacar M'Baye, *The Trickster Comes West* (Jackson: University of Mississippi Press, 2009), 103–104.

[68] Carretta discusses Cugoano's developing/competing identities in terms of his 'binomial identity' (i.e. John Stuart/Ottobah Cugoano) in his private correspondence. Carretta, 'Revisited and Revised', 84. Christine Levecq has discussed how the political messages embedded in published petitions written by black authors in late eighteenth-century America reveal that they 'were both assimilating and expanding on the revolutionary ideology that surrounded them'. Christine Levecq, '"We Beg Your Excellency": The Sentimental Politics of Abolitionist Petitions in the Late Eighteenth Century', in Stephen Ahern (ed.), *Affect and Abolition in the Anglo-Atlantic, 1770–1830* (London: Ashgate, 2013), 152.

[69] Cugoano, *Thoughts and Sentiments*, 129, 143.

Cugoano's *Evil of Slavery* when it was published in 1791. The publication's list of subscribers named 'Mr. Adams', 'Mr. Baily', 'Mr. Dent' and 'Mr. Elliott' as having bought a copy.[70] At least some of these corresponded to John Adams, James Bailey, George Dent and Bernard Eliot, all cosignatories of the Sons of Africa letters to Sharp, Fox, Pitt and Dolben in 1788 and 1789. William Green was also named as a subscriber.[71] For Cugoano's part, he was listed among the subscribers to the first four editions of Equiano's *Interesting Narrative*.[72] Subscription lists have not survived for Cugoano's 1787 tract *Thoughts on Slavery*, but given that many of London's black community travelled to Sierra Leone in the intervening years, it is fair to assume at least as many members of London's black poor read that as did his later text.

The Sierra Leone Resettlement Projects

The plan to expatriate London's 'black poor' came about as an initiative of the all-white Committee for the Relief of the Black Poor. The harsh British winter of 1785/1786 had a severe impact on many of the former Loyalists. A group of gentlemen, operating from Batson's Coffee-house at the Royal Exchange, began collecting public subscriptions on 5 January 1786 for free bread to be distributed to 'every Black in distress, who will apply'.[73] The response, in terms of both subscriptions and clients, was extensive. By 28 January, some 250 black people had availed themselves of the offer, and the list of subscribers expanded weekly.[74] But it was clear that the effects of extreme poverty went beyond hunger, and by 15 March public subscription money was being spent on medical expenses, clothing, lodging and preparation for work at sea.[75]

Despite the success of the subscriptions, it was evident that a longer-term solution was required. The Treasury Solicitor's Office began contributing £50 per week to the subscriptions by 17 April, on the understanding that the Committee begin working toward a permanent

---

[70] Cugoano, *Evil of Slavery*, [49–54].
[71] Cugoano, *Evil of Slavery*, [49–54]. For further evidence of black readerships of early black writing, see Eve Bannet, *Transatlantic Stories and the History of Reading, 1720–1810: Migrant Fictions* (Cambridge: Cambridge University Press, 2011), 139–158.
[72] Olaudah Equiano, *The Interesting Narrative*, 1st edn. (London: Johnson et al., 1789); Olaudah Equiano, *The Interesting Narrative*, 2nd edn. (London: Johnson et al., 1789); Olaudah Equiano, *The Interesting Narrative*, 3rd edn. (London: Johnson et al., 1790); Olaudah Equiano, *The Interesting Narrative*, 4th edn. (Dublin: W. Sleater, 1791).
[73] *Public Advertiser*, 5 January 1786, 5.
[74] See, for example, *Public Advertiser*, 27 January 1786, 1.
[75] *Public Advertiser*, 15 March 1786, cited in Braidwood, *Black Poor and White Philanthropists*, 69.

'solution'.[76] Over the course of the spring, Henry Smeathman, a member of the Committee and later its chair, redrafted some plans he had drawn up earlier for a mass relocation of hundreds of London's 'black poor' to the coast of Sierra Leone. This would be a means, he wrote to the Treasury Solicitor's Office, of 'removing such a burthen from the Public for ever, and of putting them in a condition of repaying this country the expense thereof'.[77] The Treasury agreed to fund the scheme to the value of fourteen pounds per head, and underwrote the cost of 'temporary relief' for black people in the capital on the proviso that every recipient of this charity money would sign up for permanent resettlement.[78]

The Loyalists were at the heart of the administration of the charity money as well as the resettlement project.[79] Indeed, a formal organisational structure for London's black community emerged through the Committee's plans to distribute the Treasury's money, borrowing the military language already familiar to many of the Loyalists. At the 24 May meeting of the Committee, it was resolved that

> the blacks and people of colour who assemble to receive the six pence a day allowed by the government for their temporary support understood to be continued till such time as they commence the voyage on the agreement with Mr. Smeathman be [ar]ranged in Companies of at least twelve each under a chosen man to be called Corporal, who can write or give account to our clerk by memory.[80]

At the next meeting on 7 June, the first eight of these 'Corporals' were named as James Johnson, Jonathan William Ramsay, Aaron Brookes, John Lemon, John Cambridge, John Williams, William Green and Charles Stoddard.[81] By July these had been joined by John Wilson, Jacob Jackson, Paul Clarke, J. W. Harris, Abraham Elliot, George Jemmison, Daniel Christopher and Thomas Holder.[82] Since this new externally imposed hierarchy was based on perceived intellectual and social weight, it might be surprising to see that Equiano and Cugoano were not put forward as corporals. For Equiano's part, he was in Philadelphia at the

---

[76] TNA, Treasury Papers, T1/631, 'B. Johnson to Geo. Rose, 1 June 1786 [Accounts of the Committee, 17 April to 1 June, 1786]'.

[77] TNA, Treasury Papers, T1/631, 'Memorial of Henry Smeathman, 24 May 1786'.

[78] TNA, Treasury Papers, T1/631, 'Commrs Navy report, that Mr. Smeathman's proposals are reasonable, 24 May 1786'.

[79] Stephen Braidwood, 'Initiatives and Organisations', 211–227.

[80] TNA, Treasury Papers, T1/631, 'Proceedings of the Committee for the Relief of the Black Poor, 24 May 1786'.

[81] TNA, Treasury Papers, T1/632, 'Proceedings of the Committee for the Relief of the Black Poor, 7 June 1786'.

[82] TNA, Treasury Papers, T1/633, 'Proceedings of the Committee for the Relief of the Black Poor, 15 July 1786'.

time, and in any case he may already have set his sights on a higher office for the voyage, which he attained on his appointment as commissary for the project in August.[83] Cugoano, in a comparatively comfortable situation as Cosway's servant, had no need of the charity money, and consequently was not eligible as a corporal. However, because of his connections to Equiano, Green and others involved in the project, he became one of its highest-profile commentators. Cugoano's writings (first published in 1787, and therefore admittedly written with the considerable advantage of hindsight) suggest that he had serious reservations about the plan from the beginning.

It must be acknowledged that black people viewed the charity-distributing Committee and the government-funded resettlement project quite separately, and in very different ways. Cugoano was quite clear in his opinions on both. In *Thoughts and Sentiments*, he acknowledged that:

> Particular thanks are due to every one of that humane society of worthy and respectful gentlemen, whose liberality hath supported many of the Black poor about London ... For they have not only commiserated the poor in general, *but even those which are accounted as beasts, and imputed as vile in the sight of others.* The part that the British government has taken, to co-operate with them, has certainly a flattering and laudable appearance of doing some good.[84]

This mention of the British government was handled with care. Cugoano had to balance his commitment to respectability with his social role as a leading figure in London's black community. Thus the British government's early support of the Committee for the Relief of the Black Poor was represented, with appreciable cynicism, as having only the 'appearance' of doing good. Similarly, no objections from black Loyalists against this early financial support were recorded in the minutes of the Committee.

Many of the black Loyalists shared Cugoano's scepticism over British intentions for the new Sierra Leone settlement. Embarkations on the three ships fitted out to convey them to Sierra Leone slowed to a crawl, even after the charity money was withdrawn from those who refused to go.[85] As another harsh winter drew in, the sight of black Loyalists in distress on the icy streets once again became commonplace for Londoners. Their reaction was less favourable than it had been the previous year. On 23 December 1786, the *Times* reprinted the opinion given by John

---

[83] Vincent Carretta, *Equiano, the African: Biography of a Self-Made Man* (Athens: University of Georgia Press, 2005), 224.

[84] Cugoano, *Thoughts and Sentiments*, 138–139 (emphasis in original).

[85] See, for example, *Morning Herald*, 3 November 1786, 2; TNA, Treasury Papers, T1/632, 'Proceedings of the Committee for the Relief of the Black Poor, 7 June 1786'.

Dunning, one of the lawyers on the losing side of the Mansfield ruling, that 'the numerous dingy-coloured faces which crouded our streets, must have their origin in our wives been terrified [*sic*] when pregnant, by the numerous Africans who were to be seen in all parts of the town.'[86] Dunning's theory seemed to suggest that dark skin could be developed *in utero* through some kind of osmotic process or, as he euphemistically implied, as a result of rape. This notion proved as popular as it was outlandish; it was echoed again and again in the reactionary press during the winter of 1786/1787. In the *Public Advertiser*, as well as the *Times* of 28 December 1786, a correspondent lamented that:

Two blacks are daily walking the streets, the one leaning on the other's shoulder, as if in great pain. This object is sufficiently disagreeable, and to our magistrates highly disgraceful. Must our wives and children be always exposed to be frightened in this manner? As soon as the wife of any Alderman or Magistrates shall have lost an heir, owing to the frequency of such horrid sights, the public will probably be relieved. – But not till then.[87]

For this correspondent, spectacles of black distress could lead to white miscarriages. An inverted pyramid of suffering was constructed, in which the physical deformity and death of countless unborn white innocents flowed upward from the distress of a tiny minority both at the bottom of and alien to the social hierarchy.

The presence of a burdened 'public' in need of 'relief' from such disagreeable and terrifying spectacles of black suffering underlined a sense of civic identity based on (white) ethnicity. The letter's allusions to 'the public', counterpoised against the frightening black beggars, suggested a form of national social self-definition redrawn along the lines of ethnic signifiers. With the ameliorative effects of the Eden Agreement of 1786 yet to reach most of the population, the social and economic burden of the nation's humiliating defeat in America seemed to be articulated in the suffering bodies of a visibly alien Other, to whom the boundaries of 'Britishness' could no longer afford to extend.[88] In other words, the desire to morally 'atone' for the loss of America began to equivocate under the economic pressures of the post-war recession. Black people, regardless of their record of supporting British interests through their military service, were now defined *against* a white British 'public'. Thus the 'public', in the imagination of the popular press, took

---

[86] *Times*, 23 December 1786, 2.   [87] *Public Advertiser*, 28 December 1786, 3.
[88] For background on the postwar British economy and the Eden treaty, see John E. Crowley, 'Neo-Mercantilism and *The Wealth of Nations*: British Commercial Policy after the American Revolution', *Historical Journal*, 33:2 (1990), 339–360, esp. 353–355.

on the character of a racially homogenised society from which black people, former British military or not, were emphatically and by definition excluded.

Black people did not need to suffer to become 'sufficiently disagreeable' objects in the eyes of the British press. Those who were not pathogenic were parasitic, and black people in the comparatively comfortable position of domestic service such as Cugoano were seen to be depriving 'real' British citizens of work. On the day after the *Public Advertiser* piece appeared, the *Morning Post* published an article complaining that 'When so many of our own young men and women are out of employment ... it is abominable that aliens, and more particularly Black aliens, should be suffered to eat the bread of idleness in Gentlemen's houses.'[89] Here again, the nationalist rhetoric of supporting formerly 'British' soldiers and sailors had given way under the weight of carrying it out in practice. British people had sympathised with the black Loyalists and helped them as much as they were willing to. But permanent asylum was never the preferred solution. By December 1786, the message emerging from the press was as consistent as it was shrill: it was time for the black Loyalists to leave.

Even with so much vitriol targeted at them, London's black people remained reluctant to board the ships. While Smeathman was responsible for the expedition, the project had been popular, but after his death in July 1786 enthusiasm waned. This was possibly because the Loyalists themselves came to recognise that their relocation was rooted at least as much in political expediency as in altruism. Cugoano articulated the sentiments of his peers the following year:

What with the death of some of the original promoters and proposers of this charitable undertaking ... and by the adverse motives of those employed to be the conductors thereof, we think it will be more than what can be well expected, if we ever hear of any good in proportion to so great, well-designed, laudable and expensive charity.[90]

The Loyalists' distrust of government influence slowed down embarkations, and despite the charity money being stopped altogether after 31 October 1786, the ships remained at anchor in the Thames until 16 January 1787, when they sailed half-full to Spithead in preparation for their voyage.[91]

[89] *Morning Post and Daily Advertiser*, 29 December 1786, 2.
[90] Cugoano, *Thoughts and Sentiments*, 140–141.
[91] Braidwood, *Black Poor and White Philanthropists*, 145.

The problems with the project went deeper than a failure to convince black people that they would be better off in Sierra Leone. Many of the settlers who had initially signed up for the project were, in the event, reluctant to go. Lack of communication from the Committee and an increasingly draconian approach from the Treasury Solicitor's Office made many of them nervous. On 15 December 1786, the *Morning Herald* reported that

> some of the leaders of the seven hundred poor Black [*sic*] who had signed an engagement to go to a Free Settlement on the coast of Africa, submitted the new system, intended for their government in Ethiopia, to the consideration of the Right Hon. Lord George Gordon, and requested his advice and opinion on the subject, before they sailed from England. His Lordship advised them *not to go*.[92]

Gordon, best known for instigating the anti-Catholic riots of 1780, was not the obvious choice for the 'black poor' to select as their advisor. Newspaper reports show that condemned prisoners and those under sentence of transportation appealed to him at around the same time to intercede in their sentences.[93] The *Times*, dependable in its dismissive attitude toward black suffering, parodied this sudden flurry of requests on 12 January 1787: '*Lord George Crop* knows not what to do, or where to turn himself – *Newgate Prisoners*, *Botany Bay convicts*, and *vagabond Blacks*, solicit his divided and distracted attention.'[94] Connections may have been made between some of the free black Loyalists and Gordon through black 'Botany Bay convicts', such as 'Peter, a black man', or Francis Othello.[95] In any case, the leaders of the 'black poor' bound for Sierra Leone, according to various newspaper reports, visited Gordon in Newgate prison several more times during December and January.[96] They even published a letter addressed to him in the *Morning Herald*, drawing the public censure of the new superintendent of the expedition, Joseph Irwin.[97]

The British authorities were so keen to fill vessels bound for Sierra Leone that they quickly acceded to demands made by the corporals that

[92] *Morning Herald*, 15 December 1786, 3.
[93] See, for example, *Public Advertiser*, 25 December 1786, 2; *General Evening Post*, 6 January 1787, 4.
[94] *Times*, 12 January 1787, 2.
[95] *Old Bailey Proceedings Online*, s17860531-1, 'Punishment summary, 31 May 1786', available at www.oldbaileyonline.org. My assumption that Francis Othello was black is based solely on his surname. Pybus has reconstructed more individual biographies of black convicts transported to Australia. Pybus, *Epic Journeys of Freedom*, 89–102.
[96] See, for example, *Morning Herald*, 2 January 1787, 3.
[97] This letter is unfortunately no longer available in any major collection. For Irwin's response, see *Morning Herald*, 13 January 1787, 4.

certain black prisoners be released from gaol to take part in the voyage.[98] This accommodating spirit, intended to kick-start the mass expatriation of London's black community, now appeared suspect for entirely new reasons, and the corporals began to see parallels between their own and the convicts' situations. A number of the Loyalists had undergone the horrors of the middle passage once already, and they were not keen to be transported in comparable conditions again. Matters were not helped when it became apparent that the Royal Navy ship HMS *Nautilus*, which was assigned to escort the settlers to Sierra Leone, had only just returned from scouting the West African coast for a suitable site to build a new penal colony.[99] In contrast, Gordon had intervened on behalf of the Botany Bay convicts so spiritedly that his actions led to a seditious libel conviction in 1787.[100] If the contracts the 'black poor' had signed did indeed turn out to amount to the same bonded servitude as that meted out to convicts, they were unlikely to find a more forceful or better-qualified advocate.

While it is unlikely that Cugoano ever boarded the ships bound for Sierra Leone, it is likely that he was among the 'Chiefs of the Black Poor' who visited Gordon. The lengthy criticisms Cugoano gave of the Sierra Leone voyage in his *Thoughts and Sentiments* demonstrated a keen but distrustful interest in the proceedings of the project. Equiano certainly wrote to him to keep him up to date with the latest problems aboard the ships.[101] And according to the *Morning Chronicle*, 'Mr. John Stuart', described as one of 'the principal persons concerned in the abolition of the Slave Trade', visited Gordon in Newgate in January 1788 'and requested his Lordship to look over and revise all the publications, and appeals lately printed on their [the abolitionists'] behalf'.[102] While it is and was a common enough British name, Cugoano was the only leading abolitionist figure active in London in 1788 known as John Stuart.

There is another social link between Cugoano and Gordon. Even though he was not keen to promote the fact, Thomas Hardy, secretary

---

[98] See, for example, TNA, T 1/636, 'Proceedings of the Committee for the Relief of the Black Poor, 6 October 1786'.

[99] Braidwood, *Black Poor and White Philanthropists*, 131. Emma Christopher has discussed the rejection of West Africa as a suitable site for a convict settlement. Emma Christopher, 'A "Disgrace to the Very Colour": Perceptions of Blackness and Whiteness in the Founding of Sierra Leone and Botany Bay', *Journal of Colonialism and Colonial History*, 9:3 (2008), available at http://muse.jhu.edu/journals/journal_of_colonialism_and_colonial_history/v009/9.3.christopher.html

[100] See George Gordon, *The Whole Proceedings on the Trials of Two Informations Exhibited ex Officio by the King's Attorney-General against George Gordon, Esq.* (London: M. Gurney, 1787).

[101] *Public Advertiser*, 4 April 1787, 3.   [102] *Morning Chronicle*, 19 January 1788, 3.

of the London Corresponding Society and landlord of Cugoano's correspondent and collaborator Equiano, was an old friend of Gordon. In a passage deleted from the published version of his memoirs, Hardy described how he was 'well acquainted with Lord G. Gordon' and 'always much entertained and expressed a sincere respect for the many admirable virtues of that misguided but much injured, and oppressed man'.[103] While Equiano did not lodge with Hardy until 1790, it is possible that he or Cugoano had met him by 1786 through mutual radical friends – such as Gordon's cousin and legal counsel Thomas Erskine – and that Hardy introduced them to Gordon.

Though the *Morning Herald*'s assertion that 'there are very few now left aboard, except such decoy blacks as are paid by government to go out with enormous salaries' was an overstatement, Gordon's advice further slowed embarkations at London.[104] By the time the ships sailed to Spithead on 16 January 1787, only 459 people had embarked – well short of the 675 who had signed the agreement and received the charity money after 3 June 1786.[105] A combination of severe weather and mismanagement by Irwin and Equiano caused further delays at Spithead and forced the ships to dock again at Plymouth for repairs. Here, Equiano was dismissed from his post as commissary (see Chapter 2), and it was not until 9 April 1787 that the ships finally set sail for Sierra Leone without him.[106]

A week later, an unsigned letter written by Cugoano appeared in the *Public Advertiser*.[107] It represented a blistering attack on the management of the project, couched in even more critical terms than Equiano's:

We find his Majesty's servants have [taken] away the Commissary's commission [from Mr.] Vasa. He came up from Plymouth to complain, and is now gone back again to take his effects on shore. The memorials of all the Black people, which they have sent up from Plymouth, represent that they are much wronged, injured, and oppressed natives of Africa and under various pretences and different manners have been dragged away from London and carried captives

---

[103] BL, Add. MSS. 65153A, 'Manuscript Copy of Memoirs of Thomas Hardy', ff. 8–9.
[104] *Morning Herald*, 15 December 1786, 3.
[105] Braidwood, *Black Poor and White Philanthropists*, 148.
[106] Carretta, *Self-Made Man*, 231.
[107] 'by Cugoano': This letter was paraphrased heavily in *Thoughts and Sentiments*. While Cugoano freely drew on sources without citing them elsewhere in the text, this passage is paraphrased, with the same key points made in a different order (see in the main text below). This, in conjunction with the chronological proximity to Equiano's letter, plus the fact that it appeared in the same newspaper, strongly suggests that the 6 April letter was written by Cugoano in response to the news of his friend's dismissal from the voyage. Braidwood also asserts that the letter 'may well have been written by Cugoano'. Braidwood, *Black Poor and White Philanthropists*, 158.

to Plymouth, where they have nothing but slavery before their eyes, should they proceed to Africa or the West Indies under the command of the persons who have charge of them.[108]

Cugoano's lines of communication with the black settlers on board the ships put him in a position, as he saw it, to represent their views in the press. His articulation of the understandable fear of re-enslavement reflected the Botany Bay rumours as well as Gordon's response to the contracts when he reviewed them in December 1786. He simultaneously highlighted the hypocrisy of the British government with regard to their support of slave forts on the West African coast: 'They cannot conceive, say they, Government would establish a free colony for them, whilst it supports its forts and factories to wrong and ensnare, and to carry others of their colour and country into slavery and bondage.'[109] But Cugoano has misjudged the public mood. He approximated the broad public support for the relief of the 'black poor' in early 1786 with a popular turn against the slave trade. Perhaps naively, he assumed that his suggestion that the enslavement process was beginning in London, and that passengers were 'carried captives to Plymouth', would direct public indignation toward the project. He reckoned, wrongly, that humanitarian feeling would overcome the financial burden and social inconvenience represented by the 'black poor'.

Cugoano's letter went on to criticise the white managers of the project personally, stating that 'the contract, on Mr. Smeathman's plan' had 'not been fulfilled ... but a Mr. Irwin has contrived to monopolize the benefit to himself.'[110] Even though, according to the Committee's July 1786 minutes, the corporals declared that 'there is no man in whom they can now repose the same confidence and trust as in Mr. Joseph Irwin', they were then judging him solely on Smeathman's recommendation.[111] Once they were aboard the ships, relations broke down very quickly. Cugoano's impressions of Irwin could not have been helped when another old friend, William Green, was ejected from the voyage in Plymouth following a row with him.[112] Given the fact that several of Cugoano's known associates were on board the ships at Plymouth – including Green and Cugoano's fellow members of the Sons of Africa, Equiano, Daniel Christopher and George Mandeville – it is safe to assume that his information was coming directly from them. In a thinly

---

[108] *Public Advertiser*, 6 April 1787, 2.   [109] *Public Advertiser*, 6 April 1787, 2.
[110] *Public Advertiser*, 6 April 1787, 2.
[111] TNA, Treasury Papers, T1/634, 'Proceedings of the Committee for the Relief of the Black Poor, 15 July 1786'.
[112] Braidwood, *Black Poor and White Philanthropists*, 152.

veiled reference to Irwin in his *Thoughts and Sentiments*, Cugoano blamed 'some disagreeable jealousy of those who were appointed governors' for the project's problems.[113]

Cugoano went on to reiterate his comparison between the coercive methods used to ensure black people boarded the ships and the process of enslavement:

Many more of the Black People still in this country would have, with great gladness, embraced the opportunity, longing to reach their native land; but as the old saying is, A burnt child dreads the fire, some of these unfortunate sons and daughters of Africa have been severally unlawfully dragged away from their native abodes, under various pretences, by the insidious treachery of others, and have been brought into the hands of barbarous robbers and pirates, and like sheep to the market, have been sold into captivity and slavery.[114]

Two forms of coerced migration here were purposefully conflated by the repetition of the euphemistic phrase 'under various pretences', a device Cugoano had also used in his *Public Advertiser* letter. In his hands, the phrase had sufficient elasticity to encompass both the brute-force approach of kidnap associated with the slave trade and the more subtle forms of coercion imposed in the execution of the resettlement attempt. Similarly, the comparative distinction between 'captivity' and 'slavery' recalled that the project had, in effect, divested the settlers of their freedom once they boarded the ships. While he accepted the charitable and humane intentions of the project in principle, the ends remained resolutely unjustified by means too similar to enslavement to be worth differentiating from it.

Such harsh criticism of the government may seem at odds with Cugoano's attempts to court 'establishment' figures such as Burke and Pitt. But he managed to incorporate the analogy between the Sierra Leone project and transatlantic slavery into his model of respectability by invoking the patriotic myth of a national love of freedom.[115] He redefined cardinal measures of alterity away from visible, extrinsic signifiers such as skin colour and toward intrinsic personal characteristics such as morality. Thus, slave traders, not black Loyalists, fell outside the boundaries of morally upstanding, charitable and benevolent 'Britishness'. Cugoano

---

[113] Cugoano, *Thoughts and Sentiments*, 140.
[114] Cugoano, *Thoughts and Sentiments*, 141.
[115] Nicholas Hudson discusses 'establishment' antislavery rhetoric in relation to the 'patriotic image of Britons as a freedom-loving people' in Nicholas Hudson, '"Britons Never Will Be Slaves": National Myth, Conservatism, and the Beginnings of British Antislavery', *Eighteenth-Century Studies*, 34:4 (2001), 559–576.

countered the collective 'public' identity based on whiteness, as engineered in the popular press, with one based on a supposedly shared national intuition for moral justice. Service in the public interest demanded incorporation into public society. Thus he reminded his readership that many of the black people aboard the ships, 'by various services either to the public or individuals, as more particularly in the course of the last war, have gotten their liberty again in this free country', but explained that they were 'afraid of being ensnared again; for the European seafaring people in general, who trade to foreign parts, have such a prejudice against Black People, that they use them more like asses than men, so that a Black Man is scarcely ever safe among them'.[116] Here, Cugoano renegotiated the racialized terms of villainy and victimhood expressed by the press during the winter of 1786/1787. Readers assuming a degree of exaggeration regarding dehumanising attitudes toward black people needed only look at a misguided humanitarian essay published two years later in *Woodfall's Register* entitled, without irony, 'Cruelty to Horses, and Asses, and Negroes' to see the literal truth behind his assertion.[117]

Of course, it is a now well-documented fact that this first attempt to establish a 'Province of Freedom' in Sierra Leone ended in catastrophic failure. Events in Sierra Leone between 1787 and 1791 have been well rehearsed by historians, who broadly agree that the settler population was devastated by a combination of unfortunate timing, mismanagement, bad luck, poor communication with local Temne peoples and infighting.[118] By 1790, the settlers' new home in Sierra Leone, Granville Town, was deserted, with all the inhabitants dead, enslaved or seeking refuge as employees of local African or European slave traders.

In 1791, a new Sierra Leone Company was established in London with the aim of reviving the project's fortunes. This time the company received the full backing of the government from a very early stage in its development. Meanwhile, a black Loyalist from Nova Scotia named Thomas Peters had arrived in London to petition Secretary of State William Grenville for 'some Establishment where [black people in Nova

---

[116] Cugoano, *Thoughts and Sentiments*, 141.
[117] *Diary or Woodfall's Register*, 29 December 1789, 1.
[118] See, for example, Wallace Brown, 'The Black Loyalists in Sierra Leone', in Pulis (ed.), *Moving On*, 103–134; Braidwood, *Black Poor and White Philanthropists*, 181–225; Walker, *The Black Loyalists*, 94–115; John Peterson, *Province of Freedom: A History of Sierra Leone 1787–1870* (London: Faber and Faber, 1969), 17–27. The classic account of the establishment of Sierra Leone is Christopher Fyfe, *A History of Sierra Leone* (Oxford: Oxford University Press, 1962), esp. 13–25.

Scotia] may obtain a competent settlement for themselves'.[119] This convenient piece of timing was seized on by the new Company, and in 1791 they sent John Clarkson, younger brother of the abolitionist Thomas Clarkson, to Nova Scotia in order to convince some of the black people there to relocate to Sierra Leone.[120] Among their number was a preacher named Boston King.

Cugoano felt more comfortable with the plans of this new Sierra Leone Company. In *Evil of Slavery*, the passages decrying the failures of the original 1786/1787 project had been removed. By comparison, the passages dealing with Irwin remained in every edition of Equiano's *Interesting Narrative* up to the 1794 ninth edition, the last to be published before his death in 1797.[121] Cugoano was so keen on the new project that he even wrote to Sharp, volunteering to go to New Brunswick to convince some of the black Loyalists there to participate in the venture:

as there is several ships now going to new Brunswick I could wish to have your answer that I might be able to gived [*sic*] the black settlers there some kind of answer to their request, the generality of them are mediately the natives of africa who Join the british forces Last war, they are consisting of different macanicks such as carpenters, smiths, masons and farmers, this are the people that we have imediate use for in the Provence of freedom.[122]

The fact Cugoano knew that black people in Canada were actively seeking a new home suggests that he was in contact with Peters. He was certainly communicating with a large black community in London, since *Evil of Slavery*, unlike *Thoughts and Sentiments*, was explicitly addressed to his 'Gentlemen Countrymen and brother Sufferers' and written in the collective first-person throughout.[123] It is not unreasonable to assume, given Cugoano's close associations with a number of black Loyalists in London, that he had met Peters through mutual friends or at one of the 'black Loyalist pubs', such as the White Raven on Mile-End Road or the Yorkshire Stingo. An awareness that the impetus for this new phase of the Sierra Leone project came from black people themselves goes some way to explaining Cugoano's apparent *volte-face* on the issue of resettlement. But his objections to the original plans were founded largely in the coercive nature of the government's involvement. A broader view is

[119] TNA, Correspondence of Secretary of State, 1790–1792, CO 217/63, 'Enquiry into the Complaint of Thomas Peters', cited in Walker, *The Black Loyalists*, 95.
[120] See Brown, 'The Black Loyalists in Sierra Leone', 106–109; Walker, *The Black Loyalists*, 115–144.
[121] Olaudah Equiano, *The Interesting Narrative*, 8th edn. (London, 1794), 343–347.
[122] Gloucestershire Archives, Granville Sharp Papers, D3549/13/1/S36, 'John Stuart to Granville Sharp, n.d.'
[123] Cugoano, *Evil of Slavery*, 5.

therefore needed to explain his esteem for the Sierra Leone Company, which was *more*, not less, incorporated with Pitt's administration than the Committee had been.

First, the new Company could boast Sharp as its first chair. This represented a far greater degree of involvement than he had taken in the first attempt at resettlement. While he had directed funds toward the Committee for the Relief of the Black Poor in 1786 and took an active interest in the developments of the first project, he was not as closely involved at that stage as is sometimes suggested.[124] In fact, the Committee's minutes never mentioned him attending a single meeting. Even though his plan for the government of the new territory (based on a medieval system of land-sharing called frank-pledge) was adopted by the settlers, and the first town named for him, his influence over the 1786/1787 project was largely indirect.[125] By contrast, the new Sierra Leone Company had come about primarily because of his actions. It was first conceived under the name of the St. George's Bay Company as a means of organising relief for the ailing settlement. Later, reorganised and renamed the Sierra Leone Company, it was viewed explicitly as a way to set up alternative forms of trade with Africa to compete with the slave trade.[126] Sharp had been the driving force behind the St. George's Bay Company, and he was responsible for the involvement of a number of abolitionists in it. When the organisation became fully incorporated in July 1791, Sharp remained a director and was instrumental in the election of Henry Thornton – a member of SEAST and former member of the Committee for the Relief of the Black Poor – as the Company's chairman.[127] Just as with Smeathman during the first half of 1786, Cugoano's personal regard for Sharp reassured him as to the motives of this new project.

Second, Cugoano's perception was that the government's reasons for becoming involved had changed since he published *Thoughts and Sentiments* in 1787. In the intervening years, Wilberforce had successfully moved for a Privy Council inquiry into the slave trade and Dolben had

---

[124] Walker, for example, suggests that the project came about largely because of Sharp and that he was among the individuals who staged collections for London's 'black poor' in early 1786. Walker, *The Black Loyalists*, 96–97.

[125] For Sharp's system of Frankpledge, see Granville Sharp, *An Account of the Constitutional English Polity of Congregational Courts* (London: B. White and C. Dilly, 1786). Sharp's plan for the government of Sierra Leone, in the form of a response to Smeathman's plan, was entitled 'Memorandum on a Late Proposal for a New Settlement to Be Made on the Coast of Africa' and was published as an appendix in the same volume, 262–282.

[126] See Braidwood, *Black Poor and White Philanthropists*, 225–250; Walker, *The Black Loyalists*, 94–114.

[127] Walker, *The Black Loyalists*, 103.

implemented tighter regulations on overcrowding in slave ships. Evidence against the slave trade gathered by Clarkson and others was introduced into Commons from 1789, and in 1791 Wilberforce introduced the first parliamentary bill for abolition.[128] The process of abolishing the slave trade seemed well under way. Cugoano was already considering the details of post-abolition economics, proposing that 'should the abolition of that horrific traffic take place, as it ought, next sessions of Parliament; that there may be a plan adopted to meet the general approbation of our African friends'.[129] His optimism was palpable in the opening address of *Evil of Slavery*, in which he offered thanks to 'these truly worthy and humane gentlemen (viz. Mr. Wm. Wilberforce and Mr. Grenville [*sic*] Sharp) with the warmest sence of gratitude, for their beneficient and laudable endeavours'.[130] Claiming to represent all formerly enslaved people, he now lionised parliamentary abolitionists for beginning to effect the changes he had campaigned for since at least 1786, expressing confidence in their success as inevitable and forthcoming:

> The part that has been taken lately by the generous senator WILLIAM WILBERFORCE esq. to co-operate with the British parliament, in behalf of the oppressed Africans, and many other gentlemen, ... shews the aimiable intentions of that august and much revered Assembly; we, as part of the sufferers, cannot but rest with the strongest confidence, and hope that the end of so laudable exertions, are the total abolition of that horrible traffic.[131]

These effusions were written after 1787 and inserted into the newer *Evil of Slavery* pamphlet. Combined with the fact that he had volunteered to become involved in the 1791 project, these additions – and the removal of the passages criticising the 1786/1787 project – suggest that Cugoano had significantly reassessed his position on government involvement in resettling Loyalists in Sierra Leone.

It was against a backdrop of shrill press antagonism that the first expedition had sailed from London in 1787, led by white people with no proven commitment to antislavery and whom many of the black settlers did not trust, and funded by a government which appeared to be reacting more to widespread xenophobia than to the worsening humanitarian crisis affecting the homeless black Loyalists on London's streets. This first plan, as Cugoano saw it, was that the 'black poor' 'were to be hurried away at all events, come of them after what would'.[132] But in 1791, the Sierra Leone Company was an organisation run by

---

[128] Anon., *The Speeches of Mr. Wilberforce … on a Motion for the Abolition of the Slave Trade* (London: John Stockdale, 1789).

[129] Cugoano, *Evil of Slavery*, 7.   [130] Cugoano, *Evil of Slavery*, 5.

[131] Cugoano, *Evil of Slavery*, 7.   [132] Cugoano, *Thoughts and Sentiments*, 140.

committed abolitionists (some of whom he knew personally) and funded by a government which appeared to be progressing quickly with the abolition of the slave trade. While he was understandably unwilling to publicly endorse the project after the catastrophe of the 1786 venture, his private involvement demonstrated a quiet optimism regarding the government's intentions at Sierra Leone.

The influx of black Loyalists into London after 1783 significantly bolstered the capital's black population. As a well-educated and socially well-connected domestic servant, Cugoano met with black Loyalists such as William Green in order to interpose in individual cases of illegal re-enslavement and quickly established himself as an advocate for black rights. The relationships between Loyalists and black intellectuals formed the basis of the Sons of Africa, the first black political organisation in Britain. When he wrote *Thoughts and Sentiments* in 1787, Cugoano directed copies to policymakers and socially significant figures such as the Prince of Wales and William Pitt, encouraging them to promote a widespread revaluation of black intellectual capabilities. His writing reflected the increasing involvement of black people in domestic political radicalism, including protest and organised resistance to arrests. These forms of radicalism emerged in part as a reaction to racial discrimination as well as the disproportionate rates of poverty and crime affecting black people in London.

Cugoano was also highly critical of the government's chosen method of dealing with the new social crisis presented by the 'black poor'. Both his and Equiano's reactions to the 1786/1787 project demonstrated that many black people in London felt deeply jaded by the execution of the design, in which the Committee gave relief only on the extraction of a promise to go to Sierra Leone, and publicly requested that white people cease giving money to starving black beggars in order to encourage them aboard the ships.[133] Cugoano's work in particular gave voice to the legitimate (and ultimately justified) concerns held by the black settlers that they might be re-enslaved once they got to Africa and pointed out the hypocrisy of the government funding the scheme while it supported slaving castles a few miles down the West African coast. The 1786/1787 attempt at resettlement was, in Cugoano's appraisal, a kow-towing reaction to the xenophobic reports of the British press, rather than a legitimate humanitarian endeavour. However, his view of the 1791 attempt to relocate black Loyalists in Nova Scotia to Sierra Leone was altogether

---

[133] *Public Advertiser*, 14 December 1786, 1.

more positive, since the British government appeared by then to be far more committed to the abolition of the slave trade. The 1791 attempt took the establishment of an alternative African trade, and the under-mining of the slave trade, as its primary objective, whereas the 1786/1787 attempt saw it as merely an additional benefit of solving the local social crisis represented by London's 'black poor'. As demonstrated by his plan to establish a school for black people in London, Cugoano worked ever in the interests of his fellow former slaves.[134] Even though he required patronage for his writing, he remained resolute in his principles, and as his stinging criticism of the government's hypocrisy in supporting the slave trade shows, he was unwilling to compromise them even for the sake of the respectability he so carefully cultivated in his correspondence.

[134] Cugoano, *Evil of Slavery*, 47.

8   Robert Wedderburn and London's Radical Underworld

Cugoano's powerful advocacy for black people in Britain prefigured the emergence of an even more trenchant and charismatic black radical. Robert Wedderburn, the son of an enslaved Jamaican mother and a Scottish slave-owner, was among the most outspoken voices in both the abolition and reform movements of the early nineteenth century. In a writing and preaching career that spanned the first three decades of the century, he became one of the most infamous men in the country for his extreme views on slavery and liberty. If Cugoano as a political commentator remained relatively obscure to establishment figures (especially when compared with his more media-savvy friend Olaudah Equiano), then Wedderburn's extraordinary ultra-radical activities brought him rather more attention from the government than he bargained for. Most acutely in the winter of 1819–1820, when Britain seemed to be teetering on the brink of revolution, the Home Secretary knew exactly who Robert Wedderburn was.

Part of Wedderburn's double-edged success came down to timing. Unlike Cugoano, he operated in a period of British popular politics characterised by extremes, both of radical 'direct action' and of government suppression. Through a combination of pamphleteering and oratory, Wedderburn carved out a position for himself as a leading member of London's working-class radical community during the politically tumultuous 'Peterloo years' of the late 1810s. He acted as one of the most important individual links between working-class activism and the rarefied world of parliamentary antislavery politics. Unlike earlier black writers, Wedderburn never courted the approval of, or support from, 'respectable' authority figures, either within or peripheral to his own networks. In fact, he usually framed his antislavery sentiments in conscious opposition to dominant British cultural ideals of politeness, restraint and respectability. In both his radical and antislavery work, Wedderburn remained an uncompromising and distinctive black voice.

He often attributed his lifelong rejection of authority to two traumatic episodes from his childhood. The first happened when he was four.

Recounting it more than fifty years later, his rage was still palpable: 'I have seen my poor mother stretched on the ground, tied hands and feet, and FLOGGED in the most indecent manner, though PREG-NANT AT THE SAME TIME!!! her *fault* being the not acquainting her mistress that her master had *given her leave to go to see her mother in town!*'[1] The second came when he was eleven. His maternal grand-mother, an Obeah woman known as Talkee Amy, was flogged, again in the sight of the young Wedderburn, for apparently bewitching her master's smuggling ship and causing it to be apprehended by the colonial authorities.[2] These two instances of violence toward maternal figures imbued him with a fierce independent streak – and a passionate hatred of slavery.

His father, James Wedderburn, sold his mother, Rosanna, while she was pregnant with Robert. James eventually paid for Robert's release from slavery in 1765, when the boy was two years old.[3] As soon as he was able, he left the plantation near Kingston and 'travelled as a jobbing millwright throughout the different parts of Jamaica', spending eighteen months in Spanish Town and 'the like period in Port-Royal' before joining the Royal Navy as a Gunner's Mate.[4] After serving for the British during the American Revolutionary War, he came to settle in Britain during the late 1770s, marrying Elizabeth Ryan in London in November 1781.[5] He was pressed into service once more, aboard the HMS *Poly-phemus*, and undertook a final tour of duty in the West Indies before returning to London to find work as a tailor and raise a family.[6]

Wedderburn had been raised as a Christian and, much like Gronnio-saw, Equiano, Cugoano, Jea, and Prince, believed that 'if he could once get to a Christian country, he should be happy'.[7] But when he arrived he was disappointed by the squabbling and divisions between the vari-ous denominations. Eventually, he came to reject all religious authority,

[1] *Bell's Life in London and Sporting Chronicle*, 29 February 1824.

[2] Robert Wedderburn, *The Horrors of Slavery* (London: R. Wedderburn, 1824), 11.

[3] Jamaica Archives, Spanish Town, 1B/11/6/9, 'Manumission of Slave Registers', ff. 37–38. Cited in Nadine Hunt, 'Remembering Africans in Diaspora: Robert Wedderburn's "Freedom Narrative"', in Olatunji Ojo and Nadine Hunt (eds.), *Slavery in Africa and the Caribbean: A History of Enslavement and Identity since the Eighteenth Century* (London: I. B. Tauris, 2012), 178.

[4] Robert Wedderburn, *An Address to the Right Honourable Lord Brougham and Vaux* (London: John Ascham, 1831), 4, 3.

[5] Guildhall Library, London, St. Katherine Kree, P69/KAT2/A/01/MS7891/1, 'Register of Marriages, 1754–1785', no. 335.

[6] TNA, Admiralty Records, Ships' Pay Books, ADM 34/602, 'Polyphemus, 18 Apr 1782 – 28 Jun 1783', f. 1. Wedderburn was listed as supernumary aboard the *Polyphemus*, but he himself later claimed to have been a gunner.

[7] [Cannon], *The Trial of the Rev. R Wedderburn*, 7–8.

arriving at his own Unitarian free-thinking position. At around the same time, Wedderburn became involved with members of the 1790s radical scene, and it was through these individuals that his ideas first found their way into print. Over the next three decades, he rose to prominence as one of the most recalcitrant, insurgent and influential working-class advocates of radical political reform and antislavery activism in the country. Since the pioneering work of Iain McCalman, academics working on Wedderburn's life have tended to take one of two main approaches. Historians of popular radicalism consider him as first and foremost a radical concerned with domestic political reform, for whom antislavery agitation was part of a wider package of anti-establishment sentiment.[8] On the other hand, historians of diaspora, literary critics and cultural theorists have focused on Wedderburn's antislavery writing as a manifestation of his African ancestry and/or his ethnic status as a free black man in Britain.[9] However, historians have yet to examine how Wedderburn's discourses, spoken and printed, related to 'mainstream' parliamentary abolitionism. In the same way, Wedderburn's insurrectionary antislavery writing has been seen as having been influenced by the Haitian Revolution without a full account of the impact of slave uprisings on the British political climate in which he wrote.[10] Similarly, while

---

[8] Iain McCalman, 'Anti-Slavery and Ultra-Radicalism in Early Nineteenth-Century England: The Case of Robert Wedderburn', *Slavery and Abolition*, 7:2 (1986), 99–117; Iain McCalman, *Radical Underworld: Prophets, Revolutionaries and Pornographers in London, 1795–1840* (Cambridge: Cambridge University Press, 1988), 97–238; David Worrall, *Radical Culture: Discourse, Resistance and Surveillance* (Hemel Hempstead: Harvester Wheatsheaf, 1992), 129–146, 165–178.

[9] Sue Thomas, *Telling West Indian Lives: Life Narrative and the Reform of Plantation Slavery Cultures 1804–1834* (London: Palgrave Macmillan, 2014), 97–118; Hunt, 'Remembering Africans in Diaspora', 175–198; Alan Rice, 'Ghostly and Vernacular Presences in the Black Atlantic', in Susan Manning and Eve Bannett (eds.), *Transatlantic Literary Studies 1680–1830* (Cambridge: Cambridge University Press, 2012), 154–168; Edlie Wong, *Neither Fugitive nor Free: Atlantic Slavery, Freedom Suits and the Legal Culture of Travel* (New York: New York University Press, 2009); Peter Linebaugh, 'A Little Jubilee? The Literacy of Robert Wedderburn in 1817', in John Rule and Robert Malcolmson (eds.), *Protest and Survival, the Historical Experience: Essays for E. Thompson* (London: Merlin Press, 1993), 174–220.

[10] See, for example, Helen Thomas, *Romanticism and Slave Narratives* (Cambridge: Cambridge University Press, 2000), 255–271; Hilary Beckles, 'Slave Ideology and Self-Emancipation in the British West Indies, 1650–1832', *Bulletin of Eastern Caribbean Affairs*, 10:4 (1984), 1–8; Robin Blackburn, *The Overthrow of Colonial Slavery 1776–1848* (London: Verso, 1988); Hilary Beckles, *Freedoms Won: Caribbean Emancipations, Ethnicities and Nationhood* (Cambridge: Cambridge University Press, 2006); Gelien Matthews, *Caribbean Slave Revolts and the British Abolitionist Movement* (Baton Rouge: Louisiana State University Press, 2006). While Peter Linebaugh and Marcus Rediker have acknowledged the effects of the Barbadian rebellion of 1816 on Wedderburn's radical periodical *The Axe Laid to the Root*, it has so far gone unacknowledged that his autobiographical account, *The Horrors of Slavery*, was published in the wake of the Demerara uprising

Wilberforce's influence on Wedderburn has been the subject of some speculation, there has been no attempt to compare their approaches to emancipation.[11] There has also been little exploration of how Wedderburn's writing, particularly the relationship between his antislavery and radical work, developed and changed during his career. This is despite the well-established fact that both the radical and abolitionist movements of which he was a part were practically unrecognisable in 1831 from what they had been in 1817.[12] This chapter therefore takes into account how shifts in the landscapes of abolitionism and radicalism on both sides of the British Atlantic affected Wedderburn and his writing, delineating his position in overlapping networks of British radical and antislavery activism.

Radicalism and Antislavery Combined, 1817–1821

The first stirrings of Wedderburn's subversive literary talents were directed not at the political establishment but at the established church. His earliest known work, *The Truth Self-Supported* (1802), decried religious conservatism (including that increasingly represented by the Methodists) in terms reminiscent of nothing so much as the reformist pamphlets of the early 1790s[13]. It was no coincidence that *The Truth Self-Supported* was published by William Glindon and George Rieubau, veterans of the 1790s radical scene. The text represented a confluence of the printers' and author's interests: its politics were similar to texts Glindon and Rieubau had been publishing for years, while its Unitarianism and opposition to Methodist and Anglican 'establishment' respectability served Wedderburn's interests as a religious free-thinker. As a result, *The Truth Self-Supported* struck a note of insurrectionary millenarianism and solidarity

of 1823. Peter Linebaugh and Marcus Rediker, *The Many-Headed Hydra: The Hidden History of the Revolutionary Atlantic* (London: Verso, 2000), 302–305.

[11] McCalman, 'Introduction', 1–3; Wong, *Neither Fugitive nor Free*, 79.

[12] See, for example, Worrall, *Radical Culture*, 165–178; for the changing radical movement (with specific reference to Spenceanism), see Malcolm Chase, *The People's Farm: English Radical Agrarianism 1775–1840* (Oxford: Oxford University Press, 1988); for the changing abolitionist movement, see Seymour Drescher, *Abolition: A History of Slavery and Antislavery* (Cambridge: Cambridge University Press, 2009), 245–266.

[13] Robert Wedderburn, *The Truth Self-Supported; or a Refutation of Certain Doctrinal Errors Generally Adopted in the Christian Church* (London: W[illiam] Glindon and G[eorge] Riebau, [1802]). There is some disagreement as to the date of publication here. Eighteenth Century Collections Online and the British Library list the item as being published in 1795, but McCalman, an authority on British radical publishing and Wedderburn in particular, lists it as 1802 in his edited collection of Wedderburn's works. See Wedderburn, *The Horrors of Slavery and Other Writings*, 65.

Figure 8.1 Detail from wedding certificate of Robert Wedderburn
and Elizabeth Ryan, 5 November 1781, showing 'the mark
of Robt. Wedderburn'. Guildhall Library, London, St. Katherine
Kree, P69/KAT2/A/01/MS7891/1, 'Register of Marriages,
1754–1785', no. 335.
Courtesy of London Metropolitan Archives, City of London.

with the oppressed which was to resurface in Wedderburn's later anti-slavery work: 'however he is rejected and despised, there is a day coming, when his friends and his enemies will know ... that he is possessed with power, by authority of the Father, to condemn the one, and reward the other.'[14] Wedderburn's childhood experiences of slavery were apparent here, but even a cursory reading of this text poses questions regarding how much control he had over its final form. Aside from its perfectly reflecting the interests of both publishing partners, the text was written in third person and furnished with a formal introduction to the writer, 'a West-Indian, son of James Wedderburn, Esq. of Inveresk'. It is likely that Wedderburn dictated the text to his publishers or a third party, who then wrote it down and prepared it for print.

Once again, we encounter the question of literacy in determining black authorial agency. Peter Linebaugh and Eric Pencek have both examined this issue at length, but it is worth exploring further here in the light of some new manuscript evidence.[15] Wedderburn was not literate enough to sign his own name on his wedding certificate in 1781 (see Figure 8.1). By the 1830s, his literacy had improved, but he never attained the quality of written communication demonstrated in *The Truth Self-Supported*. 'The Works of Mr. Spence I have lent and lost', he wrote to Francis Place in 1831, 'has to the bust, Edwards inform me that Mr. Galloway give him the orders to make about fifteen'.[16] Wedderburn's competency

[14] Wedderburn, *The Truth Self-Supported*, 8, 3.
[15] Peter Linebaugh, 'A Little Jubilee?'; Eric Pencek, 'Intolerable Anonymity: Robert Wedderburn and the Discourse of Ultra-Radicalism', *Nineteenth-Century Contexts*, 37:1 (2015), 61–77.
[16] BL, Add MSS. 27808, Place Papers, 'Robert Wedderburn to F[rances] Place, 22 March 1831'.

in written English was moderate, and never reached the standard expected of a professional polemicist. Indeed, both manuscript and printed sources written by him reveal a marked deficiency in conventional early nineteenth-century English grammar and spelling. However, since he was the subject of numerous spy reports, examples of his spoken discourse have been preserved and can be compared against the texts published under his name.[17] As a result, it is possible to gauge the extent to which any particular text was subject to editorial intervention, since Wedderburn's written style, like Cugoano's, tended to reflect his oratory rather than grammatical convention. In the case of *The Truth Self-Supported*, the frequent use of elevated rhetoric and specialist religious terminology was so common that one contemporaneous reader found it to be 'unintelligible jargon'.[18] This stood in marked contrast to Wedderburn's forceful and direct spoken style, which, along with its use of the third-person throughout, indicated that *The Truth Self-Supported* was likely to have been heavily edited.

Limited literacy was not necessarily a barrier to Wedderburn's political engagement. In 1813, he came into contact with veteran radical orator Thomas Spence. A former leading member of the London Corresponding Society and United Englishmen, Spence had spent the first decade of the nineteenth century attempting to restart the effectively suppressed radical movement in Britain.[19] A new cohort of young, working-class reformers gravitated toward this charismatic speaker, including Wedderburn and his future publishers Richard Carlile and Thomas Davison. Spence also mediated introductions between these new revolutionaries and some of the older radicals from his days in the corresponding societies of the 1790s, including the Thomas Evans and (another of Wedderburn's future publishers) Andrew Seale. Together the group (known as the 'Spencean Philanthropists' after 1814) hosted rough, loud debates in public houses and published cheap political pamphlets and broadsides. It was in this environment that Wedderburn first rose to prominence and developed the oratorical skills which he later put to use agitating for the abolition of slavery.

When Spence died in 1814, Wedderburn and his fellow Spencean Philanthropists vowed to continue his work. After a short-lived co-editorship of a 'penny weekly' named *Forlorn Hope*, Wedderburn struck out on his

---

[17] See, for example, *Axe Laid to the Root*, no. 1 (1817); TNA, Home Office Papers, HO42/195, cited in Wedderburn, *The Horrors of Slavery and Other Writings*, 114–115.

[18] The marginalia are from the BL's copy of *The Truth Self-Supported* (BL, General Reference Collection 4226.cc.47).

[19] H. T. Dickinson, 'Spence, Thomas (1750–1814)', in *ODNB*, available at www.oxford dnb.com/view/article/26112.

own in 1817 with a new periodical named *The Axe Laid to the Root*. In it, he accommodated Spencean land reform within his own distinctive brand of antislavery rhetoric. He made much of his Jamaican ancestry and of witnessing his mother and grandmother being abused by tyrannical white overseers. His distinctive anti-establishment swagger pervaded much of the *Axe*'s six issues, beginning in the first, when he charged 'all potentates, governors, and governments of every description' of the 'felony' of 'wickedly violat[ing] the sacred rights of man – by force of arms, or otherwise, seizing the persons of men and dragging them from their native country, and selling their stolen persons and generations'.[20] The mention of that ever-divisive Painite refrain, 'the sacred rights of man', drew his condemnation of slavery and his hatred of 'all potentates, governors, and governments' together in terms reminiscent of Cugoano's work. However, Wedderburn's vision of Jamaican emancipation took on the character not of reform from within but of revolution from below. In this respect he was a far more radical figure than any earlier black writer.

The year 1817 was an especially dangerous time to be seen to be encouraging slave resistance. Uprisings, always a threat in the West Indian colonies, became an increasingly common occurrence as it became apparent that the Abolition of the Slave Trade Act of 1807 impacted little on the lives of most of the enslaved. One of the largest of these, Bussa's rebellion in Barbados in April 1816, resulted in the death of at least one white colonist, and the Royal Navy were called in to quell the rebellion. By the time the *Axe* was produced, news of the fighting in Barbados had made it across the Atlantic.[21] Despite a disproportionate response from the Navy in which up to 900 of the enslaved were killed in battle or executed, newspaper reports in London took a fiercely loyalist and unsympathetic line on the revolt. There was much talk of 'a perfidious league of slaves', 'pillaging and destroying the buildings' and generally 'pursuing a system of devastation which has seldom been equalled'.[22] The West Indies interest, keen to make political hay from the carnage, linked the uprising to the slavery registration bills introduced by Wilberforce and James Stephen in 1815. The bills, intended as 'a first small step' toward emancipation, were ultimately

[20] *Axe Laid to the Root*, no. 1 (1817), 1–3.
[21] TNA, Commonwealth Office Papers, CO 28/85, 'James Leith to Earl Bathurst 30 April 1816'. For a full discussion of the Demerara uprising, see Michael Craton, *Testing the Chains: Resistance to Slavery in the British West Indies* (Ithaca, NY: Cornell University Press, 1982), 254–266.
[22] *Morning Post*, 6 June 1816, 2; Drescher, *Abolition*, 231–232.

rejected in Lords following the Barbados rebellion.[23] Opinion pieces appearing in the wake of the rebellion deployed a racialized discourse which suggested that 'the natural indolence and ferocity of the passions of Negroes' made the uprising inevitable in such a political environment.[24] Thus, the immediate effect of the Barbados uprising in Britain was to diminish popular support for abolition and galvanise the proslavery lobby, for whom the rebellion merely manifested black slaves' inherently violent nature.

Perhaps it is for this reason that Wedderburn's advice to Jamaican slaves in 1817 echoed, to some extent, the approach of his contemporary John Jea, expounding a pacifist revolution:

My advice to you, is, to appoint a day wherein you will all pretend to sleep one hour beyond the appointed time of your rising to labour; ... let it be talked of in your market place, and on the roads. The universality of your sleeping and non-resistance, will strike terror to your oppressors. Go to your labour peaceably after the hour is expired; and repeat it once a year, till you obtain your liberty.[25]

Wedderburn recognised two things. First, he saw the need to reaffirm the capacity for reason and restraint in black West Indian slaves, especially in the context of Bussa's rebellion (and, of course, the deteriorating situation in Haiti). As such his writing provided a rare counterpoint to proslavery writers keen to link abolitionism with 'the natural indolence and ferocity' of black slaves. 'Oh, ye oppressed', he wrote, 'use no violence to your oppressors, convince the world you are rational beings, follow not the example of St. Domingo ... leave revengeful practises for European kings and ministers.'[26] As long as stereotypes of black violence and savagery persisted, Wedderburn understood that to encourage the same violent political action in Caribbean slaves as he could (and would) in British labourers would ultimately be counter-productive.

The second thing Wedderburn recognised was the need to terrify slave-owners. Indeed, on first reading, the moderation he promoted in his first article appeared to be contradicted by the violence of a second, printed directly after it. In this second article, he issued a darkly threatening warning to Jamaican planters that 'the fate of St. Domingo awaits you'. Indeed, he utilised the negative stereotypes appearing in the papers

[23] See, for example, Matthews, *Caribbean Slave Revolts and British Abolitionism*, 28–29; Drescher, *Abolition*, 232–233; Hilary Beckles, 'Emancipation by Law or War? Wilberforce and the 1816 Barbados Slave Rebellion', in David Richardson (ed.), *Abolition and Its Aftermath: The Historical Context* (London: Frank Cass, 1985), 80–104; Linebaugh and Rediker, *The Many-Headed Hydra*, 302–305.
[24] *Morning Post*, 7 June 1816, 3.   [25] *Axe Laid to the Root*, no. 1, 4.
[26] *Axe Laid to the Root*, no. 1, 3–4.

following the 1816 Barbadian rebellion to intimidate imagined planto-cratic readers, threatening that their slaves 'will slay man, woman, and child, and not spare the virgin, whose interest is connected with slavery, whether black, white, or tawny'.[27] The radical character of this second article might seem to undermine the coherency of the pacifist plan out-lined in the first. But the key difference between these articles lies in their imagined readerships. The second was nominally directed at planters, intended to weaken their confidence in the institution of slavery. It stood to reason that the revolution imagined in this article would be violent. On the other hand, the first, more moderate article was supposedly intended to be read by slaves, Wedderburn's '[d]ear countrymen and relatives', and was intended to convince them of the benefits of Spenceanism as well as the dangers of 'vengeful practises'. The Jamaican revolution imagined in *this* article was bloodless.

Eric Pencek has pointed out that print culture in Wedderburn's radical circles emphasised heterodox discursive styles and blurred distinctions between numerous authorial identities.[28] This was enacted in the *Axe* most explicitly in an imagined correspondence between Wedderburn and his half-sister in Jamaica, Elizabeth Campbell, in which she recounted the spread of Spencean radicalism through the island and the colonial gov-ernment's attempts to suppress it. In reality, this never happened, and it is most likely that Wedderburn wrote both sides of the correspondence.[29] Similarly, while nominally addressed to slaves and planters, his two visions of revolutionary Jamaican emancipation were actually both intended for a metropolitan audience. In fact, no evidence has emerged to suggest that a single copy of the *Axe* was ever read in Jamaica. By inhabiting such diverse authorial personae, Wedderburn was able to suggest that two separate authors, based on either side of the Atlantic, had written for the *Axe*. This gave the impression of an international group of activists dedi-cated to inciting a Jamaican revolution – with realistically diverse views on how that might look. Wedderburn hoped as much to inspire metro-politan confidence in transatlantic political radicalism as to encourage slave resistance in the Caribbean.

This authorial fluidity elicits further questions about the editorial processes at work in Wedderburn's published writing. The *Axe*, despite

---

[27] *Axe Laid to the Root*, no. 1, 12.   [28] Pencek, 'Intolerable Anonymity', 61–77.
[29] *Axe Laid to the Root*, no. 4 (1817), 49–52; *Axe Laid to the Root*, no. 6 (1817), 64–96. McCalman and Pencek concur that this correspondence is fictitious, though Campbell herself may have been real. Wedderburn, *Horrors of Slavery*, 102 n. 1. Linebaugh and Rediker have not questioned the authenticity of the letters but do not cite any docu-mentary evidence suggesting that they were genuinely written by Campbell. Linebaugh and Rediker, *The Many-Headed Hydra*, 287–326.

its authorial schizophrenia, was uniformly riddled with halting prepos-
itions and unresolved clauses. Stylistically, it bore little resemblance to
The Truth Self-Supported, suggesting that the two texts underwent quite
different editorial processes. Where *The Truth Self-Supported* was stylistically refined and full of jargon, the articles in the *Axe* seemed to better
reflect oral than written discourse. These articles were direct and simply
put, though all hampered by an evident lack of grammatical training.
Take, for example, the unresolved first sentence of the very first issue:

> Be it known to the world that I, Robert Wedderburn, son of James Wedderburn,
> esq. of Inveresk, near Musselborough, by Rosannah his slave, whom he sold to
> James Charles Shalto Douglas, esq. in the parish of St. Mary, in the island of
> Jamaica, while pregnant with the said Wedderburn, who was not held as a slave,
> (a provision made in that agreement, that the child when born should be free.)[30]

Wedderburn's 1817 periodical, then, bore little evidence of professional
editorship. Might it therefore be understood as more closely reflecting his
own approach to antislavery and radical activism than his earlier tract?

Useful comparisons can be drawn with Wedderburn's public speeches.
Unusually for a black, impoverished (and thereby doubly marginalised)
writer, a number of accounts of these oratorical skills survive. Spies
working for the Home Secretary, Lord Sidmouth, reported that Wedderburn often took the lead at Spencean debates in pubs around London.
His business as a tailor was going well, and in 1816, he and his family
lived in comfortable lodgings in the West End, at Smith's Court, just off
Great Windmill Street.[31] Early in 1818, in partnership with the new
leader of the Spencean Philanthropists, Thomas Evans, Wedderburn
took out a joint licence at a chapel on Archer Street to use as a base for
Spencean activities. During the same year, he'd had himself ordained as a
Unitarian minister. This afforded the chapel a degree of protection from
Sidmouth's increasingly draconian anti-radical legislation by appealing
to the Doctrine of the Trinity Act of 1813, which granted freedom of
worship to religious dissenters. Nevertheless, the partnership between
Wedderburn and Evans was not to last long. Evans had already been
arrested under suspicion of planning the Spa Fields riots of December
1816, and after habeas corpus was suspended again in March 1817 he
was held without trial until the following spring. He emerged from prison
anxious about being held accountable for any insurrectionary activities,
and began to steer the Spencean Philanthropists toward a more moderate

---

[30] *Axe Laid to the Root*, no. 1 (1817), 3.
[31] London Metropolitan Archives, Holborn St Giles in the Fields, DL/T/036, 'Register of
Baptisms', Item 024.

position. In particular, Evans wanted to distance himself from the less respectable elements of the society.[32] Wedderburn, meanwhile, was growing ever more violent in his speeches. On 2 November 1818, a government spy named James Hanley reported that Wedderburn's 'language is so horridly blasphemous at Archer St every Tuesday afternoon – that the Spenceans themselves are apprehensive of a prosecution – some of them wish him to withdraw his name from the society.'[33] When Wedderburn was finally ejected from the Archer Street chapel in January 1819, he well and truly burned his bridges by helping himself to the benches and desks. He was accosted in the street by Evans, and a fight ensued. Incensed, Wedderburn published two handbills within weeks, insulting Evans's wife and describing him as a 'two-faced politician' and 'an apostate'.[34] These handbills included an advertisement for debates to be held at Wedderburn's new hayloft chapel at Hopkins Street, Soho.

Freed from Evans's restraining influence, Wedderburn continued to hold ever more inflammatory debates at his new hayloft. His audience by now was rife with spies looking for an opportunity to bring him to prosecution on a charge of treason or sedition. Even though his Unitarian licence afforded him only flimsy legal protection, Wedderburn was emboldened by the fact that the focus of many of his debates, ostensibly, was on the slightly less provocative question of Caribbean slavery. On the evening of 9 August 1819, a meeting was held debating the questions, 'Can it be murder to kill a tyrant? ... Has a slave an inherent right to slay his master, who refuses him his liberty?'[35] Either of these questions could apply to British working-class 'wage slavery' as much as West Indian slavery, but Wedderburn's reaffirmation of his ethnic status as 'the offspring of an African' in advertisements for the event suggested that the question under discussion was the legitimacy of West Indian insurrection.

Wedderburn's opening comments on the night were a mixture of domestic and colonial politics. The literal enslavement of black Africans served as both a product of and metaphor for the tyranny of white landowners, creating obvious resonances for the working-class audience. These resonances did not go unnoticed by government spies. As the Reverend John Chetwode Eustace wrote to the Home Office the next day, 'Yesterday evening I proceeded to Hopkins St. Chapel to hear the

[32] McCalman, *Radical Underworld*, 131.
[33] TNA, Home Office Papers, HO42/158, 'Report', ff. 383–384.
[34] TNA, Home Office Papers, HO42/202, 'Robert Wedderburn, *A Few Lines for a Double-Faced Politician* (London: E. Thomas, 1818)', f. 6; TNA, Home Office Papers, HO42/190, 'Robert Wedderburn, "A Few Plain Questions for an Apostate"', f. 73.
[35] 'Handbill, 9 August 1819', cited in Wedderburn, *The Horrors of Slavery and Other Writings*, 113.

question discussed whether it be right for the People of England to assassinate their rulers, for this my Lord, I conceive to be the real purport of the question tho' proposed in other terms.'[36] Eustace may have brought his own prejudices against Wedderburn and the Spenceans to his reportage of the evening's debate, since another spy, J. Bryant, reported Wedderburn speaking explicitly about the transatlantic slave trade and its links to British political corruption:

Wedderbourne – rose – Government was necessitated to send men in arms to West Indies or Africa which produced commotion. They would employ blacks to go and steal females ... This was done by Parliament men – who done it for gain – the same as they employed them in their Cotton factories to make slaves of them.[37]

Eustace took Wedderburn's imagined West Indian uprising as a mask for a British revolution, assuming him to be more concerned with domestic politics than antislavery. Given the print and distribution networks surrounding the *Axe*, it is unlikely that Eustace was familiar with Wedderburn's existing antislavery corpus. If he had, he might have realised that Wedderburn saw the West Indies as having legitimate potential to demonstrate the usefulness and desirability of national political reform – and violent revolution – in their own right. Unlike Eustace, Wedderburn thought about the West Indian colonies as more than simply a surrogate for Britain.

Eustace also assumed that the attendees at Hopkins Street were more parochial in their concerns than was actually the case. When the final question was taken, 'has a Slave an Inherent right to slay his master who refuses him his Liberty?' almost all the hands in the room were raised in favour. The posters for the following week's debate proclaimed the result without any hint that the question was allegorical, and additionally that 'a numerous and enlightened assembly' had 'expressed their Desire of hearing of another sable Nation freeing itself by the Dagger from the base tyranny of their Christian Masters'. Moreover, 'Several Gentlemen declared their readiness to assist them.' According to Bryant, when the 'sense of the meeting was taken', Wedderburn declared, 'I can *now write home and tell the Slaves to Murder their Masters as soon as they please.*'[38] The explicit mention of 'another sable nation' in a revolution recalled not

---

[36] TNA, Home Office Papers, HO42/191, cited in Wedderburn, *The Horrors of Slavery and Other Writings*, 116–117.
[37] TNA, Home Office Papers, HO42/195, cited in Wedderburn, *The Horrors of Slavery and Other Writings*, 114–115.
[38] TNA, Home Office Papers, HO42/192, 'Handbill', f. 119; TNA, Home Office Papers, HO42/195', cited in Wedderburn, *The Horrors of Slavery and Other Writings*, 115.

only revolutionary Haiti but also Wedderburn's plan for the establishment of a Spencean utopia in Jamaica, published two years earlier in the
Axe. To characterise Wedderburn's investment in antislavery as a mere
decoy for his 'true' aim of British political and social reform, even in this
single instance, was to ignore the largest part of his affirmed political
outlook.

Encouraged by Eustace's account, the Home Office looked to prosecute Wedderburn for holding this debate on the grounds that it was
seditious. When queried by Sidmouth himself, the Law Officers sum-
marily declared the meeting lawful, since the question being debated was
not explicitly designed to incite unrest among British subjects.[39] Wedderburn's entanglement of British politics with the slavery debate had
kept him from prosecution. It is a matter for speculation as to whether
the Law Officers would have come to the same decision over Wedderburn's meeting in the tense political atmosphere following the Peterloo
massacre, which took place a mere six days later. Certainly, public
outrage bolstered the ranks of meetings like Wedderburn's after Peterloo,
but the Home Office reacted by tightening restrictions on them, notably
with the introduction of the repressive 'Six Acts' in November 1819.[40] It
was now obvious to Sidmouth that the Hopkins Street Chapel was a
centre for anti-establishment and perhaps even revolutionary agitation.
Firebrands such as Wedderburn, wherever they imagined their revolutions taking place, were now seen as a potential threat to home security,
and it was only a matter of time before he was arrested.

Evidence of sedition and blasphemy at Hopkins Street was amassing,
even as Sidmouth's net drew tighter round Wedderburn's circle. The
trial for sedition of Wedderburn's friend Richard Carlile was in the news;
a loophole in the law meant that he was entitled to read aloud the entire
text of Thomas Paine's banned *Age of Reason* to the jury, which could
then be legally published as minutes of court proceedings. However,
when Carlile offered to show some of the inconsistencies of Christian
doctrine by reading extended passages from the Bible, an understandably
tired Justice Abbot disallowed it.[41] On 28 October 1819, Wedderburn,

---

[39] TNA, Treasury Solicitors' Papers, TS25/2035/20, 'Opinion of Law Officers regarding
the legality of a meeting held for the purpose of debate at Hopkins Street Chapel,
London', f. 136.
[40] For an overview of the Six Acts, see Anon., *Abstract of the Six Acts of Parliament (Passed in
the Month of December 1819)* (London: George Ayre and Andrew Strahan, 1820). The
effects of the Six Acts on British literary culture are discussed in James Chandler,
England in 1819: The Politics of Literary Culture and the Case of Romantic Historicism
(Chicago, IL: University of Chicago Press, 1998), 42–43.
[41] Philip Martin, 'Carlile, Richard (1790–1843)', in *ODNB*, available at www.oxforddnb
.com/view/article/4685.

now completely jaded by the established church, reacted to this news by staging another debate. The question under discussion this time was 'Whether the refusal of Judge Abbott [*sic*] to Mr. Carlile's reading the Bible in his defence was to be attributed to a respect he had for the Scripture or a fear that the absurdities and falsehoods it contained should be exposed?' On the night, Wedderburn's usual anti-clericalism ran through his diatribe, as well as a close association between radical politics and truly Christian actions:

[Y]our fat gutted parsons priests or Bishops would see Jesus Christ damned or God almighty either rather than give up their Twenty or Thirty thousand a year ... but what did He teach us what did He say Acknowledge no King (he was a Reformer) ... He said acknowledge no Rabbi (no priest) no he knew their tricks and he says stand it no longer.

At one point, Wedderburn even cast Jesus Christ as a radical reformer, making the radical reformer Henry Hunt into a messianic figure in his stead:

Times were bad then and Christ became a Radical Reformer. Now I never could find out where he got his knowledge but this much I know by the same Book that he was born of very poor parents, who like us felt with him the same as we now feel, and he says I'll turn Mr. Hunt and then when he had that exalted ride upon the Jack Ass to Jerusalem the people ran before him crying out *HUNT FOR EVER!!!*[42]

The speed at which Wedderburn switched the focus of this debate from religion to politics was breakneck. Anti-clericalism was one thing – for a registered Unitarian preacher it might even be explainable as necessary – but to proclaim Hunt as being similar to Jesus and at the same time to explicitly call Jesus Christ a 'Radical Reformer', all in the shadow of Peterloo, was practically to invite prosecution.

Still, Wedderburn persisted in giving anti-authoritarian and anti-clerical speeches at Hopkins Street, binding the British government and missionary activity to the worst excesses of slavery and injustice whenever he could. On 10 November 1819, for example, the question was raised, 'which is the greater crime, for the Wesleyan missionaries to preach up passive obedience to the poor black slaves in the West Indies, or, to extort from them at the rate of 18,0-0-0 per annum, under pretence of supporting the gospel.' A Home Office spy named Richard Dalton recorded what Wedderburn had to say: '[T]he Missionaries that was sent from London by the secretary of State for the Home Department and for no other motives than to extort money for by the great Weslyans

---

[42] TNA, Treasury Solicitors' Papers, TS11/45, 'R v. Robert Wedderburn, publisher'.

pretending to preach the Gospel to the poor devils and passive obedience to the planters there masters'.[43] Wedderburn was mistaken when he assumed any formal link between British government and Wesleyan missions in the West Indies, but his speech illustrated how closely he now linked anti-clericalism with antislavery. It also highlighted how the furore surrounding the rebellion in Barbados stifled the radical element of his earlier abolitionism. Wedderburn had not felt able to openly incite violent slave resistance in the *Axe* when it was published in late 1817, but two years later he was quite happy to decry the Methodists' pacifist antislavery position to a public assembly of dozens.

Among the audience on 10 November 1819, by special invitation from Wedderburn, were two other Jamaican-born black political radicals. One of them was the young William Davidson, who three months later achieved a degree of infamy as one of the 'Cato Street conspirators'. Wedderburn and Davidson had much in common: they had both witnessed at close quarters the horrors of plantation slavery; they had both served in the Royal Navy; they both trained as artisans in Britain (Wedderburn as a tailor, Davidson as a cabinet-maker); and they both mixed in the same radical social circles. They had mutual acquaintances, not least Arthur Thistlewood, who was executed alongside Davidson for high treason following the failed conspiracy to assassinate the cabinet in 1820. So close were they that McCalman has surmised that Wedderburn would 'almost certainly' have taken part in the Cato Street conspiracy, and presumably would have been hanged and beheaded along with Thistlewood and Davidson, if he were not under such close scrutiny from government spies.[44]

Given the vast amount of evidence against Wedderburn, it seems puzzling as to why the Home Office waited so long to prosecute him. Even though the first slavery debate on 9 August 1819 was decided not to have been illegal in principle, Home Office spies continued to amass evidence against him for months before he was finally arrested in late November 1819. Sidmouth was behind this seemingly strange decision: by waiting to arrest Wedderburn, he was able to secure a prosecution under new, harsher sedition laws. The timing of the arrest, along with the continued suspension of habeas corpus, ensured that Wedderburn could be held without trial for two months, while the courts were at Christmas recess. In the meantime, the Blasphemous and Seditious Libels Act was

---

[43] TNA, Home Office Papers, HO42/196 cited in Wedderburn, *The Horrors of Slavery and Other Writings*, 126–127.

[44] McCalman has discussed the relationship between the two men at length. McCalman, 'Introduction', 23–28; McCalman, 'Anti-Slavery and Ultra-Radicalism', 107–112.

updated to allow tougher sentencing in December 1819, ostensibly as a reaction to Peterloo. Sidmouth, already personally involved once in trying to bring Wedderburn to court back in August 1819, knew about the forthcoming changes to the law when he ordered the arrest in November – after all, it was his office that introduced them. Wedderburn was tried in February 1820, just in time for the new laws to be applicable to his case. Despite entering into recognizances of £100 for himself and a further £50 each from two others in early February, he was free for only a few weeks of the winter of 1819/1820.[45] He was convicted of blasphemous libel on 25 February.

One of Wedderburn's underwriters was almost certainly his future publisher George Cannon, a liberally educated radical active in both anti-clerical and anti-establishment circles since at least 1812. He was a regular attendee at Hopkins Street and published a number of anti-clerical works under Wedderburn's name, as well as acting as his editor for at least one other.[46] Cannon also took responsibility for drafting Wedderburn's defence against the blasphemous libel charge in court. Historians have tended to represent the relationship between the two men as more mutually beneficial than was actually the case. For example, McCalman suggests that 'Wedderburn could experience the pleasure of seeing himself represented in print as "Reverend Robert Wedderburn, VDM", a scholar, theologian and member of the republic of letters' as a result of Cannon's ghost-writing.[47] Yet Wedderburn was only to experience that 'pleasure' from within the cell into which Cannon had, intentionally or not, helped to place him.

Cannon's disastrous handling of Wedderburn's defence, first at the trial on 25 February 1820 and then at the sentencing on 9 May the same year, practically ensured his client's imprisonment. On each appearance at court, Wedderburn's defence consisted of two parts: a spontaneous speech given by the defendant himself without notes and an address composed in advance by Cannon and read out by the clerk. Wedderburn, whose 'demeanour throughout the trial', according to the *Morning Chronicle*, 'was extremely respectful', sought to ameliorate his part in the alleged blasphemy by referring to his own status as 'the offspring of a

---

[45] *Morning Post*, 7 February 1820, 2.
[46] Robert Wedderburn, *Letter to Solomon Herschel, Chief Rabbi of England* (London: T. Davison 1820); Robert Wedderburn, *Letter to the Archbishop of Canterbury* (London: T. Davison 1820); Robert Wedderburn, *High-Heel'd Shoes for Dwarfs in Holiness* (London: T. Davison, 1821); Robert Wedderburn, *Cast-Iron Parsons* (London: T. Davison, 1820).
[47] McCalman, 'Introduction', 28.

female slave, by a rich European planter'.[48] On the grounds that 'he had received no education' as a consequence of his situation at birth, Wedderburn moved that he was not to be held accountable for his misinterpretation of the Bible.[49]

Cannon's part of the defence could not have been in greater conflict with Wedderburn's, nor more inflammatory. Citing numerous canonical writings and scriptural references, he sought to persuade the jury (and at the sentencing, the magistrate) that the Bible did in fact contain a number of inconsistencies. 'I defy the most inveterate of my enemies that can be found among the innumerable fanatics of the day', Cannon's defence read, 'to prove that I have ever written, or spoken a single word derogatory to the honour of the Deity; for as Plutarch justly observes, it is far less infamous to deny the existence of a Supreme being, than to entertain dishonourable and degrading notions of him.'[50] This line of argument had three significant effects. First, the appeal to classical authorities completely undermined Wedderburn's argument for mitigation on the grounds of his being uneducated. Second, it aggravated the offence by repeating a number of the supposed blasphemies for which Wedderburn was on trial. Third, it provided a public forum for Cannon's own sceptical philosophies, and even allowed him to advertise another of his ghost-written tracts, *A Letter to the Archbishop of Canterbury*, to an incredulous courtroom.[51]

Despite a recommendation to mercy from the jury 'in consequence of his not having the benefit of parental care', the magistrate Justice Bailey sentenced Wedderburn to two years in Dorchester gaol. He left little doubt as to which part of the defence was responsible for this harsh sentence. 'When persons stand upon the floor of this court to answer for an offence', he pronounced, 'it is possible they may diminish the quantum of punishment, by proving that they have repented of their crime; but you still persist in justifying it, which is an aggravation of your crime.'[52] For his part, Cannon made sure to maximise his financial profit and intellectual prestige from Wedderburn's imprisonment, publishing full accounts of both the initial trial and the sentencing hearings, with verbatim reports of his own sections of the defence. In addition, he republished an earlier tract named *A Dissertation on the Moral Sense* under

---

[48] *Morning Chronicle*, 26 February 1820, 3; [Cannon], *Trial*, 7.   [49] [Cannon] *Trial*, 7.
[50] [Cannon], *Trial*, 9.
[51] Erasmus Perkins [pseud. George Cannon] (ed.), *The Address of the Rev. R. Wedderburn, to the Court of King's Bench at Westminster* (London: W. Mason, 1820), 10–11.
[52] Cannon, *Address*, 15–16.

the new title *A Few Hints Relative to the Texture of Mind and the Manufacture of Conscience*, with an introduction directing the tract to Bailey.[53]

Wedderburn began his sentence at Dorchester on 16 May 1820, leaving his wife Elizabeth and their six children to provide for themselves.[54] Possibly out of his desperation to make money to support his family, he maintained his relationship with Cannon during at least the first year of his sentence. While in prison in 1820, he wrote a short anti-Anglican tract entitled *Cast-Iron Parsons* and sent it to Cannon to edit and forward to Davison for publication.[55] But the professional relationship between the two men did not last long beyond Wedderburn's incarceration, and *Cast-Iron Parsons* was the last project on which they collaborated.

Radicalism and Antislavery Divided, 1821–1831

Of all Wedderburn's contacts, one stood out as a beacon of establishment respectability: William Wilberforce. As might be expected, their first meeting, which took place in Wedderburn's cell at Dorchester, was engineered by the aging evangelical politician. As part of his connection with the Society for the Suppression of Vice, Wilberforce had been visiting incarcerated radicals since 1816 – especially those of deist or sceptical bent – in an attempt to reform them and bring them back to faith in God and loyalty to the government.[56] This bore him, at best, mixed results. One can easily imagine the reception he received, for example, during his visit to the recalcitrant sceptic Carlile in Dorchester in the spring of 1820.[57] The reasons for radicals' dislike of Wilberforce are easy to spot: his opposition to an enquiry into the Peterloo Massacre was well known, as was his 'unflinching support' for Sidmouth's Six Acts. Indeed, when 'soft tactics' failed him, Wilberforce was not afraid to exercise his considerable influence within the Home Office to prosecute sceptics and deists to the full extent of the new laws. When he

[53] George Cannon, *A Few Hints Relative to the Texture of Mind and the Manufacture of Conscience* (London: T. Davison, 1820).
[54] Dorset History Centre, Dorchester Prison, NG/PR1/D2/1 'Dorchester Prison Admission and Discharge Records, 1782–1901', 111. This record contains a rare description of Wedderburn: 'A man of colour, broad nostrils, a cut on the left side of the forehead, a slight cut across the bridge of the nose. Lusty.'
[55] Wedderburn, *Cast-Iron Parsons*. While this tract, as McCalman puts it, 'does seem to catch something of [Wedderburn's] authentic voice and outlook', it was heavily copyedited and contains none of the linguistic idiosyncrasies that characterise, for example, the *Axe*.
[56] Robin Furneaux, *William Wilberforce* (Vancouver: Regent College Publishing, 2005), 371–375.
[57] John Pollock, *William Wilberforce* (London: Lion, 1977), 258, cited in McCalman, 'Introduction', 36 n. 8.

found he was unable to prevail on Carlile to repent for his anti-Christian publishing, for example, he pursued his prosecution relentlessly, 'with an eagerness which in another man would be deemed vindictive'.[58] When he discovered that Jane Carlile's trial for publishing seditious libel (namely her husband's *Republican*) had been postponed for several months, he personally intervened at the Home Office to bring it forward.[59] These personal interventions, as much as his vocal support for Sidmouth's repressive legislation, his piousness and his anti-vice politicking, made Wilberforce a deeply and especially unpopular Tory MP among London's working-class radicals.

The accusation most frequently levelled at him from radical quarters was 'that he loved the black slaves yet did nothing for the white "wage slaves" of Britain'.[60] The radical publisher George Midford, for example, characterised Wilberforce as 'one of your regular humanity-mongers ... whose stock of charity is so bare, that it never begins at home', while bemoaning his 'large stock of compassion' for '*niggers*, felons, and gaol-birds'.[61] Obviously this was not so much a cause for friction between him and his fellow antislavery campaigner Wedderburn. In addition, the two men found they shared some, limited, political common ground in their mutual support for Queen Caroline.[62] As a result, Wilberforce was able to make more headway with Wedderburn than he had with other radicals. In *The Horrors of Slavery*, which Wedderburn dedicated to Wilberforce, the author thanked the evangelical for his 'advice' as well as 'two books beautifully bound in calf'.[63] The exact nature of their conversation, however, is unknown. McCalman suggests that Wilberforce advised Wedderburn 'to devote himself to the urgent cause of emancipating his West Indian brethren instead of squandering his talents on blaspheming God and subverting the King'.[64] Yet Wilberforce would surely have been aware that the very subversive actions for which Wedderburn was incarcerated were irrevocably bound up with his antislavery activism. Clearly, Wilberforce was keen to establish a relationship with the blaspheming, radical child of a slave, but evidence suggests that his motives went beyond a mere desire to save Wedderburn's soul.

---

[58] Ann Stott, *Wilberforce: Family and Friends* (Oxford: Oxford University Press, 2012), 196.
[59] Wilberforce House, Hull, Wilberforce Letters, 16/15 'William Wilberforce to Olivia Sparrow, 20 July 1820'.
[60] Pollock, *William Wilberforce*, 255.
[61] *Rambler's Magazine, or Fashionable Emporium of Polite Literature*, 2 (1823), 324–325.
[62] For Wilberforce's support for Queen Caroline, see, for example, Stott, *Wilberforce: Family and Friends*, 197–200.
[63] Wedderburn, *Horrors of Slavery*, 1.   [64] McCalman, 'Introduction', 1.

The loyalist, evangelical character of Wilberforce and his abolitionist contemporaries (Hannah More, Thomas Fowell Buxton and others) made the antislavery cause unpopular among working-class and free-thinking radicals. Wedderburn, on the other hand, was in a social position to stir up working-class opposition to slavery. His ethnic status and personal experiences as 'the offspring of a slave' gave him unassailable moral legitimacy among an artisanal audience – the same audience who dismissed the 'Clapham Saints' as apathetic to the hardships of the British working classes. Wilberforce wanted to cultivate Wedderburn's 'popular talents' for spreading opposition to slavery. Yet Wedderburn's insistence on mixing his powerful antislavery rhetoric with religious scepticism and political radicalism was not only unacceptable to Wilberforce, but it had also prevented him from preaching emancipation by landing him in prison. Wilberforce wanted to separate Wedderburn's antislavery and anti-establishment sentiments.

The effectiveness of Wilberforce's intervention has been dismissed by some historians, who can point to Wedderburn's continued presence at radical meetings and contributions to sceptical publications after his release from Dorchester as evidence of his continuing commitment to 'unrespectable' radicalism.[65] Others have seen Wilberforce's visit as a 'watershed moment' in Wedderburn's writing career, when his focus shifted away from domestic political radicalism and toward antislavery rhetoric. Edlie Wong, for example, acknowledges that 'Wedderburn's autobiography marked a departure from the radical propaganda that characterised his earlier work', even stepping beyond the mandate of available evidence to assert that Wilberforce specifically 'suggested that he pen an autobiography'.[66] However, this approach runs the risk of both minimising Wedderburn's earlier antislavery output and ignoring his later political radicalism. It also risks oversimplifying the nature of Wilberforce's influence over Wedderburn, who had been agitating for the abolition of slavery under his own initiative since at least 1817.

This is not to say that Wedderburn remained entirely unmoved by Wilberforce's visit. A close investigation of the writing produced by Wedderburn after his time in Dorchester shows a far more marked division between his political radicalism and antislavery activism. The *Axe Laid to the Root* and the antislavery speeches given at Hopkins Street sought to promote West Indian emancipation within the ideological

---

[65] See, for example, McCalman, 'Introduction'; McCalman, 'Anti-Slavery and Ultra-Radicalism'; Linebaugh, 'A Little Jubilee?'; Hunt, 'Remembering Africans in Diaspora'.
[66] Wong, *Neither Fugitive nor Free*, 64.

framework of radical anti-establishment rhetoric. However, Wedderburn's post-1820 works presented a much more 'respectable' moderatism when dealing with the issue of slavery. Clearly, he had no intention of being arrested again. His time in jail had been financially trying for his family: he was still in Dorchester when his son Jacob was baptised on 14 January 1822, and Elizabeth and the children had been forced to move to cheaper lodgings on New Compton Street, near Seven Dials.[67] Wedderburn therefore continued to be an active non-publishing supporter of radical, sceptical and deist politics, but crucially he kept these activities separate from his commitment to antislavery. This would explain the relative absence of anti-clericalism or insurrectionary rhetoric in his autobiography *The Horrors of Slavery*, published in 1824. True, the text was still distributed through a relatively narrow network of former Spencean Philanthropists and sold chiefly by Carlile and Davison, but its actual content steered well clear of the specifics of domestic political radicalism.

Of course, *The Horrors of Slavery* was not published in a political vacuum. Like the *Axe*, it was written in the wake of a major slave revolt in the West Indies. The uprising in Demerara in August 1823, itself apparently fuelled by false rumours of an emancipation act being passed in British parliament, began to feature heavily in the slavery debate in Britain, just as the Barbados uprising before it had.[68] Parliamentary abolitionists including Fowell Buxton (who later that year established the cautiously named Society for the Mitigation and Gradual Abolition of Slavery) and the Foreign Secretary George Canning took the uprising in Demerara as evidence of the folly of immediate emancipation. On 20 March 1824 Canning addressed the Commons, warning of the horrors awaiting those who would instantly abolish slavery: 'The men who would emancipate the negro, without previous preparations', he said, 'would be like *Frankenstein*, who had formed a giant without a mind, and trembled before the creature he had formed.' This was met with shouts of 'hear, hear' from the benches. Fowell Buxton followed Canning's speech with a number of examples of torture and abuse suffered by slaves under British masters. For example, 'by the law and custom of the West Indies, a *female Negro may be stripped naked, laid upon the ground, and, held down by four others*, in the presence of father, husband, or son, whipped with the cart whip.'[69] For the parliamentary section of the antislavery movement, the

[67] London Metropolitan Archives, Holborn St Giles in the Fields, DL/T/036, 'Register of Baptisms', Item 042.
[68] For a full discussion of the impact of the 1823 uprising on the British antislavery movement, see Matthews, *Caribbean Slave Revolts and the British Abolitionist Movement*, 135–179.
[69] *Bell's Life in London and Sporting Chronicle*, 21 March 1824.

Demerara uprising was evidence of the dangers of over-harsh treatment of the slaves and the necessity of educating and Christianising slaves as a prerequisite for their self-government.

While it hardly radicalised the abolitionist movement, the Demerara uprising altered the character of public discourse in Britain surrounding slave emancipation. The 'perfidious league of slaves' appearing in the mainstream British press in the wake of the Barbados rebellion in 1816 had by October 1823 been replaced by a group of merely 'unfortunate men'.[70] The more sympathetic representations of the Demerara uprising may have stemmed from the central involvement of a white missionary named John Smith in the insurrection. Smith was convicted of complicity in the rebellion on 19 November 1823 and sentenced to death with a recommendation to mercy. But the King's reprieve, signed on 14 February 1824, arrived too late, and Smith died of consumption while in custody.[71] The death of a white British clergyman provoked antislavery (though not necessarily abolitionist) discourse in both popular and parliamentary forums, including Henry Brougham's lengthy speech in Commons on 1 June 1824 calling for an inquest into Smith's death and an amelioration of conditions for the enslaved.[72] The Demerara uprising and Smith's death emboldened the parliamentary arm of the British emancipationist movement to more openly and unapologetically support gradual abolitionism, and softened popular attitudes toward rebelling slaves in the West Indian colonies.[73] For Canning, Fowell Buxton and Brougham, the immediate abolition of slavery remained out of the question; it not only would have physically endangered the planters but also would have morally weakened the slaves themselves.

This view was quite at odds with the vision of Jamaica as a revolutionary republic outlined by Wedderburn in the *Axe* seven years earlier. Nevertheless, he did have an impact on the parliamentary debate surrounding slavery. Fowell Buxton's illustrative example of female slaves being whipped in front of their sons bore a striking resemblance to an anecdote of Wedderburn's published three weeks previously in *Bell's Life in London*, detailing how as a child he had witnessed his mother 'stretched on the ground, tied hands and feet, and FLOGGED in the most indecent manner'. While *Bell's*, a gaudy sporting weekly, specialised in sensationalist news items and was not particularly targeted at well-to-do gentlemen like Fowell Buxton, its consistent antislavery stance may

---

[70] *Morning Post*, 6 June 1816; *Morning Chronicle*, 16 October 1823.
[71] Craton, *Testing the Chains*, 288–289.   [72] *Morning Chronicle*, 2 June 1824, 5–6.
[73] See Craton, *Testing the Chains*, 267–290; Matthews, *Caribbean Slave Revolts and the British Abolitionist Movement*, 28–58.

very well have brought it to the MP's attention. The detail of a mother being flogged in the presence of her son, while a common enough occurrence on slave plantations, was specific enough to suggest a connection between Wedderburn and Fowell Buxton's anecdotes.[74]

Wedderburn's letter was to prove the seed of *The Horrors of Slavery*, published later in the same year. While the uprising in Demerara had stimulated interest in antislavery politics, Wedderburn's motives for publishing an autobiography were more personal than political. While sharing his own personal experiences had certainly won him the support of the editor at *Bell's*, his habit of 'naming and shaming' the perpetrators of such atrocities – in this case his father James Wedderburn – irked his (white, legitimate) paternal half-brother Andrew Colvile. In the *Axe*, Wedderburn had already named their father as a rapist and abuser of his slaves.[75] But the *Axe* was a specialist publication designed to be distributed among an already-established market of radicals and radical-sympathisers, and as such it is unlikely that Colvile, a respectable West India merchant based between Jamaica and London, ever came across it. *Bell's*, on the other hand, was a tabloid-style newspaper with a very large circulation. Their line in sensationalist news stories along with their staunch antislavery position suited Wedderburn's letter perfectly. It also alienated the proslavery lobby as well as the rest of the taste-conscious, socially aspirant middle class to which most of them belonged. Indeed, by 1828 an increasingly 'respectable' Richard Carlile would be 'mortified that such a paper as *Bell's Life in London* should be the leading paper, as to the extent of circulation'.[76] Colvile himself acknowledged rather disdainfully that the paper needed to be 'put into [his] hands' before he took notice of it, but its market share could hardly be ignored.[77] To see his father maligned in such a public forum deeply offended Colvile, and he drafted a response to Wedderburn, printed in the same paper on 21 March 1824.

Colvile's letter was a personally malicious attack on Wedderburn's mother. In it he described Rosanna as a 'negro woman-*slave*', a 'troublesome' 'cook' with 'so violent a temper that she was continually quarrelling with the other servants, and occasioning a disturbance in the house'.[78] Colvile flatly denied Wedderburn's accusation that Rosanna

---

[74] The practice of publicly flogging enslaved women featured frequently in abolitionist literature of the 1820s, but Fowell Buxton's and Wedderburn's accounts were nevertheless strikingly similar. See Henrice Altink, *Representations of Slave Women in Discourses on Slavery and Abolition, 1780–1838* (London: Routledge, 2007), 131–139.

[75] *Axe Laid to the Root*, no. 1 (1817), 3.   [76] *Lion*, 1:5 (1828), 144.

[77] *Bell's Life in London and Sporting Chronicle*, 21 March 1824.

[78] *Bell's Life in London and Sporting Chronicle*, 21 March 1824.

'was FORCED to submit to [James Wedderburn], being *his Slave*, though he knew she disliked him'.[79] Rather, he called upon well-established racist stereotypes of sexual profligacy among black slaves in an attempt to undermine Wedderburn's claim to kinship with him. According to Colvile, 'several years' after James Wedderburn had sold Rosanna, 'this woman was delivered of a mulatto child, and as *she could not tell who was the father*, her master, in a foolish joke, named the child Wedderburn.'[80] Were this true (and the fact that James Wedderburn paid £200 in 1765 to have Robert and his brother James Jr. emancipated suggests that it was not), it would have been, at best, a spiteful assault on the character of a rape victim.[81] Colvile had hardly endeared himself to the editor of *Bell's* when he chastised them for 'lending yourself to be the vehicle of such foul slander upon the character of the respected dead', referring to Wedderburn's statements about their father rather than his own insinuations about Rosanna. However, it was his sign-off, threatening that 'in the event of your not inserting this letter in your Paper of next Sunday ... I have instructed my Solicitor to take immediate measures for obtaining legal redress against you', that piqued Wedderburn to respond directly.[82]

Wedderburn's reply was published the following week, systematically disproving Colvile's claims and challenging him to '*show fight* before the Nobs at Westminster'. Wedderburn took the opportunity to announce that he would 'publish my whole history in a cheap pamphlet', in order to 'give the public a specimen of the inhumanity, cruelty, avarice, and diabolical lust of the West-India Slave-Holders'. *Bell's* ran the letter accompanied by an endorsement running to more than a thousand words.[83] Colvile, repeatedly upbraided and humiliated in the most public setting imaginable, had nothing to say in response.

Wedderburn, on the other hand, had a great deal more to say on the subject. His promised autobiography, *The Horrors of Slavery*, was published within weeks. In it, Wedderburn included the entire exchange from *Bell's*, inviting the reader to 'judge which had the best of the argument'.[84] Interestingly, Wedderburn chose to reproduce the accompanying *Bell's*

---

[79] *Bell's Life in London and Sporting Chronicle*, 29 February 1824.

[80] *Bell's Life in London and Sporting Chronicle*, 21 March 1824.

[81] Jamaica Archives, Spanish Town, 1B/11/6/9 'Manumission of Slave Registers', ff. 37–38, cited in Hunt, 'Remembering Africans in Diaspora', 178.

[82] Jamaica Archives, Spanish Town, 1B/11/6/9 'Manumission of Slave Registers', ff. 37–38, cited in Hunt, 'Remembering Africans in Diaspora', 178; *Bell's Life in London and Sporting Chronicle*, 29 February 1824; *Bell's Life in London and Sporting Chronicle*, 21 March 1824.

[83] *Bell's Life in London and Sporting Chronicle*, 21 March 1824.

[84] Wedderburn, *The Horrors of Slavery*, 18.

editorials promoting only amelioration for slaves' conditions, as the paper 'wished not an *instantaneous* emancipation'.[85] He also included a narrative account of his own life, detailing, among other things, his father's 'very disgusting' seduction of his female slaves, 'like a bantam cock upon his dunghill', the whippings he witnessed administered to his mother and aged grandmother, and the unchristian lack of charity displayed by Colvile when he applied to him for financial help after coming to Britain.[86] Yet this catalogue of evils was a strangely depoliticised tract – at least in terms of domestic reform. The public exchange with Colvile had led Wedderburn to respond in a manner that vindicated his mother's character while exposing the morally degenerative effects of slavery for both enslaved and slaver.

Wedderburn's impetus in writing *The Horrors of Slavery* came from not his well-known political and ideological opposition to the institution but his personal outrage at Colvile's letter. 'Oppression I can bear with patience', he stated, 'but when to this is added insult and reproach from the authors of my miseries, I am forced to take up arms in my own defence, and to abide the issue of the conflict.'[87] *The Horrors of Slavery* was thus a publication primarily concerned with a personal 'conflict' with Colvile. Of course, this conflict arose from and fed back into the broader transatlantic debate surrounding slavery, but *The Horrors of Slavery* was first and foremost a personal vindication.

In truth, Wedderburn no longer saw the abolition of slavery as an aim in which he himself could take a lead role in achieving. He recognised that the radical circles in which he moved were becoming increasingly ambivalent toward the antislavery movement, while the parliamentary abolitionists were making steady progress in improving conditions for slaves. As Canning had pointed out in Parliament, a system of Christian moral education for slaves was proving very successful in Trinidad and was considered a preparatory step toward emancipation.[88] More to the point, the swift and brutal suppression of the slave revolts in Barbados and Demerara illustrated quite clearly that the kind of mass political mobilization Wedderburn had envisaged for Jamaica in 1817 was not likely to result in success. The only route to the abolition of slavery which seemed realistic in 1824 was through the introduction of new legislature in the House of Commons, and the now-infamous Wedderburn could expect limited sympathy there.

[85] *Bell's Life in London and Sporting Chronicle*, 29 March 1824.
[86] Wedderburn, *The Horrors of Slavery*, 22–23.
[87] Wedderburn, *The Horrors of Slavery*, 5.
[88] *Bell's Life in London and Sporting Chronicle*, 21 March 1824, 2.

In his dedication to Wilberforce, Wedderburn placed the onus for using his life experiences in the cause of abolitionism squarely on the shoulders of the parliamentary movement: 'Receive, Sir, my thanks for what you have done: and if, from the following pages, you should be induced to form any motion in parliament, I am ready to prove their contents before the bar of that most Honourable House.'[89] The reverence paid to Parliament in this quotation contrasted sharply with the anti-establishment speeches in which Wedderburn had specialised during his time at Hopkins Street. Not once in *The Horrors of Slavery* did he criticise the British government, either for their continuing involvement in slavery or for any of his own personal difficulties while living under their rule.

Indeed, after his release from Dorchester, ultra-radical rhetoric disappeared altogether from Wedderburn's printed output, though he continued to associate with radical networks for at least another nine years. In 1828, a scurrilous article appeared under Wedderburn's name in Carlile's sceptical periodical *The Lion* entitled 'The Holy Liturgy, or Divine Service upon the Principles of PURE CHRISTIAN DIABOLISM'. This sarcastic article described a fictional sect that worshipped the Devil, since the 'GOD OF HELL and "OF THIS WORLD,"' partakes in part of our character and imperfections, and is consequently, from his power superior to ours, a *Being to be feared, to be worshipped*'.[90] This short article appeared as part of a series written largely by Carlile in support of Robert Taylor, a sceptic who had been imprisoned on charges of blasphemy. But while Wedderburn's rough preaching style was extremely popular during his Hopkins Street days, radical and anti-clerical luminaries strove for a more genteel approach in the late 1820s. When he read Wedderburn's piece in *The Lion*, Taylor wrote to Carlile in response. While praising the article for its 'exquisite sarcasm', he lamented that '[i]f Wedderburn's measure of talent were but served up in a better looking vessel, or some that have ten-fold his talent would but bring it forth with half his courage and honesty, we should not want rich intellectual feasts.'[91] This was as clear an indication as any that Wedderburn had fallen out of step with his radical contemporaries on the issue of respectability. His limited education, low socioeconomic status, public association with known pornographers including Cannon and increasingly frequent appearances in court were becoming embarrassing to his radical friends.

Racist attitudes were also gaining popularity across all socioeconomic strata of British society, and Taylor's suggestion for the need of a

---

[89] Wedderburn, *The Horrors of Slavery*, 3.   [90] *Lion*, 1:12 (1828), 359–361.
[91] *Lion*, 1:13 (1828), 395.

Figure 8.2 George Cruikshank, *The New Union Club*, 1819,
hand-coloured etching, 312 mm × 482 mm.
Courtesy of the Lewis Walpole Library, Yale University.

'better-looking vessel' to lead his and Carlile's anti-clerical operations
can be read in this context. Wedderburn had already been the subject of
more than one form of racist satire. He was almost certainly the central
figure of George Cruikshank's 1819 print 'The New Union Club' (see
Figure 8.2), in which he was depicted standing on a table gesticulating
with one hand while grabbing his genitals with the other. The image
satirised the pretentions of both black radicals and parliamentary abolitionists, reimagining a dinner held by the African Society as a grotesque
carnival of drunkenness and interracial sexual profligacy, with Wedderburn and Wilberforce presiding as chief revellers.[92] When Wedderburn
had appeared in court as a plaintiff in February 1823, attempting to
reclaim some money he had been swindled out of by his editor George
Midford, a reporter skewered him with a lengthy and derisive description
even before describing the case. Wedderburn was mocked both for the

---

[92] Marcus Wood has examined the racist stereotyping of 'The New Union Club', including
its utility for galvanising working-class racism, at length. Marcus Wood, *Blind Memory:
Visual Representations of Slavery in England and America 1780–1865* (Manchester:
Manchester University Press, 2000), 165–172.

colour of his skin and his cultural aspirations, the inference being that the two were incompatible:

Mr. Robert Wedderburn – or Robertus Wedderburn, as he delighteth to designate himself, is a man of colour – something the colour of a toad's back; plomp and puffy as a porpoise, and the magnitude of his caput makes it manifest that nature cut him out for a counsellor, had not the destinies decreed that he should cut out cloth.[93]

These caricatures of Wedderburn demonstrate a popular perception of him, both as a political reformer and more prominently as a black public figure. Both represented the perceived ridiculousness of Wedderburn's pretentions to cultural and intellectual parity with his white peers. It did not matter that in reality his speeches at Hopkins Street were no more or less dignified than those of his white radical contemporaries, such as Hunt or Carlile. Their ambitions of respectability met with some success, even without the benefit of associations with well-to-do individuals, as Wedderburn had when he met Wilberforce in 1820. Such an ambition, if Wedderburn ever held it, was rendered unattainable in the popular imagination by nothing so much as the colour of his skin.

By 1830, Wedderburn's continuing commitment to antislavery agitation (and especially his vocal support of relatively privileged parliamentary abolitionists) alienated him further from his former radical contemporaries, who saw it as an unwelcome distraction from the cause of improving conditions for the 'wage-slaves' in British manufactories. Carlile's shift against abolitionism was a good indicator of how even Wedderburn's closest ultra-radical allies became hostile to the cause. Carlile's preface to the memoir of Robert Blincoe, a young British 'wage-slave', appearing in *The Lion* in February 1828 demonstrated that his position was, at best, ambivalent:

The religion and the black humanity of Mr. Wilberforce seem to have been entirely of a foreign nature. Pardon is begged, if an error is about to be wrongfully imputed; but the Publisher has no knowledge, that Mr. Wilberforce's humane advocacy for slaves, was ever of that homely kind, as to embrace the region of the home-cotton-slave-trade.[94]

The reference to Wilberforce's 'black humanity' was reminiscent of Cruikshank's representation of him presiding over 'The New Union' of abolitionists and debauched black people, in the bottom right-hand corner of which a black pauper could be seen kicking a white sailor out

---

[93] *The Hull Packet and Original Weekly Commercial, Literary and General Advertiser*, 3 March 1823, 3.
[94] *Lion*, 1:5 (1828), 145.

of the room (Figure 8.2). By February 1829, Carlile had incorporated out-and-out anti-black racism into his anti-clerical rhetoric. Following on from an anecdote about baboons stealing supplies from soldiers stationed at the Cape of Good Hope, Carlile suggested that 'if it be necessary to send missionaries to any part of Africa, it is necessary to send them to these baboons, who are as near to humanity as the negroes.'[95] Finally, Carlile began lending his support to the proslavery lobby, and by 1834 he was printing and selling proslavery pamphlets.[96]

Not all working-class radicals in the 1820s supported the proslavery position. The anti-abolitionist sentiments of Wedderburn's circle in particular may have had more to do with the essentially evangelical nature of the abolitionist movement of the 1820s and 1830s than mere political partisanship. A constant thread linking the work of Spence, Evans, Carlile, Davison, Cannon and indeed Wedderburn himself was religious scepticism and the criticism of all forms of clergy. Considering the drive toward 'respectability' in radical circles from the mid-1820s onward, the opposition of Wedderburn's circle (though not he himself) to the abolitionist movement might be thought of as emerging as an adjunct to their attack on religious dogmatism. Yet despite sharing their disdain for the clergy, Wedderburn gradually became ostracised from this ultra-radical circle. His appreciation for the antislavery work of the 'saints' in Parliament made him appear inconsistent in his political line, while his rough take on domestic politics looked increasingly old-fashioned. Early in 1828, he had established a new preaching house in Whites Alley, Chancery Lane, but found himself unable to compete with his new, respectable-radical contemporaries.[97] By June the same year, the chapel had closed down. Wedderburn's former circle was less inclined than ever to associate with him.

The decisive break came on 11 November 1830, when Wedderburn was tried for 'keeping a disorderly house' – probably a brothel – in Featherbed Lane, in which the prosecution reported that 'the character of the house was clearly proved'. Despite Wedderburn's repeated insistence that 'he kept, and should always keep, a house for destitute women,' he was convicted and sentenced to twelve months' hard labour. It is telling of how obscure Wedderburn had become that the news reporter on the case had confused him with one of his former circle, erroneously stating that he was 'one of the persons tried with Thistlewood for the

---

[95] *Lion*, 3:6 (1829), 168–170.
[96] Ryan Hanley, 'Slavery and the Birth of Working-Class Racism in England, 1814–1833', *Transactions of the Royal Historical Society*, 26 (2016).
[97] McCalman, 'Introduction', 30–31.

Cato-street conspiracy'.[98] In any case, this decidedly unrespectable conviction led to a permanent fracture between Wedderburn and the ultra-radical underworld with whom he had associated for fifteen years or more. While he continued to hold an interest in radical activities – for example, attending an anti-clerical speech given by Taylor in 1834 – he never again took a lead role in the movement for political reform in Britain.[99]

Wedderburn's second stint in prison gave him time to produce one final tract on the issue of slavery, *An Address to the Right Honourable Lord Brougham and Vaux*. Written in January 1831 and only recently rediscovered, this text represents an extensive revision of Wedderburn's stances on both slavery and political activism, in the light of which the latter part of his political life must be re-examined.

Now beneath the notice of his former circle, Wedderburn was free to pursue his own line on antislavery. Even Davison and Carlile, who had sold all of Wedderburn's previous writing from their shops, wanted nothing to do with his *Address*. Instead, it was published by John Ascham, a jobbing publisher and bookseller who had proved his radical credentials by selling pirated editions of Percy Shelley's *Queen Mab* – the so-called Chartist Bible. Wedderburn's final printed work represented a remarkable and disturbing reassessment of his position on slavery and its abolition.[100] The fiery articles of the *Axe*, fuelled by the insurrectionary zeal of the Barbados uprising, saw a slave-led revolution in Jamaica as both desirable and necessary. *The Horrors of Slavery*, published in the wake of the Demerara uprising amid a vitriolic personal spat between Wedderburn and his half-brother, illustrated the evils attendant on the continuation of slavery, inferring if not directly stating that its parliamentary abolition was at hand. The *Address*, on the other hand, represented if anything an unusually *moderate* viewpoint on emancipation, at times even flirting with anti-abolitionist sentiments.

After giving a brief biographical sketch, detailing the events of his childhood with none of the anger that characterised *The Horrors of Slavery*, Wedderburn set out his position: 'I have always considered, that the condition of slaves was far superior to that of European labourers, and therefore could never hold my hand up to support those ignorant fanatics, who were so frequently troubling parliament with petitions

---

[98] *Lancaster Gazette and General Advertiser*, 13 November 1830.
[99] McCalman, 'Introduction', 34.
[100] For an analysis of the authorship and publication history of this text, and a transcript, see Ryan Hanley, 'A Radical Change of Heart: Robert Wedderburn's Last Word on Slavery', *Slavery & Abolition*, 37:2 (2016), 432.

against slavery.'[101] This might seem to mirror Carlile's earlier statements regarding Wilberforce's supposed neglect of the rights of British labourers, but Wedderburn went on to advertise his 'equitable plan for the emancipation of the slaves' in terms of 'the benefit and safety of the proprietors, as well as ... the advantage of the overseers and book-keepers'.[102] This could hardly be more at odds with the anti-establishment, working-class principles that underpinned the radical movement of the 1810s and 1820s to which Wedderburn had once belonged.

Wedderburn went on in his *Address* to present a comprehensive ameliorationist argument, absolutely rejecting the prevailing abolitionist position – by this time even supported by moderates such as Fowell Buxton – of immediate universal emancipation. His Spencean roots showed through in his emphasis on land-ownership as the foundation of political worth, but much of his argument echoed the paternalism of the proslavery lobby. For Wedderburn, slaves' exclusion from owning personal property shielded them from the worst difficulties faced by European labourers:

Now, as slaves, they are landholders; but when free, they will be dispossessed of this necessary foundation of human happiness ... In a state of slavery, there is no seizing for rent or taxes, no casting into prison for debt, no starving families obliged to destroy themselves, or their offspring, for want of provision; excepting in a few instances, no separation of relatives takes place: in war or peace there is no alteration of the situation of the slaves; ... no remorse for crimes, that being unknown to them; as slavery does not admit of such – their time being fully occupied with work, and they being amply provided with every thing necessary for their comfort.[103]

Like a number of contemporaneous proslavery advocates, Wedderburn's support for the continuation of slavery was predicated on the notion that slaves would be putatively less comfortable and secure in the event of immediate emancipation. He still needed to demonstrate, however, his conviction that the continuation of slavery was not only beneficial but desirable to the slaves themselves. To this end, he produced examples of 'four intelligent slaves' turning down opportunities to abscond, 'preferring slavery in Jamaica, to freedom in this country'.[104] Wedderburn here placed the slave's voice into the debate around emancipation as he always had, but now suggested, disturbingly, that the interest of slaves and slave-owners were held in common.

---

[101] Wedderburn, *Address to Lord Brougham*, 4.
[102] Wedderburn, *Address to Lord Brougham*, 4.
[103] Wedderburn, *Address to Lord Brougham*, 4–5.
[104] Wedderburn, *Address to Lord Brougham*, 7.

Wedderburn went on to attack the methods of abolitionist orators, seeming to turn on the position he himself had occupied at Hopkins Street and in *The Horrors of Slavery*. 'It is easy for an orator to work upon the feelings of his auditors, respecting the supposed horrid state of slavery', he wrote, presumably drawing on his own experiences as an antislavery preacher, 'without any consideration of the West India proprietors' right by law.'[105] Apparently forgetting the descriptions of slave punishments he himself had given in *The Horrors of Slavery*, he went on to attack the 'advocates of slave emancipation' of the 1790s for the 'base practise' of 'exhibiting pictures of the different modes of punishing slaves, with the intent of making horrified impressions upon the public in general'.[106] Wedderburn went on to explain that he had rarely seen such torture employed during his time in Jamaica.

It is difficult to see why Wedderburn chose to represent West Indian slavery in such a sanitised manner, or why he suddenly began to value the property rights of the slave-owner as equal to the human rights of the slave, stating for example that 'it is quite just to set the slave free, and it is equally unjust to rob the master of his value.'[107] This change in stance once again raises the possibility of externally imposed changes to the text. However, in 1831 there was very little motive for any such edition. Wedderburn was no longer a central figure in London's radical scene, and with parliamentary abolitionists increasingly agitating for immediate emancipation, the moderate plan presented in *The Address* was hardly controversial. While a comparison with a manuscript letter written by Wedderburn during the same year strongly suggests that the *Address* was copy-edited, there was little in its content to indicate that editorial intervention went beyond basic grammatical corrections.[108]

If Wedderburn's stance on immediate emancipation had been reversed since he wrote the *Axe*, it should be noted that he retained some of his old principles in the *Address*. While he did now argue for the continuation of West Indian slavery as an institution, *The Address* did not discount the possibility of future slave emancipation. For example, Wedderburn placed emphasis on the centrality of black agency and self-emancipation as a means to the gradual and 'equitable' abolition of slavery: 'I hold it right that a slave ought to have a law made in his favour, to demand his release from his master when he can purchase his freedom, or that he can

---

[105] Wedderburn, *Address to Lord Brougham*, 7.
[106] Wedderburn, *Address to Lord Brougham*, 11.
[107] Wedderburn, *Address to Lord Brougham and Vaux*, 7.
[108] See BL, Add MSS., 27808, 'Robert Wedderburn to F[rances] Place, 22 March 1831'.

choose another owner.'[109] Wedderburn brought forward from the *Axe* a conviction that black people should be involved in the judiciary process, suggesting that 'the slaves, under certain limitations, have the right of giving evidence, and sitting as jurors.'[110] Indeed, the very conditions outlined in the *Address* for the continuation of West Indian slavery were a realigning of legal and political rights to give slaves opportunities to earn their own money by, for example, curing bacon and growing extra corn crops in fallow fields, thus enabling them to purchase their own freedom on a case-by-case basis. Wedderburn's *Address* was unique among the vast numbers of pro- and antislavery pamphlets published in the early 1830s in that it offered his promised 'plan for the emancipation of the slaves' without requiring the abolition of slavery.

Wedderburn also renewed his attack on the conduct of Methodist missionaries in the West Indies, by linking their 'extorting money from the slaves, under the pretence of directing them to heaven' to the continuation of their enslavement.[111] Wedderburn's suggestion to the Methodists to atone for what he saw as their extortion of the slaves was again linked to his plan for self-emancipation. Methodist missionaries, according to Wedderburn, 'ought to be honest enough to pay back these monies, so long received by them, into a savings' bank, to enable their black brethren to purchase their freedom'. Wedderburn's plan even included a proviso to prevent 'deluded slaves' from being swindled in such a manner, 'to see that the property of their slaves is not extorted from them by any pretence whatsoever'.[112] Wedderburn envisaged a cooperative movement toward the simultaneous peaceful self-emancipation of the slaves and compensation for the planters, completely bypassing the need for a single parliamentary bill imposing emancipation on planters from above.

Regardless of his misguided new approach, Wedderburn had matured as a writer since he last published without significant editorial intervention in 1824. Moreover, his ability to mould his message to his intended readership, attuned to the global political context of the time, had obviously been sharpened. The Baptist War was still eleven months away when Wedderburn wrote his *Address* in January 1831, and the prospect of immediate abolition, even as it gained momentum, was causing friction in Parliament. Brougham might not initially seem the obvious person to whom to address such a pamphlet, since he no longer held a vote in the

---

[109] Wedderburn, *Address to Lord Brougham and Vaux*, 5.
[110] Wedderburn, *Address to Lord Brougham and Vaux*, 6–7.
[111] Wedderburn, *Address to Lord Brougham and Vaux*, 8.
[112] Wedderburn, *Address to Lord Brougham and Vaux*, 14.

House of Commons. Yet the Lord Chancellor shared many of Wedderburn's objectives, including parliamentary reform and the abolition of slavery. Famously, he had acted as the 'Queen's lawyer' during the Queen Caroline affair, earning him plaudits among the radicalised working classes.[113] As Lord Chancellor, he wielded significant influence in both the upper and lower houses, especially among reforming Whigs. Like Wedderburn, he was critical of the Established Church, to the extent that one clergyman judged 'his present appointment [to the office of Lord Chancellor] one of the severest blows which could have been inflicted on the Church of God'.[114] Perhaps most importantly, Brougham, like Wedderburn, had kept a close eye on the rebellions taking place in the West Indies in 1816 and 1823.[115] On 1 June 1824, for example, he had delivered a marathon speech in Commons calling for an inquest into John Smith's death and recommending that the slaves in Demerara be educated in preparation for their gradual emancipation.[116]

Wedderburn ensured that his embarrassing conviction did not immediately prejudice the socially and politically elite Brougham against him by simply bending the truth. 'The cause of my imprisonment', he stated, 'arises from having let out furnished lodgings, though I did not reside on the premises; I was made to suffer through the misconduct of the tenants, who unfortunately (for them and myself) were addicted to drunkenness and noise; which gave rise to the indictment against me for nuisance.'[117] Wedderburn had mitigated his own crimes and presented himself as, of all things, a respectable, moderate gradualist.

In reality, however, extreme poverty and ever-decreasing social capital continued to drag Wedderburn deeper into criminality. On his release, he set up another 'house for destitute women' – in reality a brothel and pornography shop – at No. 8 Field Lane, in the notorious area of Saffron-Hill.[118] In February 1832, only three months after his release from prison, he was in court again. This time he had been indicted for the much more serious crime of attempting to 'burke' (garrotte) a woman named Mary Ann Jevitt at his house. A local landlord, hearing a cry of 'murder' coming from Wedderburn's house at nine o'clock on the morning of 11 February, had rushed to the house on Field Lane and found Jevitt with her arms and

---

[113] Michael Lobban, 'Brougham, Henry Peter, first Baron Brougham and Vaux (1778–1868)', in *ODNB*, available at www.oxforddnb.com/view/article/3581.

[114] *Morning Post*, 25 November 1830.   [115] Craton, *Testing the Chains*, 289.

[116] *Morning Chronicle*, 2 June 1824, 5–6.

[117] Wedderburn, *Address to Lord Brougham*, 15–16.

[118] 'Waddington said that part of the house was kept as a brothel, and in the front Wedderburn sold obscene books and prints, some of which, the most filthy that can be imagined, the officer produced.' *Morning Post*, 13 February 1832.

legs bound by a cord, which was also wrapped tightly around her neck. She 'appeared to be in a dying state'. By this point a local constable named Waddington had arrived, and upon Jevitt informing him that Wedderburn had bound her, he took Wedderburn into custody. At court, Wedderburn stated that Jevitt had come to the house, drunk and raving, at seven that morning, pulling the clothes from the beds and throwing water over the lodgers. Wedderburn admitted to tying her arms and legs and placing her in a cellar, 'to keep her there until she became sober'. He did not reply to the magistrate's questions regarding the cord around Jevitt's neck.[119] The following Monday, when Jevitt was well enough to come to court, she accused Wedderburn, along with his associates John Dunningham and William Rose, of a sustained and violent attack in which she was punched, kicked and beaten with a log of wood. Wedderburn this time responded that he had bound her arms and legs 'to prevent her laying violent hands upon herself', insisting that 'my intentions were good, though the law appears to be against me'. Dunningham and Rose made no defence.[120]

The magistrate found all three men guilty, though he regretted 'that the law did not justify him in dealing with them to the extent their brutality deserved'. Each was fined a mere £5 each, to be imprisoned for two months in the event of default. Given Wedderburn's desperate poverty, it is unclear as to whether he was able to pay this fine. In any case, he did not immediately go free. This may have proved beneficial to his safety. When Wedderburn's female associate Ann Whittingham stepped out into the street following the hearing, she was mobbed 'and nearly every part of her dress torn from her back, and no doubt she would have been killed on the spot had it not been for the timely assistance of some officers.'[121] Wedderburn, who had once made his living exciting crowds of working-class radicals into states of furious indignation, now in his dotage had himself cause to fear mob justice. While he maintained an interest in anti-clerical and anti-establishment politics, Wedderburn never again attained the degree of respect and infamy he had accrued during his Hopkins Street days, and he died in poverty and near-total obscurity in December 1834 or early January 1835 – though not without the satisfaction of seeing a bill for the emancipation of his 'oppressed countrymen' passed in Parliament. He was buried in London on 4 January 1835.[122]

It is impossible to consider Wedderburn's early antislavery work without the context of the politically radical social circles in which he mixed.

---

[119] *Morning Post*, 13 February 1832, 4.   [120] *Morning Chronicle*, 21 February 1832.
[121] *Morning Chronicle*, 21 February 1832.   [122] Thomas, *Telling West-Indian Lives*, 116.

Politically galvanised by Thomas Spence in 1814, the anti-establishment views inculcated by Wedderburn's traumatic childhood experiences of slavery found expression in political radicalism and abolitionism. Bussa's rebellion in Barbados in 1816 provided the catalyst for an innovative plan for a bloodless slave-led revolution in his home country of Jamaica, published in his periodical *The Axe Laid to the Root* in 1817. In Wedderburn's plan, the tropes of Spence's imagined agrarian utopia – common land-ownership, free universal education, abolition of both capital and corporal punishment – were enmeshed with his own hatred of plantocratic tyranny and Christian hypocrisy. The result was a text which struggled to present a coherent imaginary, vacillating between millenarian insurrectionism (when addressed to the planters) and pacifist stoicism (when addressed to the slaves). The furore surrounding Bussa's rebellion combined with the contraction in popular support for slave emancipation effectively prevented Wedderburn from inciting in Jamaica the type of armed insurrection seen in Barbados the preceding year. Nevertheless, the language and tone of the *Axe* bears much resemblance to the politically radical publications of his British peers.

While the threat of a prosecution for sedition hung over Wedderburn as a producer of published tracts, his status as a licenced Unitarian minister afforded his verbal discourse a degree of protection from the Home Office's increasingly draconian anti-radical approach. The dissolution of his partnership with Thomas Evans and the increasingly moderate remnants of the Spencean Philanthropists in the summer of 1819 marked the beginning of a period of blatant anti-government and anti-clerical activism which fed from and back into a militant perspective on abolition. Lord Sidmouth, who had tried and failed to indict Wedderburn on charges of sedition for holding a radical abolitionist meeting on 9 August 1819, responded by targeting him with a blasphemy charge, leading to his imprisonment for two years from May 1820.

Either his time in custody or a visit from Wilberforce led Wedderburn to re-examine the relationship between his radicalism and abolitionism, and after 1822 he no longer blended the two together. For example, when in 1824 he responded to an antislavery article in the popular newspaper *Bell's Life in London*, he gave anecdotes from his own life on a plantation without comment on the rebellion in Demerara, even though that was what had prompted the initial article. Similarly, *The Horrors of Slavery*, published in 1824, contained no discernible call for radical mobilisation, armed or otherwise, in either Britain or the West Indies, limiting itself instead to a recitation of Wedderburn's own experiences under the system of slavery. Yet even though *The Horrors of Slavery* was published and distributed through Wedderburn's existing radical social network, working-class support for abolitionism was waning while anti-black racism became more pervasive across Britain's entire social topography. Wedderburn himself had been the target of racist caricature in both news reportage and satirical visual culture, and by 1828 such ideas had permeated his own social network. The anti-abolitionist and increasingly racist character of the radical network of which Wedderburn was a part made his associations with them and Wilberforce's parliamentary abolitionists incompatible. Given the increased emphasis placed on 'respectability' by radicals such as Carlile and Taylor, Wedderburn's earlier association with the pornographer George Cannon, and especially his conviction in 1830 for running a brothel, led to his ostracisation from their network.

Under these social circumstances Wedderburn was able to devise a highly pragmatic and unusually moderate model for gradual slave emancipation, published in early 1831 as *An Address to Lord Brougham*. Like the *Axe*, this tract emphasised the centrality of slave agency in effecting emancipation. However, the *Address to Lord Brougham* had been purged of all trace of the insurrectionary zeal and anti-authoritarian tone which had characterised Wedderburn's early antislavery work, favouring instead a measured, respectful attitude designed to maximise the chances of its being taken seriously by its titular addressee. More importantly, perhaps, it represented the extent to which Wedderburn had divorced himself from his radical peers, pursuing instead a system of slave emancipation from within the existing British West Indian colonial political establishment.

The seediness of Wedderburn's subsequent alleged criminal behaviour as much as his obscurity indicates that by 1832 his social and political capital were well and truly expended, though it tells us little about how the *Address to Lord Brougham* was received. Nevertheless, in his thirty-year writing career, Wedderburn was the most prolific black author of the period. For as long as he was able to accommodate his antislavery discourse within the framework established by his radical peers in London, Wedderburn remained an influential actor in a network of working-class political mobilisation. However, following his imprisonment between 1820 and 1822, he recognised that the cause of abolition transcended the social boundaries of class. His social circle, unable to reconcile his consolidated abolitionist position with their own developing ideas of class and race – both of which demanded a Manichean negative against which to function – rejected him. Wedderburn's final, misguided position on slavery was defined by neither his relationship to his peers nor his own experiences, but rather by what he saw as a pragmatic commitment to the cause of freedom for slaves in the West Indies.

Conclusion

James Olney suggests that if one were to read dozens of American slave narratives, 'a sense not of uniqueness but of overwhelming *sameness* is sure to be the result ... [one] is sure to come away dazed by the mere repetitiveness of it all: seldom will [one] discover anything new or different but only, always more and more of the same.'[1] While scholars have since challenged Olney's assessment of American slave narratives, he could hardly have said the same of early black British writing.[2] To be sure, a number of discursive elements and themes recurred throughout much of the corpus – slavery of course being one of the most obvious. Yet black British life narratives, in many cases less closely managed by white abolitionists, tended to be more idiosyncratic in nature, more picaresque in their accounts of their authors' transatlantic and global travels and usually less self-consciously 'representative' of the 'slave experience' than those produced in the antebellum United States, particularly during the early and mid-nineteenth century.[3] Our investigation into how and why some of these works were produced in Britain reveals early black authors to have engaged in a comprehensively diverse range of social, political, epistemological, cultural, doctrinal, aesthetic, spiritual and scholarly concerns. Far from being marginal figures interested solely in the issues of race and slavery, black intellectuals were invested in the full spectrum of British life. They were significant, often central, actors in British and international networks as distinct and varied as the Countess of

---

[1] James Olney, '"I Was Born": Slave Narratives, Their Status as Autobiography and Literature', in Charles T. Davis and Henry Louis Gates Jr. (eds.), *The Slave's Narrative* (Oxford: Oxford University Press, 1985), 148.

[2] See, for example, John Ernest, 'Introduction', in John Ernest (ed.), *The Oxford Handbook of the African American Slave Narrative* (Oxford: Oxford University Press, 2014), 6–7.

[3] For abolitionist influences on American slave narratives, see Barbara McCaskill, 'Collaborative American Slave Narratives', in Ernest (ed.), *African American Slave Narratives*, 299–310. For a comparison of British and American black writing, see Kyle T. Bulthuis, 'Oceanic Barriers: The British-American Divide among Revolutionary Black Atlantic Writers', *History* 102:352 (2017), 576–596.

Huntingdon's Calvinist connexion and London's 'radical underworld'.[4] It was the unique character of the connections they made in these networks that gave their work both personality and discursive value. With this in mind, the continuities and formal qualities that historians and literary critics have used to bind early black autobiographies together into a corpus – their 'overwhelming *sameness*' – becomes less significant than the specific, interdependent contexts in which they were each produced. An appreciation of these contexts helps to reveal the individuality – the messily *human* characteristics – of these authors and their diverse literary productions.

Nevertheless, some networks and concerns were more widely influential among black writers than others. Evangelical Christianity, and particularly Methodism, was a significant factor in almost all the writing under discussion: Ukawsaw Gronniosaw and Ottobah Cugoano were both professed Calvinists; Boston King and John Jea were Episcopal Methodists operating within British Arminian networks; and the rational Unitarianism pervading Robert Wedderburn's later works grew partly from his disdain for Methodism. Manifestly, the comparative readiness of certain networks to support the publication of black autobiography was related to their stances on slavery and abolition. The most commercially successful and widely read black writing was marketed as antislavery literature. Some authors, including Ignatius Sancho, Olaudah Equiano and Mary Prince, became reasonably well known as spokespersons or avatars for the wronged and enslaved African. This did not mean, however, that all black writers unilaterally wrote abolitionist literature. Gronniosaw's Calvinist devotional autobiography largely reflected the paternalist pro-slavery stance of his patrons and peers. King's memoir, while clearly critical of slavery, was extremely careful not to appear anything like a 'radical' abolitionist text, since the Methodists in his network were keen to promote good relations with 'respectable' Tories, especially William Wilberforce. Similarly, Jea's antislavery rhetoric, while always present, was subordinated to his evangelising mission when he was in Britain – a tendency which became especially pronounced during his time in Liverpool. Conversely, the most outwardly *abolitionist* authors in this study – Cugoano, Equiano, Prince and Wedderburn – depended far less on evangelical networks for the publication of their work, and the most widely read had little to say on the subject of religious nonconformity.[5]

The conflict between political radicalism and antiradicalism provided another fruitful environment for black writing during this period. Like evangelical groups, reformist and conservative networks alike saw supporting the publication and/or distribution of black writing as a means of demonstrating their commitment to the ideal of liberty. Thus, all black writing produced in support of either side of this broad political divide espoused antislavery sentiments. However, the writing supported by groups with non-reformist interests – King's 'Memoirs', for example – tended to avoid advocating immediate or universal emancipation, instead emphasising the need for patience and forbearance on the part of the enslaved. Given his stance on the American Revolution, Ignatius Sancho might be understood to fall at least partly into this category. On the other hand, authors like Equiano, Cugoano and Wedderburn turned to the language of the new working-class radical movements of which they were part and applied it to the problem of transatlantic slavery. The corruption and 'tyranny' of the British government, for these authors, was manifested in their cruelty toward slaves and their brutal suppression of slave uprisings. These authors tended to advocate (or at least imagine) direct, revolutionary and often violent action as the best means to securing freedom from both literal slavery and political oppression.

One concern shared by all black writers during this period was that their intellectual and spiritual capacities were understood as being equal to those of their European peers. This is an orthodox finding, but this study has more specifically highlighted the prevalence of the notion of *respectability* in black writing. To be sure, Wedderburn was less concerned with respectability than most, but he was still careful to emphasise his rhetorical sophistication, and he was deeply invested in being perceived as an especially intelligent man. Certainly, his final published text, *An Address to Lord Brougham and Vaux*, demonstrated a far greater desire for establishment acceptance than his earlier work. All of the black authors we have looked at here used their publications to challenge essentialist notions of Africans as less intellectually capable than Europeans. Sancho, Equiano and Prince were widely celebrated – and sometimes scrutinized and publicly attacked – for their successes in this undertaking. Moreover, through their intercessions in overwhelmingly white print culture, they were able to carve out for themselves a social situation well within the boundaries of self-defined 'polite', 'respectable' and 'intellectual' British networks.

Despite these achievements, it is evident that the period 1770–1830 did not see a smooth teleological increase in either creative agency or editorial control for black writers. Nor were the two necessarily coterminous. For example, Sancho, one of the earliest writers under discussion, had among the greatest degree of control over the original composition of his correspondence, but the least editorial influence over the published *Letters*, since they were edited posthumously. Conversely, Jea, one of the latest, declared absolute editorial control but was unable to enforce it due to his limited literacy; he needed an amanuensis to record his *Life*. Perhaps unsurprisingly, a correlation existed between the financial dependency of an author and the extent of a network's influence over the text: white interlocutors and editors appear to have moderated texts more heavily when the authors in question were financially dependent on them.

This study has demonstrated that black intellectuals participated in a broad array of British concerns between 1770 and 1830, extending well beyond abolitionism. However, it also prompts a reconsideration of the nature of the British anti- and proslavery movements. Formalised and semi-formalised groups such as SEAST and the West India proprietors have often been seen as metonyms for two binary, neatly opposed factions in which everyone who wanted to abolish the slave trade and slavery stood against everyone who wanted to retain these systems.[6] This book suggests that it would be more useful to conceive of these 'two movements' rather as consisting of numerous, competing, conflicting and sometimes untidily overlapping networks of interest and influence.[7] In compiling the microhistories of individual authors, this study has demonstrated that these various networks thought about slavery and ethnicity in endlessly adaptable ways. Writings by Gronniosaw and Sancho, for example, bear little in common beyond the fact that their authors were black and formerly enslaved. At times, they both complained of the miseries of slavery. At others, they both saw it as necessary, either to the conversion of African pagans or to shoring up Britain's economy after the loss of America. After the mid-1780s, black writing ceased to argue that the system was necessary, but its antislavery messages were no more unified. While Equiano and Prince were attached to formalised antislavery organisations, they were in the minority of black authors. Cugoano and Wedderburn, for example, envisioned the system of slavery ending in the violent destruction of the slave-traders. King and Jea saw freedom as best achieved through forbearance and prayer. Each of these authors'

---

[6] See, for example, Steven Tomkins, *Clapham Sect: How Wilberforce's Circle Transformed Britain* (Oxford: Lion, 2010), 66–74, 80–90, 223–233; Adam Hochschild, *Bury the Chains: The British Struggle to Abolish Slavery* (London: Macmillan, 2005), 106–121.

[7] See, for example, the relationship between the Wilberforce family and the slave-trading Hibberts and Pinneys, discussed in Katie Donington, 'The Benevolent Merchant? George Hibbert (1757–1837) and the Representation of West Indian Mercantile Identity', PhD thesis, University College London (2013), 176–178; Anne Stott, *Wilberforce: Family and Friends* (Oxford: Oxford University Press, 2012), 232–244.

texts reflected different networks of British people, each with a different way of thinking about slavery.

In this sense it may be more appropriate to think about British pro- and antislaveries in the plural, rather than the singular. This approach is especially useful when considering contexts specific to localities beyond the boundaries of London. Three of the authors under discussion in this study – Gronniosaw, King and Jea – spent more time out of London than in it, and so were largely influenced by attitudes toward slavery, politics, art and religion that were not necessarily reflective of those in the metropolis. This was most pronounced in Jea's work, since he moved from an area where slavery accounted for much of his congregation's employment to an area where its suppression was a source of intense local pride. However, King's geographical location at Kingswood School, near Bristol, in some measure accounted for the extent to which his work represented the 'respectable' antislavery voice so expedient to Thomas Coke and his circle. Similarly, Gronniosaw lived the last years of his life in Kidderminster and Hertfordshire, where Selina Hastings's influence was strong, and his *Narrative* was published in the Calvinist hotspot of Bath. Because so many eighteenth-century networks were spatially as well as ideologically bounded, an acknowledgement of the quite specific geographies of black writings in Britain enables a greater understanding of them as both material objects to be bought and sold and discursive artefacts to be read and understood.

In this sense, this study also highlights how attention to influential networks can shed light on writing from this period produced by apparently 'marginal' figures. Investigations into the production and dissemination of working-class autobiography, for instance, share many of the same methodological challenges and practical questions around authorship, authority and authenticity in the face of limited literacy, conflicting interests, and financial dependence. Like black writing, working-class autobiography frequently appeared in the pages of nonconforming religious bulletins and radical periodicals, each with their own editorial agenda.[8] (In some cases, the same individuals involved in bringing black writing to press, such as the political radical Richard Carlile or the Methodist publisher George Whitfield, were also involved in the production of other forms of 'marginal' autobiography.) As we have seen in the case of Mary Prince, women writers – particularly working-class women

---

[8] See D. Bruce Hindmarsh, *The Evangelical Conversion Narrative: Spiritual Autobiography in Early Modern England* (Oxford: Oxford University Press, 2005); Emma Griffin, *Liberty's Dawn: A People's History of the Industrial Revolution* (New Haven, CT: Yale University Press, 2013).

writers – had also to negotiate patriarchal systems of oppression and social organisation, just as black authors had to negotiate ideas of racial difference and racial prejudice.[9] Reading early black British writing through its networks of production reminds us that marginalised voices are rarely left to posterity without mediation. The response of some historians has been to caveat their own analyses or to seek to verify the bare facts related in such life-writing through recourse to archival sources, validating the experiences of their authors as 'truthful'.[10] Yet such texts are rarely read for what – and why – they *are*, rather than what we as historians might like them to be. We might turn to the stories of how these (auto)biographies were produced, as texts and as cultural artefacts, to answer these questions. Closer attention to the influential networks responsible for publishing the life stories of working men and women, children, and ethnic 'Others' from all over the world may yet yield surprising insights about British culture and society.

Early black writing was affected profoundly by the networks of association and influence that surrounded each author. While evangelical and political networks exerted the most extensive and direct forms of influence, the interventions of these outside parties resulted in a diversity of effects. Black authors wrote texts that ranged from proslavery Calvinist devotionals to radically insurrectionary abolitionist polemics. All of these texts shared a desire to demonstrate the respectability, intelligence and spiritual parity of their black author-protagonists. However, just like the abolitionist movement, progress was neither smooth nor linear regarding black authorial and editorial control over their work. The individual character of their surrounding networks still deeply influenced black writers in Britain on the eve of abolition, just as they had when slavery was only rarely challenged. In the meantime, black writing had become unilaterally critical of slavery, but not within any single overarching aesthetic or political tradition. This reflected the multifaceted and dynamic nature of antislavery activism in Britain. As the period progressed, black authors took on an increasingly central role in the organisation, facilitation and popularisation of these activities. Black intellectuals like Gronniosaw, Sancho, Cugoano, Equiano, King, Jea, Prince and Wedderburn provided links between the debates over slavery and a wide range of other, seemingly disparate British interests. Through them, networks as disparate as

---

[9] See Amy Culley, *British Women's Life Writing, 1760–1840: Friendship, Community, and Collaboration* (Basingstoke: Palgrave Macmillan, 2014).

[10] See, for example, Jane Humphries, *Childhood and Child Labour in the British Industrial Revolution* (Cambridge: Cambridge University Press, 2015).

the Hampshire Methodist circuit and the ultra-radical debating clubs of London could engage in the same conversations, however differently they articulated their views. What this study has set out to demonstrate, above all, is that through their interactions with local, national and global networks of influence, black authors and their works helped to shape British society, just as they themselves were shaped by it.

Select Bibliography

Primary Sources

Manuscripts

The Bodleian Library, Oxford, UK
MSS British Empire
    Manuscripts of the Anti-Slavery Society

The British Library, London, UK
Additional Manuscripts
    Francis Place Papers (Add. MSS. 27808)
    Manuscript Copy of Memoirs of Thomas Hardy (Add. MSS. 65153A)
    Minute Books of the Committee for the Abolition of the Slave Trade (Add. MSS 21254–21255)
    Stephenson Papers: The Letters of Ignatius Sancho (Add. MSS. 80977)
General Collections
    'Marginalia', in Wedderburn, Robert, The Truth Self-Supported *(4226.cc.47)*
Loan Collections
    Miss Elizabeth Sancho, Daughter of Ignatius Sancho (Loan 96 RLF 1/583)

Cheshunt Foundation, Westminster College, Cambridge, UK
Selina Hastings Correspondence

Dorset History Centre, Dorchester, UK
Dorchester Prison
    Dorchester Prison Admission and Discharge Papers, 1782–1901 (NG/ PR1/D2/1)

Gloucestershire Records Office, Gloucester, UK
Sharp Family Papers
    Granville Sharp Papers (D/3549/13)

Guildhall Library, London, UK
St. Katherine Kree Parish Records
  Register of Marriages, 1754–1785 (P69/KAT2/A/01/MS7891/1)

Hampshire Records Office, Sussex, UK
Microfiche Collections
  Copy of Portsea St Thomas Parish Register (Fiche 248)
  Gosport Holy Trinity Parish Register (Fiche 11, Fiche 12)
Parish Registers
  Exbury Parish Register (50M80/PR1)
Opinions of Law Officers
  Albert Pell (W/D6)

Huntingdon Library, California
Wilberforce: Slavery, Religion & Politics

John Rylands Library, Manchester, UK
Methodist Collections
  John Wesley, Copy Letters (1977/609)
  John Wesley Letters (1977/617)
  John Wesley Letters, Main Sequence (1977/613)
  Selina Hastings, Countess of Huntingdon Papers (1977/504)

Kingswood School Archives, Bath, UK
School Account Books
  Account Books for 1794
  Account Books for 1795
  Account Books for 1796

London Metropolitan Archives
Holborn St Giles in the Fields
  Register of Baptisms (DL/T/036)

The National Archives, London, UK
Admiralty Records
  Minutes of Admiralty Board (ADM 1/163)
Commonwealth Office Papers
  Barbados, Original Correspondence (CO28/85)
  Correspondence of Secretary of State (CO217/63)
Home Office Papers
  Disturbance Papers (HO42/195, HO42/158, HO42/190, HO42/191,
    HO42/192, HO42/196, HO42/182, HO42/202)
Treasury Solicitors Papers
  Law Officers' and Counsel's Opinions (TS25/2035/20)
  Treasury Correspondence (T1/631, T1/632, T1/633, T1/634, T1/635)
  Treasury Solicitor and HM Procurator General, Papers (TS11/45)

Local Parish Records
  Worcestershire (RG 4/3374)
Guy Carleton, 1st Baron Dorchester Papers
  'The Book of Negroes' (30/55/100/10427)

National Royal Navy Museum, Portsmouth, UK
Admiralty Library
  Selected Parliamentary Papers for 1818

Norfolk Record Office, Norwich, UK
Manuscript Letters
  General (MC 5D)

Wilberforce House Museum, Hull
William Wilberforce Letters

Periodicals and Newspapers

Arminian Magazine
The Axe Laid to the Root
Bell's Life in London and Sporting Chronicle
Boddely's Bath Journal
The Chartist
La Chronique de Jersey
Edinburgh Magazine and Review
Felix Farley's Bristol Journal
Gazetteer and New Daily Advertiser
General Evening Post
Gentleman's Magazine
Giant Killer, or Anti-Landlord
Hampshire Telegraph
*The Hull Packet and Original Weekly Commercial, Literary and General
  Advertiser*
The Lancaster Gazette and General Advertiser
Lancaster Gazetteer
The Lion
Liverpool Mercury
Lloyd's Evening Post
London Advertiser
London Chronicle
London Evening Post
The London Magazine, or Gentleman's Monthly Intelligencer
Methodist Magazine
Missionary Magazine
Monthly Miscellany
Monthly Review, or Literary Journal
Morning Chronicle

Morning Chronicle and Daily Advertiser
Morning Herald
Morning Post
Morning Post and Daily Advertiser
Pig's Meat: Containing Lessons for the Swinish Multitude
Public Advertiser
Sentimental Magazine
St. James's Chronicle or the British Evening Post
The Diary: or Woodfall's Register
The Times
Weekly Miscellany
Wesleyan Methodist Magazine
World

Printed Primary Sources

Anon. *Nocturnal Revels* (London: M. Goadby, 1779).
  A Particular Account of the Insurrection of the Negroes of St. Domingo (London: Assemblée Générale, 1792).
  A Select Collection of Poems: With Notes, Biographical and Historical (London: J. Nichols, 1772).
  Some Account of the Proceedings at the College of the Right Hon. the Countess of Huntingdon, in Wales, Relative to Those Students called to go to her Ladyship's College in Georgia (London, 1772).
  The Speeches of Mr. Wilberforce, . . . on a Motion for the Abolition of the Slave Trade (London: John Stockdale, 1789).
Cannon, George, *A Few Hints Relative to the Texture of Mind and the Manufacture of Conscience* (London: T. Davison, 1820).
Capitein, Jacobus, *The Agony of Asar: A Thesis on Slavery by the Former Slave Jacobus Elisa Johannes Capitein, 1717–1747*, trans. and ed. Grant Parker (Princeton, NJ: Markus Wiener, 2001). Originally published 1747.
Clark, Ewan, *Miscellaneous Poems* (Whitehaven: J. Ware & Son, 1779).
Clarkson, Thomas, *The History of the Rise, Progress and Accomplishment of the Abolition of the African Slave Trade* (London: Longman et al., 1808), 2 vols.
  Reflexions sur la traite et l'esclavage des Negres, trans. Antoine Diannyere (Paris: Royez, 1788).
  Thoughts and Sentiments on the Evil of Slavery (London: Kirkby et al., 1791).
  Thoughts and Sentiments on the Evil and Wicked Traffic of the Slavery and Commerce of the Human Species (London, 1787).
Equiano, Olaudah, *The Interesting Narrative of the Life of Olaudah Equiano, or Gustavus Vassa, the African* (London: 1789).
  The Letters and Other Writings of Gustavus Vassa (Olaudah Equiano, the African): Documenting the Abolition of the Slave Trade, ed. Sapoznik, Karlee Anne (Princeton, NJ: Markus Wiener, 2014).
Fox, William, *The Complete Writings of William Fox: Abolitionist, Tory, and Friend to the French Revolution* (Nottingham: Trent Editions, 2011), ix–xvii.

Frelinghuysen, Theodorus, *Forerunner of the Great Awakening: The Sermons of Theodorus Jacobus Frelinghuysen*, ed. and trans. Joel Beeke (Grand Rapids, MI: William Eerdman, 2000).

Fyfe, Christopher (ed.), *'Our Children Free and Happy': Letters from Black Settlers in Africa in the 1790s* (Edinburgh: Edinburgh University Press, 1991).

Gronniosaw, Ukawsaw, *A Narrative of the Most Remarkable Particulars in the Life of James Albert Ukawsaw Gronniosaw* (Bath: W. Gye and T. Mills, [1772]).

Hammon, Briton, *Narrative of the Uncommon Sufferings and Surprizing Deliverance of Briton Hammon* (Boston: J. Green and J. Russell, 1760).

Hammon, Jupiter, *An Evening Thought: Salvation by Christ, with Penetential Cries* (New York, 1760).

Hoare, Prince, *Memoirs of Granville Sharp* (London: Lilerton and Henderson, 1820).

Jea, John (ed.), *A Collection of Hymns* (Portsea: James Williams, 1816).

Jea, John *The Life, History and Unparalleled Sufferings of John Jea, the African Preacher* (Portsea: John Williams, [1815/1816]).

Kilham, Alexander, *The Hypocrite Detected and Exposed; and the True Christian Vindicated and Supported* (Aberdeen: J. Chalmers, 1794).

 The Progress of Liberty, amongst the People Called Methodists. To Which Is Added, the Out-lines of a Constitution (Alnwick: J. Catnach, 1795).

King, Boston, 'Memoirs of the Life of Boston King', in Anon., *The Methodist Magazine* [1799], 157–161, 209–213, 261–265.

Long, Edward, *The History of Jamaica*, 2 vols. (London: T. Lowndes, 1774).

Marrant, John, *A narrative of the Lord's wonderful dealings with John Marrant, a black, born in New-York in North-America* (Dublin: B. Dugdale, 1790).

Nichols, John (ed.), *Literary Anecdotes of the Eighteenth Century* (London: J. Nichols, 1812–1814), 9 vols.

Perkins, Erasmus [Cannon, George] (ed.), *The Address of the Rev. R. Wedderburn, to the Court of King's Bench at Westminster* (London: W. Mason, 1820).

 (ed.), *The Trial of the Rev. R. Wedderburn, (A Dissenting Minister of the Unitarian Persuasion,) for Blasphemy* (London: W. Mason, 1820).

Prince, Mary, *The History of Mary Prince, a West Indian Slave* (London: F. Westley and A. H. Davis, 1831).

Sharp, Granville, *A Representation of the Injustice and Dangerous Tendency of Tolerating Slavery* (London: Benjamin White, 1769).

Simmons, Henry, *Third Letter to the Right Hon. Earl Grey, First Lord of the Treasury &c. on the Question of Negro Emancipation* (London: Richard Carlile, 1834).

Spence, Thomas, *The Rights of Man, First Published in 1783* (London: T[homas] Spence, 1793).

Sterne, Laurence, *Letters of the Late Laurence Sterne* (London: T. Beckett, 1775).

Wedderburn, Robert, *An Address to the Right Honourable Lord Brougham and Vaux* (London: John Ascham, 1831).

 Cast-Iron Parsons (London: T. Davison, 1820).

 High-Heel'd Shoes for Dwarfs in Holiness (London: T. Davison, 1821).

 The Horrors of Slavery (London: R. Wedderburn, 1824).

 Letter to the Archbishop of Canterbury (London: T. Davison 1820).

Letter to Solomon Herschel, Chief Rabbi of England (London: T. Davison 1820).

The Truth Self-Supported; or a refutation of Certain Doctrinal Errors Generally Adopted in the Christian Church (London: W[illiam] Glindon and G[eorge] Rieubau, [1802]).

Wesley, John, 'Farther Thoughts on Separation from the Church', *The Arminian Magazine*, 13 (1790), 215–216.

A Short Account of the School, in Kingswood, near Bristol (Bristol: William Pine, 1768).

Thoughts upon Slavery (London: R. Hawes, 1774).

Wheatley, Phillis, *An Elegiac Poem. On the Death of . . . George Whitefield* (Newport, RI: S. Southwick, [1771]).

Whitefield, George, *Works of George Whitefield*, 7 vols. (London: Edward and Charles Dilly, 1771–1772).

Wilberforce, William, *The Speech of William Wilberforce Esq. . . . on the Question of the Abolition of the Slave Trade* (London: Logographic Press, 1791).

Secondary Sources

Books and Articles

Ahern, Stephen (ed.), *Affect and Abolition in the Anglo-Atlantic, 1770–1830* (London: Ashgate, 2013).

Allen, Jessica, 'Pringle's Pruning of Prince: The History of Mary Prince and the Question of Repetition', *Callaloo*, 35:2 (2012), 509–519.

Altink, Henrice, *Representations of Slave Women in Discourses on Slavery and Abolition, 1780–1838* (London: Routledge, 2007).

Andrews, William, *To Tell a Free Story: The First Century of Afro-American Autobiography, 1760–1865* (Urbana: University of Illinois Press, 1986).

Anon., 'New Light on the Life of Ignatius Sancho: Some Unpublished Letters', *Slavery & Abolition*, 1:3 (1980), 345–358.

Anstey, Roger, *The Atlantic Slave Trade and British Abolition, 1760–1810* (London: Macmillan, 1975).

'Parliamentary Reform, Methodism and Anti-Slavery Politics, 1829–1833', *Slavery & Abolition*, 2:3 (1981), 209–226.

Anstey, Roger, and Hair, P. E. H. (eds.), *Liverpool, the African Slave Trade, and Abolition: Essays to Illustrate Current Knowledge and Research* (Liverpool: Historic Society of Lancashire and Cheshire, 1976).

Banner, Rachel, 'Surface and Stasis: Re-Reading Slave Narrative via *The History of Mary Prince*', *Callaloo*, 36:2 (2013), 298–311.

Bannet, Eve, *Empire of Letters: Letter Manuals and Transatlantic Correspondence, 1680–1820* (Cambridge: Cambridge University Press, 2005).

Transatlantic Stories and the History of Reading, 1720–1810 (Cambridge: Cambridge University Press, 2010).

Barker-Benfield, G. J., *The Culture of Sensibility: Sex and Society in Eighteenth-Century Britain* (Chicago, IL: University of Chicago Press, 1992).

Barrell, John, *Imagining the King's Death: Figurative Treason: Fantasies of Regicide* (Oxford: Oxford University Press, 2000).

Beckles, Hilary, *Freedoms Won: Caribbean Emancipations, Ethnicities and Nationhood* (Cambridge: Cambridge University Press, 2006).

'Slave Ideology and Self-Emancipation in the British West Indies, 1650–1832', *Bulletin of Easter Caribbean Affairs*, 10:4 (1984), 1–8.

Bethencourt, Francisco, *Racisms: From the Crusades to the Twentieth Century* (Princeton, NJ: Princeton University Press, 2013).

Blackburn, Robin, *The Overthrow of Colonial Slavery 1776–1848* (London: Verso, 1988).

Boulukos, George, *The Grateful Slave: The Emergence of Race in Eighteenth-Century British and American Culture* (Cambridge: Cambridge University Press, 2008).

Bradley, James, 'Parliament, Print Culture and Petitioning in Late Eighteenth-Century England', *Parliamentary History*, 26:1 (2007), 98–111.

Braidwood, Stephen, *Black Poor and White Philanthropists: London's Blacks and the Foundation of the Sierra Leone Settlement 1786–1791* (Liverpool: Liverpool University Press, 1994).

Brant, Clare, *Eighteenth-Century Letters and British Culture* (London: Palgrave Macmillan, 2006).

Brown, Christopher, *Moral Capital: Foundations of British Abolitionism* (Chapel Hill: University of North Carolina Press, 2006).

Cameron, Gail, *Liverpool: Capital of the Slave Trade* (Liverpool: Picton Press, 1992).

Campbell, James, *Songs of Zion: The African Methodist Episcopal Church in the United States and South Africa* (Oxford: Oxford University Press, 1995).

Carey, Brycchan, *British Abolitionism and the Rhetoric of Sensibility: Writing, Sentiment, and Slavery, 1760–1807* (London: Palgrave Macmillan, 2005).

'"The extraordinary Negro": Ignatius Sancho, Joseph Jekyll, and the Problem of Biography', *British Journal for Eighteenth Century Studies*, 26 (2003), 1–13.

From Peace to Freedom: Quaker Rhetoric and the Birth of American Antislavery, 1657–1761 (New Haven, CT: Yale University Press, 2012).

'William Wilberforce's Sentimental Rhetoric: Parliamentary Reportage and the Abolition Speech of 1789', *The Age of Johnson: A Scholarly Annual*, 14 (2003), 281–305.

Carey, Brycchan, Ellis, Markman, and Salih, Sarah (eds.), *Discourse of Slavery and Abolition: Britain and Its Colonies, 1760–1838* (London: Palgrave Macmillan, 2004).

Carretta, Vincent (ed.), *Equiano, the African: Biography of a Self-Made Man* (Athens: University of Georgia Press, 2005).

Carretta, Vincent 'New Equiana', *Early American Literature*, 44:1 (2009), 147–160.

'A New Letter by Gustavus Vassa/Olaudah Equiano?', *Early American Literature*, 39:2 (2004), 355–361.

'Olaudah Equiano or Gustavus Vassa? New Light on an Eighteenth-Century Question of Identity', *Slavery & Abolition*, 20:3 (1999), 96–105.

Phillis Wheatley: Biography of a Genius in Bondage (Athens: University of Georgia Press, 2011).

'Response to Paul Lovejoy's "Autobiography and Memory: Gustavus Vassa, alias Olaudah Equiano, the African"', *Slavery & Abolition*, 28:1 (2007).

'Three West Indian Writers of the 1780s Revisited and Revised', *Research in African Literatures*, 29:4 (1998), 73–87.

Unchained Voices: An Anthology of Black Authors in the English-Speaking World of the 18th Century (Lexington: University Press of Kentucky, 1996).

Carretta, Vincent, and Gould, Phillip (eds.), *Genius in Bondage: Literature of the Early Black Atlantic* (Lexington: University Press of Kentucky, 2001).

Chandler, James, *England in 1819: The Politics of Literary Culture and the Case of Romantic Historicism* (Chicago, IL: University of Chicago Press, 1998).

Chase, Malcolm, *The People's Farm: English Radical Agrarianism 1775–1840* (Oxford: Oxford University Press, 1988).

Chater, Kathleen, *Untold Histories: Black People in England and Wales during the Period of the British Slave Trade, c. 1660–1807* (Manchester: Manchester University Press, 2009).

Clapp, Elizabeth, and Jeffrey, Julie (eds.), *Women, Dissent and Anti-Slavery in Britain and America, 1790–1865* (Oxford: Oxford University Press, 2011).

Coffey, John, '"Tremble, Britannia!": Fear, Providence and the Abolition of the Slave Trade, 1758–1807', *English Historical Review*, 127:527 (2012), 844–881.

Colley, Linda, *Britons: Forging the Nation, 1707–1837* (New Haven, CT: Yale University Press, 1982).

Costanzo, Angelo, *Surprizing Narrative: Olaudah Equiano and the Beginnings of Black Autobiography* (London: Greenwood, 1987).

Costello, Ray, *Black Liverpool: The Early History of Britain's Oldest Black Community, 1730–1918* (Liverpool: Picton, 2001).

Craton, Michael, *Testing the Chains: Resistance to Slavery in the British West Indies* (Ithaca, NY: Cornell University Press, 1982).

Dabydeen, David, *Hogarth's Blacks: Images of Blacks in Eighteenth Century English Art* (London: Dangaroo Press, 1985).

Dabydeen, David, Gilmore, John, and Jones, Cecily (eds.), *The Oxford Companion to Black British History* (Oxford: Oxford University Press, 2007).

David, Huw, 'Transnational Advocacy in the Eighteenth Century: Transatlantic Activism and the Anti-Slavery Movement', *Global Networks*, 7:3 (2007), 367–382.

Davis, Charles T., and Gates, Henry Louis Jr. (eds.), *The Slave's Narrative* (Oxford: Oxford University Press, 1985).

Davis, David Brion, *The Problem of Slavery in the Age of Emancipation* (New York: Alfred A. Knopf, 2014).

The Problem of Slavery in the Age of Revolution 1770–1823 (Oxford: Oxford University Press, 1999).

Davis, Michael, and Pickering, Paul (eds.), *Unrespectable Radicals? Popular Politics in the Age of Reform* (London: Ashgate, 2008).

Dickinson, H. T., *British Radicalism and the French Revolution 1789–1815* (Oxford: Blackwell, 1985).

Drescher, Seymour, *Abolition: A History of Slavery and Antislavery* (Cambridge: Cambridge University Press, 2009).

Capitalism and Antislavery: British Popular Mobilization in Comparative Perspective (Oxford: Oxford University Press, 1986).

Econocide: British Slavery in the Era of Abolition (Pittsburgh, PA: University of Pittsburgh Press, 1977).

'The Shocking Birth of British Abolitionism', *Slavery & Abolition*, 33:4 (2012), 571–593.

Edwards, Paul. (ed.), *Through African Eyes* (Cambridge: Cambridge University Press, 1966–1969).

Unreconciled Strivings and Ironic Strategies: Three Afro-British Authors of the Georgian Era: Ignatius Sancho, Olaudah Equiano, Robert Wedderburn (Edinburgh: Centre for African Studies, 1992).

Edwards, Paul, and Dabydeen, David (eds.), *Black Writers in Britain, 1760–1890* (Edinburgh: Edinburgh University Press, 1991).

Edwards, Paul, and Walvin, James, *Black Personalities in the Era of the Slave Trade* (London: Macmillan, 1983).

Ellis, Markman, *The Politics of Sensibility: Race, Gender and Commerce in the Sentimental Novel* (Cambridge: Cambridge University Press, 1996).

Ferrer, Ada, 'Haiti, Free Soil, and Antislavery in the Revolutionary Atlantic', *American Historical Review*, 117:1 (2012), 40–66.

Foster, Francis Smith, *Witnessing Slavery: The Development of Ante-Bellum Slave Narratives* (Westport, CT: Greenwood Press, 1979).

Foucault, Michel, *The Archaeology of Knowledge*, trans. A. M. Sheridan Smith (New York: Pantheon, 1972).

Fryer, Peter, *Staying Power: The History of Black People in Britain* (London: Pluto Press, 1984).

Furneaux, Robin, *William Wilberforce* (Vancouver: Regent College Publishing, 2005).

Fyfe, Christopher, *A History of Sierra Leone* (Oxford: Oxford University Press, 1962).

Gates, Henry Louis Jr, *The Signifying Monkey: A Theory of African-American Literary Criticism* (Oxford: Oxford University Press, 1988).

Gates, Henry Louis Jr, and Higginbotham, Evelyn Brooks (eds.), *African American Lives* (Oxford: Oxford University Press, 2004)

Geggus, David (ed.), *The Impact of the Haitian Revolution in the Atlantic World* (Columbia: University of South Carolina Press, 2001).

Gellman, David, *Emancipating New York: The Politics of Slavery and Freedom, 1777–1827* (Baton Rouge: Louisiana State University Press, 2006).

Gerzina, Gretchen, *Black England: Life before Emancipation* (London: John Murray, 1995).

Gilbert, Alan, *Black Patriots and Loyalists: Fighting for Emancipation in the War for Independence* (Chicago, IL: University of Chicago Press, 2012).

Gilroy, Paul, *The Black Atlantic: Modernity and Double Consciousness* (Cambridge, MA: Harvard University Press, 1993).

Goring, Paul, *The Rhetoric of Sensibility in Eighteenth-Century Culture* (Cambridge: Cambridge University Press, 2005).

Haggerty, John, and Haggerty, Sheryllynne, 'Visual Analytics of an Eighteenth-Century Business Network', *Enterprise and Society*, 11:1 (2010), 1–25.

Haggerty, Sheryllynne, *'Merely for Money'? Business Culture in the British Atlantic, 1750–1815* (Liverpool: Liverpool University Press, 2012).

Hall, Catherine, McClelland, Keith, Draper, Nick, Donington, Katie, and Lang, Rachel, *Legacies of British Slave-Ownership: Colonial Slavery and the Formation of Victorian Britain* (Cambridge: Cambridge University Press, 2014).

Hamilton, Keith, and Salmon, Patrick (eds.), *Slavery, Democracy and Empire: Britain and the Suppression of the Slave Trade, 1807–1975* (Brighton: Sussex University Press, 2009), 81–92.

Hammerschmidt, Soren, 'Character, Cultural Agency and Abolition: Ignatius Sancho's Published Letters', *Journal for Eighteenth-Century Studies*, 31:2 (2008), 259–74.

Harding, Alan, *The Countess of Huntingdon's Connexion: A Sect in Action in Eighteenth-Century England* (Oxford: Oxford University Press, 2003).

Harris, Jennifer, 'Seeing the Light: Re-Reading James Albert Ukawsaw Gronniosaw', *English Language Notes* 42:4 (2004), 43–57.

Hempton, David, *Methodism: Empire of the Spirit* (New Haven, CT: Yale University Press, 2005).

Methodism and Politics in British Society, 1750–1850 (London: Hutchinson, 1984).

The Religion of the People: Methodism and Popular Religion, 1750–1900 (London: Routledge, 1996).

Religion and Political Culture in Britain and Ireland: From the Glorious Revolution to the Decline of Empire (Cambridge: Cambridge University Press, 1996).

Heywood, Ian, and Seed, John, *The Gordon Riots: Politics, Culture and Insurrection in Late Eighteenth-Century Britain* (Cambridge: Cambridge University Press, 2012).

Hochschild, Adam, *Bury the Chains: The British Struggle to Abolish Slavery* (London: Macmillan, 2005).

Hodges, Graham Russell (ed.), *Black Itinerants of the Gospel: The Narratives of John Jea and George White* (London: Palgrave, 2002).

Hudson, Nicholas, '"Britons Never Will be Slaves": National Myth, Conservatism, and the Beginnings of British Antislavery', *Eighteenth-Century Studies*, 34:4 (2001), 559–576.

Huzzey, Richard, *Freedom Burning: Anti-Slavery and Empire in Victorian Britain* (Ithaca, NY: Cornell University Press, 2012).

Innes, Lyn, *A History of Black and Asian Writing in Britain* (Cambridge: Cambridge University Press, 2002).

Jackson, Maurice, *Let This Voice Be Heard: Anthony Benezet, Father of Atlantic Abolitionism* (Philadelphia: University of Pennsylvania Press, 2008).

James, C. L. R., *The Black Jacobins: Toussaint Louverture and the San Domingo Revolution* (London: Secker and Warberg, 1938).

Jennings, Judith, *The Business of Abolishing the British Slave Trade 1783–1807* (London: Frank Cass, 1997).

Kielstra, Paul, *The Politics of Slave Trade Suppression in Britain and France, 1814–48: Diplomacy, Morality and Economics* (London: Macmillan, 2000).

Kilday, Anne-Marie, '"Criminally Poor?" Investigating the Link between Crime and Poverty in Eighteenth Century England', *Cultural and Social History*, 11:4 (2014), 507–526.

King, Reyahn, et al. (eds.), *Ignatius Sancho: African Man of Letters* (London: National Portrait Gallery, 1997).

Klingberg, Frank, *Parliamentary History of the Abolition of Slavery and the Slave Trade in the British Colonies* (New Haven, CT, 1911).

Krishnamurthy, Aruna (ed.), *The Working-Class Intellectual in Eighteenth- and Nineteenth-Century Britain* (London: Ashgate, 2009).

Lambert, Frank, *Pedlar in Divinity: George Whitefield and the Transatlantic Revivals, 1737–1770* (Princeton, NJ: Princeton University Press, 1993).

Langford, Paul, *A Polite and Commercial People: England 1727–1783* (Oxford: Oxford University Press, 1989).

Langton, John, and Laxton, Paul, 'Parish Registers and Urban Structure: The Example of Late-Eighteenth Century Liverpool', *Urban History*, 5 (1978), 74–84.

Le Jeune, Francoise, '"Of a Negro, a Butler and a Grocer" (Jekyll, 7) – Ignatius Sancho's Epistolary Contribution to the Abolition Campaign (1766–1780)', *Etudes Anglaises*, 61:4 (2008), 440–54.

Lindsay, Lisa, and Sweet, John Wood (eds.), *Biography and the Black Atlantic* (Philadelphia: University of Pennsylvania Press, 2014).

Linebaugh, Peter, and Rediker, Marcus, *The Many-Headed Hydra: The Hidden History of the Revolutionary Atlantic* (London: Verso, 2000).

Lovejoy, Paul, 'Autobiography and Memory: Gustavus Vassa, alias Olaudah Equiano, the African', *Slavery & Abolition*, 27:3 (2006), 317–347.

'"Freedom Narratives" of Transatlantic Slavery', *Slavery & Abolition*, 32:1 (2011), 91–107.

'Issues of Motivation – Vassa/Equiano and Carretta's Critique of the Evidence', *Slavery & Abolition*, 28:1 (2007), 121–125.

'Olaudah Equiano or Gustavus Vassa – What's in a Name?', *Atlantic Studies*, 9:2 (2012), 165–184.

Maddison-Macfayden, Margot, 'Mary Prince, Grand Turk, and Antigua', *Slavery & Abolition*, 34:4 (2013), 1–10.

Makalani, Minkah, *In the Cause of Freedom: Radical Black Internationalism from Harlem to London, 1917–1939* (Chapel Hill: University of North Carolina Press, 2011).

Maniquis, Robert (ed.), *British Radical Culture of the 1790s* (San Marino, CA: Huntingdon Library Press, 2002).

Manning, Susan, and Bannet, Eve (eds.), *Transatlantic Literary Studies 1680–1830* (Cambridge: Cambridge University Press, 2012).

Matthews, Gelien, *Caribbean Slave Revolts and the British Abolitionist Movement* (Baton Rouge: Louisiana State University Press, 2006).

M'Baye, Babacar, *The Trickster Comes West* (Jackson: University of Mississippi Press, 2009).

McCalman, Iain, 'Anti-Slavery and Ultra-Radicalism in Early Nineteenth-Century England: The Case of Robert Wedderburn', *Slavery and Abolition*, 7:2 (1986), 99–117.

Radical Underworld: Prophets, Revolutionaries and Pornographers in London, 1795–1840 (Cambridge: Cambridge University Press, 1988).

Midgley, Claire, *Women against Slavery: The British Campaigns, 1780–1870* (London: Routledge, 1992).

Myers, Norma, *Reconstructing the Black Past: Blacks in Britain, 1780–1830* (London: Routledge, 1996).

Nasta, Susheila (ed.), *Reading the 'New' Literatures in a Postcolonial Era* (Cambridge: D. S. Brewer, 2000).

Nussbaum, Felicity, *The Limits of the Human: Fictions of Anomaly, Race and Gender in the Long Eighteenth Century* (Cambridge: Cambridge University Press, 2003).

Ojo, Olatunji, and Hunt, Nadine (eds.), *Slavery in Africa and the Caribbean: A History of Enslavement and Identity since the Eighteenth Century* (London: I. B. Tauris, 2012).

Oldfield, John, *Popular Politics and British Anti-Slavery: The Mobilisation of Public Opinion against the Slave Trade, 1787–1807* (Manchester: Manchester University Press, 1995).

Transatlantic Abolitionism in the Age of Revolution: An International History of Anti-Slavery, c. 1787–1820 (Cambridge: Cambridge University Press, 2014).

Palk, Deirdre, *Gender, Crime and Judicial Discretion, 1780–1830* (London: Boydell Press, 2006).

Pencek, Eric, 'Intolerable Anonymity: Robert Wedderburn and the Discourse of Ultra-Radicalism', *Nineteenth-Century Contexts*, 37:1 (2015), 61–77.

Peterson, John, *Province of Freedom: A History of Sierra Leone 1787–1870* (London: Faber and Faber, 1969).

Philp, Mark (ed.), *The French Revolution and British Popular Politics* (Cambridge: Cambridge University Press, 2004).

Reforming Ideas in Britain: Politics and Language in the Shadow of the French Revolution, 1789–1815 (Cambridge: Cambridge University Press, 2013).

Pierrot, Gregory, 'Insights on "Lord Hoth" and Ottobah Cugoano', *Notes and Queries*, 59:3 (2012), 367–368.

Pollock, John, *William Wilberforce* (London: Lion, 1977).

Potkay, Adam, and Burr, Sandra, *Black Writers of the 18th Century: Living the New Exodus in England and America* (New York: St. Martin's Press, 1995).

Prince, Mary *The History of Mary Prince: A West Indian Slave*, ed. Ferguson, Moira (London: Pandora, 1987), ii–xvi.

Pulis, John (ed.), *Moving On: Black Loyalists in the Afro-Atlantic World* (London: Taylor and Francis, 1999).

Pybus, Cassandra, *Epic Journeys of Freedom: Runaway Slaves of the American Revolution and Their Global Quest for Liberty* (Boston: Beacon Press, 2006).

Ramdin, Ron, *The Making of the Black Working Class in Britain* (Aldershot: Gower 1987).

Rawerda, A. M., 'Naming, Agency, and "A Tissue of Falsehoods" in *The History of Mary Prince*', *Victorian Literature and Culture*, 64:3 (2001), 397–411.

Richardson, Alan, and Lee, Debbie (eds.), *Early Black British Writing: Olaudah Equiano, Mary Prince, and Others* (Boston: Houghton Mifflin Harcourt, 2004).

Richardson, David (ed.), *Abolition and Its Aftermath: The Historical Context* (London: Frank Cass, 1985).

Richardson, David, Schwarz, Suzanne, and Tibbles, Anthony (eds.), *Liverpool and Transatlantic Slavery* (Liverpool: Liverpool University Press, 2007).

Rodgers, Nini, *Equiano and Anti-Slavery in Eighteenth-Century Belfast* (Belfast: Ulster Historical Foundation, 2000).

Ireland, Slavery and Anti-Slavery: 1612–1865 (London: Palgrave Macmillan, 2007).

Rule, John, and Malcolmson, Robert (eds.), *Protest and Survival: The Historical Experience: Essays for E. P. Thompson* (London: Merlin Press, 1993), 174–220.

Sancho, Ignatius, *Letters of the Late Ignatius Sancho, an African*, 2 vols. (London: J. Nichols et al., 1782).

Sandhu, Sukhdev, 'Ignatius Sancho and Laurence Sterne', *Research in African Literatures*, 29:4 (1998), 88–106.

Sandiford, Keith, *Measuring the Moment: Strategies of Protest in Eighteenth-Century Afro-English Writing* (London: Associated University Presses, 1988).

Schama, Simon, *Rough Crossings: Britain, the Slaves and the American Revolution* (London: BBC Books, 2005).

Schlenther, Boyd, *Queen of the Methodists: The Countess of Huntingdon and the Eighteenth-Century Crisis of Faith and Society* (Bishop Auckland: Durham Academic Press, 1997).

Schwarz, Suzanne, 'The Legacy of Melvill Horne', *International Bulletin of Missionary Research*, 31:2 (2007), 88–94.

'"Our Mad Methodists": Methodism, Missions and Abolitionism in Sierra Leone in the Late Eighteenth Century', *Journal of Wesley and Methodist Studies*, 3 (2011), 121–133.

'Reconstructing the Life Histories of Liberated Africans: Sierra Leone in the Early Nineteenth Century', *History in Africa*, 39:1 (2012), 175–207.

Scobie, Edward, *Black Britannia: A History of Blacks in Britain* (Chicago, IL: Johnson, 1972).

Semmel, Bernard, *The Methodist Revolution* (London: Heinemann, 1974).

Shum, Mathhew, 'The Prehistory of *The History of Mary Prince*: Thomas Pringle's "The Bechuana Boy"', *Nineteenth-Century Literature*, 64:3 (2009), 291–322;

Shyllon, Folarin, *Black People in Britain, 1555–1833* (Oxford: Oxford University Press, 1977).

Black Slaves in Britain (Oxford: Oxford University Press, 1974).

Simon, Kathleen Harvey, *Britain's Lead against Slavery* (London, 1930).

Smith, Gene, *The Slaves' Gamble: Choosing Sides in the War of 1812* (New York: Palgrave Macmillan, 2013).

Solow, Barbara, and Engerman, Stanley (eds.), *British Capitalism and Caribbean Slavery: The Legacy of Eric Williams* (Cambridge: Cambridge University Press, 1987).

Sparks, Randy, *The Two Princes of Calabar: An Eighteenth-Century Atlantic Odyssey* (Cambridge, MA: Harvard University Press, 2004).

Stott, Ann, *Wilberforce: Family and Friends* (Oxford: Oxford University Press, 2012).

Swaminathan, Srividhya, *Debating the Slave Trade: Rhetoric of British National Identity* (Farnham: Ashgate, 2009).

Sypher, Wylie, *Guinea's Captive Kings: British Anti-Slavery Literature of the XVIIIth Century* (Chapel Hill: University of North Carolina Press, 1942).

Taylor, Alan, *The Internal Enemy: Slavery and War in Virginia, 1772–1832* (London: W. W. Norton, 2013).

Thomas, Helen, *Romanticism and Slave Narratives: Transatlantic Testimonies* (Cambridge: Cambridge University Press, 2000).

Thomas, Hugh, *The Slave Trade* (New York: Simon and Schuster, 1997).
Thomas, Sue, 'New Information on Mary Prince in London', *Notes and Queries*, 58:1 (2011), 82–85.
  'Pringle v. Cadell and Wood v. Pringle: The Libel Cases over *The History of Mary Prince*', *Journal of Commonwealth Studies*, 40:1 (2005), 113–135.
  Telling West Indian Lives: Life Narratives and the Reform of Plantation Slavery Cultures (New York: Palgrave Macmillan, 2014).
Thompson, Edward Palmer, *The Making of the English Working Class* (London: Random House, 1963).
Tomkins, Stephen, *Clapham Sect: How Wilberforce's Circle Transformed Britain* (Oxford: Lion, 2010).
  William Wilberforce: A Biography (London: Lion, 2007).
Turley, David, *Culture of English Anti-Slavery: 1780–1860* (London: Routledge, 1991).
Turner, John, *Conflict and Reconciliation: Studies in Methodism and Ecumenism in England 1740–1982* (London: Epworth Press 1985).
Turner, Michael, 'The Limits of Abolition: Government, Saints and the "African Question", c. 1780–1820', *English Historical Review*, 112:446 (1997), 319–357.
Walker, James, *The Black Loyalists: The Search for a Promised Land in Nova Scotia and Sierra Leone 1783–1870* (Toronto: University of Toronto Press, 1976).
Walvin, James, *An African's Life: The Life and Times of Olaudah Equiano, 1745–1797* (London: Cassell, 1998).
  Black Ivory: A History of British Slavery (London: Harper Collins, 1992).
  Black and White: The Negro in English Society, 155–1945 (London: Allen Lane, 1973).
  'The Impact of Slavery on British Radical Politics: 1787–1838', *Annals of the New York Academy of Sciences*, 292, (1977), 343–355.
  The Zong: A Massacre, the Law and the End of Slavery (New Haven, CT: Yale University Press, 2011).
Whetmore, Alex, *Men of Feeling in Eighteenth Century Literature: Touching Fiction* (London: Palgrave Macmillan, 2013).
Williams, Eric, *Capitalism and Slavery* (Chapel Hill: University of North Carolina Press, 1944).
Wilson, Arline, *William Roscoe: Commerce and Culture* (Liverpool: Liverpool University Press, 2008).
Wong, Edlie, *Neither Fugitive nor Free: Atlantic Slavery, Freedom Suits and the Legal Culture of Travel* (London: New York University Press, 2009).
Wood, Betty, *Slavery in Colonial Georgia, 1730–1775* (Athens: University of Georgia Press, 1984).
Wood, Marcus, *Blind Memory: Visual Representations of Slavery in England and America 1780–1865* (Manchester: Manchester University Press, 2000).
  Slavery Empathy and Pornography (Oxford: Oxford University Press, 2002).
Woodard, Helena, *African-British Writings in the Eighteenth Century: The Politics of Race and Reason* (Westport, CT: Greenwood Press, 1999).
Worrall, David, *Radical Culture: Discourse, Resistance and Surveillance* (Hemel Hempstead: Harvester Wheatsheaf, 1992).
Yerxa, Donald (ed.), *British Abolitionism and the Question of Moral Progress in History* (Columbia: University of South Carolina Press, 2012).

Unpublished Theses

Donington, Katie, 'The Benevolent Merchant? George Hibbert (1757–1837) and the Representation of West Indian Mercantile Identity', PhD thesis, University College London (2013).

Field, John Langston, 'Bourgeois Portsmouth: Social Relations in a Victorian Dockyard Town, 1815–75', PhD thesis, University of Warwick (1979).

Vickers, John, 'Methodism and Society in Central Southern England 1740–1851', PhD thesis, University of Southampton (1986).

Online Sources

Legacies of British Slave-Ownership, University College London, 2014. Available at www.ucl.ac.uk/lbs.

The Old Bailey Proceedings Online, 1674–1913, Hitchcock, Tim, Shoemaker, Robert, Emsley, Clive, Howard, Sharon, McLaughlin, Jamie, et al., March 2012. Available at www.oldbaileyonline.org.

The Oxford Dictionary of National Biography. Available at www.oxforddnb.com.

Voyages: The Trans-Atlantic Slave Trade Database, Eltis, David, et al., 2008–2009. Available at www.slavevoyages.org/tast/database/search.faces.

Index